TRANSPARENCY, POWER AND CONTROL

Law, Language and Communication

Series Editors
Anne Wagner, Université du Littoral Côte d'Opale, France and
Vijay Kumar Bhatia, City University of Hong Kong

This series encourages innovative and integrated perspectives within and across the boundaries of law, language and communication, with particular emphasis on issues of communication in specialized socio-legal and professional contexts. It seeks to bring together a range of diverse yet cumulative research traditions related to these fields in order to identify and encourage interdisciplinary research.

The series welcomes proposals – both edited collections as well as single-authored monographs – emphasizing critical approaches to law, language and communication, identifying and discussing issues, proposing solutions to problems, offering analyses in areas such as legal construction, interpretation, translation and de-codification.

Transparency, Power and Control
Perspectives on Legal Communication

Edited by

VIJAY K. BHATIA, CHRISTOPH A. HAFNER
AND LINDSAY MILLER
City University of Hong Kong, Hong Kong

ANNE WAGNER
Université du Littoral Côte d'Opale, France

Routledge
Taylor & Francis Group
LONDON AND NEW YORK

First published 2012 by Ashgate Publishing

2 Park Square, Milton Park, Abingdon, Oxon OX14 4RN
711 Third Avenue, New York, NY 10017, USA

Routledge is an imprint of the Taylor & Francis Group, an informa business

First issued in paperback 2016

British Library Cataloguing in Publication Data
Transparency, power and control : perspectives on legal
communication. -- (Law, language and communication)
1. Communication in law. 2. Law--Language. 3. Semantics
(Law) 4. Semiotics (Law) 5. Discourse analysis--Social
aspects. 6. Persuasion (Rhetoric)
I. Series II. Bhatia, V. K. (Vijay Kumar), 1942-
340.1'4-dc22

Library of Congress Cataloging-in-Publication Data
Transparency, power and control : perspectives on legal communication / by
Vijay K. Bhatia ... [et al.].
p. cm.
Includes bibliographical references and index.
ISBN 978-1-4094-3284-5 (hardback)
1. Semantics (Law) I. Bhatia, V. K. (Vijay Kumar), 1942-
K213.T7365 2011
340'.14--dc23

2011024617

ISBN 978-1-4094-3284-5 (hbk)
ISBN 978-1-138-24882-3 (pbk)

Contents

List of Figures *vii*
List of Contributors *ix*
Preface *xiii*

1 Transparency, Power and Control in Legal Communication 1
Vijay K. Bhatia, Christoph A. Hafner, Lindsay Miller and Anne Wagner

PART I: THEORIZING TRANSPARENCY, POWER AND CONTROL IN LEGAL COMMUNICATION

2 Linguistic Uncertainty and Legal Transparency: Statutory Interpretation in China and Australia 13
Deborah Cao

3 The Power of Legal Conditionals in International Contracts 31
Celina Frade

4 The Directive and Persuasive Style of a Legislative Speech Act and the Transformations Thereof (Illustrated with the Polish Legal Discourse) 51
Irena Szczepankowska

5 *Zorkin v. Morschakova*: Legal Dispute in Rhetorical Terms 67
Anita Soboleva

6 A Dialogical and Polyphonic Approach to Contract Theory 85
André Bélanger and Andy van Drom

7 What EU Legislative Texts Reveal about Power, Control and Transparency 109
Colin Robertson

8 Toward an Objective Means of Measuring Governmental Legitimacy 125
M. Douglass Bellis

PART II: VISUALIZING AND CONTEXTUALIZING TRANSPARENCY, POWER AND CONTROL

9 Battle of the Sexters: Teens Celling Sex in a World Wide Web of Conflicting Laws, Values and Social Norms 147
Michelle L. Wirth

10 Visualizing the Terrorist Risk in President Bush's War on Terror and Peter Jackson's *The Two Towers* 165
Anita Lam

11 Hearing and Belonging: On Sounds, Faiths and Laws 183
Massimo Leone

12 Terror *Australis* 199
Maria Giannacopoulos

13 'The Unbearable Whiteness of Beckham': Semiotics and Political Recoding of the Contemporary Celebrity 217
David Tan

14 Warhol: Images of Infamy and Underpinning Power 243
Oliver Watts

Index *261*

List of Figures

3.1	Conditional markers	38
3.2	Position of *if p* (based on Quirk et al. 1985: 1037)	42
3.3	Mental spaces of legal conditional (based on Dancygier and Sweetser 1996: 85)	46
6.1	Tetrahedral framework of discursive contractual analysis	94
7.1	The European flag	113
14.1	Andy Warhol, *Thirteen Most Wanted Men*, 1964	244
14.2	Andy Warhol, *Double Elvis*, 1964	256

List of Contributors

André Bélanger has been teaching law at Université Laval since 2002. He was awarded a doctoral degree in Law at Université Laval, after completing a DEA at the University of Montpellier I. His research and teaching activities centre on the theory underlying contracts.

M. Douglass Bellis is Professorial Lecturer in Legislative Affairs at George Washington University in Washington DC and also Senior Counsel in the Office of the Legislative Counsel, United States House of Representatives. His education includes a Bachelor of Arts (with majors in Greek and Latin Classics and in Government) from Cornell University and a degree of Juris Doctor from Duke University. His relevant academic interests include the theory of government and its practical application to the business of parliamentary assemblies. Many of his writings, mostly available on the internet, focus on aspects of legislative drafting.

Vijay K. Bhatia is a Visiting Professor in the Department of English at the City University of Hong Kong. He is also the founding President of the Association of LSP and Professional Communication for the Asia-Pacific Rim. His research interests include the genre analysis of academic and professional discourses, including legal, business, newspaper and advertising genres, ESP and Professional Communication. He has published widely, including research articles in international journals, chapters in books, edited volumes and book monographs. Two of his books, *Analysing Genre: Language Use in Professional Settings* (1993) and *Worlds of Written Discourse: A Genre-based View* (2004), are widely used in genre theory and practice.

Deborah Cao is a Professor at Griffith University, Australia. A linguist and a legal scholar, she writes about legal theory, legal language, animal law and Chinese law. She is Editor of the *International Journal for the Semiotics of Law* and a Fellow of the Oxford Centre for Animal Ethics (UK). She also contributed to the drafting of a proposed *Law for the Prevention of Cruelty to Animals of China.* Her major books include *Chinese Law: A Language Perspective* (2004), *Translating Law* (2007), *Animals Are Not Things: Animal Law in the West* (2007) and *Animal Law in Australia and New Zealand* (2010).

Celina Frade is currently Professor of English for Specific Purposes in the Multidisciplinary Institute at the Federal Rural University of Rio de Janeiro. Her main areas of interest include legal English discourse and the design and delivery of ESP courses for graduation students and professional continuing education in general.

Maria Giannacopoulos is a lecturer in socio-legal studies at the Flinders Law School, Adelaide, Australia. Her research uses cultural theory to examine law's relationship to race and state violence. She has authored numerous essays on Australian law with a specific emphasis on the multiple collusions of law and race in the context of ongoing colonial relations.

Christoph A. Hafner is an Assistant Professor in the Department of English, City University of Hong Kong. His research interests include legal discourse, academic and professional literacy, and educational technology. He is trained as a lawyer and has acted as a tutor on legal writing and drafting courses for novice lawyers in professional legal training in Hong Kong.

Anita Lam is an Assistant Professor of Criminology at York University, Toronto. She teaches and researches in the area of cultural criminology, and is particularly interested in examining the intersection of crime, media and culture. Her dissertation research examined the production of television crime procedurals in Canada.

Massimo Leone is Research Professor of Semiotics and Cultural Semiotics at the Department of Philosophy, University of Torino, Italy. His work focuses on the role of religion in modern and contemporary cultures. His last monograph is: *Saints and Signs – A Semiotic Reading of Conversion in Early Modern Catholicism* (2010).

Lindsay Miller is an Associate Professor in the Department of English at the City University of Hong Kong. His main areas of research are in Learner Autonomy, English for Specific Purposes, and Academic Discourse. He has published widely in each of these areas.

Colin Robertson is a Scottish lawyer by profession. He works as a legal-linguistic reviser ('lawyer-linguist') at the Council of the European Union checking and revising draft EU legislative texts in English. He has knowledge of several languages, including English, French, German, Italian, Czech, Slovak and Bulgarian. He is married with two children.

Anita Soboleva is an Associate Professor of the Department of Public Policy at the National Research University-Higher School of Economics (HSE) and Chief Counsel for Legal Science and Education in the independent not-for-profit organization 'Lawyers for Constitutional Rights and Freedoms' (JURIX) in Moscow. She holds a degree in philology from Moscow State University, a law degree from Moscow Law Institute (currently Moscow State Law Academy), an

LLM in comparative constitutional law from the Central European University and a PhD in linguistics from Moscow State University. She has published widely in journals on rhetoric, constitutional law, ethnic and linguistic discrimination, philosophy of law, legal reasoning and legal interpretation. She is the author of *Topical Jurisprudence: Arguments and Interpretation in Law* (2002).

Irena Szczepankowska Ph.D. is a linguist and a Professor in the Institute of Polish Philology, the University of Białystok (Poland). She is a member of the Polish Linguistic Society and the Legal Language Commission in the Polish Academy of Sciences. She has been conducting research on the evolution of the Polish language of the law and its functioning in the social space for ten years, and has published books as well as articles in scientific magazines and collective works, including 'The Language of the Law in the First Republic of Poland', in *Collection of Court Laws*, edited by Andrzej Zamoyski (2004) and 'Law and Freedom in the Political Discourse of the Pre-Partition Republic of Poland: Basic Research Problems', *Poradnik Językowy* [Linguistic Guide], 8 (2008), pp. 75-93.

David Tan is an Assistant Professor of Law at the National University of Singapore. He holds a PhD, LLB and BCom from the University of Melbourne, and a LLM from Harvard. In the area of law, his works have appeared in journals such as the *Cardozo Arts and Entertainment Law Journal, Yale Journal of International Law* and *Harvard Journal of Sports and Entertainment Law*.

Andy van Drom is a doctoral candidate in the Department of Language, Linguistics and Translation at Université Laval. His interdisciplinary research focuses on the discursive construction and management of conflicting social identities in legal media, and political discourse.

Anne Wagner is an Associate Professor at the Université du Littoral Côte d'Opale, France. She is the Editor-in-Chief of the *International Journal for the Semiotics of Law* (Springer) and co-editor for the book series *Law, Language and Communication* (Ashgate). She is the President of the *International Roundtables for the Semiotics of Law*. She has published extensively, including papers and edited volumes, in the area of law and semiotics, legal discourse, law and culture, plain language, and legal translation.

Oliver Watts lectures in critical theory and art history at the College of Fine Arts, University of New South Wales and University of Sydney. His PhD thesis, completed in 2009 at the University of Sydney, was entitled *Images on the Limit of the Law* and looked at the imaging of sovereignty, which was called 'the effigy'. Watts has published articles on the nexus of art and law both in legal terms (terrorism, criminology and statutory issues such as copyright) and through visual studies mining the canon of art history and images to see how the image produces and performs belief in the law.

Michelle Wirth Esq. earned a Master's degree in public policy from Carnegie Mellon University and a Juris Doctorate from The Penn State Dickinson School of Law. She lives in Pittsburgh, Pennsylvania with her partner.

Preface

The overall aim of this special volume is to bring together three important aspects of socio-legal practice – law, language and communication – and identify a variety of issues and contexts to reflect on the growing importance of concepts such as *transparency*, *power* and *control* with a view to offer a range of *perspectives in legal communication.*

The issues of transparency, power and control were the central focus of the 8th International Roundtable for the Semiotics of Law organized by the Department of English, City University of Hong Kong during 1-4 December 2009, which brought together academics, scholars and practitioners from a range of disciplines such as law, public and social administration, linguistics and discourse analysis, and semiotics from more than 20 countries to reflect on the growing importance of these concepts and to identify the contexts in which these concepts assume crucial importance in the international community, and how these concerns and ideas have been examined, used and interpreted in a range of national and international contexts. Participants explored these issues from a range of overlapping concerns and perspectives, such as semiotic, rhetorical, pragmatic, sociolinguistic, psychological, philosophical and visual in diverse socio-political, administrative, institutional, as well as legal contexts.

The current volume presents a selection of the papers from the Roundtable that were chosen by keeping in mind a variety of different contexts in which these concepts give rise to some of the issues considered important in the present socio-political order and to provide an opportunity for a general discussion of issues in the semiotics of law as well as open discussions to increase our understanding of the broader context of law, language and communication.

The editors would like to express their gratitude to a number of people who contributed to the organization of the Roundtable as well as to the preparation of the manuscript in various ways. First and foremost, we would like to acknowledge the contribution from the Department of English, City University of Hong Kong for its generous financial support to make the Roundtable possible. Special thanks are due to Professor Kingsley Bolton for all his encouragement and support in various ways, including the willing deployment of secretarial staff to take care of some of the most difficult day-to-day tasks before, during and after the Roundtable.

For their invaluable support in organizing and making possible the Roundtable, special thanks also go to Chris Leung Pak Hang for designing the innovative publicity poster and programme schedule and for his management of the audio-visual facilities, as well as to Winnie Cheng Wing Yan for her support throughout the process, especially her management of a team of volunteers who made difficult tasks look so easy. We would also like to acknowledge the assistance of Brian Tang Tsz Hong and Candy Tang So Man in the final stages of preparing the manuscript for publication.

Vijay K. Bhatia, Christoph A. Hafner, Lindsay Miller and Anne Wagner

Chapter 1

Transparency, Power and Control in Legal Communication

Vijay K. Bhatia, Christoph A. Hafner, Lindsay Miller and Anne Wagner

> Could language injure us if we were not, in some sense, linguistic beings, beings who require language in order to be? Is our vulnerability to language a consequence of our being constituted within its terms? If we are formed in language, then that formative power precedes and conditions any decision we might make about it, insulting us from the start, as it were, by its prior power. (Butler 1997: 1–2)

Communication, in general, and legal communication, in particular, is an act with consequences, and comprises performative utterances with effects. There exist various ways in which actors in our society have provoked public discourse in order to unveil the unsaid or hidden mechanisms of power and control, and then to call for transparency to all citizens – that is, readability, visibility and accessibility. Legal communication encompasses complex relations across a diversity of languages, cultures and different orientations arising from their confrontations within space and time. The treatment of data and its reliability presupposes intercultural analyses with factorial typologies: linguistic, pragmatic and situational accounts. Cultural 'embeddedness' is a key notion in effective, transparent and clear legal communication, which involves analysing the power of social institutions included in the language itself but not limited to it. Bourdieu (1991: 109) posits:

> He thinks that he has found in discourse itself – in the specifically linguistic substance of speech, as it were – the key to the efficacy of speech. By trying to understand the power of linguistic manifestations linguistically, by looking at language for the principle underlying the logic and effectiveness of the language of institutions, one forgets that authority comes to language from outside, a fact concretely exemplified by the *skeptron* that, in Homer, is passed to the orator who is about to speak. Language at most represents this authority, manifests and symbolizes it. There is a rhetoric, which characterizes all discourses of institution, that is to say, the official speech of the authorized spokesperson expressing himself in a solemn situation, with an authority whose limits are identical with the extent of delegation by the institution.

The overall aim of a state is to protect the social order in which the individual liberty of the citizen is a major concern. As a consequence the state should guarantee simultaneously but also paradoxically a high level of individual freedom and an order in which such freedom is made possible and guaranteed with respect to others and within the framework of legal communication.

Legal communication serves that purpose with legal interpretation and conceptual transfer, translatability in legal texts. These activities are captivating not only for the jurists who can conceive hypotheses, but also for actors in society (amongst others: politicians, photographers, drafters, artists, translators) who have to understand the very core of the message. The participant in legal interactions is seduced by the sophisticated repartee established between the law and its medium of expression. It offers him/her the opportunity to enter the world of legal communication by his/her active participation in the comprehension of the law, but it also shows his/her vulnerability in terms of understanding, misunderstanding or even non-understanding.

The present edited collection of research papers offers an integrated perspective on the issues of transparency, power and control in legal communication. Each chapter focuses on a specific context providing a study within a specific theoretical framework to investigate how these three issues and other related concepts impact our socio-political environment in the present-day world. The volume is divided into two parts: Part I contains chapters that deal with theoretical aspects of legal communication, while Part II is a collection of chapters addressing issues of visualizing and contextualizing transparency, power and control.

Part I: Theorizing Transparency, Power and Control in Legal Communication

It is an illusion to believe in clear legal communication and legal drafting of norms. Transparency is a goal to attain in itself, but this goal is subject to legal interpretation.

> Clear, simple and precise drafting of Community legislative acts is essential if they are to be transparent and readily understandable by the public and economic operators. It is also a prerequisite for the proper implementation and uniform application of Community legislation in the Member States. (European Parliament etc. 1999: preamble (1))

Rules are not free from interpretation, from controversy (Moor 2005: 170), from social conceptions, manipulations, political beliefs and 'diplomatic' law:

> Where jurists seek precision, diplomats practice non-speak and are not averse to ambiguity. It happens more often than one might think that they fail to agree on a word simply because it does not have the same meaning for everyone. … They

> likewise encourage writing techniques that here and there allow for perpetuating interesting – and promising – contradiction. (France, Conseil d'Etat 1992 cited in Gallas 2001: 117ff)

As such the debate over legal dynamism, plurality is a never-ending story. Language has this capacity of distortion, of modifying its initial meanings which is viewed as a lexical potentiality (Cornu 2005), as 'spaces in meaning' (Fish 1989) or as an evasive criterion 'fuyance' (Gény 1922). There are two possibilities of translatability in legal communication, which are the direct consequences of the descriptive intent of the legislator:

1. What degree of flexibility is given to the user/interpreter of the rule? And/or
2. What degree of rigidity will be imposed on him/her in the application? Will he/she have the capacity to 'speak' or interpret the law?

> An appropriate interpretation is one that can be justified in terms of (a) its plausibility, that is, its compliance with the legislative text; (b) its efficacy, that is, its promotion of the legislative purpose; and (c) its acceptability, that is, the outcome is reasonable and just. (Driedger 1974: 131)

Research into the intention of the legal communication gives the interpreter a free space within the confines of the text to produce a dynamic application of the law. In his/her search for meaning, he/she essentially uses terminological, semantic and syntactic tools and takes the consequences of the application of the law into account. The interpreter integrates in his/her data collections new formulations, which are combined with specific cognitive contents. Consequently, saying that legal communication has specific, bounded meanings is not that simple, since if this were the case, laws would be too rigid and only one single meaning would exist and fit only specific circumstances (Wagner 2005).

> … whilst certainty is highly desirable, it may bring in its train excessive rigidity and the law must be able to keep pace with changing circumstances. Accordingly, many laws are inevitably couched in terms which, to a greater or lesser extent, are vague and whose integration and application are questions of practice. (*The Sunday Times v. The United Kingdom* (1979) ECHR 1: para. 49)

The criteria for legal certainty and transparency in legal communication remains subject to the power and control of government as expressed through the legal instruments that constitute the state's legal system. However, access to these important texts remains limited, as Cutts notes when he says:

> like a poor man's Martin Luther King, I have a dream. It is that every person of reasonable intelligence and literacy may sit at their kitchen table and open a

> small book or CD-ROM in which the most important laws that govern them are clearly and simply written in their original, unabridged form. I have that dream. But we stand a long, long way from making it reality. Indeed, I sometimes think the prospect is daily receding. (Cutts 2000: 11)

The chapters in Part I of this book offer theoretical insights into the social and linguistic practices that relate to issues of transparency, power and control. Deborah Cao in her chapter 'Linguistic Uncertainty and Legal Transparency: Statutory Interpretation in China and Australia' investigates linguistic uncertainty in statutory interpretation in China and Australia. Cao suggests that transparency of law serves an important function to secure the trust of the governed population. However she points out that linguistic uncertainty, defined as 'the indeterminate properties of language such as linguistic vagueness, generality and ambiguity' may make such transparency harder to achieve as it reduces predictability and stability. Of course, such linguistic uncertainty can also be useful as it provides a certain flexibility in the application of law. The chapter provides a comparative analysis of practices in China and Australia, which aim to resolve linguistic uncertainty in legislative texts. The analysis suggests that there is greater uncertainty in the Chinese system and this is attributed to a 'lack of coherent and consistent legal narrative in China, and the lack of precedent which may settle indeterminate cases in reference to a settled past legal history as it exists in English common law'. Cao argues that established legal rules and principles of statutory interpretation are yet to form in China and this means that authorities can make decisions or exempt themselves from the law, i.e. use the uncertainty to their own advantage.

Celina Frade in her chapter 'The Power of Legal Conditionals in International Contracts' discusses the use of conditionality in common law texts, especially focusing on the role it plays in contracts. Considering legal English as the main tool of international contracts to regulate legal relations and actions in multilingual and multi-legal contexts, she discusses what constitutes conditionals in this legal genre. In her view, conditional constructions seem to be the phenomena which most evidently portray the inherent power of the parties to control potential contingencies and anticipate possible (and agreed) solutions in contracts. She investigates how conditionality is manifested in international contracts in English, under a multifunctional approach comprising functional and discoursal and cognitive domains, and claims that a conditional construction *if p, then q* – takes on a restrictive value dependent upon the position of *if p* in contractual clauses thus helping in the understanding of the correlation between situations and actions by transposing discourse from one current context (the contract rendering valid in the present) into another (the contract dealing with future contingencies).

Irena Szczepankowska in her chapter 'The Directive and Persuasive Style of a Legislative Speech Act and the Transformations Thereof' focuses on the historical development of speech acts in legal contexts within Poland. Her claim is that such speech acts have been historically shaped by the communication convention of the time they were given. In Poland such legal speech acts have been influenced by the Germanic stylistics of an ortyl. The author considers if such speech acts are clear and transparent to citizens nowadays as they are often based on the concept of 'motiva evitentur': that legislators are not expected to give explanations, only declaratives and directives. Szczepankowska considers whether this antipersuasive restriction is justifiable nowadays in democratic states where citizens may want to know the motives for legal decisions, but which are not apparent because of the ways in which the legal speech acts are framed.

Anita Soboleva presents '*Zorkin v. Morschakova*: Legal Dispute in Rhetorical Terms'. The chapter provides a rhetorical analysis of the debate between two prominent Russian judges and legal scholars on the subject of judicial reform in Russia. Soboleva shows how the two judges differ in the *topoi* or commonplaces (common background knowledge, warrants) that they adopt in order to support their arguments. The chapter highlights a philosophical difference in the way the two judges approach legal interpretation, similar to the difference between the legal positivism of H.L.A. Hart and the natural justice of Ronald Dworkin. While one judge (Morschakova) approaches legal interpretation by appealing to 'higher principles of law', the other (Zorkin) prefers to rely on the letter of the law, and avoid reference to what he terms 'higher principles of expedience'. The rhetorical analysis shows differently grounded argumentation styles, with Morschakova making appeals to reason (*logos*) while Zorkin appeals to emotion (*pathos*). Soboleva argues that ultimately, appeals to emotion are unsuccessful in persuading the legal community for whom the texts are intended.

In André Bélanger and Andy van Drom's chapter 'A Dialogical and Polyphonic Approach to Contract Theory' the authors present a complex analysis of the roles of dialogism and polyphony as applied to contract theory. The authors illustrate through examples that '… polyphony concerns the traces of decisions and positions that are elaborated in a fully-fledged interaction with the other, whereas dialogism considers the elaboration of a given utterance in the verbal milieu of social representations …'. As such, when deciding on the definition of a contract we should focus on the polyphonic process rather than the dialogic mechanisms. In their analysis of the literature on dialogism and polyphony, Bélanger and van Drom develop a conceptual framework illustrated in a tetrahedral model for discursive contractual analysis in order to answer the simple question: who is thinking and speaking in the utterance of a contract? This chapter shows how the '… relationship between discourse and social factors is not direct (transparent), but manifested through a process of mediation'. In order to understand the process we have to consider the ways in which language is used by the addresser and the addressee, and that 'a mosaic of voices' interact in binding the contractual text together.

Colin Robertson presents 'What EU Legislative Texts Reveal about Power, Control and Transparency'. Robertson's chapter is based on the assumption that the European Union has been constructed using legal texts, in the form of primary treaties supplemented with a plethora of other acts and instruments, which express the will of the member states and the institutions they have created to work together in peaceful and orderly cooperation, for the benefit of all. He identifies a constructed set of arrangements in EU texts touching on issues of power, creating balancing mechanisms and arrangements for control of the exercise of power for the benefit of business, individual persons and citizens, which he claims are crucial for one's understanding of the system. The implications are for the transmission of information and transparency, while preserving the ability of the institutions to function efficiently. Drawing on the analysis of the written texts as signs, the chapter is an attempt to present a picture in terms of a series of relationships that indicate structural contexts in which issues of power, control and transparency arise. There seems to be an inherent balance, he claims, to be achieved between the need for information to the public and the ability of the institutions to work efficiently without undue pressure.

M. Douglas Bellis in his chapter 'Toward an Objective Means of Measuring Governmental Legitimacy' discusses the issue that authoritarian governments are not as stable as they sometimes appear to be, as recent events in North Africa and elsewhere show us. While they may survive for decades, people power seems sooner or later to prevail against them. At the same time, forms of government based more clearly on the consent of the governed appear to last for centuries and may indeed have a sort of permanency. What is the philosophical basis for this apparent empirical fact? During the Enlightenment in Western Europe there arose a belief that this basis was founded in the laws of nature, much as the then contemporary advances in physics were. But this belief became clichéd and discredited over time for a variety of reasons. Instead, a somewhat uneasy and subjective consensus has arisen that governments ought to be 'nice' and respect the rights of their people, though the content of those rights seems arbitrary and subject to ultimate determination by the very governments involved. Without firmer underpinnings, this consensus offers little practical guidance for the determination of the legitimacy of any given government. Perhaps the dismissal of the Enlightenment conclusions was too hasty and based on a trivialization of them rather than on their fundamental, and still persuasive, premises.

Part II: Visualizing and Contextualizing Transparency, Power and Control

Legal communication is an act of showing, sharing, accepting and transforming cultural acts. Habermas (cited in Warnke, 1995) states that in a multicultural society the inclusion of every form of life that has rights consists of the recognition for everybody to have:

> The opportunity to grow up in the world of cultural heritage and to have his or her children grown up in it without suffering discrimination because of it. It means the opportunity to confront this and every culture and to perpetuate it in its conventional form or to transform it (in Warnke 1995: 131)

The chapters in Part II seek to harness the diverse and innovative works within and across the boundaries of law, language and media in various contexts and manifestations to better visualize and contextualize transparency, power and control. Rosen (1990: 157) noted:

> That there is a complex dependency between law and culture is not just a consequence of citizens bringing to the law their cultural baggage and the law seeking a legitimacy that speaks to citizens. Social justice (or at least a morally rich pluralism) depends not only on the autonomy of law but also on the interdependencies of law and culture. Interdependence is normatively required, at least in part, because not only must the law morally matter to a culturally heterogeneous population, but also the law ought to be able to speak to those whose claims it does not currently recognize.

Michelle Wirth in her chapter 'Battle of the Sexters: Teens Celling Sex in a World Wide Web of Conflicting Laws, Values and Social Norms' presents a case study of the practice of 'sexting', where teenagers use the multimedia text message function of their mobile phones to send each other sexually suggestive self-portraits. The chapter describes a legal case (*Miller v Skumanick*) concerned with teenage girls who had engaged in sexting, and found themselves at the centre of legal proceedings as a result. Wirth performs a semiotic analysis of legal documentation, including briefs, judgments and legislation, in order to highlight problematic legal terms and the associated assumptions and world views that are brought to bear in their interpretation. The case described raises a number of interesting issues, including the issue whether a child who has engaged in sexting can be appropriately charged with a criminal offence under anti-child-pornography laws. Wirth observes that in such cases, the child appears to be simultaneously constructed as perpetrator, accomplice and victim. The case demonstrates how legal texts and their interpretations must shift and adapt to accommodate technological change. It is increasingly the case that changes in technology make possible new scenarios which have not been considered at the time that laws are passed, and such changes in technology (and attendant changes in society) lead to the introduction of unexpected ambiguities which have to be resolved by judges charged with settling legal disputes.

Anita Lam in her chapter 'Visualizing the Terrorist Risk in President Bush's War on Terror and Peter Jackson's *The Two Towers*' compares some of the political narrative used by George W. Bush's administration immediately after the events of 11 September 2001 with Peter Jackson's film adaptation of J.R.R. Tolkien's *The Lord of the Rings: The Two Towers* (2002). In her analysis of these two aspects of political and popular culture Lam presents us with comparisons between the ways in which the Bush administration presented itself to the American public by aligning itself with concepts in the film, for instance an epic adventure (against terrorism), good versus evil, light versus darkness, and surveillance in the 'new world order'. In comparing these two cultural artefacts Lam demonstrates a striking similarity in the ways of viewing life and the world. These views are based on Judeo-Christian notions and are embedded in a Western perspective of right versus wrong. In her conclusion, Lam shows how ideas of knowledge and truth are often controlled by those in power who have particular political imperatives.

Massimo Leone presents 'Hearing and Belonging: On Sounds, Faiths and Laws'. 'Belonging' is a frontier-concept in the field of present-day cultural studies on cities and religion. Although the idea of 'belonging' has been considered as central since the early development of city studies – for instance in *Human Communities* by Robert E. Park (1952) and in the other ground-breaking contributions of the Chicago 'urban ethnographers' – both social researchers and policy makers currently believe that the concepts of 'sense of belonging' and 'feeling of belonging' urgently require further investigation. The chapter deals with the issue of religious belonging in contemporary multicultural cities from the point of view of a *sensuous semio-geography*. 'Sensuous semio-geography' is an expression modelled after the title, and the contents, of Peter Stoller's book *Sensuous Scholarship* (1997), which has inspired the most interesting trends in the socio-ethnography of multicultural cities in recent years. The main idea of sensuous semio-geography is to seek to understand how a sense/feeling of religious belonging is articulated not only through visual signs (for instance, the adoption of a certain architectural style for new places of worship, as well as the adoption of a certain style of religious clothing for believers), but also through signs that involve other senses. The chapter focuses, in particular, on sounds: what is the phenomenology of soundscapes in present-day 'Western' multicultural cities? How does it compare with the phenomenology of 'non-Western' or 'non-multicultural' cities? Are such soundscapes multi-religious, mono-religious or a space of acoustic *laïcité*? How do 'sacred' and 'profane' sounds intertwine in the soundscapes of contemporary multicultural cities? What tensions arise in the management of public urban soundscapes? How do bureaucratic, administrative and legal frameworks seek to regulate these tensions?

Maria Giannocopoulos in her chapter 'Terror *Australis*' argues against the view that law can be used as a preventive weapon against terrorism. It posits law as the means through which terror can be quashed, it functions to evacuate terror from the definition of white, Australian law. But the use of language such as 'preventative weapon' and the very idea of a 'weapon' imply strength, force and power, and hence the idea that the law can be a forceful weapon that eliminates terrorism from the national domain brings forth the seeming aporia that such law is implicated in war that is disguised in the language of civility. She analyses in detail the parliamentary debates around the *Anti-Terrorism Bill* in Australia and claims that the *democratic* process through which a Bill is transformed into an Act of law reveals that even the critics of the process are instrumental in reproducing one of the primary myths of white law, that it is a location free from violence.

David Tan in his chapter '"The Unbearable Whiteness of Beckham": Semiotics and Political Recoding of the Contemporary Celebrity' examines the celebrity as a form of cultural power and its significance in identity formation (assuming the celebrity sign as an embodiment of particular meanings for the majoritarian public). He argues that certain uses of the celebrity sign may be 'political speech' protected by the First Amendment, depending on its content, form and context, which he claims, adopts the premise that the underlying rationale of the First Amendment is the advancement of a democracy where the public can freely participate in deliberating issues important to decision making. From these, he contends that the augmentation of this participatory theory of the First Amendment with cultural studies insights is likely to lead to better outcomes in cases because more speech of 'greater' constitutional value is protected – i.e. speech that contributes to an increased awareness and debate of public issues – while speech of 'lesser' value need not be accorded the same level of protection. He goes on to show that First Amendment jurisprudence, especially Supreme Court decisions, supports an overarching approach to the First Amendment in terms of a participatory theory that places the highest constitutional value on political speech, thus arguing that the various tests formulated to give effect to First Amendment goals in right of publicity claims do not accord sufficient protection to political speech because they do not adequately address how uses of the celebrity identity may contribute to the advancement of democratic deliberation and debate. This is demonstrated through an analysis of the three main judicial tests presently used to articulate a First Amendment defence in publicity claims. Tan further contends that cultural studies writings on the political significance of the celebrity semiotic sign can assist the development of First Amendment jurisprudence and judicial tests in this area. It advances the analysis by recommending ways in which the three tests may incorporate relevant insights on the recoding potential of the celebrity sign especially as used by subaltern groups or counterpublics as an integral part of political and social identity formation, thus concluding that the use of cultural studies allows current First Amendment jurisprudence to be refined to protect political speech in a manner that more effectively negotiates the competing right of the celebrity individual to exploit the commercial value of his or her identity and the right of the public to use the celebrity sign as an expressive communicative resource in a participatory democracy.

In the final chapter in this collection, 'Warhol: Images of Infamy and Underpinning Power', Oliver Watts looks at the tension between two authors of images: Andy Warhol and the state. In his examination of Warhol's *Thirteen Most Wanted Men* Warhol shows how art and the image may illuminate the hidden ideology behind neutral knowledge. Warhol showed through a strategy of differencing how the image is underpinned at any given moment by singularity and that the law cannot easily account for this shifting ground. In his analysis of the *Thirteen Most Wanted Men* issue, Watts shows how the sovereign power is invisible, it is no longer a king's body, or effigy, but merely an ideological quilting point meant to function to make politics *appear* neutral. When Warhol was challenged for usurping the sovereign authority he made the sovereign power show its hand through (censoring) violence. The violence of the law became a crack in the law's edifice at the point that it could not account for the singularity

Warhol asserted. Finally, Watts concludes that Warhol's art was not an act of insurrection or revolution but merely an ethical deconstruction through difference and iteration.

The chapters presented in this book come from authors with various disciplinary and research backgrounds, professional training and life experiences, and cover a variety of interesting and challenging issues in the field of semiotics of law. The underlying theme in all of them is the degree of transparency, power and control used in the present-day socio-legal world. The use and analysis of linguistic as well as other semiotic resources often reveal how power and control is achieved and how transparency is revealed or concealed. We believe that the issues raised in this volume are important, not only for academic study, but also for us to better understand the world we live in, and how we interact with it.

References

Bourdieu, P. 1991. *Language and Symbolic Power*. Harvard, MA: Harvard University Press.

Butler, J. 1997. *Excitable Speech: A Politics of the Performative*. London: Routledge.

Cornu, G. 2005. *Linguistique uridique*. Paris: Montchrestien.

Cutts, M. 2000. Clarity in EC Legislation. *Clarity*, 45, 10-19.

Driedger, E. 1974. *Construction of Statutes*. Toronto: Butterworths Canada.

European Parliament, the Council of the European Union and the Commission of the European Communities. 1999. Interinstitutional Agreement of 22 December 1998 on Common Guidelines for the Quality of Drafting of Community Legislation (1999/C 73/01).

Fish, S. 1989. *Doing What Comes Naturally: Change, Rhetoric, and the Practice of Theory in Literary and Legal Studies*. Durham, NC: Duke University Press.

Gallas, T. 2001. La rédaction législative multilingue dans l'Union Européenne: bilan et perspective. *LeGes – Législation and Evaluation*, 12(3), 115-129.

Gény, F. 1922. *Sciences et Techniques en Droit Privé Positif*. Paris: Recueil Siret.

Moor, F. 2005. *Pour une Théorie Micropoligique du Droit*. Paris: Presses Universitaires de France.

Rosen, R. 1990. Liberal Battle Zones and the Study of Law and the Media. *Law and Human Behavior*, 14(5), 511-521.

Wagner, A. 2005. Les apports de l'analyse linguistique dans la conception du flou et de la sécurité juridique. *La Semaine Juridique, Edition Générale*, 51, 2355-2359.

Warnke, Georgia. 1995. Communicating Rationality and Cultural Values, in *The Cambridge Companion to Habermas*, edited by S.K. White. Cambridge: Cambridge University Press, 120-142.

PART I

Theorizing Transparency, Power and Control in Legal Communication

Chapter 2

Linguistic Uncertainty and Legal Transparency: Statutory Interpretation in China and Australia

Deborah Cao[1]

Introduction

We use and interpret language in various ways each and every day. As language users, we do so according to both linguistic conventions and rules and sometimes arbitrarily and creatively. Similarly, language users in the legal process, be it lawyers, judges or legislators, employ language in ordinary, unordinary or sometimes extraordinary ways. On many levels, these legal language users do not read and interpret legal texts exactly the same way that ordinary language users do. As we know, '[l]egal texts are richly layered with meaning; its language has evolved over many centuries and its peculiar form is a result of this history and specialised use' (Johnson and Coulthard 2010: 1). However, at the same time, we are reminded that the legal world is peopled by a hierarchical mini-nation of judges, lawyers, police and law-enforcement officers and the common man and woman who walk through this strange world (Johnson and Coulthard 2010: 1). Law and justice are not a word game. They produce real and tangible impacts and consequences, sometimes profound and long-lasting, on the lives of ordinary men and women every day. As interpreters of legal texts, the courts and judges are thus constrained by rules and conventions and policies. Such rules and conventions can be linguistic and/or legal, and those that courts follow in different jurisdictions and legal systems are naturally not the same, but all in pursuit of truth and justice. Transparency of such rules is also important for public confidence in and proper functioning of the judiciary and system of justice in all societies.

One of the linguistic constraints that affect the reading of legal texts by judges has to do with the inherently indeterminate nature of language, any language. As we know, linguistic uncertainties sometimes lead to legal disputes and become matters of contention in court. However, a more fundamental issue related

1 Part of the original version of this chapter was first presented to the Legal Drafting Conference organized by the Chinese Legal Drafting Association and Australian Law Council, held in Shanghai, 2009. The author would like to acknowledge the financial support of the Chiang Ching-Kuo Foundation for International Scholarly Exchange.

to linguistic uncertainty is the question of legal transparency and ultimately accessibility to law and effectiveness and accountability of the legal system. This chapter examines linguistic uncertainty in legislative language and discusses the various implications of such uncertainty with specific reference to a comparative perspective of the Chinese and Australian legal contexts, including the different approaches of the court in this regard.

Chinese and Australian laws and legal systems are very different, with the former being a socialist legal order with Western influences and the latter part of the common law system. The Chinese and English languages are also very different, but the laws and the courts in both countries are faced with matters arising from uncertainty in legislative instruments. Both systems have developed their own approaches in dealing with these matters. Irrespective of the methods or approaches used, one fundamental question concerns the transparency of the legal systems involved. This chapter argues that linguistic uncertainty found in legislative language may reveal an aspect of transparency or the lack thereof, of the legal order and the rule of law of a particular jurisdiction. To put it another way, linguistic clarity and certainty in law and transparency are interconnected. If meanings of legislation are hard to understand or difficult to ascertain, or worse still, if such meanings are given arbitrarily to serve particular purposes, then not only accessibility to law but also justice and equality before the law may become casualties.

Linguistic Uncertainty

'Linguistic uncertainty' is used in this chapter as a general term to cover the indeterminate properties of language such as linguistic vagueness, generality and ambiguity. 'Uncertainty' is used here interchangeably with 'indeterminacy'. Essentially, a word, phrase or sentence is ambiguous if it has more than one meaning. An expression is vague or imprecise if it admits of borderline cases in actual use. To say that a concept is vague is to say that there can be no clear determination as to whether or not it applies. For instance, words such as 'tall', 'bald' and 'old', and concept words or cluster concepts such as 'just', 'legitimate' and 'reasonable' are vague. Another example is 'serious'. For instance, for the provision that 'serious consequence will result' if United Nations resolutions are not complied with, what does 'serious' entail: economic sanctions, use of force, or any other consequences? One type of vagueness is intentional vagueness, with words such as 'religion', 'vehicle' and 'fruit' (Moore 1981 and 1985). This kind of vagueness is quite common in law. Courts are often asked to define, say, 'agricultural produce'.[2] An expression is general when it is applicable to any one of a number of things whose differences are not denied or necessarily overlooked.

2 For discussions of law and vagueness and ambiguity, see Hart (1961/1994), Endicott (2000), Bhatia et al (2005) and also Cao (2004 and 2007).

Ambiguity, vagueness and generality are distinguishable, but they are also relative, and sometimes may overlap (Williamson 1994, 2001).

All languages, including Chinese and English, are inherently indeterminate. This linguistic nature is not always realized or appreciated. Ambiguity, vagueness, generality and other such features are often pervasive as well as important.

Linguistic Uncertainty in Chinese Law

There are various sources of linguistic uncertainty as far as Chinese law is concerned and I have examined them in detail elsewhere (Cao 2004). Generally speaking, three major issues of linguistic uncertainty in Chinese legislative texts deserve our attention: inherent linguistic uncertainty, certain common and peculiar linguistic usage, and legal drafting practices. In this chapter, I will briefly discuss some of these aspects with reference to Chinese legislative texts. It is commonly acknowledged that contemporary Chinese law suffers from excessive generality and vagueness. Chinese legislation has been described as having excessive generality, vagueness, omissions, undefined terms and inconsistencies (Peerenboom 2002: 247 and 251; also Ross and Ross 2000). At the same time, generality and flexibility is believed to be the essential guide in Chinese lawmaking and a guiding principle in Chinese legislative drafting (Keller 1994: 749 and 750). The justification offered for this central doctrine in Chinese legal theory is that national legislation must be general and flexible so that it can be implemented throughout the country and adapted to local conditions (Keller 1994: 749). As Keller (1994: 752) notes, Chinese lawmakers have not, in general, attempted to use legislative language supported by rules of construction to strengthen the internal structure and order of positive law. They prefer instead, particularly in relation to primary legislation, that the specific meanings attached to legislative language shift according to their contexts (Keller 1994: 752). Similarly, Chinese administrative bodies also have a preference for broadly drafted laws that leave them free to act as they see fit in specific circumstances (Keller 1994: 752).[3] In short, generality and vagueness is believed to be a prominent feature of contemporary Chinese law, often undermining the certainty and predictability of the emerging Chinese law and legal order.

For examples of some of the linguistic manifestations of generality and vagueness in Chinese law, we will look at the Criminal Code of the People's Republic of China (as amended in 2001). Some Chinese scholars have reportedly found that there are over 100 articles in the Code that contain imprecise and vague

3 As Keller (1994: 749) points out, citing Ma Xiaohong, the principles of generality and flexibility in contemporary Chinese lawmaking have a close parallel with the Chinese imperial legislative tradition. Ma Xiaohong, cited in Keller, believes that the late imperial Ming and Qing legislation was characterized by generality of language, and contemporary Chinese legislative theorists often praise and invoke the views of imperial lawmakers in support of their contemporary practices.

words and expressions. I would like to draw particular attention to the following expressions of vagueness: *qingjie yanzhong* (serious circumstances [in which an offence occurs]), *qingjie tebie yanzhong* (particularly serious circumstances), *qingjie jiaoqing* (light circumstances) *shu'e jiao da* (a rather large sum of money), *shu'e juda* (a huge sum of money). These phrases are used throughout the Code, in relation to different offences, ranging from criminal acts of murder and assault, to economic crimes, environmental crimes, intellectual property right infringement, smuggling, drug trafficking, property crimes, prostitution, pornography, bribery, abuse of office, military offence and offence endangering the state security. Other open-ended and non-inclusive expressions include *qita* (other) and *deng* (etc.).

These descriptive words are vague in Chinese or any other language. In fact, such words are typical expressions of vagueness or imprecision as they indicate borderline cases where there can be no clear determination as to whether or not the expression applies.

There are two kinds of uncertainty in the Criminal Code with regard to these words. First, these words and expressions are vague in a general sense: how 'serious' or 'light' would be considered 'serious' or 'light', or how 'large' or 'huge' would be considered 'large' or 'huge'? They are borderline cases, and the Code does not provide any further qualification or particularization. Second, these words as used in the Code differ in the specific context of use in referring to the degree or extent in different situations or offences. As the offences as specified in the Criminal Code are different, ranging from ordinary criminal offences to economic crimes, the degree or meaning of the 'seriousness' and 'lightness' or 'large' and 'huge' would also differ.

Specifically, let us look at a few examples. The recent Sun Weiming case may be used for illustration. In 2009, the defendant was charged and convicted for the offence of endangering public safety under article 115 of the Criminal Code which reads:[4]

> Article 115 Whoever commits arson, breaches a dike, causes explosion, spreads poisonous or radioactive substances, or infectious-disease pathogens or other substances, or *uses other dangerous means*, thereby inflicting serious injury or death on people or causing heavy losses of public or private, shall be sentenced to fixed-term imprisonment of not less than 10 years, life imprisonment or death. (emphasis added)

In late 2008, Sun Weiming of Chengdu, Sichuan province, killed four people and injured a number of others when he drove under the influence of alcohol and without a licence. This was otherwise a traffic offence which would normally be prosecuted under article 133 of the Criminal Code. However, due to the seriousness of the case and the circumstances of the offence, Sun was charged instead under

4 Chinese texts relied on in this chapter have been translated into English by the author.

article 115 for using 'other dangerous means' to inflict serious injury or death, which carries much heavier penalties including life imprisonment and death as opposed to a maximum of seven years' imprisonment under article 133. In article 115, the expression 'other dangerous means (*qita weixian fangfa*)' is not specified as to exactly what could be included by the Chinese court or the legislature. It is an open-ended and vague expression. Furthermore, the phrase 'heavy losses (*zhongda sunshi*)' is not specified either as to what may be considered 'heavy'. In the first instance, the Chengdu court found Sun guilty of the crime and sentenced him to death. On appeal, and also based on the Supreme People's Court opinion requested for this purpose, which supports the court decision regarding the application of article 133 in this case, the Chengdu Intermediate People's Court upheld the verdict but changed the death sentence to life imprisonment. The Supreme Court indicated that driving motor vehicles under the influence of alcohol and in disregard to the consequences of reckless driving resulting in serious loss of life may be included in 'other dangerous means' as referred to in article 133, thus subject to the punishment of life imprisonment or death sentence. For our purpose, one may say that the phrase 'other dangerous means' is general and uncertain, and it leaves ample room for interpretation or application of the law that may or may not have been envisaged by the legislature originally. Nevertheless, the recent case law in China indicates that such device has indeed been utilized in the enforcement of law and one may argue that the uncertain phrase in the law in this case served its purpose.

Since the Sun Weiming case and a number of similar cases in recent times, a proposed amendment of the relevant provisions in the Criminal Code relating to traffic offences has now been put forward to make the law clearer.

Next let us look at a few different examples of vague and ambiguous expressions, specifically, Articles 338 and 339 of the Code relating to environmental crimes:

> Article 338. Anyone who, in violation of the state regulation, releases, dumps or disposes radioactive wastes, wastes containing pathogen of contagious diseases, toxic materials or other hazardous wastes to land, water or atmosphere, causing a serious environmental pollution accident that results in serious consequences causing serious loss to public *or* private property or personal injury or death is punishable by no more than three years' imprisonment or detention, and is also punished with a fine, or is only punished with a fine; for those accidents resulting in particularly serious consequences, no less than three years' and no more than seven years' imprisonment is imposed together with a fine.

Similarly,

> Article 339. Anyone who, in violation of the state regulation, dumps, stockpiles or disposes solid wastes from overseas to China is punished by no more than five years imprisonment or detention and a fine. Anyone causing serious environmental pollution incidents, resulting in serious loss to public or private

> property or serious harm to human health, is punished by no less than five years' and no more than ten years' imprisonment and by imposing a fine. For those resulting in particularly serious consequences, more than ten years' imprisonment and a fine are imposed.
>
> Anyone who does not have the approval of the relevant departments in charge under the State Council imports without authorization solid wastes as raw materials, causing a serious environmental pollution accident that results in serious loss to public or private property or serious harm to human health, is punished by no more than five years' imprisonment or detention, and is also punished with a fine. For those accidents resulting in particularly serious consequences, no less than five years' and no more than ten years' imprisonment is imposed together with a fine.
>
> Anyone who imports solid wastes, liquid wastes and waste gas in the name of raw materials which cannot be used as such is punished under Sections 2 and 3 of Article 152 of this Act.

There are a number of linguistic uncertainties in the above two provisions involving the use of vague and general words. We can see that in both Articles 338 and 339, the words *yanzhong* (serious), *zhongda* (serious, major or heavy) and *tebie yanzhon*g (particularly serious) are used a number of times. As said above, such words are typical expressions of vagueness and imprecision as they indicate borderline cases. It is not very clear from the wording as to how 'serious' would be considered 'serious' or 'particularly serious' and these words are not further described in the Code. However, they touch on an important aspect in Chinese criminal law.

As pointed out, in Chinese criminal law, determining what constitutes a criminal and capital offence can turn on interpretations of phrases such as 'serious', 'large sum' or 'special circumstances' (Belkin 2000). These are the most obvious and most frequently used words of vagueness in the Code. These words are frequently employed to describe the degree of the seriousness of crimes, extent of harms or damage done by criminal acts and amount of money involved in crimes for the purpose of prescribing penalties and punishment. In this regard, the legal definition of crime in Chinese criminal law is relevant. Article 13 of the Criminal Code stipulates:

> A crime refers to an act that endangers the sovereignty, territorial integrity and security of the States, splits the State, subverts the State power of the people's democratic dictatorship and overthrows the socialist system, undermines public and economic order, violates State-owned property, property collectively owned by the working people, or property privately owned by citizens, infringes on the citizens' rights of the person, their democratic or other rights, and any other act that endangers society and is subject to punishment according to law. However,

> if the circumstances are obviously minor and the harm done is not serious, the act shall not be deemed a crime.

According to Wang, in this legal definition of crime, what we should notice is not only the material characteristic of a crime in China, but also the requirement as to what constitutes a crime (Wang 2004: 153). According to Chinese criminal law and, principally, for the general definition of a crime, any harmful conduct will not be treated as a crime 'if the circumstances are obviously minor and the harm done is not serious' (Wang 2004: 153). In the theory of Chinese criminal law, 'the circumstances' are closely linked with the degree of the social harmfulness caused by the conduct. In the Specific Provisions of the Criminal Code, the circumstances or the degree of the social harmfulness shall be clearly defined (Wang 2004). This is reflected in the form of actual harmful consequences and the sum of the illegal money involved. In some cases, it might be also reflected in the criminal method or criminal mind, but in these cases, the final decisive factor in what constitutes a crime is still the actual harmful consequences (Wang 2004: 153). As Wang points out, because of this requirement of 'the circumstances', Chinese criminal law builds up its unique 'guilty line' for differentiating guilty and innocent. Accordingly, most conduct which is treated as innocent in Chinese criminal law because it is below 'the guilty line' would constitute a crime in other legal systems (Wang 2004). Thus, the seriousness of an act and the seriousness of its social consequence determine whether the act constitutes a crime or not and dictate punishment accordingly, but the vague words 'serious' and 'particularly serious' in the Criminal Code may pose problems in the application of the law and in people's understanding of the law.

Therefore, it is not surprising that the Supreme People's Court issued an explanation for these words as used in the Criminal Code, *The Interpretation of the Supreme People's Court Concerning Certain Issues Related to the Specific Application of Law in Hearing of Criminal Cases regarding Environmental Pollution* (2006). The Interpretation by the Court was issued with regard to the explanation as to what constitutes 'serious loss', 'particularly serious consequences' and 'serious harm' in Articles 338 and 339, quantifying what they mean. The Interpretation states:

> Article 1. Any of the following situations falls under 'serious damage to public [or] private property' referred to in Articles 338, 339 and 408 of the Criminal Code:
>
> 1. causing damage to public [or] private property in the sum of more than 300,000 *yuan*;
> 2. causing the loss of the basic functions or permanent damage to basic agricultural land, protected forest land [or] forest land for special purposes of more than five *mu*, other agricultural land of more than ten *mu*, [or] other land of more than twenty *mu* [a Chinese measurement];

3. causing the death to forest or other forest trees of more than fifty cubic metres, or causing the death to more than 2,500 young trees;

Article 2. Any of the following situations falls under 'serious consequences of personal death [or] injury' or 'serious harm to human health' referred to in Articles 338 and 339 of the Criminal Code:

1. causing the death of more than one person, serious injury of more than three persons, [or] light injury of more than ten persons, or serious injury to more than one person and light injury to more than five persons;
2. causing the occurrence [or] spread of a contagious disease, or causing people being poisoned constituting a situation as classified in Sub-Category III of emergency public health incident as set out in the Plan of the State Emergency Response to Sudden Public Health Incidents;
3. other situations 'causing serious consequences of personal death [or] injury' or 'causing serious harm to human health'.

Article 3. Any of the following situations falls under 'particularly serious consequences' referred to in Articles 338 and 339 of the Criminal Code:

1. causing loss to public [or] private property of more than one million *yuan*;
2. causing the occurrence of situations involving water source pollution [or] people evacuation that are specified in the emergency environmental incidents in above subcategory II as stated in the Plan State Emergency Response to Sudden Environmental Incidents;
3. causing the loss of the basic functions or permanent damage to basic farm land, protected forest, special purpose forest land of more than 15 *mu*, and more than 30 *mu* of other land for agricultural use, [or] other land of more than 60 *mu*;
4. causing the death of forest or other trees of more than 150 cubic meters, or the death of more than 7,500 young trees;
5. causing the death of more than three persons, serious injury to more than ten persons, light injury to more than 30 persons, or serious injury to more than three persons and light injury to more than ten persons;
6. causing the occurrence [or] spread of a contagious disease constituting a situation above those as classified in Sub-Category II of emergency public health incident as set out in The Plan of the State Emergency Response to Sudden Public Health Incidents;
7. other situations with particularly serious consequences.

The Interpretation thus clarifies the meaning of some of the imprecise words in the Code. However, the Interpretation was issued in 2006, almost ten years after the original Code took effect.

Furthermore, in Articles 338 and 339, there are other words of imprecision, for instance, 'relevant departments', 'loss of public or private property'. Of relevance here is the fact that in Chinese statutes there are definitions but many general and vague words are not defined or described. For the example cited above, the Criminal Code does not provide any definition or description as to what may constitute 'loss of public or private property' in Article 338. The Supreme People's Court also recognized this and issued an explanation in the *Interpretation of the Supreme People's Court Concerning Certain Issues Related to the Specific Application of Law in Hearing Criminal Cases Involving Environmental Pollution* (2006):

> The 'loss of public or private property' referred to in this Interpretation includes the damage and destruction to property directly caused by the environmental polluting act, the reduction of the actual value of the property, and the costs incurred for the necessary and reasonable measures adopted to prevent the expansion of the pollution and the elimination of the pollution.

This is not to say that Chinese statutes do not have definitions. In fact, Chinese statutes normally give some definitions to the key terms at the beginning of statutes, for instance, in the Chinese Environmental Protection Law, Article 2 states:

> 'Environment' in this law refers to the total body of all natural elements and artificially transformed natural elements affecting human existence and development, which includes the atmosphere, water, seas, land, minerals, forests, grasslands, wildlife, natural and human historical relics, nature reserves, historical sites and scenic spots and urban and rural areas, among others.

But such definitions are usually restricted to a very few key terms in a statute, in the Environmental Protection Law, 'environment' is the only definition. Furthermore, one can also argue many of the terms that are used to define the key terms need definition themselves, for instance, what is considered 'wildlife' as used in the above definition.

Thus, we have seen that legal uncertainty may arise from the use of words of generality and vagueness. On the whole, in the Criminal Code, there are many other words of generality and vagueness, for instance, 'public interest', 'justified self-defence', 'wilful criminal act', 'work units concerned', 'other laws', 'other regulations'. These words are not defined or detailed. We may further note that in the judicial interpretation by the Supreme People's Court cited above, there are further linguistic uncertainties that will not be discussed here in this chapter.

Linguistic uncertainty in legislative texts is closely linked to drafting practices and principles. Regarding Chinese legislative drafting, as stated earlier, many Chinese laws, especially major national laws, treat many issues in a general way so that they can afford the flexibility for lower level legislature to enact their own local laws. For such situations, statutes need to be general. Thus, Chinese lawmakers and legislative drafters seem to deliberately take advantage of linguistic uncertainty. Notwithstanding such use, excessive use of linguistic indeterminacy and inappropriate and defective use of language may also produce unwelcome uncertainty, undermining predictability and certainty in Chinese law.

Different Approaches to Uncertainty in Legislation in Common Law Jurisdictions

For our purposes, it may be constructive to compare English legislative drafting in common law countries, such as the UK and Australia. General, vague and ambiguous words are also found in the statutes in these jurisdictions. Poor drafting may sometimes also cause problems. Three aspects are worth discussing that present an interesting contrast to Chinese law and legal culture: (1) definitions in an English statute; (2) the roles of the judiciary in statutory construction; and (3) statutory interpretation rules and principles that assist the court to identify meanings and solve disputes.

First, generally speaking, statutory provisions drafted in English in common law countries often have extensive and sometimes very specific and detailed definitions of key terms. Some statutes now have a dictionary section. Statutes from these countries may contain general and vague words and expressions, but on the whole such words are not as extensive as those found in Chinese statutes. Often when vague or general expressions are used in English statutes, they may be accompanied by qualifications or further description in the same statute. For instance, as is the case in English law, the UK Animal Welfare Act (2006), uses the general expression, 'appropriate national authority', but the general interpretation section of the Act clearly defines what 'appropriate national authority' means, that is, it refers to (a) in relation to England, the Secretary of State; and (b) in relation to Wales, the National Assembly for Wales. Another example drawn from the same Act is the use of 'local authority' which is defined in the same statute to refer specifically to, (a) in relation to England, a county council, a district council, a London borough council, the Common Council of the City of London or the Council of the Isles of Scilly; and (b) in relation to Wales, a county council or a county borough council. Some definitions can be very specific and exhaustive in statutes.

In general in such statutes, when a particular word or a phrase used is general or vague but carries legal significance, its definition is expressly contained in the same statute. The same rule generally applies when an ordinary word which may carry an uncommon meaning is used in a statutory provision. For example, the interpretation provision of the UK Animal Welfare Act defines the ordinary word 'premises' as 'any place and, in particular, includes – (a) any vehicle, vessel, aircraft or hovercraft; (b) any tent or movable structure'.

Secondly, when general, vague or ambiguous words are used, they may give rise to disagreement and litigation. In this regard, the court in common law countries plays a vital role providing certainty in cases of linguistic and legal disputes. The court is often asked to adjudicate and clarify and provide legal and authoritative meanings in cases of disagreement. The Australian High Court case of *Palgo Holdings Pty Ltd v Gowans* [2005] HCA 28 illustrates the role of the court in an interesting way.

In *Palgo Holdings Pty Ltd v Gowans*, a question arose as to the meaning of the word 'pawn' as it appeared in a statute of New South Wales (NSW) in Australia. The relevant statute is the 1996 Pawnbrokers Act (NSW). Palgo Holdings was prosecuted for conducting pawnbroking business without a licence in pursuit of the Act. However, evidence shown to the court indicated that Palgo's business should be best characterized as involving chattel mortgage, not pawn or pledge. Consequently, the question was whether the legislation was intended to capture such businesses as well, or whether Palgo's activities fell outside the regulation of the Act. Specifically, the 1996 Pawnbrokers Act (NSW) repealed the Pawnbrokers Act 1902 (NSW), the Second-hand Dealers and Collectors Act 1906 (NSW) and the Hawkers Act 1974 (NSW). The 1902 Pawnbrokers Act extended its reach beyond transactions of pawn and pledge to also cover transactions where money was advanced 'upon interest, or for or in expectation of profit, gain, or reward … upon security, whether collateral or otherwise, of any article taken … by way of pawn, pledge, or security'. However, this definition was not used in the 1996 Pawnbrokers Act. Section 6 of the 1996 Pawnbrokers Act provided that a 'person must not carry on a business of lending money on the security of pawned goods except in accordance with a licence held by the person'. Section 3 defined a pawnbroker as 'a person who carries on a business of lending money on the security of pawned goods'. However, critically, the 1996 Act did not provide a definition of 'pawn' or 'pawned goods'. This became the focus of contention. Thus, the issue before the court was whether the word 'pawn' or 'pawned goods' should be given its popular meaning or whether it should be given a different, specialized and technical legal meaning, because it was used by the law-maker in a specific legal context.

The court held in the majority judgment of McHugh, Gummow, Hayne and Heydon JJ that the High Court of Australia holds the view that if words used in a statute have a general common law meaning, they may be given that meaning if the statute does not provide an alternative definition. The court noted that 'pawn' has a recognized and long-established legal meaning,[5] and the court went back to ancient Roman law and English common law to trace its origin and meaning. The court pointed out that, as with any question of statutory construction, it is necessary to begin with the legislative text itself.[6] The court found that pawns or pledges are distinguished from chattel mortgages, and the property rights thus created, and the rights of the lender and borrower are fundamentally different between the two types of security, and thus the word 'pawn' could not include two forms of security that are mutually exclusive. The court held that, for words that have long-established legal meanings, if the parliament intends to depart from the established legal meanings, then that departure needs to be reflected in the legislation by the use of a definition that is appropriate to the context.[7] In the instant case, the legislation failed to provide a definition different from the long established common law meaning for the word 'pawn' even though the legislature may have intended otherwise, and as Palgo's activities could not be described as such as falling under the regulation of the legislation, Palgo's conviction was quashed. As a direct result of the High Court

5 *Palgo Holdings Pty Ltd v Gowans* [2005] HCA 28, at [9], per Kirby, J.

6 *Palgo Holdings Pty Ltd v Gowans* [2005] HCA 28, at [9], per Kirby, J.

7 *Palgo Holdings Pty Ltd v Gowans* [2005] HCA 28.

decision, the relevant state parliament, the NSW legislature, subsequently amended the Act to correct the problem.[8] Thus, we have seen that in this case, the poorly drafted statute failed to achieve its intended purpose and had to be amended.

Thirdly, in many instances, otherwise seemingly ordinary words in legislation may require the court to provide authoritative interpretation as to their precise legal meanings. For instance, many words in the Australian Constitution have particular legal meanings and are understood and applied by the court with reference to their legal meanings. Words such as those found in section 51 of the Constitution that the court has been asked to interpret over the years include 'insurance', 'bills of exchange', 'promissory notes', 'bankruptcy', 'insolvency', 'copyrights', 'trade marks', 'naturalisation', 'aliens', 'corporations', 'trading corporations', 'marriage', 'divorce', 'conciliation' and 'arbitration'. So, how does the court identify and find meanings and what are the guiding principles or philosophy for the court in statutory interpretation?

By way of illustration, in a 2004 case, *Singh v Commonwealth of Australia* [2004] HCA 43, Gleeson CJ of the High Court explained:

> The concepts which those terms signify, in the context of the Constitution, can only be identified by reference to legal usage and understanding. Thus, when a dispute arose as to whether an incorporated local government authority that sold electrical appliances was a 'trading corporation' within the meaning of s 51(xx), the question was not resolved by consulting a dictionary, and looking up the meaning of the noun 'corporation', and the verb 'to trade'. This Court held that, although the authority in question was a corporation, and although it traded, it was not a trading corporation. In reaching that conclusion, the Court looked to the history of the development of corporations law, and noted that, at and around the time of Federation, legal authorities treated trading corporations and municipal corporations as entities of a different kind. The relevance of contemporary legal usage was that it formed part of the context in which the expression 'trading corporations' was adopted, and an understanding of the context was necessary to a conclusion about the constitutional meaning of the expression. Furthermore, … some expressions used in the Constitution, such as 'a writ … of prohibition', or 'patents of inventions', have no meaning other than as technical legal expressions. A knowledge of the law, including legal history, is indispensable to an appreciation of their essential characteristics.[9] (citations omitted)

This example illustrates the application of one statutory interpretation principle – the contextual approach. *Contextual interpretation* means that the meaning of words in legislation is not derived by taking a word in isolation and construing it as if it existed in a vacuum.[10] In a statute, a word (if undefined) normally takes its meaning from the

8 See Pawnbrokers and Second-hand Dealers Amendment Act (NSW).

9 *Singh v Commonwealth of Australia* [2004] HCA 43 at [10] per Gleeson, CJ.

10 *Palgo Holdings Pty Ltd v Gowans* [2005] HCA 28, at [37], per Kirby, J.

surrounding text.[11] Words are not to be taken out of the context and the context can be legal, cultural and historical. As pointed out by Gleeson CJ, meaning is always influenced, and sometimes controlled by context, and the context may include time, place and any other circumstances that could rationally assist understanding of meaning.[12] This also includes the immediate context of the legislation, and in the case of the Australian Constitution, the context includes the whole of the instrument, its nature and purpose, the time when it was written and came into legal effect, other facts and circumstances, including the state of the law, within the knowledge or contemplation of the framers and legislators who prepared the Constitution or secured its enactment, and developments, over time, in the national and international context in which the instrument is to be applied.[13]

Another important principle for the elucidation of contested statutory language that guides the High Court is *purposive interpretation*, that is, a purposive, not a literal, approach in statutory construction:[14]

> A search for the grammatical meaning still constitutes the starting point. But if the grammatical meaning of a provision does not give effect to the purpose of the legislation, the grammatical meaning cannot prevail. It must give way to the construction which will promote the purpose or object of the Act.[15]

As *Palgo* illustrates, the High Court has also placed a limit on the purposive approach. The legislature is restrained by meanings accumulated in the legal history and culture. If the legislature intends to achieve its purpose, it needs to express it in a proper manner in the legislative text.

The High Court case *Singh v Commonwealth of Australia* also illustrates the complex roles of the court. It involves the definition of the word 'alien' in the Australian Constitution. The proceedings challenge the validity of section 198 of the Migration Act 1958 (Cth), which provides for the removal of unlawful non-citizens in its application to the plaintiff, a non-citizen born in Australia to Indian parents. Without going into the details of the case, the Commonwealth contended that section 198, in its application to the plaintiff, is a valid law made pursuant to the power conferred upon Parliament by section 51(xix) of the Constitution, that is, the power to make laws with respect to 'naturalization and aliens'. The plaintiff's case was that, notwithstanding her Indian citizenship and her lack of Australian citizenship, by virtue of the fact that she was born in Australia, she was not an alien, thus, it was beyond the legislative competence of the Parliament to

11 *Palgo Holdings Pty Ltd v Gowans* [2005] HCA 28, at [37], per Kirby, J.

12 *Singh v Commonwealth of Australia* [2004] HCA 43 at [12] per Gleeson, CJ.

13 *Singh v Commonwealth of Australia* [2004] HCA 43 at [12] per Gleeson, CJ.

14 For discussion of statutory interpretation in Australia, see Corcoran and Bottomley (2005), and Gifford (1990). For discussion of common law statutory interpretation in general, see Cross et al. (1995) and Bennion (2002).

15 *Palgo Holdings Pty Ltd v Gowans* [2005] HCA 28, at [35], per Kirby, J.

treat her as such. For our purpose, in relation to the role of the court in interpreting the Constitution, Gleeson CJ pointed out:

> Everyone agrees that the term 'aliens' does not mean whatever Parliament wants it to mean. Equally clearly, it does not mean whatever a court, or a judge, wants it to mean. When a judicial decision is made in the course of judicial review of legislative action, for the purpose of determining constitutional validity, it is made by reference to a standard other than current public opinion. In a representative democracy, the will of Parliament is the most authentic and legitimate expression of public opinion. It may be imperfect, but it is through the political process, culminating in legislative action, that public policy is formed and imposed. It is not the role of the judiciary to give effect to an understanding of public opinion in opposition to the will of Parliament. When a law enacted by Parliament, which represents, or purports to represent, current community values, is declared unconstitutional and invalid, the judicial arm of government is imposing a restraint upon the power of a democratically elected legislature by reference to a written instrument, the Constitution. The source of the restraint is the legal effect of the instrument, not the will of the judiciary. The legal effect of the instrument is determined by the meaning of the text.[16]

The court held that Singh was an alien, and the Commonwealth had the power under section 51(xix) of the Constitution to make the relevant valid law applicable to her. The lesson for us here is that the role of the court in Australia is to interpret law made by the legislature, but the court and the legislature are both restrained by the text of the law in identifying meanings of the text. Meanings of words change over time in ordinary discourse as well as in law. The court is guided by the interpretive principles long established by the court in this endeavour.

Legal Implications of Linguistic Uncertainty

Language used in law as in other areas is characterized by indeterminacy, or 'open textureness' as Hart calls it, with a core of settled meaning and a penumbra of uncertainty (Hart 1961/1994). The English legal language is not immune from imprecise and ambiguous expressions. English legal jargon such as 'fair and reasonable', 'due process of law' is vague and elusive. So are abstract legal expressions such as 'justice', 'due diligence' and 'reasonable endeavours'. Languages are inherently uncertain. For our purpose, for Chinese language and Chinese law, Chinese law should not be more uncertain than English law, but in reality, it is more uncertain, at present and for the foreseeable future. Major reasons, I believe, are the lack of coherent and consistent legal narrative in China, and the lack of precedent which may settle indeterminate cases in reference to

---

16 *Singh v Commonwealth of Australia* [2004] HCA 43

a settled past legal history as it exists in English common law. Legal rules and judicial interpretation I refer to here, as we have seen in the foregoing, differ from legislative interpretation practised in China when the Supreme People's Court issues binding legislative interpretation to define statutory provisions. This is very different from case law determined on the basis of legal dispute and precedent. It is noted that legal systems and legal cultures differ and the interpretative practices of the judiciary in different countries also differ and are influenced by the indigenous and complex political, cultural and institutional factors of each country.

Endicott (2000), in his study of indeterminate language and law in English, points to a paradox in law. On the one hand, Endicott notes, for law and rule of law, there is a consensus about the requirements: law must be open, clear, coherent, prospective and stable (Raz 1979 and Fuller 1969). Law that fails to meet these requirements would not be law, and a legal system that lacks them to some degree is defective in a legal sense (Endicott 2000: 185). So, either such linguistic unclarity, be it vagueness, ambiguity or generality, must be eliminated in the language used in law, or law and rule of law cannot be attained and arbitrary government will result. On the other hand, linguistic uncertainty is inherent in language, and cannot be eliminated, thus is ineliminable from a legal system (Endicott 2000: 190). Furthermore, law commonly appeals to moral considerations, and such general moral evaluative considerations are necessarily vague. This is the most important source of vagueness in law (Endicott 2003: 114, and also Endicott 2000). Not every law needs to be vague, but all legal systems necessarily have vague, general and uncertain laws. In fact, it is inconceivable for a community to be completely regulated with precise and exact laws (Endicott 2000: 190). Given the above dilemma, Endicott argues that a vague law does not necessarily represent a deficit in the rule of law. By the same token, replacing a vague law with a precise law does not necessarily bring a community closer to the ideal of the rule of law (Endicott 2000: 191). But what is important here is that the judiciary plays a critical role in making law certain and stable.

In China's case, due to historical reasons and the influence of the civil law system and legal, political, cultural and institutional reasons, established legal rules and principles of statutory interpretation are yet to form as they exist in common law formulated over the centuries. It is fair to say that uncertain laws enable authorities to make decisions or exempt their actions from the law as it happens not infrequently throughout China's modern history. In China, courts in recent years have started to formulate interpretive rules, but they are not systematic and not binding. There is not yet a coherent body of legal principles or rules of statutory interpretation which may be necessary as part of the construction of the emerging legal order in China.

Relevantly, poor and improper use of language in court decisions by judges has also been a problem in China. It was reported in the Chinese media that some court judgments contain linguistic errors and that some courts feel too embarrassed to publish poorly written decisions. Such linguistic errors include ungrammatical or wrong usage, use of slang, inappropriate use of words, accidental omission or addition of words, typographical errors, punctuation errors, impropriate use of classical Chinese mixed with colloquialisms, mistakes in writing litigants' names, among others.[17] It was reported that some judges in Sichuan Province were accorded with disciplinary and financial sanctions in 2004 for linguistic errors in their judgments after the court in Sichuan held that a linguistic error in a court decision may make the judgment a wrong decision. Further improvement of legal drafting standards by all concerned will undoubtedly reduce some of the uncertainties in Chinese law, even though indeterminacy in language and law can never be eliminated, in Chinese and other tongues.

In short, linguistic uncertainty is part of law, but the law is also concerned with establishing unitary and universally applied meanings; accordingly, the courts have devised rules of construction to resolve such uncertainties. Linguistic or grammatical meanings and legal meanings are not necessarily the same. By the same token, ordinary interpretation and legal interpretation are not the same. It is appropriate to quote the words of a judge from the New South Wales Court of Appeal, Priestley JA, who noted that the purpose for which courts seek to discover the meaning of a text is different from the purpose of a literary critic or an historian.[18] He wrote,

> Courts have to decide the meaning of texts in a way that will affect the property or civil rights of the parties before the court directly, and which may have an effect on the property or civil rights of many parties not before the court …
>
> Courts, unlike literary critics, are not usually in a position to start afresh, even if so disposed, every time the meaning of a particular text is being considered. No doubt every successive reader of both a literary and a legal text will come to it with a somewhat different perception of its possible meaning than anyone had before; the literary interpreter can take advantage of the fact that the meaning of a text can be approached as never closed; the legal interpreter is constrained when … an authoritative meaning for legal purposes has previously been seen in the text.[19]

---

17 Interestingly, in May 2009 a Chinese court found a litigant guilty of using a swear word in a statement to the court and sanctioned this litigant for using inappropriate and offensive language. Separately, in a criminal case in late 2008 by a county people's court in Anhui province, convictions were made against three offenders for sexual crimes. The court used such vague wording in its final decision that the crime was committed 'in an afternoon around February or March of 2008' (2008 年二三月份的一天下午), and this caused some considerable concern among Chinese netizens who argue that since the court and the prosecution could not be even be certain as to when the crime actually was committed, there must be some doubt surrounding the case for the convictions.

18 Priestley, JA. 1995, 'Judges as Story Tellers', paper delivered at the Law and Literature Association Conference, San Francisco, October 1995, cited in *Singh v Commonwealth of Australia* [2004] HCA 43, at [8] per Gleeson CJ.

19 Priestley, JA. 1995, 'Judges as Story Tellers', paper delivered at the Law and Literature Association Conference, San Francisco, October 1995, cited in *Singh v Commonwealth of Australia* [2004] HCA 43, at [8] per Gleeson, CJ.

In common law jurisdictions, when judges interpret law involving linguistic uncertainty, they make normative decisions. In some cases, linguistic uncertainties in law cannot be easily resolved or may not be possible to resolve linguistically. But the court is never entitled, on the principle *non liquet* (it is not clear), to decline the duty of determining the legal meaning of a relevant enactment (Bennion 2002: 14). It must provide a correct interpretation in case of uncertainty. Judicial interpretation is constrained by established laws, the legal rules and principles governing statutory interpretation, policy and other considerations. This latter point is true not just for common law judges, but for judges in all jurisdictions.

To conclude, in this chapter, there are three major aspects that can be highlighted relating to linguistic uncertainty and transparency: inherent linguistic uncertainty in either Chinese or English; linguistic clarity in legislation that can minimize uncertainty, making law accessible to all as required by rule of law; and the role of the court in cases of legislative ambiguity or unclarity in making law certain. As China is still developing its legal system, there are considerable challenges to the latter two aspects in the Chinese system. In this sense, the Chinese legal system is still defective and deficient, more so compared with the more mature common law system. Given the vast changes that have taken place in the Chinese legal order over the past 30 or so years, optimistically, perhaps rule of law is slowly emerging in China so that Chinese law one day will become transparent, open, clear, coherent and stable as it ought to be for the benefit of many millions of Chinese citizens.

References

Belkin, I. 2000. 'China's Criminal Justice System: A Work in Progress'. *Washington Journal of Modern China*, 6(2), 61-84.

Bennion, F. 2002. *Statutory Interpretation: A Code*. 4th edition. London: Butterworths.

Bhatia, V., Engberg, J., Gotti, M. and Heller, D. (eds). 2005. *Vagueness in Normative Texts*. Bern: Peter Lang.

Cao, D. 2004. *Chinese Law: A Language Perspective*. Aldershot: Ashgate.

Cao, D. 2007. *Translating Law – with Foreword by Justice Michael Kirby of the High Court of Australia*. Clevedon: Multilingual Matters.

Corcoran, S. and Bottomley, S. (eds). 2005. *Interpreting Statutes*. Sydney: The Federation Press.

Cross, R., Bell, J. and Engle, G. 1995. *Cross: Statutory Interpretation*. London: Butterworths.

Endicott, T. 2000. *Vagueness in Law*. Oxford: Oxford University Press.

Endicott, T. 2003. 'Raz on Gap: The Surprising Part', in *Rights, Culture, and the Law: Themes from the Legal and Political Philosophy of Joseph Raz*, edited by L.H. Meyer, S.L. Paulson and T.W. Pogge. Oxford: Oxford University Press, 99-115.

Fuller, L. 1969. *The Morality of Law*. New Haven, CT: Yale University Press.
Gifford, D. 1990. *Statutory Interpretation*. Sydney: The Law Book Company.
Hart, H.L.A. 1961/1994. *The Concept of Law*. 2nd edition, with a Postscript edited by Penelope A. Bulloch and Joseph Raz. Oxford: Clarendon Press.
Johnson, Alison, and Coulthard, Malcolm, 2010. 'Introduction: Current Debates in Forensic Linguistics', in *The Routledge Handbook of Forensic Linguistics*, edited by M. Coulthard and A. Johnson. London: Routledge, 1-15.
Keller, P. 1994. 'Sources of Order in Chinese Law'. *American Journal of Comparative Law*, 42(4), 711-759.
Moore, M.S. 1981. 'The Semantics of Judging'. *Southern California Law Review*, 55, 151-294.
Moore, M.S. 1985. 'A Natural Law Theory of Interpretation'. *Southern California Law Review*, 58, 277-398.
Palgo Holdings Pty Ltd v Gowans [2005] HCA 28 (High Court of Australia).
Peerenboom, R. 2002. *China's Long March toward Rule of Law*. Cambridge: Cambridge University Press.
Raz, J. 1979. *The Authority of Law*. Oxford: Clarendon Press.
Ross, C. and Ross, L. 2000. 'Language and Law: Sources of Systemic Vagueness and Ambiguous Authority in Chinese Statutory Language', in *The Limits of the Rule of Law in China*, edited by K. Turner, J.V. Feinerman and R.K. Guy. Washington, DC: University of Washington Press, 221-270.
Singh v Commonwealth of Australia [2004] HCA 43 (High Court of Australia).
Wang, S. 2004. 'Environmental Crime and Environmental Criminal Law in the People's Republic of China'. *European Journal of Crime, Criminal Law and Criminal Justice*, 12(2), 150-165.
Williamson, T. 1994. *Vagueness*. London: Routledge.
Williamson, T. 2001. 'Vagueness, Indeterminacy and Social Meaning'. *Critical Studies*, 16, 61-76.

Chapter 3
The Power of Legal Conditionals in International Contracts

Celina Frade[1]

> But, as I shall try to show, a legal duty so called is nothing but a prediction that if a man does or omits certain things he will be made to suffer in this or that way by judgment of the court, and so of a legal right.
>
> Oliver Wendell Holmes, Jr (1897: 169)

Introduction

Conditional constructions are essential for our understanding of language and how our actions are guided, and have been a central concern for linguists, philosophers and psychologists who have independently developed various perspectives and methods, but 'without a common focus' (Ferguson et al. 1986: ix). Two classic collections of papers offer discussion on various issues related to conditionality: *On Conditionals* (Traugott et al. 1986) attempts to address a multidisciplinary approach so as to combine the different perspectives and traditions; and, as 'a tribute to the first volume', *On Conditionals Again* (Athanasiadou and Dirven 1997) approaches the conceptual domain of conditionality. From linguistic to the psychological, philosophical and logical traditions, these studies reinstate the connection between form, meaning, interpretations and actions of conditionals under discoursal, pragmatic, historical, cognitive and conceptual domains, among others.

Nevertheless, the role of conditionals and the restrictive value they assume in specific discourse genres still remain an open area for linguistic research with few studies in available literature, though there has been some analyses of conditional form and meaning in economics text (Mead and Henderson 1983) and conditionality in international contracts in English (Frade 2004).[2] Most of

1 PhD in Linguistics and ESP Professor at the Universidade Federal do Rio de Janeiro, Brazil.

2 In her PhD thesis, Frade (2004) provides for a more thorough analysis of an international contract, including its origin and development in the common law tradition, its levels of textual organization and its sociocultural contexts. Here, although the discussion on conditionality is partly reproduced from the thesis, issues such as power and control were added to better serve the role of the parties in the current context of international business and commerce.

the extensive discussion on conditionals has been traditionally concerned with legislative writing in the common law system and as one of the complex features of legal English style as a whole.[3] In the particular case of contracts, and different from legislation, conditional constructions are the phenomena which most evidently portray the inherent power of the parties to constrain and guide actions so as to control potential contingencies by anticipating possible (and agreed) solutions.

International contracts are those whereby the agreement made by the parties is potentially submitted to two or more legal systems which, in turn, may provide for different rules on the same subject matter. They are generally written in legal English style and are available in model forms to be reproduced and used in international contexts by multilegal and multilingual parties. This chapter analyses the restrictive value conditionals (schematically *if p, q*) assume in international contracts dependant on the position of *if p*; it also draws on the 'mental spaces' model (Dancygier and Sweetser 1996) to improve the parties' understanding of the correlation between situations and actions by transposing discourse from one current context (the contract rendering valid in the present) into another (the contract solving future contingencies). By doing this, the chapter intends to raise the parties' awareness of their power to reinforce and reproduce institutional authority. The data selected – the Angola Production Sharing Agreement (PSA) – were drawn from a compilation of authentic modern petroleum contracts (Barnes, undated). The chapter concludes by making some considerations and implications of the research on international contracts in the current global context involving multilegal and multilingual parties.[4]

The Power of Legal Conditionals

In discussing the three kinds of power in discourse Scollon (1997: 389), in relation to one of them, considers that '*power* is the ability to frame *discourse events and utterance*'. Assuming that (both the transparent and nontransparent) power of legal English in contracts lies much more in framing *how* and *by whom* clauses are written rather than what the *rules* really mean, the focus on conditionals also intends to show how power is reinforced behind its potential and strategic use in the hands of 'institutional power-holders' (Fairclough 1989: 61).

Broadly speaking, legal conditionals are composed of a main clause (the apodosis) and a subordinate clause (the protasis) introduced by a conditional

3 See Crystal and Davy (1969), Gustafson (1975), Maley (1987) and Durán (2010). Bhatia (1982, 1983, 1984 and 1993) also refers to conditional constructions in legislative statements as 'operational qualifications, which give additional information about the execution or operation of a rule of law' (1993: 115).

4 The free English versions of the references in Portuguese are the author's responsibility.

conjunction, 'which [like] in the majority of conditional sentences in English is *if*' (Dancygier 1993: 403). They fall into only one class of conditional sentences, the so-called 'predictive' conditional, using the present tense in the protasis – *if p* – and future modal markers, usually *shall* or *may*, in the apodosis – *q*.[5] Thus, legal conditionals can be characterized in terms of *backshift*, that is, 'the time reference intended by the speaker is systematically *later* than the time referred to by the verb form in its prototypical (non-conditional) uses' (Dancygier 1993: 406). A typical legal conditional withdrawn from the data (see the following section, 'The Data') is:

> [1] If CONTRACTOR does not comply with the obligation to appoint another operator as provided in the preceding paragraph within thirty (30) days from the date when SONANGOL gave due notice to CONTRACTOR, then CONTRACTOR shall appoint as Operator the entity so designated by SONANGOL.

The tendency to think law conditionally is rather old. Evidence of conditional structures in Anglo-Saxon law dates back to the eleventh and twelfth centuries (Hiltunen 1990). On the other hand, the construction *if p, q* is considered the most important general strategy to rule syntax in legal sentences, according to Crystal and Davy (1969: 203):

> Reduced to a minimal formula, the great majority of legal sentences have an underlying logical structure which says something like 'if X, than Z shall be Y or, alternatively, 'if X, then Z shall do Y'. There are of course many possible variations on this basic theme, but in nearly all of them the 'if X' component is an essential: every action or requirement, from a legal point of view, is hedged around with, and even depends upon, a set of conditions which must be satisfied before anything at all can happen.

Legal rules turn to conditionality due to the 'need to fix the conditions so as to take right decisions' (Luhmann 1985: 28). In case of contractual rules, this tendency assumes a critical problem-solving act between the parties, in which the basic form is 'if certain conditions are fulfilled, a particular decision should be adopted' (Luhmann 1985: 28). This way of decision-making is linguistically instantiated by the conditional construction *if p, q*. With this specific format, not only does law mean a justified behavioural assumption but it also establishes a 'conditional assumption' in the sense of a *if/then* relation between sets of facts and legal consequences whose execution presumes examination and selection. This explains the reason why contractual rules constitute 'conditional programs' (Luhmann 1985: 27):

---

5 See earlier research in Coode (1845) and Bhatia (1982).

> The concept of program means that problems can be defined by specifying the restrictive conditions of their solutions ('constraints') and that they are solvable through decisions based on this definition; moreover, the programmed character means that even this definition of the problem is instantiated by decision processes and is also tested by decisions.

There are advantages to consider contractual rules as conditional programs. Firstly, in spite of not eliminating uncertainties, they become sustainable as long as they take the form of 'contingent uncertainties', that is, as long as 'the behavioral contingency and the sanction contingency' are combined into a kind of *if p, q* selective relation (Luhmann 1985: 29), Secondly, the conditional program consists of the 'opening of possible variations' which, by replacing a simple behavioural expectancy by a binary polar structure allows the change from one side to the other – the condition *if p* to the consequence *q* – 'keeping the counterpart and all the meanings intermediated by them as reference of change' (Luhmann 1985: 30). And, thirdly, conditional programs are algorithms and thus 'automated', reducing the attention and the responsibility in relation to the consequences of the decision: *if p, q* also states 'accepting its consequences without calculating or valuing them' (Luhmann 1985: 30).

Legal conditionals can also be conceptualized as an amalgamation of speech acts since they are comprised of the conjunction of two clauses describing a 'commissive collaborative act' whereby the parties commit themselves to do (or not to do) something in the future (Hancher 1979: 13). As a strategic construction, legal conditionals bind possible future actions to current decisions taken in order to effect the transaction and prevent what Austin (1962: 35) calls 'misexecutions' whereby procedures could not be correctly and completely executed by the parties.

In short, conditional constructions are essential to our understanding of how legal discourse is construed, used and interpreted. In *if p, q* the identification of an alternative world (or worlds) is possible through *p* and what is said about this world (or worlds) is in *q*. Therefore, the parties' ability of 'predicting' future contingencies in a contract and deciding upon alternative solutions is instantiated by means of legal conditionals.

The Data

The data used for this study has been drawn from an authentic petroleum contract (Barnes, undated)[6] – the Angola Production Sharing Agreement (PSA). The PSA

6 An edition of the compilation is available upon request to International Oil and Gas Law, Contracts, and Negotiations through The Southwestern Legal Foundation, P.O. Box 830707, Richardson, TX 75083, USA; Rocky Mountain Mineral Law Foundation, 7039 East 18th Ave. Denver, CO 80220, USA and Association of International Petroleum Negotiators, P.O. Box 51876, Katy, TX 77491, USA.

is considered one of the five 'modern petroleum contracts' or 'second generation contracts'[7] and, generally speaking, is used to determine a company's share of natural resources extracted from a petroleum producing country.

In the current international petroleum business, the institutional framework to regulate the commercial and legal government–company relationship is the modern petroleum contract, which has developed out of the former traditional oil concession agreements prior to the 1950s (Gao 1994). The modern petroleum contract has a dual legal character in that it is both a commercial contract like any other ordinary contract, and also an agreement which possesses public law elements as it deals with state-owned natural resources developed by an alien (see more in Frade 2007). Modern petroleum contracts operate within a national and global scale and display texturing which reflects globalized trends and 'generalized tensions between imported international practices and local traditions' (Fairclough 2001: 25-26).

Due to its length, the integral contract is not presented here but as it displays a considerable amount of conditional constructions to allow a comprehensive analysis, I have selected some representative examples drawn from the data for discussion in the next section.[8]

On Legal Conditionals

According to Dancygier (1998: 10), 'it is necessary, in describing conditionals, to choose a set of descriptive parameters'. Therefore, we will address the following basic parameters or domains to provide for an understanding of how conditionality is manifested in legal discourse: on the discourse level, conditionals will be described in terms of the relation form-function, their main conditional markers and clause order whereas on the cognitive level they will be interpreted under the mental space model out of real-world situations.

The Relation Form-Function

We can identify four main functional categories of 'conditional meaning' in legal conditionals: a) the predictive conditional; b) the directive conditional; and c) the restrictive conditional (Frade 2004). Such categories are in turn associated with a series of formal constraints as to the syntactic mobility of *if p* to better serve their communicative purposes. The main conditional patterns (and their respective examples) found in international contracts are:

---

7 The others are the Modern Concession Contract (MCC), the Risk Service Contract (RSC), the Hybrid Contract (HC) and joint-venture and their substantive content basically refers to risk, control and profit sharing (Gao 1994).

8 See also Frade (2007) on power dynamics in modern petroleum contracts.

Pattern 1: if + NP + VP [present tense] + then + NP + M + VP[9]

[2] If CONTRACTOR does not comply with the obligation to appoint another operator as provided in the preceding paragraph within thirty (30) days from the date when SONANGOL gave due notice to CONTRACTOR, then CONTRACTOR shall appoint as Operator the entity so designated by SONANGOL.

Pattern 2: if + NP + VP [present tense] + NP + M + VP

[3] If following the discovery of a Commercial Well, the subsequent Appraisal Well, or Wells, are completed as producing or injection Wells their costs shall be treated as part of the Development Expenditures for the purpose of calculating the amount of Cost Recovery Crude Oil.

Pattern 3: NP + M + if + NP + VP [present tense]

[4] SONANGOL shall make the required funds available to CONTRACTOR the amounts paid to SONANGOL pursuant to Article 4(e) of Annex C plus accrued interest, if such request is made.

It is worth pointing out that there is not a one-to-one relation between the categories and the patterns described above, except for the restrictive conditional which always occurs in Pattern 3. On the other hand, the syntactic mobility of conditions in medial position in the clause makes its formal classification impossible as they appear 'somewhere in the middle of the "consequence" clause' (Ford and Thompson 1986: 356).

A predictive conditional 'makes a statement about the logic outcome of a given situation' (Mead and Henderson 1983: 142) and is the most frequent category of legal conditionals. It orders the relation between the parties and selects, among many possible ones, the compatible and agreed outcome in the case of a given contingency. The prediction is subject to the *ceteris paribus* principle whereby the elimination or omission of 'other things' in a process implies in its non-relevance for the purpose at hand (Mead and Henderson 1983: 142).

[5] If CONTRACTOR does not comply with the obligation to appoint another operator as provided in the preceding paragraph within thirty (30) days from the date when SONANGOL gave due notice to CONTRACTOR, then CONTRACTOR shall appoint as Operator the entity so designated by SONANGOL.

In [5], the appointment of 'Operator the entity so designated by SONANGOL' eliminates any and all other possibilities stated in *q* in case of Contractor's non-compliance with the obligation stated in *if p*.

9 NP = nominal phrase; VP = verbal phrase; M = modal.

On the other hand, the directive conditional is not used to interpret the contents but rather to indicate the reader 'how to interact with the context' and has the function of initiating 'a chain of interactive references' between text-reader by means of textual-mapping either within the clause or elsewhere in the text (Mead and Henderson 1983: 153):

> [6] 3. If the conditions referred to in paragraph 2 have been met, SONANGOL may, as to any operation described in paragraph 1, give a written sole risk notice to CONTRACTOR and the latter shall have the following periods of time from the date of receipt of such sole risk notice within which to notify SONANGOL whether it elects to undertake such proposed operation as part of the Petroleum Operations:
> (a) as to any operation described in paragraphs 1(a) and (b), 48 hours or until commencement of the deepening operations, whichever occurs last;
> (b) as to any operation described in paragraphs 1(c) and (d), 3 months;
> (c) as to any operation described in paragraphs 1(e) and (f), 6 months.
>
> 4. If CONTRACTOR elects to include as part of the Petroleum Operations the operation described in the sole risk notice within the appropriate period described in paragraph 3 of this Article, such operation shall be carried out by the Operator within the framework of the Petroleum Operations under this Agreement, as a part of the current Work Program and Budget, which shall be considered as revised accordingly.

As pointed out in Frade (2004: 62), textual-mapping involves three main operations, illustrated in [6]: a) spatial and syntactic breaking up of the provision into several itemized or numbered sub-provisions (article 3 in [6]); b) indexing the various sub-provisions for ease of reference (items 3(a), (b) and (c)) and c) forward and backward intra-textual cross-referencing to place sub-provisions in a wider textual context ('paragraph 2' in article 3 and 'paragraph 3' in article 4).[10]

And finally, a restrictive conditional is always placed at the end of the clause and has the function of clarifying or restricting what is expressed in the preceding clause, as underlined in [7].

> [7] An initial Exploration Phase of four (4) Contract Years shall start from the Effective Date. One (1) successive extension of two (2) Contract years (the Optional Exploration on Phase) shall follow the Initial Exploration Phase upon CONTRACTOR's written notice to SONANGOL at least thirty (30) days before the end of the Initial Exploration Phase and if Contractor has fulfilled its obligations in respect of such Phase.

10 Bhatia (1993: 211) refers to 'textual-mapping' as a device used in legislative writing to 'reduce information load at a particular point in the expression of legislative content'.

The restrictive conditional also seems to evidence Ford and Thompson's (1986: 359-361) claim that a conditional clause appearing in final position occurs within a nominalization, as in our example above.

Conditional Markers

Legal conditionals are marked by 'a special set of boundary markers or brackets of a conventionalized kind' (Goffman 1974: 251), which we will call 'conditional markers'. Not only the conditional markers establish the beginning of a specific act but also 'a slot for signals' which will inform and define what kind of decision is to be made within the clause (Goffman 1974: 255).

Conditional markers are discursive values insofar as they 'look **simultaneously** [author's original emphasis] forward and backward – that the beginning of a clause is the end of the other and vice-versa' (Schiffrin 1987: 37). The most frequent markers occurring in legal conditionals are described in Figure 3.1:

If p	*q*
if, unless, in case (of/that) in the event (of/that), should, provided (that), except (that), only if, even if, as far as, without, except (that/as), save (that/as), as/so long as; once, when, where, notwithstanding whereas	*then* (optional)

Figure 3.1 Conditional markers

If is regarded the 'primary exponent of the conditional meaning in English' (Dancygier 1998: 14) and is also the most frequent marker in legal discourse. It is argued to have three functions: it introduces one of the clauses of a conditional construction which 'presents the assumptions *p* and *q* connected in a given cognitive domain'; it acts like a 'space builder' for conditional spaces in the mental process of space construction and it is a marker of 'non-assertiveness' (Dancygier 1998: 23). A prototypical legal *if*-conditional with a heavy noun phrase is underlined in [8].

> [8] If CONTRACTOR does not comply with the obligation to appoint another operator as provided in the preceding paragraph within thirty (30) days from the date when SONANGOL gave due notice to CONTRACTOR, then CONTRACTOR shall appoint as Operator the entity so designated by SONANGOL.

In legal conditionals, *if* is used alone as well as in combination with *even, only* and *as*. When combined with *even,* the clause *even if* specifies a non-relevant condition to its outcome (Haiman 1978). When combined with *only, only if* means '*only in cases in which*', different from *if* which means '*in cases which*', as underlined in [9].

> [9] Originals of records can be exported only with the permission of SONANGOL provided, however, that magnetic tapes and any other data which must be processed or analysed outside Angola may be exported only if a comparable record is maintained in Angola and provided that such exports shall be repatriated to Angola on the understanding that they belong to SONANGOL.

The marker *unless* introduces a negative conditional and is similar to the negative of *if* though there is a major focus on 'the conditions as exceptions', as in 'only … if not' (Quirk et al. 1985: 1093), as highlighted in [10].

> [10] All Exploration Wells referred to in this Article shall test all productive horizons agreed to by SONANGOL, and CONTRACTOR unless diligent test efforts consistent with sound industry practices indicate that it is technically impossible to reach and test all such horizons.

Other typical conventional markers, shown in [11] and [12], occur quite frequently in legal discourse: *in (the) case (of/that)* is used as future reference and understood as '*if it should happen that*'; *in the event (that)* can be replaced by *if* and, due to its extension, is considered 'stylistically awkward' (Quirk et al. 1985: 1093).

> [11] In the case of an emergency in the course of the Petroleum Operations requiting an immediate action, CONTRACTOR is authorized to take all the actions that it deems necessary for the protection of human life and the interests of the Parties. CONTRACTOR shall promptly inform SONANGOL of all actions so taken.

> [12] In the event CONTRACTOR elects to extend the Exploration Period into the Optional Exploration Phase, CONTRACTOR shall be obligated to drill obligatory Exploration Wells (other than Appraisal Wells) to objectives defined in the Approved Work Program and Budget.

The marker *should*, followed by the infinitive, is considered an alternative for the simple present to express an open conditional in formal, legal or quasi-legal contexts (Quirk et al. 1985). In [13], the clause with *should* seems to follow the standard use wherein it refers only to 'concrete events or situations' and it 'contains present decisions with respect to action to be taken in certain future circumstances' (Niewint 1989: 315).

> [13] Should the plan not be presented within the period established in the preceding paragraph SONANGOL may prepare in accordance with generally accepted practice in the international Petroleum industry and at the expense of the CONTRACTOR and the other entities, a plan for the joint development of the deposit.

The marker *provided that* is a bi-conditional expression '*if and only if*' (*iff*) very common in contracts. This expression has its origin in the first statutes and was used as promulgation formula '*It is provided that*' (Bhatia 1993: 140). Nowadays, it continues to be used as an 'all-purpose conjunction' to introduce exceptions or additional conditions to the clause at hand, as shown in [14].

> [14] Within the Initial Exploration Phase, CONTRACTOR will conduct a seismic program covering ___ kilometers of new seismic profiles. This seismic program will begin within six (6) months of the Effective Date provided that a seismic vessel is available.

Besides these more standard conditional markers, there are other markers present in the so-called 'conditionals of courses of events' which refer to different events linked by a relation of 'where' and 'when' and which can bear the same interpretation as conditional clauses with markers *where*, *when*, *whenever*, *wherever* and *once* (Athanasiadou and Dirven 1997: 63). In fact, such markers do not express conditionality but a consecutive sequence of events which may be interpreted based on our knowledge of the real-world as a sequence of conditions and, consequently, relations (Akatsuka 1985). Another interpretation is that these markers express 'general recurrent contingency', according to Quirk et al. (1985: 1089), as evidenced in [15] and [16].

> [15] When the use of material and equipment is temporary and their application on the Petroleum Operations does not justify the reduction in price under the terms indicated in numbers 11 and 12 above, they will be debited on the basis of their utilization.

> [16] Once the plan referred to in the preceding paragraphs has been prepared, the Parties and the other entities will meet and use best endeavours to reach agreement on its implementation.

Less frequent, the markers *as long as* and *so long as* combine condition and time and are semantically similar to *provided that* though less formal, implying '*if and only if*' (Quirk et al. 1985: 1083-1089). *Except (that/as)* and *save (that/as)*, more formal and stylistically restricted, combine exception with condition (Quirk et al. 1985: 1102) and introduce non-finite clauses, mainly *-ed* clauses, as in [17].

> [17] Except as otherwise provided herein, upon completion of an assignment to a non-Affiliate, such assignor shall have no further rights or obligations with respect to the interest in this Agreement so assigned.

The other conditional markers in *if p* described in Figure 3.1 are used similarly to the ones analysed here, except for the conditional construction *whereas ... now, therefore* which typically signals the rhetorical move 'recitals' in English contracts.

In relation to the main clause *q*, *then* is an optional marker in conditionals. In legal discourse, *then* is often omitted due apparently to the fact that its absence does not cause ambiguity though its conditional effect 'reinforce(s) the dependence between the assumptions of p and q' (Dancygier 1998: 181-182). Although its presence does not usually change the interpretation of the clause 'in any very obvious way', the effect of *then* 'strengthens the dependence between the assumptions of *p* and *q*' (Dancygier 1998: 181-182).

Then can also be understood as an anaphoric pronoun referring to the previous conditional clause, that is, to the structure of the main clause *then* which replaces *if* (Haiman 1978: 576). According to Schiffrin (1992), *then* provides with a link in time between the events of time in discourse and between the event and its context and, when in final position, it 'closes the clause when the progression in time in discourse stops'.

Under a pragmatic-cognitive perspective, Dancygier and Sweetser (1997: 116) claim that *then* also 'points deictically' to a specific mental space, be it a literal temporal space, a specific set of circumstances or else a specific abstract discursive contest. For the authors, 'conditional constructions are used for prediction', which is compatible with the deictic referential use of *then* to refer not only to temporal events but also to mental spaces established in the precedent *if p*. Examples [18] and [19] illustrate legal conditionals with *then* and without *then*, respectively.

> [18] If CONTRACTOR does not comply with the obligation to appoint another operator as provided in the preceding paragraph within thirty (30) days from the date when SONANGOL gave due notice to CONTRACTOR, then CONTRACTOR shall appoint as Operator the entity so designated by SONANGOL.

> [19] If following the discovery of a Commercial Well, the subsequent Appraisal Well, or Wells, are completed as producing or injection Wells their costs shall be treated as part of the Development Expenditures for the purpose of calculating the amount of Cost Recovery Crude Oil.

Example [18] depicts a specific circumstance. *Then* occupies a place in the mental space so as to raise a natural inference that *if p* cannot happen in another alternative mental space. On the contrary, in example [19], there is no obligation to establish an explicit causal relation but rather that 'their costs has no effect on the fact that the subsequent Appraisal Well, or Wells, are completed as producing or injection Wells'.

The Order of if p, q

As to Greenberg (1963: 75-84), 'in conditional clauses, the conditional clause precedes the conclusion as the normal order in all the languages'. This statement and the generic and schematic representation of conditional constructions *if p, q* can take us, erroneously, to believe that *if p* always precedes *q* and that this would be a mere syntactic option. Figure 3.2 depicts the possibilities of the mobility of *if p* order in relation to *q* in initial, medial and final position in conditional constructions.

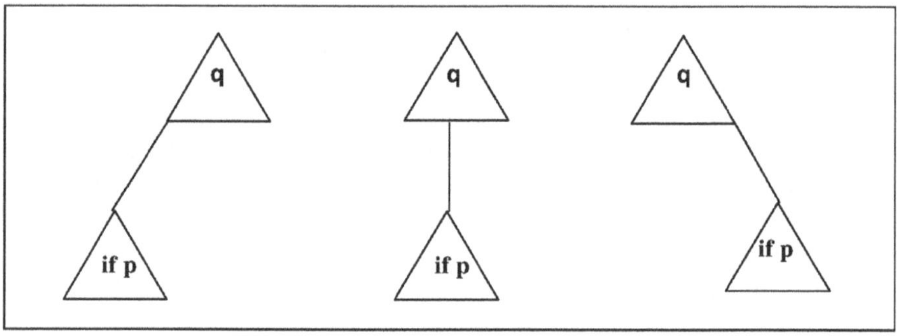

Figure 3.2 Position of *if p* (based on Quirk et al. 1985: 1037)

A brief comparative analysis of the order of *if p, q* in the old Anglo-Saxon laws and current contracts reveals important similarities and differences. At that time, it was a common strategy to expand *if* in initial position by adding a new material through coordinate and subordinate clauses, or both, achieving a relative degree of complexity, as seen in Hiltunen's (1990: 3) example in [20].

> [20] If any man is a newly enslaved penal slave, and he is accused of having stolen before he was enslaved, the accuser then has the right to give him one flogging: he can compel him to the flogging (by an oath of the mount of the stolen goods).

Differently, nowadays the tendency is to place *if p* in final position whenever there is a paratactic sequence (long or not) of conditional constructions in legal discourse. In this case, the same device is often presented by tabulated clause structure to emphasize the cumulative items and facilitate the processing of the clause, as in [21];

> [21] In the event of the occurrence of any of the following, SONANGOL can require CONTRACTOR to immediately appoint another Operator:
>
> a) if the Operator, by action or omission, commits a serious fault in carrying out its obligations and if this fault is not remedied to the satisfaction of SONANGOL within a period of twenty (28) days with effect from the date of receipt by the Operator of written notice issued by SONANGOL requesting the Operator to remedy such fault or within a greater period of time if so specified in the notice;
> b) if appropriate court action has been taken in order to obtain a declaration of bankruptcy, liquidation, or judicial dissolution of the Operator, or if sentence has been passed in court with any of the effects referred to in this paragraph;
> c) if the Operator undertakes the legal procedure established to prevent bankruptcy, or without just cause ceases payment to creditor;
> d) if the Operator terminates or if there is strong evidence that it intends to terminate its activities or a significant proportion thereof, and, as a result fails to fulfill its obligations under the Agreement.

On the whole, *if p* in initial position is of universal application and often expresses a condition which applies to the provision in the main clause *q* whereas, in other positions, 'it is more often than not a remark or an additional provision supplementing what has been stated' (Hiltunen 1990: 38). Also, Bhatia (1993), calls *if p* in initial position a 'preparatory qualification' which specifies the type of restriction to be applied to the provision in *q*, as underlined in example 22.

> [22] If SONANGOL does not exercise the right of first refusal by giving the notification referred to in paragraph 6(b) of this Article, then SONANGOL shall be deemed to have waived the right of that refusal in respect of such assignment.

In medial position, *if p* clauses are 'center-embedded clauses' resulting in serious psycholinguistic problems due to its complicated syntax (Hiltunen 1990: 33). In this position, *if p* plays the role of a comment, an explanation or a repair to something said before suggesting a type of '"impromptu" style, as if the text has been written down from spontaneous dictation' (Hiltunen 1990: 40). In contracts, *if p* in medial position also works as a 'cover term to introduce a variety of qualifications to limit or extend rights, and obligations, powers and scope of application etc.' (Bhatia 1993: 41), illustrated in [23] and [24].

> [23] Pending finalization of accounts, Development Area Profit Oil shall be shared on the basis of provisional estimates, if necessary, of deemed rate of return as approved by the Operating Committee. Appropriate adjustments shall be subsequently effected in accordance with procedures to be established by the Operating Committee.

> [24] The costs of the Commercial Well, if completed as a producing or injection Well, shall be treated as part of the Development Expenditures for the purposes of calculating the amount of Cost Recovery Crude Oil.

According to Hiltunen (1990: 40), *if p* in final position in conditional clauses tends to be less important in content and acts also as a 'comment clause'. The final position of *if p*, favours the 'final strategy' and is the most neutral, natural and varied of the three forms and has the advantage of being open (Hiltunen 1990: 40). In the old Anglo-Saxon laws, the conditional clause presents longer subordinate sequences, as in the author's example [25]:

> [25] The man who holds bookland, which is kinsmen left to him – then we establish that he may not alienate it from his kindred if there is a document or witness (to show) that he was prohibited from doing so by those men who acquired it in the beginning and by those who gave it to him; and that is then to be declared in the witness of the king and of the bishop, in the presence of the kinsmen.

On the other hand, a possible motivation for placing *if p* at the end of the clause is the tendency to introduce an 'interesting subject' in a nondependent clause, seen as an explanation, constraint or comment (Ford and Thompson 1986: 360), as in [26].

> [26] SONANGOL, by means of written notice addressed to CONTRACTOR and the other entities as aforesaid, may also require that a similar procedure to that mentioned in the preceding paragraph be adopted, in relation to other Petroleum deposits within the Contract Area, if these are commercially viable only when developed together with petroleum deposits in areas adjacent to the Contract Area.

An interesting 'test' to understand how the order of *if p, q* in legal conditionals is not merely a syntactic choice but is rather discourse-motivated is a) to approach legal conditionals as a problem-solving strategy and b) to displace the position of *if p* in the clause to check interpretation (Frade 2004). Let us examine one example from our data wherein the initial *if p* is postposed to final position:

> [27] In the event CONTRACTOR elects to extend the Exploration Period into the Optional Exploration Phase, CONTRACTOR shall be obliged to drill

obligatory Exploratory Wells (other than Appraisal Wells) to objectives defined in the Approved Work Program and Budget.

In [27], *if p* in initial position states the problem (or contingency) whose solution or alternative decision is given in the following main clause.

[28] CONTRACTOR shall be obliged to drill obligatory Exploratory Wells (other than Appraisal Wells) to objectives defined in the Approved Work Program and Budget, in the event CONTRACTOR elects to extend the Exploration Period into the Optional Exploration Phase.

Nevertheless, if we move *if p* to final position in the clause as in [28], it does not signal a problem or contingency any longer but rather constrains the preceding action.

The conclusion is that initial and final *if p* performs quite different discourse functions in legal conditionals. An initial *if p* can surely be postposed 'without disastrous consequences to the integrity of the text'; however, as well pointed out by Thompson (1985: 72-73), it is also true that some initial *if p* cannot be postposed at the risk of either giving us 'a strange text in which our expectations are frustrated'. Similar phenomena happen when transposing final *if p* to initial position as evidenced in Frade (2004).

The Linking between p and q

A conditional construction is an example of 'combination of clauses' whose propositions expressed in *p* and *q* are 'circumstantially related' (Matthiessen and Thompson 1998: 277). More particularly, it is an 'enhancing hypotactic clause' wherein the conditional clause enhances the meaning of the main clause qualifying it as a condition (Halliday 1985: 211).

The type of linking between *p* and *q* constitutes an important aspect in the interpretation of legal conditionals. They are interpreted under the 'real-world content domain' as they describe continuing events or states of affairs in the real world (Dancygier 1998: 77). Therefore, two factors contribute to shape the conditional in contracts: sequentiality and causality (Dancygier 1998: 79).

Conditional clauses with initial *if p* are obligatorily iconic of the time sequence of the events. In general, they can be characterized as 'putting things one after another', in a kind of problem-solution sequence rather than 'side-by-side' as what is contingent in the validity of the condition should come after what constitutes the condition (Dancygier 1998: 77). Likewise, causality is part of interpretation when we see the cause–effect relation between *p* and *q* referring to events in real-world from the parties' world knowledge and not pragmatically based, as in [29].

[29] In the event CONTRACTOR elects to extend the Exploration Period into the Optional Exploration Phase, CONTRACTOR shall be obligated to drill

obligatory Exploration Wells (other than Appraisal Wells) to objectives defined in the Approved Work Program and Budget.

The 'mental space model' contributes to the understanding of how the linking between *p* and *q* is related to the sequential and causal interpretation of legal conditionals. Mental spaces are built from a situation in the world to allow us to make previsions based on alternatives and their imaginary continuations. For (Dancygier and Sweetser 1996: 84), 'if we never engaged in prediction, in the construction of (and commitment to) some future scenarios as more likely than others, we could never make decisions or take actions at all'. Let us take example [30] to illustrate in Figure 3.3 how a legal conditional establishes a 'correlation of parameters that structures alternative mental spaces' (Dancygier and Sweetser 1996: 85).

[30] If CONTRACTOR comprises more than one entity, the liability of such members shall be joint and several.

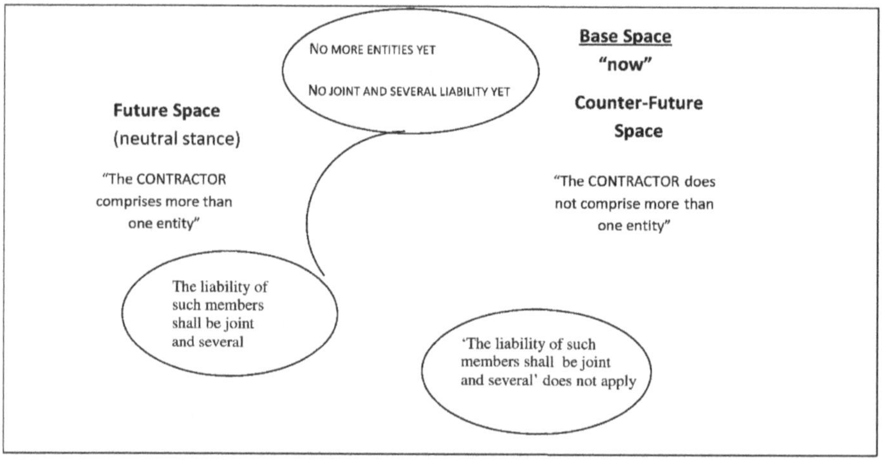

Figure 3.3 Mental spaces of legal conditional (based on Dancygier and Sweetser 1996: 85)

The conditional clause 'If CONTRACTOR comprises more than one entity, the liability of such members shall be joint and several' establishes two alternative mental spaces (both interpreted as 'potential futures' of the reader-author's Base Space): one of them, 'where CONTRACTOR comprises more than one entity' and 'the liability of such members shall be joint and several', and the other 'where CONTRACTOR does not comprise more than one entity' and 'the liability of such members shall be joint and several does not apply'. In other words, the reader does not consider a 'chain of events' but rather simply interprets the possibility of 'the Contractor comprises more than one entity or not'. According to (Dancygier and Sweetser 1996: 86),

> … the properties of mental space construction ensure that the IFF interpretation will be the normal one, since speakers [writers] and hearers [readers] will construct a minimally altered mental space, adjusting it locally as directed by the content of the if-clause.

The most salient mental space is obviously the space 'CONTRACTOR comprises more than one entity' but neither 'If CONTRACTOR comprises more than one entity, the liability of such members shall be joint and several' nor 'If CONTRACTOR does not comprise more than one entity, the liability of such members shall be joint and several does not apply' constitute a 'reasonable mental-space-structure' without the presence of two possible future spaces (Dancygier and Sweetser 1996: 86-87).

Some authors point out that the relations between *if p* and *q* may display variation in interpretation whether they are separated by a comma or not (Dancygier 1998; Thompson 1985). However, this issue will not be considered here due to the historic irregularity of punctuation in legal discourse in general and, more particularly, in international contracts.

Final Remarks

The increase in globalized commercial and business transactions has enabled researchers (other than legal) to access compilations of authentic and legally valid samples of contracts settled in English between multilegal and multilingual parties provided by sources of authority (organizations, law firms, legal advocates etc.). The result is that linguistic research on the language of the common law can now include contracts in its agenda and resource to more multifaceted insights so as to raise such parties' awareness of the strategic use of certain linguistic constructions and their control in exercising the institutional power dynamics and authority throughout the negotiation process (see Trosborg 1997).

The intended audience of my legal linguistic research on contracts, like the one presented here, is those involved in international transactions, mainly non-English-speaking parties. As modern petroleum contracts operate on a national and global scale nowadays, they seem a quite useful sample of how parties can reach the balance and complementarity of interests, rights and obligations through the understanding of how legal language is used to maintain the required symmetrical relationship. As well pointed out by Trosborg (1997: 113), each party holds 'something of value for the other party (promise and consideration)'. Therefore, it is not a matter of one party exercising power to gain authority over the other party but rather simply a matter of 'explicitly stating who does what' (Trosborg 1997: 113).

By investigating how conditional constructions *if p, q* – legal conditionals – are instantiated in international contracts, this chapter makes an attempt to contribute to the democratization of legal discourse in international contexts so as all parties enter the negotiation on the same level of control and institutional authority they are entitled to, without any potential asymmetry which may arise out of linguistic issues. The same holds for versions of original contracts in English in other languages, if required. Both texts should share the same degree of legal and discoursal prestige equalizing interpretive opportunities for the parties.

References

Akatsuka, Noriko. 1985. 'Conditionals and the Epistemic Scale'. *Language*, 61(3), 625-639.

Athanasiadou, Angeliki and Dirven, René (eds). 1997. *On Conditionals Again*. Amsterdam and Philadelphia, PA: John Benjamins.

Austin, John L. 1962. *How To Do Things with Words*. Cambridge, MA: Harvard University Press.

Bhatia, Vijay K. 1982. 'An Investigation into Formal and Functional Characteristics of Qualifications in Legislative Writing and Its Application to English for Academic Purposes'. PhD thesis, University of Aston in Birmingham, UK.

Bhatia, Vijay K. 1983. 'Simplification v. Easification: The Case of Legal Texts'. *Applied Linguistics*, 4(10), 42-54.

Bhatia, Vijay K. 1984. 'Syntactic Discontinuity in Legislative Writing and Its Implication for Academic Legal Purposes', in *Reading for Professional Purposes: Studies and Practices in Native and Foreign Languages*, edited by A.K. Pugh and J.M. Uljin. London: Heinemann Educational Books, 69-96.

Bhatia, Vijay K. 1993. *Analysing Genre: Language Use in Professional Settings*. London: Longman.

Coode, George. 1845. *On Legislative Expression: Or The Language of the Written Law*. 2008 edition, Whitefish, MT: Kessinger.

Crystal, David and Davy, Derek. 1969. *Investigating English Style*. London: Longman.

Dancygier, Barbara. 1993. 'Interpreting: Time, Knowledge, and Causation'. *Journal of Pragmatics*, 19, 403-434.

Dancygier, Barbara. 1998. *Conditionals and Prediction: Time, Knowledge, and Causation in Conditional Constructions*. Cambridge: Cambridge University Press.

Dancygier, Barbara and Sweetser, Eve. 1996. 'Conditionals, Distancing, and Alternative Spaces', in *Conceptual Structure, Discourse and Language*, edited by A.E. Goldberg. Stanford, CA: CSLI Publications, 83-98.

Dancygier, Barbara and Sweetser, Eve. 1997. '*Then* in Conditional Constructions'. *Cognitive Linguistics*, 8(2), 109-136.

Durán, Estrella Montolío. 2010. 'Discourse, Grammar and Professional Discourse Analysis: The Function of Conditional Structures in Legal Writing', in *Researching Language and the Law. Textual Features and Translation Issues*, edited by D. Giannoni and C. Frade. Bern: Peter Lang, 19-48.

Fairclough, Norman. 1989. *Language and Power*. London: Longman.

Fairclough, Norman. 2001. *Discurso e mudança social* [*Discourse and Social Change*]. Brasilia: Editora UnB.

Ferguson, Charles A., Reilly, Judy S., Meluen, Alice ter. and Traugott, Elizabeth C. 1986. 'Overview', in *On Conditionals*, edited by E.C. Traugott, A. ter Meluen, J.S. Reilly and C.A. Ferguson. Cambridge: Cambridge University Press, 3-20.

Ford, Cecilia E. and Thompson, Sandra A. 1986. 'Conditionals in Discourse: A Text-Based Study from English', in *On Conditionals*, edited by E.C. Traugott, A. ter Meluen, J.S. Reilly and C.A. Ferguson. Cambridge: Cambridge University Press, 353-372.

Frade, Celina. 2004. 'Condicionalidade no Contrato Internacional em Inglês'. PhD thesis, Universidade Federal do Rio de Janeiro, Brazil.

Frade, Celina. 2007. 'Power Dynamics and Legal English'. *World Englishes*, 26(1), 48-61.

Gao, Zhigo, J.S.D. 1994. *International Petroleum Contracts: Current Trends and New Directions*. London: Graham & Trotman/Martinus Nijhoff.

Goffman, Erving. 1974. *Frame Analysis: An Essay on the Organization of Experience*. New York: Harper & Row.

Greenberg, Joseph H. 1963. 'Some Universals of Grammar with Particular Reference to the Order of Meaningful Elements', in *Universals of Language*, edited by J.H. Greenberg. Cambridge: Cambridge University Press, 73-113.

Gustafsson, Marita. 1975. *Some Syntactic Properties of English Law Language*. Turku: Publications of the Department of English, University of Turku.

Haiman, John. 1978. 'Conditionals are Topics'. *Language*, 54, 564-589.

Halliday, Michael A.K. 1985. *Explorations in the Functions of Language*. London: Edward Arnold Publishers.

Hancher, Michael. 1979. 'The Classification of Cooperative Illocutionary Acts'. *Language in Society*, 8, 1-14.

Hiltunen, Risto. 1990. *Chapters on Legal English: Aspects Past and Present of the Language of the Law*. Helsinki: Suomalainen Tiedeakatemia.

Holmes, Oliver W. Jr. 1897. 'The Path of the Law'. *Harvard Law Review*, 10(457), 167-202.

Luhmann, Niklas. 1985. *Sociologia do Direito I*. Rio de Janeiro: Tempo Brasileiro.

Maley, Yon. 1987. 'The Language of Legislation'. *Language in Society*, 16, 25-48.

Matthiessen, C. and Thompson, Sandra A. 1998. 'The Structure of Discourse and Subordination', in *Clause Combining in Grammar and Discourse*, edited by John Haiman and Sandra A. Thompson. Philadelphia, PA: John Benjamins, 275-330.

Mead, Richard and Henderson, Willie. 1983. 'Conditional Form and Meaning in Economics Texts'. *The ESP Journal*, 2, 139-160.

Nieuwit, Pieter. 1989. '*Should* in Conditional Protases'. *Linguistics*, 27, 305-318.

Quirk, Randolph, Greenbaum, Sidney, Leech, Geoffrey and Svartvik, Jan. 1985. *A Comprehensive Grammar of Contemporary English*. London: Longman.

Schiffrin, Deborah. 1987. *Discourse Markers*. Cambridge: Cambridge University Press.

Schiffrin, Deborah. 1992. 'Conditionals as Topics in Discourse'. *Linguistics*, 30, 165-197.

Scollon, Ron. 1997. 'Attribution and Power in Hong Kong News Discourse'. *World Englishes*, 16(3), 383-393.

Thompson, Sandra A. 1985. 'Grammar and Written Discourse: Initial vs Final Purpose Clauses in English'. *Text*, 5, 55-84.

Traugott, Elizabeth C., Meluen, Alice ter, Reilly, Judy S. and Ferguson, Charles. A. (eds). 1986. *On Conditionals*. Cambridge: Cambridge University Press.

Trosborg, Anna. 1997. *Rhetorical Strategies in Legal Language: Discourse Analysis of Statutes and Contracts*. Tübingen: Narr.

Chapter 4

The Directive and Persuasive Style of a Legislative Speech Act and the Transformations Thereof (Illustrated with the Polish Legal Discourse)

Irena Szczepankowska

Introduction

The subject of this chapter is the characteristics of the genre model of legislative speech acts, as well as the indication of reasons and consequences of its style-related transformations: beginning with a directive with elements of persuasion, up to a declaration. Such a model implies a variety of semantic and pragmatic consequences.

A legislative text is regarded here as a complex message subject to schematization, that is as the realization of the 'superstructure', as understood by Teun van Dijk (van Dijk 1977, 1980, 1981), that is the global structure specific to the text type (van Dijk 1980: 128-130). 'The corresponding term of this formal model on the semantic plane is "macro-structure", specifying the global meaning of the whole discourse' (van Dijk 1981: 85) or, in other words, 'the topic of discourse' (van Dijk 1981: 197). The formal and semantic shape of the text is subordinate to its pragmatic function (communication aim) – from this perspective a legislative speech act is a macro-act composed of micro-acts interconnected in a linear and hierarchical manner. Such micro-acts form the individual stages of the communication process (for more information see Maley 1994). The historically shaped style variants of specific legislative texts which realize such global genre models depend to a small extent on individual choices of their author. On the other hand, they are determined by the communication convention applicable at that time and the common knowledge of the discourse participants, which permits mutual understanding within the given legal culture. The conventions of the genre- and style-based shaping of legal speech acts go beyond the limits imposed by individual national cultures and ethnic languages – since the system of communication rules in the field of law constitutes a specific semiotic code beyond language systems, which underlie particular legislative speech acts. Therefore, examples of texts derived from the Polish legislation can illustrate the transformation of general communication conventions against the European legal culture. This has been shaped under the influence of the principles (terms and values) of the Roman law and canon law, as well as of the models derived from the Latin rhetoric style. Moreover, beginning in the eighteenth century legal text has also been influenced by the rationalist enlightenment philosophy and the principles of logical (scientific) style, embodied in the Code Napoleon which underlay the legislation of many European nations (see Szczepankowska 2007). Local differences manifest themselves particularly in the early stages of shaping models of legislative discourse and are related to the influence of the common law of individual nations. Some such local customs – reinforced as written down codes – extended their range considerably beyond the territory occupied by the given community. For instance, the mediaeval common law originating in Saxony and the municipal law of Magdeburg significantly influenced the legislation of Central and Eastern European nations.

This chapter is comprised of two main parts. The first describes how the structure of a court verdict (ortyl) influenced the form of the genre- and style-based model of the legislative speech act in the Middle Ages by imposing the discursive nature and persuasive-directive style on the speech act. The second part presents transformations of that model which have influenced European principles of legislative techniques determined since the sixteenth century on the legislation practice, above all the 'motiva evitentur' principle (the rule stipulating that 'the legislator is not to explain its motives'). Then, the scope of its application in Polish and other European legislative acts is indicated. And finally, the change of value of that principle which is currently in progress is emphasized related to conforming the principles of legislation practice to the general requirements of democracy.

The discussion presented herein results from the conviction that research on the evolution of communication models and rules of legal discourse may contribute to better understanding between nations and taking optimal measures for improving legislation practices at both international and local level.

Directive-Persuasive Style of Legislative Speech Act

The shaping of the Polish legislative speech act in terms of genre and style was affected by the ancient common law of Slavs and the practice of public courts (rallies) where verdicts were passed, probably uttered with the use of conventional formulas, yet not reinforced locally in writing until the fourteenth century. Therefore, in the Middle Ages, a particular role was played by the Germanic stylistics of an ortyl (in German: *Urteil*). An *ortyl* is a verdict of the court in Magdeburg, forwarded to judges in Polish towns and cities which have been using German law since the twelfth/thirteenth century. Polish municipal jurors also called upon the court in Magdeburg for legal advice in doubtful cases. Municipal courts of lower instance treated such judgments as the so-called prejudicates – models of legal decisions which could be applied in similar cases. Ortyls, translated from Latin into Polish, were put together into collections which constituted the first sources of municipal law as early as the fifteenth century.[1] A court decision referred to a specific act by a defined addressee. The description of the case was typically presented as grounds for the court decision, which affected the form of the speech act composed usually of two main constituents: the *description of the case* and the *judgment*. The model ortyl structure reflected accurately the communication situation which constituted the context of the speech act. Therefore the description of the case was usually incorporated into a *framework of question* which Polish jurors asked the court in Magdeburg (by letter), and the court decision, which was a *framework of answer* from the judges. Such a superstructure is realized in the following speech act (its divisions and formulas in brackets come from the author – I.Sz.):

A (framework of question: reason)	Dalej pytaliście nas o prawo:
B (hypothesis: description of case)	Gdybymieszczaninalbogośćżałowałbyo ran(n)y albo o głowę.
C (framework of answer: effect)	Na to my przysiężnicy z Majdburku mowimy prawo:
D (directive: court judgment)	o glowę albo rany … ma dać do zagajonego sądu położonego, a tego to, co mir złomił, prawym ortelem naśladować …[2]

Eng. (A) You have asked for legal advice: (B) Should a citizen or a foreigner lodge a complaint about injury or attempt against life. (C) Thereupon, we the sworn judges of Magdeburg, hereby answer in accordance with the law: (D) The action for attempt against life or for injury … shall be brought in the court sitting in a designated place and time, and the person violating the peace shall be punished in accordance with the law.

Each of the distinguished segments of the discourse realizes a specified speech act composing the complicated macroact of the ortyl: framework of question and answer containing explicit metatextual formulas: Pol. *pytaliście nas o prawo* – Eng. *you have asked for legal advice* and Pol. *mówimy prawo* – Eng. *we hereby answer in accordance with the law*, which connote the semantic-pragmatic function of individual microacts and confer the structure of a dialogue to the entire speech act. It should be noted that the framework of question is expressed in the Polish language by a clause containing a verb in the so-called past tense, whose equivalent in the English language is the present perfect tense. Both forms stand for an already performed action, thus characterizing – from the point of view

1 The topic of transformations of structure of a single ortyl in the context of the entire collection is handled by Maria Wojtak (1998).

2 The test comes from the mid-fifteenth century; here it is presented in contemporary transcription – according to an electronic source (Najstarsze staropolskie tłumaczenie ortyli magdeburskich: 55).

of Magdeburg-based judges – the intention of the Polish jurors. The formula of answer contains a verb in the first person present tense, i.e. 'explicit performative' after Austin (1962: 32); it fulfils a creative function in the space of the current discourse; it indicates the dominating position of the act of passing a judgment in the structure of the entire speech act; and it provides for its superior communication intention. The description of the case introduced by the question is modelled by means of a predicative structure of hypothetical modality – it is visible in Polish by words composed of a conjunction and a particle: *gdyby*, *jeśliby* (in English: *if*, *should*). Therefore a specific case ('that X did P'), being an impulse for municipal jurors for seeking an opinion of a court of higher instance, is approached in the ortyl (judgement of that court) as a hypothetical event ('should X do P'), which may be treated as a type of event, thus its legal interpretation can be applied to similar cases. As a consequence, the court judgment becomes prejudicate – a judgment being a model of adjudication in analogous cases. The formulation of the decision, following the metatextual formula *mówimy prawo* (Eng. *we answer in accordance with the law*), usually contained an exponent of directive modality in the form of a modal predicate – in Polish: *ma*, *należy*, *musi*, *powinien*, *może* (in English: *is to*, *shall be*, *must*, *shall*, *may*), usually followed by an infinitive of a verb describing specific action of the directive's addressee. The description of case together with framework of question and the opinion (judgment) of the court in the framework of answer at the same time realize – at the level of macrostructure of the act of judging – the general notions of 'cause' and 'effect' ('macro-concept' as approached by van Dijk (1981: 85).

The above described standard model of text of the ortyl contained also express indicators (deictic expressions) of the sender and addressee of the text – forms of verbs in third person (*mówimy*, *pytaliście* – Eng. *we answer*, *we have asked*) and the corresponding personal pronouns (*my*, *wy* – Eng. *we*, *you*), as well as additional expressions characterizing the sender (*przysiężnicy z Magdeburga* – Eng. *the sworn judges of Magdeburg)*, more seldom the addressee (a letter containing a collection of ortyls began with the phrase *mili przyjaciele* – Eng. *dear friends*). In mediaeval collections of Polish municipal court judgments (usually written down in Latin) additional signals of the primary communication situation, i.e. court trial, appeared. The description of the subject of dispute could be presented in the form of quoted utterances of the parties (plaintiff and defendant) or witnesses (see e.g. Maisel 1959: 38-39). In texts of ortyls such utterances are preceded by an announcement clause (e.g. *Ipsa vero mater dixit …*, *Tandem filia stando dixit …*) and they usually begin with an addressative phrase: *Domine* (referring to the judge), followed by a standard declaration of the person speaking: *Hic sto, sana mente et deliberato animo*. The conclusion of judges is clearly separated from the description of the case (containing the utterances of parties) and is expressed in performative framework (e.g. *Super quo nos, consules, in Costan, diffinimus iuris sentenciam …*).

The structure of an ortyl (court judgment) is reflected most explicitly in the legislative speech act. A text which is the formulation of a legal provision represents thus a 'secondary genre' within the meaning of Bachtin (Bachtin 1986: 355), developed from the 'primary genre' of colloquial speech. The latter embraced also the field of public conferences and trials in old Slav communities. Over time, when the statutory law became the primary source of knowledge as to the norms of conduct and written communication enabled and imposed larger condensation of formulations, departure from the textual formula set by the form of ortyl gradually followed. Along with the writing, the formal variant of language and conventionalized genres of speech acts realized in court developed. In the legislative speech act, the description of a specific case corresponded to the indication of circumstances being the so-called *hypothesis* of the legal norm ('should S happen …'), whereas the court judgment assumed the nature of a *directive* (i.e. *disposition*) for the generalized addressee ('X shall do P'). The disposition could also include a formulated *sanction* ('X shall be subject to a penalty') which is to be imposed (by the court), should the directive not be performed ('should X fail to do P'). The speech act composed of the hypothesis and directive tended to be realized within a metatextual and at the same time performative framework: ('I establish that …'), which may be considered a transformed framework of answer distinguished in ortyl structure. It was often preceded by grounds (providing a cause) for the valid legislative act, corresponding to the framework of question beginning the text of an ortyl. Such a model structure is seen in an act at the beginning of the sixteenth century (at that time written down in Latin and subsequently translated into Polish), where the following constituents may be distinguished:

A (grounds)	Item providentes difficultatibus et gravaminibus subditorum nostrorum regni et magni ducatus Lythuaniae …
B (performative framework)	volumus et decernimus, ut
C (hypothesis)	quotiens opus fuerit,
D (directive)	per nos comissarii deputentur et mittantur …, ad faciendas easdem granicies et iniurias componendas …, quatenus absque querentium onere iustitia eis ministretur. (after Balzer 1906: 25)

Eng. (A) With any inconvenience and suffering of the lieges of our Kingdom and the Great Duchy of Lithuania in mind …, (B) we wish and hereby order that (C) should need arise, (D) commissars be delegated by us in order to set the limits and compensation for harm …, so that justice be done without burdening the complainants with the costs (of trial).

The above model of acts developed much earlier. The oldest written down Polish laws from 1347 also contain explicitly marked language exponents – motive, performative framework and disposition (hypothesis was omitted in general regulations). Here is an example from the collection: Statuta Casimiri Magni:

> Quia cuilibet sua defensio et titio (cum juris sit naturalis) non est deneganda; ideoquae statuimus quod in judiciis nostri Regni, quilibet homo cujuscumque sit status et conditionis potest et debet habere suum advocatum prolocutorem. (Ohryzko 1859: 30)[3]

Thus constructed provisions retain explicit signals of the sender-addressee relation (above all language exponents of the legislator: in the form of personal pronouns and verbs). The persuasive constituent (grounds) supplemented the legal directive and still in the eighteenth century played a significant role in the structure of Polish legislative speech acts, determining dialogue structure and style, essentially persuasive-directive, as in the following provision of the Constitution of 3 May 1791 (art. VI):

A (grounds$_1$)	Wszystko i wszędzie większością głosów udecydowane być powinno;
B1 (disposition)	przeto liberum veto, konfederacye wszelkiego gatunku i sejmy konfederackie
C (grounds$_2$)	jako duchowi niniejszej konstytucyi przeciwne, rząd obalające, społeczność niszczące,
B2 (disposition)	na zawsze znosimy. (Kowecki 1991: 101)

> *Eng.* (A) The majority of votes shall decide everything, and everywhere; (B2) therefore we abolish, and utterly annihilate, (B1) *liberum veto*, all forts of confederacies and confederate Diets, (C) as contrary to the Spirit of the present constitution, as undermining the government, and as being ruinous to society. (Translation into English after: New Constitution of the Government of Poland, Established by the Revolution, The Third of May: 18)

A normative speech act (disposition) is justified here by providing a general norm in the preceding clause (A), which is realized by the current act; the constituent being a parenthesis (C) additionally describes the state of affairs which is subject to change as negative – such evaluation has an obvious persuasive value. In general legislative acts, such as constitutions, the hypothesis does not usually appear, however individual provisions realize the persuasive-directive act, with

3 *Eng.* 'Because everyone is vested in defence by virtue of the natural law, we hereby establish that in courts of our kingdom, every man, regardless of class and (social) condition, may and shall have his advocate representing him (during trial).'

the formulation justifying the disposition often being more expanded than the normative clause,[4] from which it did not have to be clearly separated.

Determining the scope in which a similar text model was realized in other European (or outside European) legislative acts would require broader research on legislative tradition of various nations. Examples of discursive forming of texts can be found in mediaeval German common law (Magdeburg's and Saxon) – which became widespread in Poland – written down in collections titled Speculum Saxonum (Goldast 1613a: 126)[5] and Wilchbild (Goldast 1613b: 168).[6] The persuasive function was fulfilled by invoking general rules of law, morality, religious faith, social custom, which justify current dispositions: pragmatic motives were also provided. Until the eighteenth century Polish documents often contained explicit indication of an impulse from the citizens as a reason for establishing law – then the legislative speech act began with formulas such as *at the members' of parliament request ..., moved by complaints of our lieges ...*, proving that the given act was a product of discourse conducted between the legislator and norm addressees. Such a structure of the legislative speech act had the task to reinforce the conviction of the addressees that the law is not solely a manifestation of the ruler's (government's) will, who arbitrarily establishes limitations of freedom, but results from accounting for the needs of norm addresses or is an order of higher necessity to which the legislator is also subordinate.

4 Below is another provision from the same document, having similarly expanded justification: 'The most perfect government cannot exist or last without an effectual executive power. The happiness of the nation depends on just laws, but the good effects of laws flow only from their execution. Experience has taught us that the neglecting of this essential part of government has overwhelmed Poland with disasters. Having, therefore, secured to the free Polish nation the right of enacting over the executive power, and the choice of their magistrates, *we entrust to the King, as his Council, the highest power of executing the laws*' (art. VII [New Constitution of the Government of Poland, Established by the Revolution, The Third of May: 19-20]).

5 An example of a provision from that collection (in Latin): 'Duorum gladiorum potestatem, spiritualem scilicet & secularem, ad defendendum suum populum, Christus in sua approbavit Ecclesia; ex quibus Apostolicum spriritualem, & Romanum Imperatorem secularem habere, nemo ambigit. Ob quorum figurationem, Apostolico super equum Candidum equitare constitutum est, & in ascensu eius, à Principe sella, ne decidat, tenebitur. In quo significatur, ut si qui inobedientes Apostolico existerent, à Principe ad obediendum, et è contra, cum necessitas hoc exegerit, dummodo exercitus fuerit, compellantur' (liber I, art. I [Goldast 1613a: 126]).

6 An example of a discursive (i.e. containing an element of polemics) form of text is the following article from that collection: 'Dicitur etiam, quod nullus matris illegitimus esse possit: hoc tamen non est: quia mulier potest illegitimos ac legitimos nobilesque procreare pueros. Si est serva, potest manumitti, si est fornicaria, potest nubere & legitimos procreare' (art. IV, par. 7 [Goldast 1613b: 169]).

Causes and Effects of Genre- and Style-related Transformations of the Legislative Speech Act

As late as the end of the eighteenth century the legislative speech act was characterized by explicit persuasion. The reason should be doubtlessly sought in the above described genesis of the legislative speech act, as well as in the universal stylistic convention prevailing in Europe (particularly between the sixteenth and eighteenth centuries) – the custom to justify the communicated judgments which had originated from the theory of logic and rhetoric (*genus iudiciale* was applied also in the law establishment process). However, perhaps there existed political conditions in Poland of that period which determined the persuasive-directive and discursive models of legislative speech acts. The monarchic-republican social system (with the dominating role of parliament which established law) was favourable to the communication culture marked by the conflict between personal and citizen freedom of the representatives of the dominating stratum of the nation (the nobility) and complying with the law whose authority was subject to continuous opposition (see Szczepankowska 2008). Such a situation required that legislators pay significant attention to justifying any restrictions imposed on citizens. Absolutist countries prevailing in Europe at that time were probably less favourable to the culture of political-legal dialogue, so the persuasive constituent was exhibited in the legislative speech act to a lesser extent. The French (republican) Constitution of 24 June 1793 (see *Constitution du 24 juin 1793*), created approximately at the same time as the above quoted Polish Constitution of 3 May 1791 (Kowecki 1991), presents a definitely normative style, devoid of any elements of explicit persuasion, i.e. grounds for individual provisions formulating specific legal directives. A similar nature is displayed by the Constitution of the United States of America of 1787 (*Constitution of the United States of America. The Federal Convention of 1787*). Persuasion is limited in those documents to the preamble – a speech act which even today precedes acts of general importance (such as constitutions) – and between the sixteenth and eighteenth centuries commonly was used also in acts passed by absolutist rulers (more on the genesis and functions of preambles see e.g. Lewandowski 1996).

Already in the Middle Ages the classification of particular provisions into integrated collections used as sources of legal norms led to the alteration of the sender-addressee relation as well as to the elimination of certain repeatable framework formulas of the base model (e.g. ortyl or act) and the contamination of the constituents thereof. Individual constituents of a model legal norm – composed of the grounds, performative (modal) formula and the conditional clause comprising the hypothesis and the disposition – could be omitted in a specific act of creating a legal norm since the addressee interpolated those constituents by virtue of the conventional semantic-pragmatic implicature. For instance, defining a sanction itself in the form of the following clause ‘X shall be punished for doing P’ is sufficient to formulate a legal provision since logical inference permits reading the directive aimed at the addressee of the prohibition:

'X shall not commit P'. The strive for achieving economy in the message may serve as an explanation for the emerging omission of the performative formula, which expresses the fact of establishing the law, at the same time explicitly characterizing the genre of the speech act. If there is no present tense clause: *I (the king) establish that* ..., the binding force of an act arises solely from the message convention – the publication of the text in a specified collection of legal acts. The title of such a collection (e.g. *act, resolution, constitution, collection of laws* etc.) 'summarizes' (see van Dijk 1980: 99-100) the sequences of speech acts into a superior unit (macrostructure), which is the medium of the global meaning of the entire discourse which defines its pragmatic coherence. The transferring of the formula expressing the act of establishing a norm itself to the macrotext level prevents repeating information. It should be noted, though, that also in this case the written form of the message, and above all the intention of enacting and publishing collections of acts (codes) made it possible to execute that strive. During the period when law still rested on prejudicates which were created as oral court judgments in specific cases, the performative framework was necessary for emphasizing the causative power of those judgments as acts of legislative will; certain redundancy in oral communication is, apart from that, a functional measure of preventing misunderstandings and misinterpretations. The more important consequence of such an alteration is the impersonal stylization of a provision – the use of a performative formula, also with modal verbs (*I order, I prohibit, I permit* etc.), involved the necessity to indicate the person being the sender of the text (e.g. *we, judges of Magdeburg*; *I, king*); abandoning the phrase which identifies the sender (*it shall be ordered / prohibited / permitted*; *the act orders* etc.) permits concealing the person being the legislator. Such a stylization creates an impression that the entire responsibility for the performance of the postulated facts and states should be borne by the addressees of the norms, while the entity enacting the regulations and warranting entitlements to the addressees remains indefinite and inaccessible, even when the existence thereof is implied by such formulas as: (*sth*) *shall be ensured/guaranteed* (*to sb*) or *The Republic of Poland warrants* (*sth to sb*).

The lack of formulas explicating sender's actions in a text results in the modal predicates used in contemporary legislative texts, such as *may*, *should*, losing markedness for directiveness (volition). They function rather as exponents of objective necessity or possibility existing regardless of the will of personal entities. The formula *the law orders*, which is sometimes used by lawyers in commentaries, indicates clearly that law is a force which acts arbitrarily and independently. Also abandoning directive exponents in favour of declarative stylization of provisions contributes to the reinforcement of the asymmetry in the sender-addressee relation and to the impairment of the dialogue nature of the contemporary legislative text. Modal words: *should*, *may* etc. in such clauses as 'X should do P' merely suggest a possibility of a situation postulated by the legislator. The latter makes the arising dependent on the addressee's conduct, while the speech act without a modalizer (frequent in Polish), a formulation in indicative ('X does P') creates an impression of factuality of event (unconditional necessity). Such a procedure may be interpreted as an implicit persuasion realized at the presupposition level – assertion suggests that there is no possibility that the norm addressee fails to perform the given act. Also the future tense and any postulative structures are marked from such a point of view since they suggest that the accomplishment of the state of affairs is only possible depending on the addressee's conduct, not that the state of affairs exists by the legislator's will. The reasons for such an evolution of style should obviously be also sought in the change of the historical relation between the legislator and norm addressees. In former feudal states there was a hierarchical relation: a ruler standing in a way above the law, invoking *explicite* as the subject of a sentence with an explicit performative (*We, the king, order*), and the norm addressee subject to their will, and at the same time the executor of the act being the subject of the directive (*... that Y does P*). Since in democratic systems the legislator (parliament) is also an addressee of norms only representing other addressees, the currently generally accepted method of formulating legal provisions is the declarative speech act in third person referring solely to the generalized norm addressee, without invoking the legislator. In legal acts with general significance (such as constitutions) these are often impersonal structures whose directive function is secondary to the informative function, as in the following provision of the contemporary Constitution of the Republic of Poland:

> 1. Siły Zbrojne Rzeczypospolitej Polskiej służą ochronie niepodległości państwa i niepodzielności jego terytorium oraz zapewnieniu bezpieczeństwa i nienaruszalności jego granic
> 2. Siły Zbrojne zachowują neutralność w sprawach politycznych oraz podlegają cywilnej i demokratycznej kontroli. (art. 26 (*Konstytucja Rzeczypospolitej Polskiej z dnia 2 kwietnia 1997*: 2416))

> *Eng.*

> 1. The Armed Forces of the Republic of Poland shall safeguard the independence and territorial integrity of the State, and shall ensure the security and inviolability of its borders.
> 2. The Armed Forces shall observe neutrality regarding political matters and shall be subject to civil and democratic control. (Translation from: *Constitution of the Republic of Poland of 2nd April 1997*)

Speech acts preferred nowadays, which formulate (in Polish) only the normative disposition in the grammatical present tense, have the quality of universality and unconditional necessity. In the prototype of a legislative speech act, the act of establishing law (expressed by the explicit performative) at the same time set the initial moment of its validity and the scope of influence was restricted to the legislator's scope of power, who guaranteed its performance. A speech act devoid of such exponents may be referred to in the past, the present and the future – of course the perlocutionary effect of the speech act is meant here, not the actual scope of space-time embraced by the force of the given act, which has to be provided with relevant information as to the date of publishing and the body passing the act.

Changes in the stylistic form of the legislative speech act are also caused by the development of the principles of legislative technique. One of them is the principle known to lawyers at least since the seventeenth century under the Latin name 'motiva evitentur'. This principle provides that any introductions containing legislator's explanations as to the motives of the given law are to be avoided. It was formulated by Francis Bacon, an English philosopher, in his work of 1623 titled De Dignitate et Augmentis Scientiarum – see volume VIII, aphorism 69, which contains the following: '... prologi evitentur, et lex incipiat a iussione' (Bacon 1858: 160). Since the nineteenth century the principle has been strictly applied in European legislative acts, e.g. in the Code Napoleon, whose style significantly contributed to the change in the Polish legislative technique. The omission of any grounds for the provided legal provisions results in law losing its discursive nature, assuming the form of a steadfast speech act which leaves no room for discussion, as in the following provisions of the above mentioned code:

> (art. 2) La loi ne dispose que pour l'avenir; elle n'a point d'effet rétroactif. (*Code Civil des Français* 1804: 4)

> (art. 5) Il est défendu aux juges de prononcer par voie de disposition générale et réglementaire sur les causes qui leur sont soumises. (*Code Civil des Français* 1804: 4)[7]

The lack of any grounds for the established provisions – at the level of text itself – distorts the conviction in addressees' mind of the instrumental function of law as a norm incarnating such superior values as equity, freedom, safety, social solidarity, etc. Law itself becomes the superior value. The need to invoke higher reasons and motives for the legislative acting is expressed even nowadays in preceding important acts with a preamble, whose shape is often a result of heated social debates. That need is fulfilled, however, outside the confines of the primary legislative acts and lawyers rather do not see much normative significance in preambles (on controversies related to preambles see Lewandowski 1996). It is tolerated also in Polish legislation, though, despite being contradictory to one of the applicable principles of legislative technique (Rozporządzenie Prezesa Rady Ministrów z dnia 20 czerwca 2002: 6543), which reads (translation into English – I. Sz.):

---

7 *Eng.* (art. 2) 'The law ordains for the future only; it has no retrospective operation'; (art. 5) 'The judges are forbidden to pronounce, by way of general and legislative determination, on the causes submitted to them.'

> Expressions which do not serve expressing legal norms, in particular appeals, postulates, recommendations, admonitions or grounds for the formulated norms, shall not be used in an Act. (Sect. I, chapter 1§11).

It is obviously assumed that the legislator has important reasons to avoid providing grounds (on that topic see e.g. Lopez 1991 and Waaldijk 1987) but it is difficult to find convincing explanation in papers dealing with the theory of law. Legislative traditions of European countries vary with this respect. It should be emphasized, though, they have long incorporated the principle of justifying not only court verdicts but also any administrative decisions (see Wiener 1969). It is therefore difficult to accept that providing motives for general norms created by the legislator is more difficult and less necessary. The principle 'motiva evitentur' could be defended from the point of view of law clarity: placing additional information in the text of a legal provision apart from the directive of conduct itself may lead to stylistic complication of the speech act and, as a result, to the distortion of the primary message of the sender. Unclarity results in undesirable effects, particularly in legal communication, and legislators and linguists have long been involved in discussions on the manner of reduction thereof (see articles in the recently published collection: Wagner and Cacciaguidi-Fahy 2008). The comprehensibility of legal provisions depends, however, to a larger extent on the language and editing competence of the authors, as well as on the interpretation skills of the addressees than on the content of legal texts. An equally convincing argument for placing justifications, that is for disclosing motives for the restrictions introduced by the legislator, would be attaining acceptance by addressees. Directives are sometimes 'incomprehensible' to a lesser extent due to complicated specialized language than due to unclear or insufficiently important aim of the established law – from the perspective of addressees.

One may ponder whether the antipersuasive restriction (the rule stipulating that 'the legislator is not to explain its motives') stands in certain contradiction to the general principles of a democratic state whose citizens have the right to acquire information on the motives of any and all decisions taken by the authorities. From such a point of view the sentence 'lex iubeat, non suadeat, non doceat, non laudat' (Lopez 1991: 59) should be interpreted critically. Why did persuasion become such an undesirable constituent of a legislative act? Are the reasons for the lack of explication of motives of legislative action sufficient for approving the 'motiva evitentur' principle in contemporary social relationships and do the advantages of applying the principle outweigh the disadvantages? Such questions come to mind of contemporary addressees of legal norms who are willing to demand an explanation particularly when the freedom of conduct vested in them democratically is restricted, as can sometimes seem, without a necessary reason. Posing such question itself, realizing the existence of codified antipersuasive restriction and comparing the contemporary legislative speech act with historical communication create a dialogue situation, which may be a source of a certain 'implicature' as understood by Grice (1975). This means that such a context allows us to guess that the lack of explicit exponents of justification of established provisions in contemporary legislative speech act may result from a certain persuasive intention of the legislator. Any explicit exponents of reasoning, signals of subjectivity of a speech act (personal structures) and dialogue formulas are avoided since all those elements undermine the authority of law. They transform the unilateral relation of the norm addressee towards law – as the absolute reason – into an interpersonal relation (with disclosed legislator) which creates a framework for communication, thereby a space for a possible dispute, probably undesirable from the point of view of force of law itself.

The authority of the law is of undisputed value, particularly in a democratic country. It is, however, debatable by what means such authority is to be attained. Since the issue of explicating the motives of established law differs among legislative traditions, and particularly current legislative practices of the European Union member states, certain actions have been taken also as to adopting uniform regulations related to the edition of EU legislation documents. The attitude to the issue discussed here has already been expressed in the Treaty establishing the European Community (see Treaty Establishing the European Community, consolidated text of 2002), in article 253 (Consolidated version of the Treaty Establishing the European Union). It imposes the obligation to justify the legal acts under construction on EU bodies. Ordinances, directives and decisions adopted jointly by the European Parliament and the Council or Committee must specify the reasons for which they were passed. The lack of justification may constitute a ground for avoiding an EU legal act. EU legislation institutions have adopted guidelines as to the formation of legal acts (Office for Official Publications of the European Communities 2003), including instructions embracing the formulation of justifications. Below is one of them:

> (point 10.2) Regulations, directives and decisions must state the reasons on which they are based. The purpose is to enable any person concerned to ascertain the circumstances in which the enacting institution exercised its powers as regards the act in question (…) to give the parties to a dispute the opportunity to defend their interests and to enable the Community judicature to exercise its power of review. (Office for Official Publications of the European Communities 2003: 31)

It is emphasized here that providing motives aimed at facilitating the certainty of parties affected by the law, enabling them to defend their interests and giving courts a ground to enforce regulations concerning EU member states. Editing guidelines embrace also the sequence of individual constituents of a provision, the content of grounds, their order (e.g. numeration of motives), explicit separation of grounds from the normative part, etc. A model arrangement of constituents of an act (see: guideline 7) may be as follows: a) *title*, b) *preamble* ('means everything between the title and the enacting terms of the act, namely the citations, the recitals and the solemn forms which precede and follow them'), c) *enacting terms* ('the legislative part of the act'), d) *annexes* ('where necessary') (Office for Official Publications of the European Communities 2003: 31). A preamble, containing the justification for all contemporary regulations, constitutes an integral part of a normative text in European Union legislation. It can be accepted, therefore, that although the 'motiva evitentur' principle is still privileged in the legislative practice of certain countries, the current legislation institutions of the European Union resurrect the tradition of persuasive-directive formulation of legal provisions. Comprehensive preambles cover not only general acts (constitutions) but also any legal decisions. More attention is paid, though, to the application of a structural and stylistic template, which is supposed to facilitate the interpretation of the text (for more on the topic see Lötscher 2008), and to the application thereof by administrative and judicial institutions.

Conclusion

Despite political differences and distinct local customs, the legal culture of European countries has always displayed many similarities in terms of norms, institutions and legislative technique. This is mainly due to the heritage of Roman law and the universalizing impact of Christian ethic on social relations in European countries. Transformations of Polish legal discourse, some of which are analysed in this chapter, show how variable cultural and political circumstances influence communication between the legislator and norm addressees. The style of legislative speech acts and the communication of values performed in legal texts embrace the rules of legislation. At the level of international legal discourse the differentiation in the field of ethnorhetoric, i.e. local communication customs, is not observed. Being a member of an international political body means the obligation to adopt uniform legal regulations. In addition a certain system of values and models of social relationships together with models of public discourse have to be expressed within these rules. It may be thus presumed that the instructions adopted by EU legislation institutions concerning above all including motives of acts will lead to the reinforcement of the persuasive-normative model of speech act in legislation of individual countries (today the declarative and directive styles prevail).

Legal culture and development of specific models of discourse in the area of official communication of different nations should be an important subject of interdisciplinary research. Awareness of similarities and differences, particularly in the axiologic dimension, is a basis of mutual understanding and may contribute to reaching an effective compromise, e.g. related to a draft of the European constitution, and in a wider scope – to working out general rules of legal discourse realized in international interactions.

References

Austin, J.L. 1962. *How To Do Things with Words*. Oxford: Clarendon Press.

Bachtin, M. 1986. *Estetyka twórczości słownej*, trans. D. Ulicka. Warszawa: Państwowy Instytut Wydawniczy.

Bacon, F. 1858-1861. 'De Dignitate et Augmentis Scientiarum', in *The Works of Francis Bacon* ... vol. III, edited by J. Spedding, R.L. Ellis and D.D. Heath. London: Longmans.

Balzer, O. 1906. *Corpus iuris Polonici, vol III (annos 1506-1522 continens)*. Cracovia: Academia Litterarum.

Code Civil des Français. 1804. Paris: L'Imprimerie de la République.

Consolidated version of the Treaty Establishing the European Union. 2002. *Official Journal of the European Communities* C325 of 24 December 2002. [Online]. Available at: http://eur.lex.europa.eu/en/treaties [accessed 11 October 2009].

Constitution du 24 juin 1793. Transcription. [Online]. Available at: http://fr.wikisource.org/wiki/Constitution_du_24juin1793 [accessed 11 October 2009].

Constitution of the Republic of Poland of 2nd April 1997. 1997. [Online]. Available at: http://www.sejm.gov.pl/prawo/konst/htm [accessed 11 October 2009].

Constitution of the United States of America. The Federal Convention of 1787. Transcription. [Online]. Available at: http://www.archives.gov/exhibits/charters/constitution_transcript.html [accessed 11 October 2009].

Goldast, M. 1613a. 'Speculum Saxonum, quod Ius Provinciale vulgo Nuncupatur (...)', in *Collectio Consuetudinum et Legum Imeprialium (...)*. [Online]. Available at: http://digi.ub.uni-heidelberg.de/diglit/drwgoldast1613/0152 [accessed 25 April 2011].

Goldast, M. 1613b. 'Wichbild, sine Ius Municipale Magdeburgense (...)', in *Collectio Consuetudinum et Legum Imeprialium (...)*. [Online]. Available at: http://digi.ub.uni-heidelberg.de/diglit/drwgoldast1613/0193?sid=c401b3d80b662ea1cabcf5fbe182c9af [accessed 25 April 2011].

Grice, H.P. 1975. 'Logic and Conversation', in *Syntax and Semantics*. Vol. 3. *Speech Acts*, edited by P. Cole and J.L. Morgan. New York, San Francisco, CA and London: Academic Press, 41-58.

Konstytucja Rzeczypospolitej Polskiej z dnia 2 kwietnia 1997 r. 1997. *Dziennik Ustaw* 78, item 483.

Kowecki, J. 1991. *Konstytucja 3 Maja 1791. Statut Zgromadzenia Przyjaciół Konstytucji*. Warszawa: Państwowe Wydawnictwo Naukowe.

Lewandowski, S. 1996. 'Kontrowersje wokół preambuł'. *Studia Iuridica*, 31, 87-96.

Lopez, F.S. 1991. 'Exposiciones de motivos de las leyes: motivos para su eliminacion'. *Revista Española de Derecho Constitucional*, 11(33), 47-64.

Lötscher, A. 2008. 'Conceptual and Textual Structure in Legislative Texts', in *Obscurity and Clarity in the Law: Prospects and Challenges*, edited by A. Wagner and S. Cacciaguidi-Fahy. Aldershot: Ashgate, 129-150.

Maisel, W. 1959. *Ortyle sądów wyższych miast wielkopolskich z XV i XVI wieku*. Wrocław: Ossolineum.

Maley, J. 1994. 'The Language of the Law', in *Language and the Law*, edited by J. Gibbons. London: Longmans, 11-50.

Najstarsze staropolskie tłumaczenie ortyli magdeburskich. Transcription. In *Korpus tekstów staropolskich.* [Online]. Available at: http://www.ijp-pan.krakow.pl/pliki/OrtOssol.pdf [accessed 11 October 2009].

New Constitution of the Government of Poland, Established by the Revolution, The Third of May, 1791. 1791. London: J. Debrett.

Office for Official Publications of the European Communities. 2003. *Joint Practical Guide of the European Parliament, the Council and the Commission for persons involved in the drafting of legislation within the Community institutions*. Luxembourg: Office for Official Publications of the European Communities. [Online]. Available at: http://publications.europa.eu/code [accessed 11 October 2009].

Ohryzko, J. 1859. *Volumina Legum. Leges, statuta, constitutiones et privilegia Regni Poloniae, Magni Ducatus Lithuaniae. Vol. I (ad anno 1347 ad annum 1547)*. Petersburg: Wydawnictwo XX. Pijarów.

Rozporządzenie Prezesa Rady Ministrów z dnia 20 czerwca 2002 r. w sprawie 'Zasad techniki prawodawczej'. 2002. *Dziennik Ustaw* 100, item 908.

Szczepankowska, I. 2007. 'Prawodawczy akt mowy – konwencja stylowa i ewolucja wypowiedzi w języku polskim'. *Stil*, 6, 77-88.

Szczepankowska, I. 2008. 'Prawo i wolność w dyskursie politycznym Rzeczypospolitej przedrozbiorowej (podstawowe problemy badawcze)'. *Poradnik Językowy*, 8(657), 75-93.

van Dijk, T.A. 1977. *Text and Context: Explorations in the Semantics and Pragmatics of Discourse*. London: Longmans.

van Dijk, T.A. 1980. *Macrostructures*. Hillsdale, NY: Lawrence Erlbaum.

van Dijk, T.A. 1981. *Studies in the Pragmatics of Discourse*. The Hague, Paris and New York: Mouton.

Waaldijk, K. 1987. 'Can We Require Legislatures to State the Reasons for Their Legislative Decisions?', in *Argumentation: Analysis and Practices*, edited by F.H. van Eemeren, J.A. Blair, R. Grootendorst and C.A. Willard. Dordrecht: Foris, 110-118.

Wagner, A. and Cacciaguidi-Fahy, S. 2008. *Obscurity and Clarity in the Law: Prospects and Challenges*. Aldershot: Ashgate.

Wiener, C. 1969. 'La motivation des décisions administratives en droit comparé'. *Revue International de Droit Comparé*, 4, 779-795.

Wojtak, M. 1998. 'Teksty w tekście – o pewnym typie relacji kontekstualnych (na przykładzie ortyli magdeburskich)', in *Tekst. Analizy i interpretacje*, edited by J. Bartmiński and B. Boniecka. Lublin: Wydawnictwo Uniwersytetu Marii Curie-Skłodowskiej, 85-97.

Chapter 5
Zorkin v. Morschakova: Legal Dispute in Rhetorical Terms

Anita Soboleva

Introduction

On 19 July 2003 the liberal *Novaya Gazeta* newspaper published a full-page interview under the title '... And There Is No Trial. Doctor Morschakova's Diagnosis', in which well-known journalist and lawyer Leonid Nikitinsky discussed the problems of the Russian judicial system with Professor Tamara Morschakova. The next day Professor Valery Zorkin responded to the publication by bringing his article 'Caution: Demolition of the Law!' to the official *Rossiiskaya Gazeta* daily, which published it on July 22. One week later, *Novaya Gazeta* reproduced the article. This academic dispute in newspapers between two legal scholars on details of the judicial reform[1] would probably not have become an event for Russian legal society, if it were not for the posts of the polemists: Professor Zorkin at that time was, and up to the current moment is, a Chairman of the Constitutional Court, while Professor Morschakova was a Vice-Chairperson of that court from 1995 to 2002, and since then has been working as a counsel to the Court as a judge in resignation.

This public polemic, which continued in journals and at conferences, revealed the dramatic difference in views of these opponents on the question of whether there are any standards beyond the letter of the law which influence the judge's choice in so-called 'hard cases', and if so, who it is that defines the admissibility and legitimacy of these standards, and how. Other points of disagreement between

1 The concept of judicial reform in Russia was approved in 1991 by the Supreme Soviet of the RSFSR and aimed to bring about democratic change of the judicial system and administration of justice. Since then serious legislative changes have been made, which introduced procedural guarantees in criminal cases, judicial control over actions and decisions of the executive and law enforcement bodies. Measures to improve financial maintenance of courts and judges have been undertaken. However, many strategic problems remained unresolved. In 2006 a new program, 'Development of the Russian Judicial System', was adopted, which set forth priorities for the last phase of judicial reform aimed at strengthening the independence of judges, improving the transparency and accessibility of courts, raising public trust in the judicial system and safeguarding the enforcement of judicial decisions.

them, including the methods of judicial reform in Russia, the correlation between law and politics, and the limits of judicial discretion, follow from their position on the first issue.

In addition, this polemic provokes interest from a rhetorical point of view because 'a man's method of argument is a truer index to his beliefs than his explicit profession of principles' (Weaver 1953: 58). Rhetorical analysis of the speech acts of prominent public personae also helps us to identify, understand and employ in our own activities the techniques of engaging language as a means of social control and power. How persuasive are their logical and emotional appeals? Does the social status and political power of public personae influence our adherence to their ideas and our consent to their propositions? If such actors propose and defend some policy – in our case a policy on reforming the judiciary during society's transition to democracy – what is more persuasive: their policy arguments or their political status and controlling powers?

From the philosophical point of view, the dispute was about 'transcendental substances' (in Zorkin's terms) or 'principles of higher law' (in Morschakova's terms), which the judge may or may not use as legitimate grounds for judicial decisions. Speaking in rhetorical terms, it was about 'commonplaces' (*loci* in Latin, *tópoi* in ancient Greek) in legal reasoning and, more generally, in Russian culture.

The term *tópos*, or commonplace, was used in ancient rhetoric to designate 'places' from which arguments can be drawn (Cicero 1949: 382-383). *Tópoi* can be variously characterized as (1) commonly shared values, (2) generally accepted views, (3) premises, (4) any propositions that we take for granted without discussion, or (5) landmarks in topography of argumentation. In any of these senses, they can be considered as an initial basis for further arguments that makes possible the achievement of agreement (Soboleva 2007: 51).

Perelman and Olbrechts-Tyteca applied the notion of 'topics', or *loci*, to 'premises of a general nature that can serve as the bases for values and hierarchies' (Perelman and Olbrechts-Tyteca 1969: 83). As implied values, they participate in the justification of most of the choices we make. Because values are not unquestionable truths, each person, who uses some value as a basis for his or her decision, can always be required to justify it. Moreover, each *topos* (*locus*, commonplace) can be confronted by one that is contrary to it, and any society (or court, or group of judges) can be characterized 'not only by the particular values it prizes most but by the intensity with which they adhere to one or the other of a pair of antithetical *loci*' (Perelman and Olbrechts-Tyteca 1969: 83-84).

Theodor Viehweg considered ancient topical method as a method of problem-solving and decision-making in law (see Viehweg 1993). He investigated in detail the correlation between the topical system of reasoning and legal prudence, and showed quite convincingly how a topical approach served to locate premises which might be shared by disputing parties as generally accepted, relevant, permissible and defensible. He was also one of the first who noticed that a topical approach enables the analyst to adjust the 'natural', or 'ordinary' language of legal statutes

– by means of interpretations and reinterpretations – to legal practice. As far as problem-solving in law, in its turn, cannot be separated from interpretation, *topoi* for inventing legal arguments can also be considered as the commonplaces for interpretation of legal texts. Thus, topical jurisprudence is an attempt to apply the methodology of rhetoric to the investigation of legal texts and legal reasoning, and represents the union of rhetoric and philosophy of law (Soboleva 2007).

In addition to *tópoi*, rhetoric operates with a number of stylistic categories, which can be used for the analysis of discourse from the point of view of its persuasive effect on the audience, and which will be considered later in this chapter.

For the reconstruction of the debates two pairs of publications were chosen: the first dialogue took place in *Novaya Gazeta* in 2004 (Nikitinsky 2004; Zorkin 2004) and the second in the monthly *Vlast* in 2009 (Morschakova 2009; Zorkin 2009). In both cases the articles by Zorkin appeared as responses to publications by Morschakova, which is why they were characterized by subjectively-oriented dialogism. Morschakova uses questions asked by journalist Leonid Nikitinsky (in the first article) and proposals of imprisoned oligarch Mikhail Khodorkovsky (in the second one) as an opportunity to present her own views to a wide, yet clearly defined audience, consisting of the readers of the two liberally oriented publications – educated people with a critical approach to life and power. Zorkin writes not so much for the usual audience of the above-mentioned publications, as for his personal opponent Morschakova, for his supporters in bodies of power, and for the general public. This last audience will learn of his ideas through their reproduction in other printed media and internet sources. It was not by chance that Zorkin decided to disseminate his response to Morschakova through another, government owned, publication *Rossiiskaya Gazeta*. It was important for him to move the discussion to another public space, to present his views not simply to a wider audience, but to an audience which inherently differed in its composition from the readers of *Novaya Gazeta*. This implication can be drawn from the analysis of style, types of arguments, rhetorical schemes and tropes he deploys.

Judges' Adherence to Values and Judicial Decision-making: The Unity of Law and Rhetoric in Action

The first text for analysis is Morschakova's interview (Nikitinsky 2004), which she devoted to the 'peculiarities of Russian Femida'. She strongly criticized the Russian judicial system for failing to guarantee judicial independence and fair trials. She also expressed her views on constitutional justice and tried to explain the sources of arguments that had governed her choice in decision-making during more than ten years of her term in office as a judge.

In the very beginning she stated that about 50 years ago when she had been studying in the Soviet law school, it was the 'sphere of the proper [*должного*], not of the real [сущего]' that had attracted her in law. In her opinion,

> this is the lawyer who must say: what is written in the statute, is wrong and is a lie. If legislative norms contradict the general principles of law, the law should be placed higher.[2] (Nikitinsky 2004: 6)

She recalled that in 1969 Professor Shargorodsky said in a conference in Leningrad: 'Legal science starts where it says "No" to the legislator'. Ever since, Morschakova has considered this motto to be the main idea of constitutional justice.

When the Constitutional Court of the Russian Federation was created in 1991, she became one of its first judges. She mentioned that at that time the members of the court had been inspired by the ideals of the law-based state, supremacy of the Constitution and the priority of individual freedoms. From the very beginning the judges faced politically sensitive cases, two of which provoked much debate among her colleagues in court, legal scholars and politicians. These were the cases about the constitutionality of Yeltsin's Decree on prohibition of the Communist Party in 1991[3] and the constitutionality of Yeltsin's Decree on constitutional reform in Russia in 1993.[4] Though the Constitutional Court, in Morschakova's opinion, is not a political court but a court of law, its decisions once adopted become political facts. On the one hand, she denies the influence of politics on judicial reasoning; on the other hand, she admits that Constitutional Court decisions may pursue certain political goals. This two-fold approach led her to act differently in the two above-mentioned cases.

In the famous decision on the prohibition of the Communist Party of the Soviet Union (the so-called CPSU case), made in 1991, the Court refused to find the prohibition of the Communist Party constitutional. In this case Morschakova agreed with the other judges. Here is the rationale of her choice:

> I would have, probably, wished such a ban, but my juridical idealism prevented me from doing so. Is it possible to prohibit an ideology? Probably not, even if it is a Bolshevist one. An ideology must be defeated by another ideology within the framework of democratic elections. As for a party, it can be prohibited only by a court decision, yet not by a decision of the Constitutional Court, but of

---

2 Translation of the quotes from Russian into English is made by the author. As a general rule, a literal translation is provided. Figures of speech and deviations in syntactic structure are reflected when used by the authors of the articles as rhetorical tools.

3 Judgment of the Constitutional Court of the Russian Federation of 30 November 1992. Art. 3424. *Viestnik Konstitutsionnogo Suda*, 1993.

4 On compliance with the Constitution of the Russian Federation of the actions and decisions of the President of the Russian Federation B.N. Yeltsin, which relate to his Decree 'On step-by-step constitutional reform in the Russian Federation' of 21 September 1993 no.1400 and his Address to the Russian people of 21 September 1993. Opinion of the Constitutional Court of 21 September 1993. *Konstitutsionnyi Sud Rossiyskoi Federatsii: Postanovleniya i opredeleniya 1992-1996* [*Constitutional Court of the Russian Federation: Judgments and Decisions 1992-1996*]. 2001. Moscow: Jurist, 87-91.

> an ordinary one, in which the facts and violations of law should be proved. (Nikitinsky 2004: 6)

So, political considerations did not govern her choice in the CPSU case.

In the second case, the Constitutional Court assembled for an emergency session in September 1993, in which it found President Yeltsin's Decree on stage-by-stage constitutional reform unconstitutional and President Yeltsin subject to impeachment. This time Morschakova, as distinct from Zorkin and the majority of judges, based her choice on what she called 'higher law', which she put above the literal interpretation of the constitutional text. In her interview of 2004 she explained her position:

> I was governed by Shargorodsky's words: the Law and the Court start where they say 'No' to the legislator. Yes, President Yeltsin by his Decree de facto abrogated the Constitution existing at that time. But what was it at that time? What, for instance, did an amendment, saying that the Congress of Peoples' Deputies has the power to take any case for its consideration, mean? A higher principle of separation of powers does exist. And at that moment the Constitutional Court was obliged to rise above the legislation, let it be the Constitution itself, and to judge from the position of the higher law. (Nikitinsky 2004: 7)

Here we come to the main issues of the dispute: (1) whether judges can use in their reasoning some categories beyond the legal text, especially when the statutory text is clear and unambiguous; and (2) if so, who should define what these categories are (and how), and where should they be found in order to avoid arbitrariness in judicial decision-making.

The first of these two questions has been discussed time and again by legal scholars in different countries, and though no universal agreement has been reached, the general understanding was formed that lawyers may find support for their decisions by appealing to the aim of the law, changes in historical situation, political and legal doctrines, social theories, moral values or general principles of law in order to adjust an out-dated statutory text to the idea of justice in a changing social context (see, for instance, Aarnio and MacCormick 1992; MacCormick and Summers 1991). The major requirement is to secure the adherence of the audience, which includes other judges, lawyers, parties to a legal dispute, legal scholars and so on, to the decision made, but this adherence can only be achieved when the decision is based on commonly shared values. If such values do not exist, any value-judgment becomes refutable.

As far as Russian post-communist society is highly fragmented and is characterized by the absence of a commonly accepted system of values, because Soviet values have been confuted and new ones have not yet been created, any appeal to values or doctrines, whether democratic, communst, liberal, religious or any, other, provokes resistance from a certain part of the population. In this situation it is unclear which values should be promoted and praised most. Aristotle's answer was that commonplaces should comply with generally accepted views and seem credible to all, or to most of the people, or to wise ones – all of them, or the majority of them, or the most well-known among them (Aristotle 1989: 104a, para. 10). The Russian problem is that the wisest and most well-known among constitutional judges differ in their approach to the value-oriented decision, though they might share the same values. This manifest opposition between them makes us ask whether we can find any values at all, which might unite Russian society at the current moment.

Zorkin (2004) started his response by praising the law and the Western legal tradition and by remarking that law is 'undoubtedly, a Western category'. Freedom, equality, fraternity were ideals and goals of all Western revolutions. Equality and, in the first place, equality before the law, was the most important. He declares:

> Law is the same for everyone! Law is implacable and incorruptible! Law is supreme! Equality before the law is the only type of absolute equality, compatible with the market economy and political democracy. If there is no such equality, society dies. (Zorkin 2004: 10)

He further emphasizes:

> Let the world perish, but law triumph! A philosopher, who insisted on that, was not a world-execrator. He simply understood that without law the world would die finally and irrevocably. (Zorkin 2004: 10)

Thus, from the very beginning Zorkin clearly stated that for him 'Law' *per se* is a higher value. Further he reveals his disagreement with any decisions based on considerations of political expediency and proclaims his adherence to strict observance of the existing laws whatever they might be at the moment:

> To defend law – always and in everything. To struggle in order to let Russia take the law barrier. And become a truly law-based state. To be aware, how far this ideal is from reality. To patiently reduce this distance – that is for me to be a judge in general and to be a constitutional judge in the first place. (Zorkin 2004: 10)

Strict adherence to law understood as a corpus of written texts leads him to explicit and emotional negation of any attempts to interpret law in a wider context:

> I do not accept when under slogans of protection of the law someone consciously pursues law-destructive activities in the strict legal and general ethical sense of this word. When this demolition of law is exercised by an educated judge, a supporter of the protection of human rights, who has pretensions of proclaiming adherence to liberal views and values, it is three times unacceptable. (Zorkin 2004: 10)

His choice is:

> Both Law and Russia, not Either Law or Russia. (Zorkin 2004: 10)

But it should be mentioned that legal norms, established or sanctioned by the state power, are just the first, lowest layer of the legal system. Sometimes it is enough to apply them literally to resolve the case, but in other cases strict interpretation may lead to an obviously unjust decision. Zorkin does not challenge this postulate: in his lecture 'Constitutional Grounds for the Law-based State in Russia' (Zorkin 2009) he admits that 'it is necessary to apply legal norms in the limits of reality, otherwise it [reality] will confute all the norms'.

But 'limits of reality' may require the application of the standards of another level, which are higher than written rules. The problem is, where and how to look for these standards in order to secure the stability and constituency of the legal system, functioning in compliance with the understandings of the society about what is just and unjust, on one hand, and to avoid arbitrariness in judicial decision-making, if we can apply in practice standards other than rules, on the other.

In this respect the dispute between Tamara Morschakova and Valery Zorkin resembles the polemics between Ronald Dworkin (1997) and H.L.A. Hart (1994), as described below.

Principles Higher than Rules?

Ronald Dworkin asserts that legal systems are not capable of exhaustive reduction into patterns of rules alone. Along with rules, and often operating so as to modify them or even nullify their effect in particular cases, there are also general principles, to which courts will have recourse in cases to which the unmodified application of a 'rule' would not be possible without injustice. In addition to principles, Dworkin suggests policies, that is general goals which courts attribute to society and the recognition of which may play some part in shaping their decisions in difficult cases, as one more standard. His challenge to Hart's legal positivist position was built on a consideration of 'hard cases', in which lawyers in fact 'make use of standards that do not function as rules, but operate differently as principles, policies, and other sorts of standards' (Dworkin 1997: 22).

While rules can be changed or repealed by legislative bodies in the process of deliberation, principles are not susceptible to deliberate alteration. Rather, at any particular time it is precisely a body of principles which underlies any given body of rules, as principles inherently possess a stability which rules do not enjoy. As distinct from a rule, a principle does not set out the conditions which make its application necessary.

> Rather, it states a reason that argues in one direction, but does not necessitate a particular decision ... There may be other principles or policies arguing in the other direction .... (Dworkin 1997: 26)

When contravening considerations are absent or less weighty, the principle may be decisive – and this is exactly what happened in Russia, when the old Soviet rules came into contradiction with the new democratic values and principles.

As distinct from Dworkin's position, Zorkin challenges the existence of principles, which may be placed higher than legal norms, enacted by the legislative power. He writes:

> In her interview Madam Morschakova makes some 'principle of higher law' a cornerstone. In fact, this is an uncovered analogy of the higher expediency ... I argue categorically, that the idea of the higher law as it has been developed by Madam Morschakova can in practice only be turned into revolutionary 'troikas' and tribunals. (Zorkin 2004: 10)

Someone, in his view, may count on being allowed to use these tribunals against an undesirable government, but:

> troikas and tribunals have their own internal logic. Their execution ditch swallows exactly those people who have been wishing to use them for their specific momentary purposes. (Zorkin 2004: 10)

Zorkin states that Morschakova's idea of 'higher expediency' led her to justify the shooting of the Parliament in 1993. The Constitutional Court by a majority of votes refused in 1993 to use the logic of revolutionary expediency. In Zorkin's view, Morschakova, who wrote a dissenting opinion, revealed her intent to practice the law of revolution:

> When blood is justified by higher principles of revolutionary expediency, this is immoral. Those who try to make this position compatible with the apology of law, try to give a new chance to violence. (Zorkin 2004: 10)

Theoretically, Zorkin does not deny the existence of some higher principles, but considers them to be dangerous:

> I understand that there is some higher sense above the law, which was differently understood by Hegel and Kant. But I also know, that any new attempt to appeal to transcendental legal consciousness leads to lawlessness and to the subordination of law to a certain higher expediency. (Zorkin 2004: 10)

The positions of both sides are now clearly stated. Many values are undoubtedly shared by both opponents, such as democracy, the rule of law, civil rights and liberties. But as Perelman and Olbrechts-Tyteca fairly noted, most values are indeed shared by a great number of people, but a particular group of people 'is characterized less by which values it accepts than by the way it grades them' (1969: 81). Morschakova and Zorkin have different degrees of acceptance of values from the same list, and put them into hierarchies differently.

'Law' (as a compilation of written texts) for Zorkin is of higher value than 'Politics' or 'Morality'. Morschakova is ready to sacrifice 'Law' in the narrow sense (as the letter of the law) for 'Law' understood in a wider context, which includes 'Maxims of Law' (mainly consisting of procedural rules), 'Principles of Law', and 'Legal Concepts' (for instance, the 'separation of powers').

The second point of disagreement for them is the source of principles, which might be accepted as premises of a very general nature by all judges. Where and how can we find these 'higher principles'?

Zorkin argues that his opponent cannot provide the 'name' of this 'transcendental substance', which she calls 'higher law', and that she keeps it secret. In his view, this contradicts any legal and democratic forms. He compares this approach with criminal society, where members follow some unwritten common understandings, called 'conceptions [понятия]', according to which they know who is good and who is bad, who is a crony and who is a stranger, who is progressive and who is reactionary. 'Commonplaces' of their subculture are known only to the members of their closed circle; only members of this circle can apply them and they are applicable only to the members. Zorkin suggests that the 'higher principles of law' or transcendental substances that rule Morschakova's decisions are known, probably, only to herself and 'are provided to members of her salon, seemingly, on terms of special trust' (Zorkin 2004: 10).

The question for Zorkin is how to become a member of this 'salon'. At least, in Soviet times, the Bolshevists' logic with its values and hierarchies (or, in rhetorical terms, with its system of commonplaces, or *topoi*) was developed in a significant number of works by Marx, Engels and Lenin, and was known to the public. In our case who will decide the terms of admittance to the salon? Zorkin finds it quite worrying, for instance, that in her interview Morschakova stigmatized all Saint-Petersburg legal scholars as 'reactionaries' and thus, obviously, refused them admittance to the circle of those having knowledge about 'higher principles' of law.

Dworkin answers to arguments of this sort that it is impossible to demonstrate the authority and weight of a particular principle in the same way as that of a rule, by pointing to its origin – to an act of Congress or to a decision of a court. But it does not follow from this that principles cannot be binding or obligatory. In order to determine the weight of principles we can, instead, turn to practices and understandings. The origin of legal principles, as Dworkin argues, 'lies not in the particular decision of some legislature or court, but in a sense of appropriateness developed in the profession and the public over time' (Dworkin 1997: 40). This is a possible answer to Zorkin's question of where Morschakova's 'transcendental substances' can be drawn from.

More *Topoi* for Greater Judicial Choice

Interestingly enough, the Russian Constitutional Court with Valery Zorkin as its Chairperson in many cases uses *de facto* arguments from values, concepts and other 'illusory categories' of the same kind as Morschakova's higher principles of law. In many cases the Court refused to declare provisions unconstitutional, if their plain meaning was *prima facie* inconsistent with the Constitution. It preferred to make a statement that the provision should be assigned a new meaning and that it must be read differently, in its 'constitutional legal meaning', while preserving the old wording.

Paradoxically, Zorkin does not seem to notice that the search for 'constitutional legal meaning' outside the words of the Constitution involves a certain risk, equal to the application of Morschakova's 'higher principles': the 'constitutional legal meaning' like the 'revolutionary legal sense' applied elsewhere in Soviet times may be relied upon to justify any decision, because it does not rest upon the consideration of all arguments, drawn from different commonplaces. When it is applied as a primary and basic (rather than an auxiliary and additional) criterion, the legal provision loses any relation to its wording, and this means that there is no criterion left to evaluate the objectivity of interpretation. The Constitutional Court becomes the sole keeper of some kind of sacred knowledge about the sense and meaning of the constitutional provisions, and one can only hope that in considering complaints it is guided by the ideas of the protection of human rights and limitation of powers.

If the decisions involve more commonplaces, the dispute from the level of whether we can, generally speaking, use some principles of higher law and where we can find them, moves to another level: what kind of values, doctrines, general principles of law, comparative perspectives, international standards, legal concepts, social doctrines, pragmatic considerations, historical perspectives, statistical data, moral attitudes and so on can be relevant to this particular case and how can we put all these considerations into a hierarchy and define which arguments from the above-mentioned list seem stronger? In this case we will not need to choose between the letter of the law (Zorkin's legalism) and principles of law (Morschakova's axiology). Both approaches will become simply two arguments from a wider list, where the number and weight of all the arguments *pro* and *contra* will govern the judicial choice.

Pathos v. Logos

The two authors differ significantly also in the arrangement of their material and the style of their publications. While Morschakova's style is neutral and typical for academic publications, Zorkin's style attracts attention due to its unusual choice of words, unusual composition of sentences and abundance of figures of speech. We can find examples of so many devices for the 'dressing of thought' that his texts can be used to exemplify practically all chapters in the rhetoric textbooks.

Morschakova places her stake on the rationality of the readers. In the first publication, her interview to newspaper *Novaya Gazeta*, she discusses the flaws of judicial reform and the situation with respect to the rule of law in Russia. In the second publication, under the title 'These Proposals Are Fully Realizable' (Morschakova 2009), she comments on suggestions for strengthening the judiciary made by Mikhail Khodorkovsky in his 'Russia Waiting for Court', which had been published a few days earlier in the same monthly. From the rhetorical point of view the arrangement of the second article follows the classical scheme (Corbett and Connors 1999: 259).

In a short introduction she mentions that there is no disagreement in Russian society on the necessity of judicial reform, though different circles have different expectations for its realization. Then the main thesis follows, which serves to prepare the audience for the position of the rhetor on the main point: 'In given conditions judicial reform should precede the entire process of modernization.' Then in narration she writes retrospectively about the stages of judicial reform in post-communist Russia and marks its positive achievements. Further she describes the current situation ('the reform … failed or, what is the same, brought the opposite results …'), lists the proposals made by Khodorkovsky on how to reform the judicial community and strengthen the independence of judges, adduces proofs why his proposals are 'absolutely realizable', and refutes opposing views. These statements are followed by: a recapitulation (without the support of the public legal consciousness the reforms cannot be realized; it is hardly possible to expect that the initiatives will appear by themselves; the initiatives should come from the powers that be; wide public discussion of the reforms is necessary); appeals (to society, power and the professional legal community); and a conclusion (the proposals are vitally necessary, realizable, have positive effect, and society will support the ideas aimed at fair trial). The support of society is guaranteed by the ethical dimension of the reform: 'Society educates the power [government] to serve socially justified interests in a high moral aspiration.'

Of the three modes of persuasion which rhetoric employs, namely rational appeal (logos), emotional appeal (pathos) and ethical appeal (ethos), Morschakova primarily relies on logos. She enumerates the proposals made by Khodorkovsky and discusses them in more detail, trying to prove their validity or voidness. In doing so, she deploys the following types of arguments: the argument of direction – she divides the pursuit of an end, namely the independence of judges, into several steps to be made and measures to be undertaken in order to obtain this final goal; the argument to the meaning – she explains, why these measures will enhance the judges' status and strengthen their independence; and the pragmatic argument – she provides reasons, why the proposed measures fit into the system of society's expectations and are useful for judges themselves.

From a stylistic point of view the texts are characterized by a low number of figures of speech and tropes, especially in the second publication. Two proverbs and rare rows of antitheses are among the few exceptions to this pattern. The phrase 'it is not the persons who should provide guarantees against the laws, but, just the opposite, the laws create guarantees against undue behaviour of persons' contains, in addition to antithesis, an antimetabole (repetition of words, in successive clauses, in reverse grammatical order). Epithets which she uses do not have specific author's features and have the function of adding more precision ('petty and problematic amendments'). We come across a rhetorical exclamation ('Where this "to decide"?'), allusion to the well-known Russian proverb 'Суд не на осуд, а на рассуд [Trial is not to convict but to decide]' and some rhetorical questions ('To what extent can such proposals be realized at all? Aren't they utopian for Russia?'). However, the appeal to emotions takes place only in the first example, while in the second case the author signifies to her audience that she will further provide an answer and adduce reasons for its justification.

There are few metaphors in either publication, and these metaphors represent the court as an organism: 'Doctor Morschakova's diagnosis' suggests that the court system is ill. Further we have a metaphoric row extending the meaning: the sick body needs the 'healthening effect of jury trials' and 'recovery medication, which can change the whole judicial system'; the reform is needed 'as oxygen'.

As distinct from the *dispositio* of Morschakova's texts, Zorkin's main thesis in the first publication is formulated not in the beginning, but after several lengthy introductions, which can be more fairly called digressions, because they do not relate directly to the topic of judicial power. In the first article the introduction splits into three parts: the author's view on the past conflict between two superpowers – the USSR and the USA; the author's statements on the West as 'a pioneer of law as the centre of socium'; and deliberations about the unattainability of the higher ideal in general and the higher ideal of law in particular. We can suppose that the author needed such a long introduction in order to introduce his system of commonplaces (*topoi*). They follow from the text as several pairs of interrelated notions with internal conflict in each of the pairs: 'someone somewhere/we here and now', 'Western law/ideal', 'ideal/reality'. All successive arguments push us to make a conclusion that an ideal is something deserving admiration, but any attempt to put it into practice will inevitably lead to destruction – in the author's cognitive model this antinomy is irreconcilable.

The initial statement which opens the text – 'The question about the destiny of law in Russia is not to be discussed on this level. Here another format is required …' – has not been developed any further. The main thesis can be found in a postulate 'To defend law always and in everything – that is what it means to be a judge in general and a constitutional judge in the first place.' But the question about what kind of law must be defended, in the author's view, should not arise before a lawyer.

The expectations of a reader to see the arguments for and against the proposals made by his colleague do not pan out: in Zorkin's stylistics it is pathos, not logos, which rules the discourse; the text consists of appeals to the audience's emotions and not to the audience's reason and understanding. However, while trying to gain the adherence of the readers by touching their emotions, he makes a typical rhetorical mistake: he starts to be driven by emotions himself, though the highly tensioned emotional state of a rhetor does not necessarily create the same emotions in the audience.

We can define the emotional appeal as a main mode of persuasion in Zorkin's rhetoric by analysing the *dispositio* of his publications (arrangement of the material), types of arguments and style of presentation, which is flourishing with figures of speech and tropes. His stylistics is better suited to oral speech in public or to propaganda before a universal audience, for instance at a meeting with a big crowd of people, than to a presentation before a specialized audience, united by a common intellectual background, a similar educational level and joint interests, because the participants in public events usually have neither the time, nor the possibility, nor the special skills (inherent to the expert community) to critically evaluate the arguments.

Both Zorkin's texts are characterized by an abundance of figures of speech – 'those patternings of words which represent departures from the ordinary way of speaking' (Corbett and Connors 1999: 469). The texts contain a lot of parallelism and antitheses, often in combination with metaphors: 'Pooled Cash Fund [общак] knows, who is good and who is bad, who is ours and who is alien, who is progressive and who is reactionary'; 'If a rich man violates the law – the law will turn a rich man into a prisoner, and tuxedo his – into a prisoners' robe'; '… not as a reactionary hawk, lashing out at the reforming pigeon, but as a man and professional' and so on. The phrase 'Big cynicism can exploit someone's idealism. But idealism does not turn into cynicism because of that', appears to be an example of antimetabole. The inverse word order ('tuxedo his') also adds emotional overtone to the phrase.

In addition, Zorkin often makes use of the scheme called parenthesis, which interrupts the normal syntactical flow of the sentence: 'she puts herself aside from a circle of persons who are in charge (let it be just intellectually) for the quality of judicial reform'; 'this admiration of Western law dictated my attitude to the Soviet system (which contained a lot of unlawfulness [неправового])' and many other examples. Use of this device is justified in certain cases, for instance, to add precision or emotional charge to the sentence, revealing the author's very personal attitude to the ongoing dispute, but excessive use of it in general, for example 16 times in the second text (Zorkin 2009) alone, distracts the reader from the main problems of the discussion.

The most notable stylistic feature of Zorkin's texts is a variety of different schemes of repetition – both the repetition of words and of syntactic structures. Some of them are used to add tempo and rhythm or to underline the importance of the thought, for instance gradatio ('insistently articulated, disclosed, described') or enumeratio ('any real human rights defender – here for me a confederate, a companion, a co-brother in this holy war …'). Some of them add grace to the text, delight the reader. We meet such schemes as anaphora ('When such activity is undertaken by new Peter Verkhovensky … When by fact this law is trampled under foot by ordinary criminal bandito … When, at least, this law-undermining is made by …'), epistrophe ('Let us put aside … peculiarities … All these are, nevertheless, just peculiarities'), repetition of similar words in a medial position ('If a rich man violates the law – the law will turn a rich man into a prisoner'); anadiplosis ('It is not my personal opinion. It is the personal opinion of the significant part of that professional legal community …'; 'The West is a subject, resting on Rome. Rome Catholic and Rome Antique'). Indeed, many schemes of repetition may be very beautiful, but when they are excessively used, they may eliminate the persuasive character not only of a professional dispute, but also of a political agitprop. For instance, Zorkin's style is notable for the frequent use of polyptotons – repetitions of words derived from the same root in one or several neighbouring sentences: 'our intelligentsia … preserved the sense of taste. And can evaluate from its taste position the following passage …' [Наша интеллигенция … сохранила чувство вкуса. И может оценить с этой вкусовой позиции пассаж …]. However, as with any other types of repetition, the use of polyptoton runs the risk of creating unjustified circumlocution, as for instance, in the following phrase: 'I have in mind an unrealizable trinity, which has become the highest manifestation and pole star of all bourgeois revolutions … Critics of these revolutions spoke a lot about the unrealizability of an ideal. But, alack, an ideal is never realized in our reality entirely.'

Metaphors are few, as distinct from what one would expect in texts where the main emphasis is on pathos. Zorkin's main metaphorical model is a model of nature and the elements. Law in these elements is a ship which needs, in order to sail, sails and wind. In this model there is no actor, only the incomprehensible, unknown nature of water or fire. There is 'depth of ill-being', there is 'historical energy', there is the 'heating of history', the 'furnace of terrible convulsions'. In this cognitive model, where the subject is absent, the questions which Zorkin asks do not look surprising: 'Who will be the subject, who will join with these technologies? How can this subject be constituted in these historical circumstances at all?' He blames Morschakova for not asking herself these questions, when she deliberates on the methods of judicial reform.

Indefinite actors are met frequently in both publications: 'If it [convergence] failed, it means, that someone wanted it to fail, and this someone disposed huge resources and possibilities for it'; 'such metamorphosis seems desirable for someone. This "someone" may think …'. Euphemisms are also used to create the image of an unknown enemy: 'creators of new oppositionism [создатели новой оппозиционности]'; 'apologists of revolutionary expediency, who mum into liberal garments'; 'zealots of pogroms and genocides, calling themselves knights of protection of sovereignty of a person and rights-and-freedoms [ревнители погромов и геноцидов …, называющие себя рыцарями защиты суверенитета личности и правосвобод]'.

Zorkin's arguments are built, first of all, on attempts to compromise the position of his opponent. He invokes analogy as a means to achieve this goal. For instance, he draws an analogy between the views of Morschakova and those of Hitler, because in her article she called the Leningrad academic school of law 'reactionary'. In Zorkin's view, by doing so, she singles out a group of persons on the grounds of belonging to a certain region, which can lead, in the long run, to consequences comparable with ethnic cleansing. But any analogy is refutable, and especially this one: an academic school is composed of researchers and professors sharing common scientific views and united by common scholarship and collaboration, rather than each and every individual academic from a particular region. To call the academic school 'reactionary' does not mean calling for the extermination of its progenies.

The analogy is refutable also in the following case: 'In her interview, Professor Morschakova uses as a cornerstone some "principle of higher law". This is, in fact, uncovered analogy of the higher expediency ....' But, as mentioned above, principles and policies (including political goals) are very different standards in legal interpretation. It follows that the consequences of decisions made on the grounds of principles will differ from the consequences of decisions made on the grounds of political motives. Thus, the transitivity argument built by Zorkin, namely 'the principle of higher law – higher political expediency – revolutionary troikas and tribunals – execution ditch', becomes invalid, because the logical relation between the first and the second links of the syllogistic chain breaks.

Pragmatic arguments used by the author also deserve consideration. Zorkin evaluates the proposals made by Morschakova in terms of unfavourable consequences: he intimidates us with the demolition of Russia, beatings, travesty of justice, shooting people dead at the edge of the ditch, but does not adduce any convincing explanations why all these horrors should necessarily take place if the provisions of statutes will be supplemented by other standards, for instance, by 'not realizable', let it be at the current moment, principles of justice and equality, which he mentions in his articles.

Most of the argument types we meet in Zorkin's articles are traditionally described by rhetoricians as fallacies. They are either not related to the subject matter of the dispute, or contain deceptive reasoning.

Zorkin likes to deploy the argument of incompatibility. For instance, he argues that criticism of the existing legal system by his opponent is incompatible with her high status as a judge. Sometimes he combines this argument with attacks on the personality of his opponent (argument *ad personam*[5]), which may be softened by polite compliments: 'educated judge', 'high professional in the sphere of jurisprudence', who 'cannot but know that ...'. Sometimes this incompatibility argument is accompanied by sarcastic euphemisms: 'a person, who is not deprived of affiliation with the bodies of state power', 'discussion by this "legal person" of the quality of Constitutional Court ...' and similar descriptions. The implications

5 This type of argument is usually called 'ad hominem'. I use the distinction, drawn by Perelman and Olbrecht-Tyteca (1969: 111) : 'Argument ad hominem must not be confused with argument ad personam, which may be defined as a personal attack on the opponent and which aims essentially at disqualifying him.'

about the invalidity of the proposals made by Morschakova do not follow from such assertions.

In the second article, 'Law Is Not a Thing in Itself', the author stresses the useless character of any discussions and insists on the impossibility of building a dialogue, when it engages non-professionals (references to Mikhail Khodorkovsky). For the justification, why judicial reforms cannot be solely at the discretion of legal professionals, I have nothing to add to the remarks made by Andras Sajó, who argued that in defining the quality of shoes the interests of the expert shoe-makers should be left aside: 'It is *my* foot that is aching, these are *my* shoes that are soaked through, and all these pains just because of the shoemaker's "expert opinion", which serves his convenience! Corporatism is the dictatorship of shoemakers' (Sajó 1999: 5).

Another example of fallacies we find is the so-called 'reading in hearts', when instead of criticizing the reasoning, the author tries to find the hidden personal motives underlying the proposals. Thus, Zorkin addresses M. Khodorkovsky: 'You personally lost something, because the courts in a certain moment turned out to be in resonance with up-to-the-minute political conjuncture unfavourable for you ... When courts took decisions in your favour in the commercial cases which you had initiated, you liked their dependence, didn't you?'

There is one more fallacy, called the 'stake on false shame', when the reasons for or against the proposition are substituted by the phrases 'You must know ...' or similar. In the analysed texts, for instance, we find: 'A lawyer cannot but understand, what juridical personality is. A lawyer cannot technologize the state of jurisprudence without asking the question, who will be a subject, who will conjoin with these technologies?' (in this example, notice also the use of vague, technical lexis to convey a knowledgeable, 'scientific' impression); 'A legal professional (of course, a serious lawyer and not a newcomer or drop-out), who is asked to do something in jurisprudence, will always answer ...'. The author relies on the fact that no one lawyer will agree to be considered a non-professional or a newcomer-drop-out, and thus will not challenge the incorrect use of the term, while non-lawyers simply do not know what 'juridical personality' is. Again, rational appeals are absent here.

Fallacies are used to create the emotional atmosphere of a discussion when people are disposed to accept as proven what has only been asserted without critical analysis of what has been said. However, such arguments do not work in the expert community. Deploying them, one can achieve the adherence of the audience only in the case of a universal audience. That is why such arguments are used in sermons or in propaganda, because such texts are built on the repetition of certain postulates and emotional appeals to the audience.

Conclusion

This study illustrates the way in which a rhetorical analysis of legal argument can advance our understanding of the positions of the polemists. In the articles analysed, Zorkin and Morschakova adopt irreconcilable positions with respect to their understanding of democracy and its values. Morschakova is not ready to trade democratic values for so-called 'stability', while Zorkin uses 'stability' as a shield against radical steps on Russia's way to democracy. These different priorities are reflected in their debate about 'higher principles of law' or, as Zorkin would prefer, 'higher principles of revolutionary expediency'. In addition, Zorkin and Morschakova adopt different modes of persuasion, with Morschakova relying primarily on appeals to reason (*logos*) and Zorkin on appeals to emotion (*pathos*). Informal discussions with members of the legal community suggest that, in spite of the use of numerous stylistic devices, unusual schemes, tropes and other 'dressings of thought' (such as use of personal neologisms and own double-word epithets – 'technologize', 'newcomer-drop-out', 'law-destroying', 'world-exterminating hate', 'dominant-legal slogan', 'rights-and-freedoms [правосвободы]'), the articles by Zorkin did not seem persuasive to the professional legal community. Furthermore, although Zorkin was concerned to engage a wider, universal audience in the debate about judicial reform, his rhetorical attempts to persuade this audience were also largely unsuccessful. The more general public remained untouched, because in order to get interested in these lengthy articles, one had to understand the relevant *topoi*, or commonplaces. One had to know the uneasy history of the development of the Russian Constitutional Court and understand the numerous allusions used in the text. For people lacking background knowledge of Russian constitutional history and its conflicts, these articles lose the subject matter.

References

Aarnio, A. and MacCormick, D.N. (eds). 1992. *Legal Reasoning Vol. II*. Aldershot: Dartmouth.

Aristotle. 1989. *Topica*. Cambridge, MA: Harvard University Press (Loeb Classical Library).

Cicero. 1949. *De Inventione; De Optimo Genere Oratorum; Topica*. Cambridge, MA: Harvard University Press (Loeb Classical Library).

Corbett, E.P.J. and Connors, R.J. 1999. *Classical Rhetoric for the Modern Student*. New York: Oxford University Press.

Dworkin, Ronald. 1997. *Taking Rights Seriously*. Cambridge, MA: Harvard University Press.

Hart, H.L.A. 1994. *The Concept of Law*. 2nd edition. Oxford: Oxford University Press.

MacCormick, D.N. and Summers, R.S. (eds). 1991. *Interpreting Statutes*. Aldershot: Dartmouth.

Morschakova, T. 2009. 'Eti predlozheniya absolyutno realizuyemy' ['These Proposals Are Fully Realizable']. *Vlast*. [Online, 29 June]. Available at: http://www.kommersant.ru/doc.aspx?DocsID=1192668 [accessed 17 January 2010].

Nikitinsky, L. 2004. '… I suda net: Diagnos doktora Morschakovoi' ['… And There Is No Trial: Doctor Morschakova's Diagnosis']. *Novaya Gazeta*. [Online, 19-21 July]. Available at: http://2004.novayagazeta.ru/nomer/2004/51n/n51n-s16.shtml [accessed 17 January 2010].

Perelman, C. and Olbrechts-Tyteca, L. 1969. *The New Rhetoric: A Treatise on Argumentation*. Notre Dame, IN: University of Notre Dame Press.

Sajó, A. 1999. *Limiting Government: An Introduction to Constitutionalism*. Budapest: Central European University Press.

Soboleva, A. 2007. 'Topical Jurisprudence: Reconciliation of Law and Rhetoric', in *Interpretation, Law and the Construction of Meaning*, edited by A. Wagner, W. Werner and D. Cao. Dordrecht: Springer, 49-63.

Viehweg, T. 1993. *Topics and Law*. Frankfurt am Main: Peter Lang.

Weaver, R.M. 1953. *The Ethics of Rhetoric*. Chicago, IL: Regnery/Gateway.

Zorkin, V. 2004. 'Ostorozhno: Pravorzrushitel'stvo' ['Caution: Demolition of the Law!']. *Rossiiskaya Gazeta*. [Online, 22 July]. Available at: http://www.rg.ru/2004/07/22/zorkin.html [accessed 17 January 2010].

Zorkin, V. 2009. 'Pravo – ne viesch v sebie!' ['Law Is Not a Thing in Itself!']. *Vlast*. [Online, 6 July]. Available at: http://www.kommersant.ru/doc.aspx?DocsID=1196420 [accessed: 17 January 2010].

Chapter 6
A Dialogical and Polyphonic Approach to Contract Theory

André Bélanger and Andy van Drom

Introduction

In a postmodern society, dominated by the overconsumption of services and the proliferation of adhesion contracts, it seems both necessary and unavoidable to investigate whether the contractual underpinnings of positive law have lost their juridical sense. Indeed, it should not be forgotten that, before producing economy, the contractual relationship creates legal standards: a vital normative relationship that should not be concealed. To address this theoretical shortfall, one of whose effects is the crisis of the contract (Jamin and Mazeaud 2003), we seek to establish a new contractual paradigm that is not based on an individualist understanding of the contract – the meeting of two opposing minds and the consideration of the facts that have brought about this *fusion* to establish the contract's obligational content – but rather on the specifically intersubjective, social and human nature of the contract. With this in mind, we seek to contribute to a normative revitalization that falls within the scope of an ongoing project of legal modernity, rather than being abandoned to the mere needs of neoliberal economy.

Dialogism, by favouring the issue of the intrinsic otherness of the interpretative exercise that sustains all contracts, then appears as a stimulating theoretical approach in countering the contemporary reification of the contracting parties. As an interpretative method, it can allow for a renewal of our juridical understanding of the contract. It reveals the difficult, yet all too human, creation of a (micro) community sensible of the intersubjectivity that cannot but unite the parties subscribing to the contract. Indeed, our main criticism towards contemporary contract theory concerns the fact that it is unable to make room for *two* socialized and personified individuals. The viewpoint we suggest consolidates several advantages of the dialogic interpretation of the contract. By no longer regarding the contractual agreement as a mass-produced economic good realized as demultiplied monologic discourse, but as a private legal standard inevitably shared by the two contracting parties because of its legal status, we want to reconsider the interpretation of contracts within the framework of voluntarism itself. The contract is thus reduced to its very essence; a negotiating space of complex volitions within the frame of a social fact that is not primarily technical or economical, but human. Through dialogism, each contracting party can inscribe its full legal capacity in the normative process, and evolve from an abstract entity devoid of complexity to a genuine actor within the elaboration, the comprehension and eventually the interpretation of the contractual agreement. To this end, the current chapter explores the dialogic and polyphonic approaches within the contractual genre.[1] This can be considered to constitute an innovative doctrinal angle for, as Fabrice Bin observes:

> Otherness ... is not an integral part of conventional legal culture. But if the concept is not to be found in the jurist's gun belt, it is not utterly absent from the armory. However, doctrinal works treating jointly of law and otherness have a distinctive tendency to import their legal toolbox into another science and not vice versa. (Bin 2004: 183)

In order to avoid this pitfall, our analysis of the literature on dialogism and polyphony aims to establish the outline of a set of theoretical tools borrowed from linguistics, in order to determine the relevant vocabulary to adapt and apply to contract theory. When applied to language, the notions of dialogism and polyphony concern the non-uniqueness of the speaking subject,[2] in other words, the presence of several voices in an utterance which – at least apparently – has a single empirical producer. These notions thus refer to a simple question: who is speaking and thinking in the utterance that is the contract? The well-known postulate of the uniqueness of the speaking subject[3] according to which the utterance solely renders the words of its producer is invalidated as soon as one does not consider the utterance producer to be a physical entity, but rather the sum of his discursive representations contained within the utterance. First and foremost, this signifies that, rather than functioning as a homogenous representation of what is expressed by the speaking subject, meaning should be interpreted as an 'abstract dialogue' in praxematic terms, or as an 'orchestrated concert of voices' in polyphonic terms.

Apart from what distinguishes the two approaches from one another, the dialogic and polyphonic conceptions of language invariably consider that meaning integrates certain extrinsic voices, certain enunciative elements said to be *heterogeneous* (Authier-Revuz 1995), and that it establishes various relations of

---

1 In the first of the three sections that make up our research project, we have tried to situate the interpretation of the contract within a methodological and conceptual framework with a larger scope than what is usually adopted by jurists, in order to highlight the intersubjective nature of contemporary contracts. See (Bélanger et al. 2010).

2 The *Dictionnaire d'analyse du discours* explains that every speaking person is 'likely to have two types of identity: a social [extra-linguistic] identity and a discursive [intra-linguistic] identity. Social identity defines the speaking subject as he who produces an utterance who takes the floor ... Discursive identity defines the speaking subject as a linguistic entity expressing itself through the execution of the enunciative process' (Charaudeau and Maingueneau 2002: 556).

3 '... a postulate that, for me, seems to be a (generally implicit) prerequisite to everything that we call "modern linguistics" today, a term that covers at the same time comparatism, structuralism, and generative grammar' (Ducrot 1984: 171).

responsibility (Dendale and Coltier 2005) or, on the contrary, of *non-responsibility* (Perrin 2004) towards these *points of view*. Analyses differ sometimes, especially as the locus of this enunciative heterogeneity is concerned: the word, the sentence, the utterance itself, or even, as in our case, the contractual text as a whole. On the one hand, these different interpretations are simply a reflection of the complex structure that is language, and its likeliness to be approached from different angles. On the other hand, the various theorizations of dialogism and polyphony reflect Bakhtin's complex thought, from which they stem.

Finally, it should be emphasized that, unlike certain authors,[4] we consider dialogism to be a phenomenon that is ubiquitous within language, and which encompasses the phenomenon of polyphony. The functional definitions of contractual dialogism and polyphony that we propose (see 'Dialogism and Polyphony within the Contract' below) are a reflection of this theoretical postulate. Based on this conceptual framework, considered within the scope of a vision of discourse as social practice (see 'Discursive Otherness and Social Fact' below), we investigate the *raison d'être* of these linguistic phenomena in the contractual realm (see 'The Purposefulness of Dialogic and Polyphonic Phenomena within the Contract' below), and ultimately, we seek to integrate these concepts into the field of private law (see 'Dialogical and Polyphonic Considerations at the Heart of the Contractual Bond' below).

Discursive Otherness and Social Fact

Intuitively, we can observe that language occupies an increasingly vital place within our society. Its economic importance has considerably grown throughout the postindustrial era. As stated by Giddens (1991), this evolution has led to an increased awareness of language use that seems to be the cause of a more conspicuous control of linguistic production. The need to study language within this large social context has become imperative.

Acknowledging this economic importance of language has led us to consider discourse as a form of 'social practice' (Fairclough 2003: 26). This conception of discourse involves a *dialectic relationship* between a discursive event and the social situation that frames it: the discursive event is shaped by its social context, but it also shapes it in turn. In Fairclough's terminology (Fairclough 1992), the discourse is *socially constitutive* and *socially shaped.* That being said, the

4 Dendale and Coltier (2006: 288) conclude that 'of the two concepts, that of dialogism is clearly more specific than that of polyphony, the latter being able to incorporate … that of dialogism'. Perrin (2004), Nowakowska (2005), and Amossy (2005), amongst others, share this conception.

relationship between discourse and social factors is not direct, but manifested through a process of *mediation*.[5]

Critically analysing discourse, then, 'is essentially making visible the interconnectedness of things' (Fairclough 1997: 747) with the primary purpose of 'demystifying' and 'deciphering' discourse (Zijderveld 1979). This type of analysis emphasizes the need for interdisciplinarity in order to obtain an in-depth understanding of the function of language in the process of constituting and transmitting knowledge and social organization. Through the analysis of both transparent and opaque structural relationships that are present within discourse, we can thus retrace the different discursive voices that constitute the contractual text and that, according to contract theory, give rise to the meeting of minds.

The notion of genre is intrinsically linked to that of discourse as social practice (Fairclough 1992: 65-86). 'A genre is a way of acting in its discourse aspect … Genres can be identified at different levels of abstraction: highly abstract "pre-genres" such as Narrative or Report [or Contract], which generalize over many different forms … at a more concrete level, disembedded genres …, and situated genres' (Fairclough 2003: 216). We limit ourselves here to the most general level and consider the contract to be a discursive genre realized as 'an objectivised enunciation presenting a multi-voiced intertext' (Moirand 2007: 126) of which the scriptor remains in charge. This observation, in turn, encourages us to further investigate the notion of polyphony within the contractual phenomenon.

Even if the contract is drafted in an objectivized style, its *intertext*[6] is made up of several voices (the contracting parties, the law, the jurisprudence etc.); this contributes to the building of memory domains that are constantly updated through the linguistic and semiotic forms, which are indicators of concealed

5 'CDA sees discourse – language use in speech and writing – as a form of "social practice". Describing discourse as social practice implies a dialectical relationship between a particular discursive event and the situation(s), institution(s) and social structure(s), which frame it: The discursive event is shaped by them, but it also shapes them. That is, discourse is socially constitutive as well as socially conditioned – it constitutes situations, objects of knowledge, and the social identities of and relationships between people and groups of people. It is constitutive both in the sense that it helps to sustain and reproduce the social status quo, and in the sense that it contributes transforming it' (Fairclough and Wodak 1997).

6 In the *Dictionnaire de l'analyse du discours*, *intertext* is defined as a set of texts linked through intertextual relationships that are more or less easily linked to identifiable sources. As soon as the sources are fuzzy, we are rather dealing with *interdiscourse*. It is important to note here that the interdiscourse is to be thought of as a pattern of constraints and inevitable previous discourses, whereas the intertext appears as a place of possibility, albeit infused by previous statements, but nevertheless subject to the choice of the speaker. We conclude that the concept of intertext is close to a polyphonic understanding of the discourse, whereas the interdiscourse rather refers to a dialogic understanding. Having said this, the distinction is not consistent with all literature; therefore Genette's (1982, 1987) notion of *transtextuality* might be more convenient, since it encompasses the two others.

intersubjectivity, and which take part in the pragmatic orientation of the discursive genre that is the contract. This editorial genre is characterized by a specific form of dialogic construction that combines *interactional dialogism*, which manifests itself in the way it accounts for the interrogations that the scriptor/speaker imagines his addressees to have (cf. the notion of superaddressee, see below), and *interdiscursive dialogism*, which manifests itself in the recourse to established knowledge in the field, i.e. to the law.

Even if utterances always have an addressee, 'the author of the utterance presupposes, more or less consciously, a higher superaddressee' (Bakhtin 1986: 126). In other words, the enunciator does not only aim his utterance at empirical addressees of the communication situation that is concerned, whether they be physically or virtually present. The enunciator also enters into a dialogue with the prototypical representative of the language community to which he belongs or to which he speaks:

> The author can never turn over his whole self and his speech work to the complete and *final* will of addressees who are on hand or nearby … and always presupposes (with a greater or lesser degree of awareness) some higher instancing of responsive understanding that can distance itself in various directions. Each dialogue takes place as if against the background of the responsive understanding of an invisibly present third party who stands above all the participants in the dialogue (partners). (Bakhtin 1986: 126)

The contractual text then becomes a mosaic of voices made up of a multitude of intertextual threads, and the horizontal thread of the discourse appears, implicitly or explicitly, as fractured. The scriptor proves to be the administrator of this multi-voiced intertext (dialogism) as he must negotiate with the presumed statements of his addressees and with his own statements (polyphony); a difficult balance between opaqueness and transparence acting as centrifugal/centripetal forces (De Santis 2001: 1).

Thus the scriptor finds himself under duress to negotiate between the predictable discourses of his presumed readers, the multiplicity of convened alien discourses and the conscience of a superaddressee. These are the discursive constraints of the utterance situation, which should not be confused with its social parameters.[7] This inner negotiation with diverse alien discourses, which is conscious only to a

7 It is important to distinguish the social worlds (the political world, the scientific world, the law), which are themselves made up of diversified language communities, 'functioning as *institutions that regulate the language practices which the members of the group are subjected to and which are actualized in the discursive genres as well as in the utterances that are shared within the language community*, whether these rules be implicit or explicit' (Moirand 2007: 94-95). This implies that the standpoint of an observer external to a given language community, as long as he does not share the same imaginary, could never recognize a power as legitimate, for he does not recognize himself in it (Bissot 2002: 3).

certain extent, can only be captured through the apparent traces of dialogism and polyphony that emerge within the textual materiality. This brings us to the functional description and definition of these two concepts.

Dialogism and Polyphony within the Contract

The respective role and meaning of dialogism and polyphony within discourse are the objects of an on-going debate between praxemeticians and polyphonists.[8] Even if, in principle, they roughly apply to the same empirical facts, the choice of one notion above the other is anything but indifferent. On the one hand, followers of dialogism base their approach on the image of dialogue and the inevitable exchange with others' utterances, a metaphor dear to Bakhtin. On the other hand, the proponents of the notion of polyphony and the musical metaphor it indirectly evokes, emphasize the speaker's active part in enunciative staging. The voices that polyphony invokes can surely enter into dialogue, metaphorically speaking, but they can also interact in an entirely different manner. As a consequence, despite the precise use that Bakhtin has made of polyphony, the notion is often thought to be less restrictive, less oriented, and thus more generally applicable than that of dialogism (Perrin 2006). Nevertheless, all theorists concur to say that the two notions presently suffer from a certain conceptual instability: 'there are almost as many understandings of this notion [of polyphony] as there are linguists who make use of it,' (Nølke et al. 2004: 14) 'the use of the term dialogic is very common today …; but its scientific edge sometimes seems a little blunted' (Bres 2005: 47). Following the example of Vincent (2006: 127), we conclude that it is more appropriate to critically assess the existing conceptual frameworks rather than elaborate new theories.

Our comparison of the three main theories of dialogism and polyphony (Bélanger et al. 2010) has led us to the conclusion that the perceived differences revolve around the corpus and the methods used, rather than the linguistic phenomena at stake, because the signs of polyphony are, for the proponents of polyphony (Ducrot 1984), the same as those invoked by Bres (2005) in favour of dialogism. Nevertheless, in light of our rationale, it is important to underline the fact that the debate on the respective definitions of polyphony ('Polyphonic Traces within the Contract' below) and dialogism ('Dialogic Traces within the Contract' below) draws on persistent dichotomies: between language and discourse, between discourse and text, and between linguistic description and discursive interpretation:

> The complexity of phenomena seems to impose a dichotomizing approach at all levels, as if one should distinguish at all costs the nearby solid pedestal of linguistic phenomena from the shaky ground of interpretations, which linguists concede to literary critics: resulting in Bres and Nowakowska's distinction between dialogism and polyphony, and Nølke's distinction between linguistic polyphony and literary

8 The reader will find the summary of the debate in (Bres 2005).

> polyphony. … The central point of the debate, apart from the opposition between language and discourse, is the double question concerning the pertinent level for the marking of phenomena of heterogeneity, which are not only a matter of grammar, but also concern interactions, as well as the establishment of the levels on which to situate interpretation, as soon as one ponders on language phenomena … within discourse. (Rabatel 2006: 166-167)

In light of these considerations, it is not only pertinent but also inevitable to establish a holistic and philosophic reflection on dialogism, with a descriptive intent that remains faithful to Bakhtinian thought. Conversely, polyphony's meticulous and contextual analyses allow us to pinpoint the heterogeneity of the contract more precisely. Therefore, our aim is to attain the establishment of functional definitions that sustain an understanding of otherness within contract theory, integrating and reconciling dialogism and polyphony through a concrete analytic model.

Dialogic Traces within the Contract

We have previously established that *represented dialogism*, uncovered through observables found in the textual thread, hinges on 'another level of heterogeneity: a completely different one, extricated and theorized in non-linguistic approaches to language, which recognize … the constitutive character of all speech' (Authier-Revuz 2004: 51). This *constitutive heterogeneity* represents the field of theoretical reflections which underpin human sciences. It may be thus perceived through such notions as *dialogism* (Bakhtin) as well as *discursive memory*, which derives from a rereading of Foucault (Foucault 1969).

Words, formulations and statements conveyed by the different actors' discourses are considered to be memory carriers in and of themselves, rather than the actors who utter them. This is in agreement with the notion of dialogism as conceived by Bakhtin, for whom words are not 'neutral' but always 'inhabited', infused with the statements of others. This is the type of heterogeneity that the notion of *hyperstructure*, subordinate to that of genre,[9] explicates. It is a global heterogeneity, expressed through a common thematic unity, because words, formulations and statements are bound to function as echoes from one document to another inside the same *hyperstructure*, revealed more precisely by the formal and semantic links weaved from a discursive unit to another.[10]

9 'The hyperstructure is an intermediate and optional structuring element of information …. Its origin is situated in an explosive or implosive process' (Lugrin 2001: 69). In our case, the discursive genre is the contract, which encompasses a number of hyperstructures, such as the mass contract, the lease, the forward commodity contract, etc., each with its own parameters.

10 Moirand (2007: 12) observes that these links 'function as *recollections* only for speakers who are able to decode the allusion to previous or external statements'.

The mechanism of *discursive memory* emphasizes 'the fact that each discursive production … circulates priorly uttered formulations' (Courtine 1981: 52). Thereupon, it takes part in the dialogic orientation that is constitutive of every utterance:

> The discourse meets with the discourse of the other on all the roads that lead to its object, and it cannot avoid entering into a live and intense interaction with it. Only the mythical Adam, approaching with the first discourse a pristine and as yet unspoken world, the solitary Adam could indeed avoid this mutual reorientation according the discourse of another which takes place on the road to the object. (Todorov 1981: 98)

In the space occupied by a single text, one might find observables of the quasi clandestine presence of transverse discourses (the interdiscourse that is the result of the dialogic mechanism), that replace, surround or even infiltrate discourses that are explicitly represented (the intertext that is the result of the polyphonic mechanism). This leads us to the difference between prior constructions (the vertical axis) and what is established by the enunciator in the intradiscourse (the horizontal axis). With the interrogation on the function of recollections conveyed by the memory of words or by transverse discourses, one ventures beyond the scope of description, towards the field of interpretation. Indeed, at this stage, the reception by ordinary readers, whose principal aim is not necessarily to analyse, should be questioned in light of the conscious command of polyphony by any speaker.

Polyphonic Traces within the Contract

The term polyphony focuses on a multitude of voices that are apparent within discourse. Unlike the constitutive heterogeneity of dialogism, the polyphonic heterogeneity implies the fact that the speaker puts the voices/points of view that he summons in his discourse on stage:

> Every conversation is full of transmissions and interpretations of other people's words. At every step one meets a 'quotation' or a 'reference' to something that a particular person said, a reference to 'people say' or 'everyone says,' to the words of the person one is talking with, or to one's own previous words, to a newspaper, an official decree, a document, a book and so forth. (Bakhtin 1981: 338)

Based on the idea that polyphony refers to an apparent coexistence of voices/points of view in discourse, we postulate that polyphony occurs as soon as two discursive voices coexist within the same discourse. The speaker (or scriptor) is represented as the one through whom the utterance exists and the one who is in a direct relationship with the deictic core, in other words, the set of spatiotemporal coordinates that define the utterance as a singular event. The speaker is thus the one that can utilize shifters, but also the one who can conceal them by means of discursive strategies (Wodak et al. 1999).[11] In this conception, polyphony is compatible with a vision of dialogism accepting the fact that the speaker establishes his viewpoint from words and points of view that can be expressed in terms of enunciators who represent individual or collective discursive beings, identifiable or not. Finally, we emphasize that the speaker always establishes a double presence for himself within the text: he is at the same time the producer of the utterance who manages the enunciative links of responsibility, and one of the enunciators expressing a point of view.

Proposing a Set of Functional Definitions and an Analytic Model

Based on our readings and reflections, we propose the following applied functional definitions:

- *Contractual dialogism* refers to the constitutive enunciative relationships that every contract maintains with anteriorly produced utterances in the contractual discursive genre (and more specifically within the hyperstructure to which it belongs) – interdiscursive relationships – as well as with ulterior utterances that its addressees might produce – the interactional relationships. Dialogic signs may be opaque or transparent and are present on the discourse level, often without the speaker's knowledge, whilst opening up on major sociopragmatic issues.
- *Contractual polyphony* concerns the enunciative staging by the scriptor/speaker, who hides behind an objectivized style in order to express his point of view as well as those of the enunciators that he wishes to represent. It is a discursive strategy rooted, on one hand, in the linguistic level and whose effects are apparent, on the other hand, at the social level via a process of discursive mediation.

To illustrate the functional definitions that we have established as well as the concrete analysis that we propose, we have conceived a conceptual framework of contract analysis summarized in a tetrahedral model (Figure 6.1). The equal weight of the three plane faces symbolizes the equal importance of each of its components within our analysis. Indeed, a complete and exhaustive analysis should concern the linguistic, discursive, and socioreferential dimensions of the contractual phenomenon, which correspond, respectively, to the following primary objectives: description, interpretation and explanation.

11 It is important to note here that the term *strategy* does not necessarily imply the existence of a speaker who would consciously control the totality of his communicative behaviour.

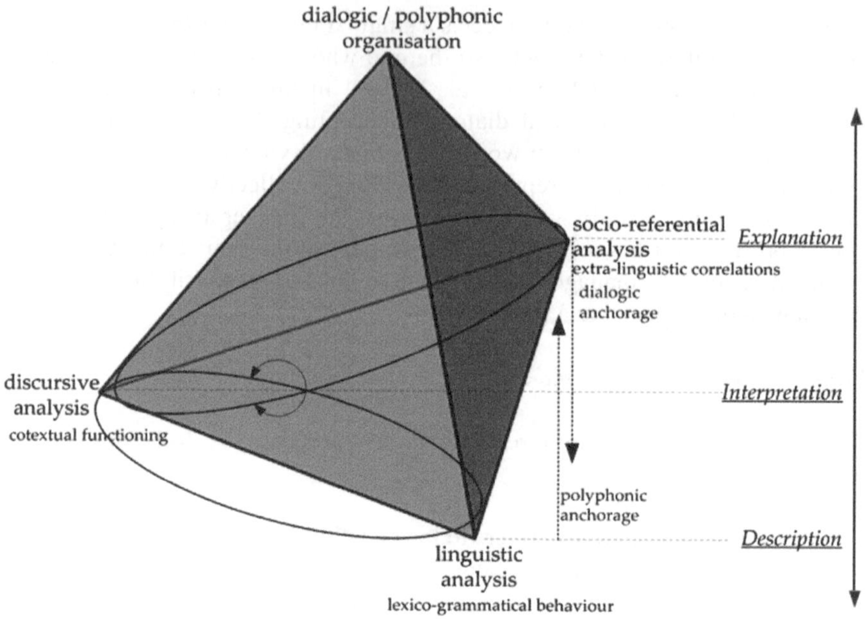

Figure 6.1 Tetrahedral framework of discursive contractual analysis

The analysis we propose draws on a bottom-up methodology firmly rooted in linguistic description, starting from a number of language parameters (preestablished or *ad hoc*, depending on the particular analysis' requirements)[12] that make up the polyphonic structure of the contract under consideration.

First of all, we comprehensively describe the semantic and semiotic forms that make up the different discursive units at the local level as well as the enunciative threads that they weave in the *horizontal order* of the discourse (the order of the text, its linearity; referring to the notion of intratextuality) and in the *vertical order* of the discourse (the transverse discourses to which these units refer explicitly [polyphony] or implicitly [dialogism]; referring to the notions of intertextuality,

12 Dividing textual materiality into typographically distinct subgroups will be enough, *a priori*, to distinguish the discursive units on which the analysis is based, but a linguistic analysis can only characterize them *a posteriori*, after having described the forms that make them up on the local level. A first identification of local phenomena will result from the study of exploratory corpuses; this study only will allow for an identification of the lexico-grammatical observables of the analysis. These are characterized by the two categories that refer to the essential functions of language: representation and communication. At the same time, these observables constitute signs of contextualization, extracted within the analysed texts, or extrapolated based on external considerations, such as social parameters, which intervene during the formulation of interpretative hypotheses.

interdiscursivity and interdiscursive memory). Updating the different voices and points of view that occur within the text in question allows us to access the level of cotextual (and subsequently discursive) interpretation, where dialogic and polyphonic phenomena meet. Working from these linguistic and discursive observations, we are able to establish and justify socioreferential explanations.

In essence, we first focus on local linguistic facts in order to fuel the analysis of the global (the utterance, the hyperstructure, the genre), leading to a comprehensive interpretation informed by these partial transversal descriptions that must be articulated in accordance with the established hypotheses that we reestablish and validate in light of our subsequent observations.

Exemplification

In accordance with the functional definition that we have established, polyphony is based on the notion of an intentional speaker/scriptor, likely to use discursive strategies to obtain adhesion by discursively staging other enunciators' utterances and points of view. Dialogism does not involve the speaker taking responsibility of the utterance by positioning himself in relation to a number of points of view, but rather in relation to anterior and ulterior discourses in a manner that partially escapes his clear conscience. In other words, if polyphony concerns decision-making and position-taking in a fully assumed interaction with the other, dialogism concerns the framing and elaboration of a given utterance within the verbal milieu of social representations.[13] Following Amossy, we can then conclude that:

> … the speaker is at the same constituted by speech of the other which he remains unaware of … as well as an intentional subject mobilizing voices and points of view to inter-act with his allocator … Far from being contradictory, these two conceptions represent two complementary facets of the speaking subject and suggest his bond to the social which is expressed at the same time through his determinations, his individuation, and his intention to speak, which is also an intention to act. (Amossy 2005: 69)

By means of illustration, we discuss an example that we have elaborated previously (Bélanger et al. 2010): 'The lawyer gave up pleading.' We can easily imagine two follow-up phrases to this statement, one expressing a positive opinion, the other a negative opinion. However, these same extensions seem more problematic with a second example modelled on the first, 'the lawyer gave up smoking':

1. + 'Fortunately, the lawyer gave up pleading.' (His speeches are rather tedious.)

13 Following Durkheim, *social representations* are defined as 'modes of practical thought oriented towards communication, comprehension and control of the social, material, and ideal environment' (Jodelet 1989: 361).

2. + 'Unfortunately, the lawyer gave up pleading.' (His speeches are very passionate!)
3. + 'Fortunately, the lawyer gave up smoking.' (It is a bad habit.)
4. ? 'Unfortunately, the lawyer gave up smoking.' (It is a good habit.)

The polyphonic analyses[14] of the four statements are similar:

> LOC > l_0 and ON
> [ON] (TRUE (The lawyer pleaded/smoked before))
> [l_0] (TRUE (The lawyer does not plead/smoke anymore))

However, the difference in content between examples 1 and 2, on the one hand, and examples 3 and 4, on the other hand, explains the fact that example 4 seems problematic, with regard to social representations. Indeed, our society generally accepts the discourse according to which smoking is bad for one's health. This transverse discourse nestles itself, in line with the way dialogism functions, at the heart of statements 3 and 4, which inevitably alters their scope as social practice. Thus, the speaker remains the stage director of the utterance, but he is inevitably influenced by the social representations of the language community to which he belongs:

> SOC > LOC > l_0 and ON
> [SOC] (TRUE (Smoking is not healthy))
> [ON] (TRUE (The lawyer smoked before))
> [l_0] (TRUE (The lawyer does not smoke anymore))

The Purposefulness of Dialogic and Polyphonic Phenomena within the Contract

We now go beyond theorization and further explore the *raison d'être* of dialogic and polyphonic phenomena within the contractual discursive genre. At the same time, these reflections will help us bring important precisions regarding our previous definitions and illustrate them through our corpus of authentic contract extracts.

Max Weber has described *rationalization* as a form of social organization within which social action is no longer oriented towards meaning, value or belief, but

14 We adopt a hybrid, simplified nomenclature based on the frameworks of polyphonic analysis proposed by Ducrot (1984) and Nølke et al. (2004). More specifically, we consider each utterance to be discursively constructed by LOC (locutor as constructor), who stages different enunciators and their points of view. These enunciators may include the locutor himself (l), other individuals (e) or collectives (ON). LOC can uphold links of responsibility (TRUE) or non-responsibility (FALSE) with the different points of view (POV) expressed in the utterance.

towards strategy (Weber 1977). Rationalization is based on whether action is efficient and whether it has reached its purpose, rather than evoking the questions whether it is good or veracious. The result is that rationalized social action is constructed as a step-by-step procedure, accomplished through the deployment of legalist norms aimed at fulfilling the action's purpose in a more efficient and economical manner. Hence, interaction no longer links the members of a society through *consensual social representations* (Jodelet 1989), but rather through the deployment of common practices and procedures. Furthermore, meaning loses its scope and becomes fragmented and heterogeneous whilst social action becomes more homogeneous and regimented. This is what Zijderveld has called 'the supersedure of meaning by function in modernity' (Zijderveld 1979: 7).

Eloquent examples are plentiful in the field of contract law; indeed, a multitude of contract types focusing on ownership, finances, insurance, work etc. are in circulation. A unified relationship between contracting parties no longer governs the cohesion of the contractual phenomenon. On the contrary, there are more and more formal rules dictating how this relationship should be verbalized. This leads us to postulate that there are less contractual procedures, formats and templates (which subsequently become more powerful) and more instantiations of contractual discourses and texts (which subsequently become blurred). In short, we observe discursive heterogeneity and generic, formal homogeneity.

It is precisely within this context that the present crisis of the contract should be situated. Indeed, how can the contract continue to be considered as the product of the meeting of the minds of two parties in an era when the contractual genre becomes more and more homogenized and standardized? Or, in Prémont's words, in the context of mass contracts, is it possible to consider the obligational relationship as a genuine multi-voiced legal creation (viz. the birth of the contractual obligation), and therefore as the result of the wills of the contracting parties and not as a trope (Prémont 2003)?

The consideration of language production as social practice is thus imperative. Every discourse, text and semiotic representation of the world, no matter how abstract, must be interpreted as a representation of social practice. As Malinowski states: 'Even in the most abstract and theoretical aspects of human thought and verbal usage, the real understanding of words ultimately derives from active experience of those aspects of reality to which the words belong' (Malinowski 1935: 58). Given the increased economic importance of the contract within the postindustrial era, the demonstration of the existence, role and evolution of its dialogic and polyphonic character should be uncovered through the analysis of the contract as a discourse which both pertains to and transforms social practice.

Van Leeuwen's conceptual framework of discourse as *transformed social practice* helps us understand the pertinence of the study of polyphonic discursive traces in the contract (Van Leeuwen 2008). Van Leeuwen draws on Weber's social postulates which he relates to Bernstein's concept of recontextualization (Bernstein 1981) and Foucault's notion of the discourse as social cognition (Foucault 1977). In this way, discourse as social cognition becomes a means of textually representing social practice. In line with the idea that social practices become more and more regularized, van Leeuwen identifies ten elements that allow us to identify an action or a social practice:

> a set of actions performed in a sequence that may be fixed to a certain degree;
> a performance mode providing directives for different sequences;
> a set of participants in preestablished roles;
> their eligibility conditions;
> their presentation styles;
> time;
> location;
> its eligibility conditions;
> the resources and tools necessary to perform the action;
> their eligibility conditions.

According to this model, then, the contract as social practice requires:

1. the gathering of at least two parties; the establishment of an agreement; the drafting, reading, and signing of the contract, etc.
2. the reading of the contract must precede its signing, etc.
3. the contracting parties
4. e.g. the person who wishes to get car insurance must own a car
5. e.g. when a contract is signed in person, it is concluded by a handshake
6. the time of the contract signing (e.g. during opening hours)
7. the place of the contract signing (e.g. the head office of the insurance company)
8. the headquarters of the company must be an office, etc.
9. paper, pen, etc.
10. the pen provided by the insurance company will not bear, for instance, a picture of a cartoon character, but rather the logo of the company in question.

All these elements are subject to a recontextualization chain acting as a filter between the social practice and the resulting discourse, which makes it possible to find more or less explicit traces in the discourse that is the contract. Recontextualization can add, erase, rearrange or even substitute certain elements.

Polyphony thus constitutes one of the transformational processes that allow us to analyse the roles of participants and their conditions of eligibility via discursive traces, as will be shown in the next pages with examples of contractual clauses. We will observe traces of eligibility conditions of the participants enumerated in the Lexicon, where personal pronouns reveal the presence of the different participants. Whilst polyphony can be explained as a direct trace of the social practice that discursively results in a contract, dialogism remains indirect and often blurred. The link between the contract as discourse, on the one hand, and as social practice, on the other hand, that van Leeuwen's theory allows us to make (Van Leeuwen 2008), is therefore entirely compatible with the definitions and the conceptual framework that we have previously established. In the following section, these theoretical reflections and practical observations, both linguistic and sociologic in nature, will be applied to various examples of contractual clauses.

Dialogical and Polyphonic Considerations at the Heart of the Contractual Bond

To summarize, in this contribution we are looking to develop the notions of dialogism and polyphony, as well as tailoring and applying them to the field of contract law. We have established an original conceptual framework that draws on ScaPoLine terminology and methodology to fuel our concrete analyses, and which considers discourse as a social practice in order to account for the apparent link between the contract (as discourse) and society. In so doing, we are hoping to stimulate the debate that will allow us to go beyond theorization and inform a number of concrete analyses on samples of contracts in order to confirm our hypotheses concerning the dialogic and polyphonic character of the contract. Given the exploratory nature of this contribution as well as its space constraints, we will henceforth focus on those dialogical and polyphonic parameters that have an obvious incidence on the contractual relationship (van Leeuwen's participants as well as their eligibility conditions and their presentation styles). After reflecting upon the importance of intra- and extralinguistic considerations in the construction of the contractual bond ('The Weight of Intra- vs. Extralinguistic Considerations' below), we will analyse the discursive staging of the relationship between the contracting parties in a number of authentic clauses ('Discursive Traces of the Contractual Relationship' below).

The Weight of Intra- vs. Extralinguistic Considerations

The completed linguistic analyses can be situated at the basis of the tetrahedron that constitutes our conceptual framework. However, before describing a selection of authentic sample clauses, it is important to question whether the institutional discursive identity expressed through the contract refers to fixed, pre-discursive, complementary roles such as landlord–tenant, insurer–insured, employer–employee, etc. Do institutional identities encompass every identity that is represented in the discourse produced in an institutional context? Is it possible to linguistically identify what is institutional? Fairclough (2003) argues that the discursive interaction produced in specific social situations is a reflection of macrosocial forces. Every analysis of institutional interactions should then be rooted in a critique of the institutions involved and of their structures, which shelter the power relations that define the institutional identity.

Having said this, the *institution* is hard to define. Intuitively, it is associated with a physical building (the head office of an insurance company) or with an organizational structure, such as the judiciary power practised in a court of law.

Agar (1985: 164) defines the institution as 'a socially legitimate expertise and the individuals authorized to implement it'. This definition is suggestive of the binary and asymmetrical sociodiscursive roles created by the institutional context: the 'expert' or representative who holds authority versus the 'non-expert' or client who must bend to institutional norms.

The idea that the institution holds enormous power over the rights of individuals and can impose a high degree of bureaucracy on its interactions (e.g. the contract) is discussed in social theories of Althusser and Habermas, amongst others. These theories describe a power that is unilaterally imposed by one of the parties, the dominant one, on the second party, the subordinate one. However, other theorists have adopted points of view that are more balanced and that treat of institutional power in a context of persuasion, compromise and cooperation (e.g. Foucault), which is in accordance with Gramsci's idea of hegemony.

Discursive Traces of the Contractual Relationship

The case of 'we' vs. 'you' We have previously defined the contractual discursive genre as 'drafted in an objectivized style [whose] intertext is made up of several voices (the contracting parties, the law, the jurisprudence, etc.)'.[15] Nevertheless, our concrete analyses encourage us to specify the nature of this 'objectivized style'. Indeed, during our study we have encountered different degrees of objectivization, which mainly concern the difference between the contracts that define the contracting parties in terms of 'we' and 'you' (ex. 1), and those designating the two concerned parties in the third person (the insurer, the insured) (ex. 2):

> Example 1:
> *Through this contract and in return for the payment of a premium, we [insurer] cover you [insured] against the risks defined or enumerated hereafter and to which you [insured] are generally exposed as lessee.* (A1)[16]

---

15 The current contribution draws on a two-year interdisciplinary research project grounded in the particular social context of Quebec civil law. The selection of examples discussed below seeks to respect the prevalence of French language contracts in Quebec, and consolidates the intrinsic relationship between the initial methodological and theoretical setup of our research. To this end, the original French clauses are provided as footnotes and are translated into English in the running text. The extracts from corpora A1 and A2 are authentic clauses of standard insurance contracts, which we consider to be paradigmatic of contemporary contractual reality: produced on a large scale, they are characterized by a power imbalance between the parties. In order to enlarge the scope of the present chapter, we have also added a number of examples taken from internet telecommunication service provider Skype's end user license agreement, an English contract aimed at an international audience. The complete document can be accessed at the following address: www.skype.com/intl/en/legal/eula/ (accessed 11 August 2009).

16 Par ce contrat et moyennant le paiement de la prime, nous [assureur] vous [assuré] couvrons contre les risques définis ou énumérés ci-après et auxquels vous [assuré] êtes

Example 2:
This policy is a legal access insurance consisting in providing the Insured with legal assistance as well as the necessary financial means to help him find an amiable or legal solution to disputes, as defined hereafter. (A2)[17]

The first example allows for an immediate extralinguistic identification of the discursive actors during the reading of the contract, which may inspire a certain degree of conviviality given that the we/you dichotomy is found in everyday language. At the same time, and for the same reasons, the power relations seem more explicit. The opposition between the two parties is clearly preserved in the use of pronouns; 'we' is realized here under the locutor-inclusive form [insurer] and the interlocutor-exclusive form [insured], whereas the realization of 'you' undergoes the reverse process. The third-person formulation is literally more difficult to access; the extralinguistic identification occurs in two stages rather than one; the polyphonic passage occupies a more important place in the interpretation process. This intermediate stage may, however, hide the unequal power relations to a certain extent.

It should be observed that these differences in interlocutionary relations have an impact on the polyphonic traces only; the dialogic traces function identically in the two excerpts where, for example, there are discursive recollections concerning the concepts of *premium*, *lessee*, *amiable solution* and *legal solution*, whose meaning here refers to what is understood in Quebec society (and which can greatly differ, for example, from a contract using the same terms, but drafted in another country).

Dialogic traces of shared representations We have seen that the dialogic processes may orient themselves either toward anterior discourses, or towards anticipated ulterior discourses, be they implicit (constitutive) or explicit (exposed):

Example 3 – constitutive dialogism:
The Insured designated in DECLARATIONS and, if they domicile or reside under the same roof as him, his spouse or de facto spouse, the members of their family and the minors whom they have in custody. (A2)[18]
Example 4 – exposed dialogism:
a) his spouse:
...

---

généralement exposé en tant que locataire. (A1).

17 Cette police est une assurance de protection juridique consistant à fournir à l'Assuré une assistance juridique de même que les moyens financiers nécessaires, pour l'aider à trouver une solution amiable ou judiciaire à des litiges, le tout tel que ci-après défini. (A2).

18 L'Assuré désigné aux <u>CONDITIONS PARTICULIERES</u> et, s'ils sont domiciliés ou s'ils résident sous le même toit que lui, son <u>conjoint légal</u> ou <u>de fait</u>, les membres de leur famille et les <u>mineurs</u> dont ils ont la garde [nous soulignons]. (A2).

Is considered spouse, (s)he who has become such as a result of a legally contracted marriage or by the fact, for a person, of residing permanently over a period of more than a year with a person of different or same sex whom (s)he introduces publicly as his (her) spouse. (A1)[19]

We observe that, in example 3, the Insurer makes reference to the notions of *spouse*, *de facto spouse* and *minor*. As we have mentioned before, these are concepts that may differ from one society to another, and in the Québécois context, there is therefore a dialogic link between this text and its *interdiscourses* which have contributed to its definition beforehand.

In example 4, even if the Insurer seeks to define the same concept, *spouse*, the mechanism of representation is different as the *interdiscourse* is represented here within the text itself; resulting in exposure of the dialogic process. Moreover, it is no longer oriented towards a prior text, but rather towards the anticipated question of the *superaddressee* who is looking for the legal definition of the term *spouse*.

In regard to the notion of superadressee (see also discussion in section 1), analysis of the discursive traces left by the locutor allows us to observe that, in the case of the mass contract, the images of the superaddressee are less virtual and idealized than we would expect them to be in other discursive genres. Indeed, when scrutinizing these discursive representations closely, we notice that they are not necessarily a result of the locutor's efforts to create a mental prototype image of his actual target audience in order to adjust his utterance accordingly, but rather a result of his efforts to make individual aspiring clients adhere to a set of constraints that allow them to access clientship. This is well illustrated by the following passages from the Skype End User License Agreement which can be seen to make up the eligibility conditions of participants as described in van Leeuwen's framework:

> **3.3 Utilization of Your Computer:** Skype Software may utilize the processor and bandwidth of the computer (or other applicable device) You are utilizing, for the limited purpose of facilitating the communication between Skype Software users.
> **No Access To Emergency Services:** Skype is not a replacement for Your ordinary mobile or fixed line telephone. In particular, apart from in the very limited circumstances set out in paragraph 3.5 of the Terms of Service, Skype does not allow You to make emergency calls to emergency services.
> **8.6 Language:** The original English version of the Terms may have been translated into other languages. In the event of inconsistency or discrepancy

19 *a) son conjoint;[...]*
Est considéré comme conjoint, celui ou celle qui l'est devenu par suite d'un mariage légalement contracté ou par le fait, pour une personne, de résider en permanence depuis plus d'un an avec une personne de sexe différent ou de même sexe qu'elle présente publiquement comme son conjoint. [nous soulignons] (A1).

> between the English version and any other language version, the English language version shall prevail.

These clauses illustrate the different constraints that the locutor seeks to impose on prospective addressees (clients) and which may remain implicit to a certain extent. Whereas some constraints appear as obvious (in order to use software, the prospective client should own a personal computer or have one at his or her disposal), others concern arbitrary rules that are unilaterally imposed (user cannot dial emergency numbers and should thus subscribe to another telephone service). Finally, some images seem optional, but can be held against the client should problems arise (users should be able to understand English, because the End User Agreement in languages other than English does not have any legislative value).

Polyphonic staging of compromise and common ground *Polyphony does not concern the enunciative links that the text (the contract) maintains with its prior and later interdiscourses, but rather the ties that the speaker creates within the text itself. Thus, when revisiting our first two examples, it can be observed that in example 1, the role of the Insurer has been blurred by making use of a strategy of personification through which the contract (the policy) becomes the agent, and the Insured becomes the patient of the action that is described.*

Example 2 represents the extralinguistic roles of the contracting parties by resorting to the use of first- and second-person pronouns. It is interesting to note that 'you' is used as a second-person singular form of politeness here ('vous êtes généralement exposé' ['you are generally exposed']), whereas 'we' automatically makes reference to a collective. This observation could be interpreted as a desire to represent multiple voices that speak as one, leading to an imbalance between the contracting parties (and therefore to an imbalance within the 'meeting' of minds).

Moreover, it should be noted that although a sense of equality between the contracting parties may be suggested on a textual (and thus, more explicit) level, unequal power relations can often be traced back on the sentence level (which remains more implicit). The following example illustrates the locutor's intention to lay out the contract in a manner that suggests equal responsibilities for both contracting parties by including a section that seems to emphasize the client's expectations, yet when looking at the sentence level, it becomes obvious that on the sentence level, the client remains most often the patient of the action described, whereas the locutor maintains an active role as the subject of the sentence:

> 3. What You should and should not expect from Skype
>
> **3.1 No Warranties:** Installing Skype Software enables You to communicate with other people. Skype cannot guarantee that You will always be able to communicate with other people, nor can Skype guarantee that You can communicate without disruptions, delays or communication-related flaws or that all Your communications shall always be delivered to other people.

A final strategy consists in suggesting the agreement between the contracting parties with regard to the interpretation of a certain element, via the use of the third person 'one', although it is clear that the speaker is the one who remains in control of the discourse and who stages the agreement of the insured with his interpretation of the 'road trailer', especially as the content of this definition is not renegotiated with each client, but rather is a preestablished fact:

> Example 5:
> *We cover ... boats, road trailers, snowplows ... One understands here, by 'road trailer', a vehicle that has no room whatsoever for loading and is only used to carry the machinery and equipment with which it is permanently fit.* (A1)

Conclusion

We have established that linguistic polyphony entails the notion of an intentional scriptor/locutor resorting to discursive strategies aimed at obtaining the addressees' adherence through a discursive staging of their words and points of view; conversely, dialogism does not necessarily call for a locutor taking responsibility for an utterance by positioning himself in relation to a number of external points of view. Rather, it is the mechanism that sees the locutor negotiate his own way in the already-said and the yet-to-be-said, according to a linguistic process that partially escapes his consciousness. In other words, polyphony concerns the traces of decisions and positions that are elaborated in a fully-fledged interaction with the other, whereas dialogism considers the elaboration of a given utterance in the verbal milieu of social representations. In consequence, when investigating the nature of the 'meeting of minds' that constitutes the core of the definition of the contract, we should focus on polyphonic processes, for dialogic mechanisms are beyond the scope of the speaker and manifest themselves inevitably in all types of texts. Our examples have illustrated several strategies used by the speaker to stage the content of the contract and the relationships that the contracting parties maintain with this content. Throughout these different strategies, however, we notice a continuity concerning the power of the speaker, since he is the one who remains solely responsible for the text and makes a selection out of the points of view that he wants to represent. When we transpose this responsibility from the linguistic to the socio-discursive level, we can conclude that, from a polyphonist perspective, the contract should continue to be considered as a 'agreement of wills' because the points of view of the different discursive actors are represented within the contract. However, an important precision should be made here: given that the physical producer of the (mass) contract automatically appropriates the role of speaker for himself, he is the one who bears the final responsibility of its content. Thus, the will of the client gets considerably blurred, which consequently alters the contractual relationship.

References

Agar, M. 1985. 'Institutional Discourse'. *Text*, 5, 147-168.

Amossy, R. 2005. 'De l'apport d'une distinction: dialogisme *vs* polyphonie dans l'analyse argumentative', in *Dialogisme et polyphonie; Approches linguistiques*, edited by J. Bres et al. Bruxelles: De Boeck, 63-74.

Authier-Revuz, J. 1995. *Ces mots qui ne vont pas de soi*. Paris: Larousse.

Authier-Revuz, J. 2004. 'La représentation du discours autre: un champs multiplement hétérogène', in *Le discours rapporté dans tous ses états*, edited by J.-M. Lopez-Muñoz, S. Marnette and L. Rosier. Paris: L'Harmattan, 35-53.

Bakhtin, M. 1981. 'Discourse in the Novel', in *The Dialogic Imagination*. Translated by Caryl Emerson and Michael Holquist. Austin, TX and London: University of Texas Press.

Bakhtin, M. 1986. 'The Problem of Speech Genres', in *Speech Genres and Other Late Essays*. Translated by Vern W. McGee. Austin, TX: University of Texas Press.

Bélanger, A., V.-D. Moraru and A. Van Drom. 2010. 'Les apports de la linguistique à la théorie des contrats: Prolégomènes à une interprétation dialogique et polyphonique du contrat'. *Les Cahiers de droit*, 51(1), 51-82.

Bélanger, A. and A. Van Drom. 2011. 'Les apports de la linguistique à la théorie des contrats: Panorama des principales théories de dialogisme et de la polyphonie à inscrire au sein du phénomène contractuel'. *Cahiers de droit*, 52(1), 37-70.

Bernstein, B. 1981. 'Codes, Modalities and the Process of Cultural Reproduction: A Model'. *Language and Society*, 19, 327-363.

Bin, F. 2004. 'L'altérité en droit public', in *Penser l'altérité: ouvrage pluridisciplinaire*, edited by A. Lordon. Aix-en-Provence: Presses universitaires d'Aix-Marseille, 178-204.

Bissot, H. 2002. *La transparence sacrée ou le secret révélé: le principe dialogique comme mode de légitimation du pouvoir*. Paris: Université Paris 1 Panthéon-Sorbonne.

Bres, J. 2005. 'Savoir de quoi on parle: dialogue, dialogal, dialogique; dialogisme, polyphonie', in *Dialogisme et polyphonie; Approches linguistiques*, edited by J. Bres et al. Bruxelles: De Boeck, 47-62.

Charaudeau, P. and D. Maingueneau (ed.). 2002. *Dictionnaire d'analyse du discours*. Paris: Seuil.

Courtine, J.-J. 1981. 'Analyse du discours politique'. *Langages*, 62, 9-128.

Dendale, P. and D. Coltier. 2005. 'La notion de prise en charge ou responsabilité dans la théorie scandinave de la polyphonie linguistique', in *Dialogisme et polyphonie; Approches linguistiques*, edited by J. Bres et al. Bruxelles: De Boeck, 125-140.

Dendale, P. and D. Coltier. 2006. 'Éléments de comparaison de trois théories linguistiques de la polyphonie et du dialogisme', in *Le sens et ses voix; Dialogisme et polyphonie en langue et en discours*, edited by L. Perrin. Metz: Université Paul Verlaine, 271-299.

De Santis, A.D. 2001. 'Caught between Two Worlds: Bakhtin's Dialogism in the Exile Experience'. *Journal of Refugee Studies*, 14(1), 1-19.
Ducrot, O. 1984. *Le dire et le dit*. Paris: Minuit.
Fairclough, N. 1992. *Discourse and Social Change*. Cambridge: Polity Press.
Fairclough, N. 1997. *Media Discourse*. London and New York: E. Arnold.
Fairclough, N. 2003. *Analysing Discourse: Textual Analysis for Social Research*. London and New York: Routledge.
Fairclough, N. and R. Wodak. 1997. 'Critical Discourse Analysis', in *Discourse as Social Interaction*, edited by T. van Dijk. London, Thousand Oaks, CA and New Delhi: Sage, 258-284.
Foucault, M. 1969. *L'archéologie du savoir*. Paris: Gallimard.
Foucault, M. 1977. *Language, Counter-Memory, Practice*. Ithaca, NY: Cornell University Press.
Genette, G. 1982. *Palimpsestes: la littérature au second degré*. Paris: Seuil.
Genette, G. 1987. *Seuils*. Paris: Seuil.
Giddens, A. 1991. *Modernity and Self-identity: Self and Society in the Late Modern Age*. Stanford, CA: Stanford University Press.
Jamin, Ch. and D. Mazeaud (ed.). 2003. *La nouvelle crise du contrat*. Paris: Dalloz.
Jodelet, D. 1989. *Les représentations sociales*. Paris: Presses universitaires de France.
Lugrin, G. 2001. 'Le mélange des genres dans l'hyperstructure'. *SEMEN*, 13, 65-96.
Malinowski, B. 1935. *Coral Gardens and Their Magic*. Vol. 2. London: Allen and Unwin.
Moirand, S. 2007. *Les discours de la presse quotidienne: observer, analyser, comprendre*. Paris: Presses universitaires de France.
Nølke, H., K. Fløttum and C. Norén. 2004. *ScaPoLine; La théorie scandinave de la polyphonie linguistique*. Paris: Kimé.
Nowakowska, A. 2005. 'Dialogisme, polyphonie: des textes russes de M. Bakthine à la linguistique contemporaine', in *Dialogisme et polyphonie; Approches linguistiques*, edited by J. Bres et al. Bruxelles: De Boeck, 19-32.
Perrin, L. 2004. 'Polyphonie et autres formes d'hétérogénéité énonciative: Bakthine, Bally, Ducrot, etc.'. *Pratiques*, 123-124, 7-26.
Perrin, L. (ed.). 2006. *Le sens et ses voix. Dialogisme et polyphonie en langue et en discours*. Metz: Université Paul Verlaine.
Prémont, M.-C. 2003. *Tropismes du droit: logique métaphorique et logique métonymique du langage juridique*. Montréal: Thémis.
Rabatel, A. 2006. 'Genette, les voix du texte et la dialogisation'. *Recherches linguistiques*, 28, 165-188.
Todorov, T. 1981. *Mikhaël Bakthine, le principe dialogique*. Paris: Seuil.
Van Leeuwen, T. 2008. *Discourse and Practice: New Tools for Critical Discourse Analysis*. Oxford: Oxford University Press.

Vincent, D. 2006. 'Polyphonie et interaction', in *Le sens et ses voix; Dialogisme et polyphonie en langue et en discours*, edited by L. Perrin. Metz: Université Paul Verlaine, 127-142.

Weber, M. 1977. *The Theory of Social and Economic Organization.* New York: Free Press.

Wodak, R., R. de Cillia, M. Reisigl and K. Liebhart. 1999. *The Discursive Construction of National Identity.* Edinburgh: Edinburgh University Press.

Zijderveld, A.C. 1979. *On Clichés: The Supersedure of Meaning by Function in Modernity.* London: Routledge.

Chapter 7
What EU Legislative Texts Reveal about Power, Control and Transparency

Colin Robertson[1]

Introduction

The 8th International Roundtable for the Semiotics of Law (IRSL 2009) held on 1-4 December 2009 at City University of Hong Kong took as its theme 'Transparency, Control and Power: Issues in Legal Semiotics'. This posed a question what one might say in respect of the European Union from a semiotic point of view. The 'European Union' has become an important sign in modern European life (Robertson 2010). It has exercised immense power over the life of each European state and beyond since the mid-1950s and continues to do so (Richardson 2006). It has developed continuously since the founding treaties and continues to do so. It has come into being as an answer to centuries of unhappiness stemming from struggles over power and control (Blockmans 1997, Davies 1996) and it aims at imposing order and system, dialogue and negotiation in accordance with carefully designed rules, having the force of law, which all member states acknowledge as binding on them (Berry and Hargreaves 2007).

The European Union has been constructed using legal texts, in the form of primary treaties supplemented with a plethora of other acts and instruments (http://eur-lex.europa.eu/en/index.htm), which express the will of the member states and the institutions they have created to work together in peaceful and orderly cooperation, for the benefit of all. It seemed a good idea to explore these texts and see what they say about power, control and transparency. As signs the treaty texts and the words they contain should point clearly to the intentions and will of their creators. Further, since these texts are legislative and lay down norms and rules that the member states, by signature and ratification, accept as binding and enforceable, then they should express rights and obligations capable of being enforced through the courts of law.

Therefore one should be able to identify a very carefully constructed set of arrangements touching on issues of power, creating balancing mechanisms and arrangements for control of the exercise of power. Ultimately the whole set of arrangements should be for the benefit of business, individual persons and citizens. That means that everyone needs to be able to know the rights and duties affecting

1 The views expressed in this chapter are solely those of the author.

them and be able to understand the system so as to enhance its efficacy. This, in turn, implies transmission of information and transparency, while preserving the ability of the institutions to function efficiently. Once again there is an inherent balance to be achieved between the need for information to the public and the ability of the institutions to work efficiently without undue pressure. This chapter places a focus on the written texts, as signs, and explores issues of power, control and transparency on the basis of what they say, as indicators. As the field is large, the scope here is restricted to primary treaty texts with the aim of presenting a picture in terms of a series of relationships that indicate structural contexts in which issues of power, control and transparency arise. (The consolidated texts of the Treaty on European Union and the Treaty on the Functioning of the European Union are printed in Official Journal of the European Union C 115 of 9 May 2008 and available on-line through http://europa.eu which is the web portal for the European Union.)

The primary EU treaties are, not surprisingly, heavily concerned with relations of power and control: the balance of powers between member states in the EU institutions, between the EU institutions themselves, between the EU and national levels. Further, the EU treaties apply to many particular domains of activity. Each domain has a power balance, negotiated in the texts, and the exercise of all the EU tasks is subject to constant monitoring and control by the participants to ensure that the law is complied with. Recourse to the European Court of Justice is available to that end (http://curia.europa.eu/). However, the EU is more than just an intergovernmental organization; it has a relationship with citizens. In order to obtain acceptance and support by citizens the EU must demonstrate that it can be trusted to perform its tasks correctly and an important part of this is to ensure that the citizen is also able to find out, check and control. This is the function of 'transparency'. The overall aim should be to achieve balance, a harmony, which matches the aims and aspirations laid down in the treaties and the EU symbols, such as the flag. This is a factor underlying the success of the EU.

Foundation in the EU Treaties

The legal foundation of the European Union consists in the set of primary treaties which have been negotiated, signed, ratified and implemented over half a century by European states. Starting with the Treaty establishing the European Coal and Steel Community, followed by the Treaty establishing the European Economic Community and the Treaty establishing the European Atomic Energy Community in the 1950s there has been a continuous series of treaties amending, updating, refining and extending the founding treaties (see for example http://www.unizar.es/euroconstitucion/Treaties/Treaty_Const.htm). The most recent of these is the Lisbon Treaty (Official Journal of the European Union C 306 of 17 December 2007; rectification in Official Journal C 81 of 29 March 2010). Currently, after the entry into force of the Lisbon Treaty on 1 December 2009, there are three main primary treaties: Treaty on European Union (TEU) (see Official Journal C 83, 30 March 2010, page 13 for the consolidated text), the Treaty on the functioning of the European Union (TFEU) (see Official Journal C 83, 30 March 2010, page 47 for the consolidated text) and the Treaty establishing the European Atomic Energy Community (TEAEC) (see Official Journal C 84, 30 March 2010, page 1 for the consolidated text). Attached to these are protocols, annexes and declarations which deal with specific matters. Another foundation text is the Charter of Fundamental Rights of the European Union (see Official Journal C 83, 30 March 2010, page 389). There have been many changes and developments over the years: for example the European Economic Community, which became the European Community, has, with the Lisbon Treaty, ceased to exist and been subsumed into the European Union. These changes in name indicate changes in orientation and substance, as set out in the treaty texts. At the time of writing, many things are new and so it is too early to comment in detail, but one can look at signs from past texts and make extrapolations, for much remains unchanged, and the new arrangements build on the old ones.

At the same time, while the foundation treaties have been revised and extended, the European Union has expanded its territory and membership of states through a succession of accession treaties over the years. An accession treaty is a legal instrument which takes all the legal threads that bind existing member states in the EU and extends them item by item to the new member state. They are complex and semiotically interesting texts, since they provide a horizontal cross-section picture of EU law as it stands at the moment of accession (see for example OJ L 236 of 23 September 2003 and L 157 of 21 June 2005 for the last two accession treaties). For the present context, however, it is sufficient to note that accession treaties have served to extend the scope of EU law, and therefore to extend the issues underlying the theme of this chapter, to additional territories and populations. It can also be commented that if there has been continuous enlargement, as indeed there has been, it is because the EU and its system of law reflects things which are sought after, not just economic security and prosperity, but also a way of organizing affairs which aims at being equitable, supportive and efficient: the key here lies in concepts such as equality and balance, both to be achieved through negotiation.

The Search for Balance through Negotiation

The EU is a multicultural organization; this arises from having, currently, 27 member states and is visible just by looking at the names and geographic and linguistic origins of representatives appointed by the institutions, for example Commissioners of the European Commission and Members of the European Parliament. It is also made obvious by listening to debates, for example of the European Parliament, where different speakers talk in their own language. This linguistic equality, or balance in linguistic power, is supported by extensive arrangements to provide for language interpretation and translation (see

Commission Directorate-General for Translation website: http://ec.europa.eu/dgs/translation/index_en.htm). The EU is multilingual and currently works and makes laws in 23 languages: this can be seen from the final articles of EU treaties which indicate the 'authentic languages' (which means that they are to be treated as a source text for legal interpretation and not as a translation) and it can be seen from the different language versions of the EU legislation, judgments of the Court of Justice of the European Union, and many other texts, that are published in 23 language versions by the Official Journal of the European Union. This is a sign pointing towards equality and balance between different languages and the respective cultures, but it is also a sign pointing towards transparency, insofar as the citizen of any EU member state can find out the EU laws that apply; they need just to look at the paper versions or search the internet under http://eur-lex.europa.eu or the general portal for all information about EU matters: http://europa.eu.

Of course, by ensuring easy access to information about its activities the EU is also aiming to extend its control over the conduct of affairs where it has been given powers under the treaties. And this brings us to an important point, for the situation is not one way; it is not a case of information going one way, say from top down or from the centre outwards. Reality is more complex; there are flows in many directions. A flow of information to the citizen allows for control over the citizens – the legal system of each member state reinforces that, for example through doctrines such *as 'Ignorantia legis neminem excusat!'* (Ignorance of the law excuses no one; no one can opt out of the legal system – this is perhaps the ultimate statement of power for a legal system; stating it in Latin enhances this power.) (See *inter alia* http://definitions.uslegal.com). On the other hand, the access to this information enables citizens to exercise some control too, through mechanisms provided by law (EU law and national law). So one comes into a context of relationships, of mutuality and of power flows coming to and fro between participants in processes being undertaken. As the saying goes '*It takes two to tango*' and that can be applied here too; power is exercised in a relational context. It is this relational context, on a very large and complex scale, which underlies the arrangements of the European Union. The details can be studied by looking at the signs. They are the product of intercultural negotiation over half a century, built against a background of centuries of pragmatic experience.

The search for balance is evident from a range of EU signs. The foundation is the concept of solidarity and working together. We can find linguistic instances of this from the wording of the treaties; for example the preamble to the TEU contains the following indicators: '*ending of ... division of the European Continent*', '*solidarity*', '*union*'. Similarly, the preamble to the TFEU contains expressions such as: '*balanced trade and fair competition*', '*reducing the differences existing between the various regions*', '*solidarity*'.

Not all EU signs are linguistic. One of the most widely seen, and potent, symbols of the EU is its flag, with the circle of gold stars on a blue background (Figure 7.1).

Figure 7.1 The European flag

The flag carries meaning. It is symbolic, but its meaning is indexical:

> Blue signifies the heaven of the west. The 12 stars represent all EU member states; 12 is the representation of perfection. The stars are in a circle, like a round table conference, to symbolise that everyone in Europe is equal. (Poels 2003)

(Interestingly, the square and circular shapes also have ancient significations in Chinese culture: the circle represents heaven and the square represents earth; but there are also other significations of these shapes: see for example http://www.whats-your-sign.com).

How Is Balance Achieved?

How do the member states and the institutions strive to achieve this balance? The linguistic foundation has been mentioned, but there are other ways. In particular, the member states have created the EU institutions and given them some power, while retaining some power for themselves. Each treaty is an act, and therefore sign, of transfer of power. Member states delegate to institutions certain functions, certain rights and obligations, which involve allowing those institutions to have power over them; for example to make regulations, directives, decisions, which are binding on them, and recommendations and opinions, which are not binding (see Article 288 TFEU). Yet the member states also maintain some control over the exercise of these powers by participating in each institution. For example, the European Parliament has elected members from each member state; the European Commission has Commissioners from each member state; the Council is under the direction of and comprises the member states; whether at European Council level of Heads of States or Council level, with ministers and a rotating six-monthly Presidency; the Court of Justice of the European Union has Judges and Advocates-General appointed from the national legal professions. The treaty texts, for example Articles 13 to 19 TEU and Articles 223 to 287 TFEU, set out the rules, backed up by implementing acts and decisions of a more technical nature. Thus, on inspection, one finds that within each EU institution there are arrangements that aim at balances in member state participation. This means one can see the EU as a complex matrix of relationships between the member states, both between each other and within the institutions. But there are more relationships and more balances of power to be handled, as will be seen shortly.

How are the balances handled? How does the system work? The first aspect is that of deciding, through negotiation, which fields or matters are best managed jointly at the EU level or at the individual member state level. The signs of the results of these negotiations are to be found in every single EU legislative text, starting with the primary treaties. Each treaty contains a delegation of powers; the institutions may only do what they have been allowed to do by the member states and in the ways set out in the treaties. The member states control, because they have to approve EU legislation through a voting procedure in the Council (see Article 238 TFEU, for example). The institutions also have controls through their respective legal services whose task is to ensure the EU rules and methods are followed.

The treaties set out a framework and this is supplemented by detailed rules in secondary legislation (for example: regulations, directives, decisions as referred to in Article 288 TFEU) that set out how the powers are to be exercised. The texts are normative, but they also are instructive: they indicate what is to be done, and by whom, in a multitude of different situations that can and do arise. They set out the procedures to follow and the rights and obligations that apply. They transmit that information; they can be seen as messages (see Gallas 1999, Robertson 2009). That is why the EU institutions have been given law-making functions; so as to strengthen the arrangements and enhance control. This is supplemented by control and enforcement by, and through, the courts, in particular the Court of Justice of the European Union, but also the national courts. They exercise legal control. In a financial context, it is the European Court of Auditors that exercises control.

Six Relationships

If one searches for relationships to identify balances of power within a context of EU law, then there are many possible candidates depending on how far one wishes to go into the fine-tuning of the arrangements. The relationship between member states has been mentioned, as well as their relationship with the EU institutions, but one can mention more. For the present purpose it is proposed to list six principal types of relationship that point to the structure of organization at the EU level:

1. between member states
2. between member states and the EU institutions
3. between the EU institutions
4. between the EU institutions and business, industry, citizens
5. between the EU and its member states and the rest of the world
6. between the EU institutions and their staff

We can look briefly at some features of these relationships, bearing in mind that there is very much more that could be said; one needs only to visit http://europa.eu to see for oneself.

Between Member States

The starting point of the EU is the fact that initially six, then more, European states joined together to pool resources and work together in a joint European venture, embodied in the EU treaties, but backed up by other international agreements and arrangements; for example those relating to avoidance of double taxation of the earnings of people and businesses. The member states have relationships outside the EU context; they conduct business, cultural and sporting activities together and they are members of many international organizations, such as the United Nations (http://www.un.org) and the Council of Europe (http://www.coe.int) which is frequently confused with the European Union. They also have relationships inside the EU context. The EU treaties regulate the 'internal' EU relationships and formalize them. Power within the EU is shared according to formulae laid down in the treaties covering matters such as: numbers of Commissioners, Council voting rights, numbers of MEPs, numbers of Judges and Advocates General (see TFEU generally for details).

The member states are signatories to the EU treaties and all of them must ratify a new treaty in order for it to exist in law. In the case of the Treaty establishing a Constitution for Europe (Official Journal of the European Union, C 310, 16 December 2004; see also http://europa.eu/scadplus/constitution/index_en.htm) that did not happen as not all member states ratified it, so it did not come into force. The reasons have been amply set out elsewhere and need not concern us here (see for example 'French Say Firm "No" to EU Treaty' at http://news.bbc.co.uk/2/hi/europe/4592243.stm). Yet the experience revealed the way in which internal national factors in individual member states have impacts at the EU level. Thus the implications of power and control extend beyond the legal boundaries of the EU and national contexts; there is deep intermixity.

Between Member States and the EU Institutions

The member states created the EU institutions by treaty, like parents bringing forth offspring, and in so doing created a relationship with them. The image of 'family' is interesting in this respect as not only do the offspring not always do what the parents want, but European relations sometimes seem to take on dynamics resembling those of many families. Again, one can turn to the primary treaties to find the signs; the EU treaties regulate the overall relationships, including those between the member states and the institutions and individual secondary acts fill in details for specific fields of action. Thus, for example, the institutions are empowered to make binding legislative acts. Art 288 TFEU lists them and indicates their main legal effects:

- regulation: general application; binding; directly applicable;
- directive: binds member states addressed as to the result to be achieved, but form and methods left to the member states;
- decision: binding on person specified;
- recommendations and resolutions: not binding.

There are many other provisions. A notable one concerns the power of the Commission to propose EU legislation (see Art 289(1) TFEU). This limits the right of a member state to seek to impose its will. The Commission has regard to the whole Union context and proposes legislation accordingly; each member state defends its interests in the ensuing negotiations on the text. Thus the institutions are given the 'space' to exercise the tasks placed on them and the discussions and negotiations take place in a structured and therefore ritualized and controlled way.

Between the EU Institutions

The EU treaties create and regulate the institutions. These are listed in Article 13(1) TEU: European Parliament, European Council, Council, European Commission, Court of Justice of the European Union, European Central Bank, Court of Auditors. Each institution has a defined role/field of power (laid down by treaty text, see for example Articles 13 to 19 TEU). These can be summarized briefly in the following terms:

- European Parliament: discusses, reviews, debates, votes, determines the budget and enacts legislation jointly with the Council;
- European Council: overview, general political direction of EU, and foreign affairs;
- Council: reviews, directs, determines budget and adopts legislation jointly with the European Parliament;
- Commission: proposes initiatives, checks and controls national

implementation, drafts legislation and most importantly supervises competition in the EU market;
- Court of Justice: judicial review, legal control, interpretation of the meaning of EU legal texts;
- European Central Bank: managing the euro; central bank coordination and monetary policy issues;
- Court of Auditors: controlling EU expenditure.

In addition to the EU 'institutions' there are two 'advisory' bodies: the Economic and Social Committee and the Committee of the Regions; and an investment bank: the European Investment Bank. Articles 223 to 287 TFEU tell us more about each institution and how it is to act.

If we now return to the central theme of this chapter, Art. 13(2) TEU says:

> Each institution shall act within the limits of the powers conferred on it in the Treaties, and in conformity with the procedures, conditions and objectives set out in them. The institutions shall practice mutual sincere cooperation.

Here we see treated the question of the relationship between the institutions and the imposition of an obligation to work together in cooperation and not in competition. Each institution has its sphere of activity laid down by treaty; these spheres are different and complementary. There is thus an allocation of power, in line with the allocation of functions between the institutions; each exercises control over its area of responsibility, within the extent of power conferred matching the degree of control granted. The European Parliament and Council agree together on the annual budget; they also jointly agree on EU ordinary legislation under Article 288 TFEU, in respect of which the Commission has the sole right of proposal (Art 289 TFEU). The Court of Justice of the European Union is the final court, has ultimate control, for interpreting EU law. The Court's case law is important as a source of rules that bind everyone. It was the Court which first decided that EU law could take precedence over national law.[2] EU law was thereby placed at a higher level of power than national law. This brings us back to the relationship between institutions and member states. In particular, in the legal context it opened the question of the power relationship between EU law and national law, especially as regards national constitutional law which is the pinnacle, or foundation, of national legal systems. Could it be possible for member states through EU law to circumvent the protections, guarantees and safeguards built into national constitutions? A lively topic and the debate continues; a recent case by the German Constitutional Court in the context of German ratification of the Lisbon Treaty examined these issues in detail (for information in English, see http://eulaw.typepad.com/eulawblog/2009/07/german-constitutional-court-and-

2 *Van Gend en Loos v. Nederlandse Administratie der Belastingen* [1963] ECR 1, see http://law.suite101.com/article.cfm/what_was_van_gend_en_loos_about.

lisbon-treaty-ratification.html). For the present purpose, however, it can just be noted how issues which seem to arise from one relationship, for example between institutions, can have implications for other relationships, for example with member states and their citizens. There is a constant flux and flow between the constituent parts. In this respect the EU has become inseparable from the member states and that extends inside the member states. This can be made clearer from a consideration of the next relationship to be discussed.

Between the EU Institutions and Business, Industry, Citizens

So far in this chapter there has been no mention of the matters on which the issues of power and control come to bear; that is to say the policies and decisions within the policy fields. This is the field of action; the place where the results of the interplay are manifested. We can form an idea of the full range of policy domains in which the EU now has competence, and therefore powers, just from glancing at the table of Contents of the Consolidated Version of the Treaty on the functioning of the European Union in Official Journal C 83 of 30 March 2010 (which contains rectifications made to the Lisbon Treaty published in OJ C 81 of 29 March 2010). The list extends over most areas of modern governmental activity and includes among others: internal market, free movement of goods; customs cooperation; agriculture and fisheries; free movement of persons; services and capital; an area of freedom, security and justice; transport; competition; employment; social policy; culture; public health; consumer protection; industry; environment.

The relationship between the EU and business, industry and the citizens comes from the implementation of EU policies in the different policy sectors. Here one typically finds that there is a national dimension as well as an EU dimension. Thus business, industry and the citizens find themselves involved with a national legal dimension as well as an EU legal dimension. That consideration raises questions about the distribution of functions between the national and EU levels, about which EU or national laws apply, about whether all the applicable EU laws, such as directives, have been implemented in the national legal system and if so whether this has been done in conformity with EU law, as well as the practical effects of the EU and national arrangements combined on business, industry and the citizens. This is a domain of political, as well as legal, economic and social discourse.

The EU treaties do specifically address the EU's relationship with citizens. Article 9 TEU refers to 'equality of citizens' and that they should receive 'equal attention from the institutions'. Article 10(1) TEU says that the functioning of the Union is founded on representative democracy; Article Art 10(2) says that citizens are directly represented at the Union level in the European Parliament. Article 10(3) says that every citizen has a right to participate in the democratic life of the Union and decisions are to be taken as openly and as closely as possible to citizens. Article 10(4) refers to political parties at the European level as contributing to forming European political awareness and to expressing the will of citizens of the Union. In addition to those provisions, one should mention the Charter of Fundamental Rights of the European

Union adopted by the European institutions (Official Journal of the European Union C 83, 30 March 2010). This sets out a series of human rights which are intended to be applied in the context of EU law; they are referred to in the Lisbon Treaty. What the precise scope and effects of the Charter will be remains a question for the future, and will depend on the attitude adopted by the courts. One can note, however, that the Charter already reflects accepted principles of law in the member states.

Other indicators regarding the EU's relationship with citizens can be seen in Article 11 TEU which requires the institutions to give citizens and representative associations the opportunity to make their views known and to consult them; the Article also provides for a citizen right (over a million from different Member States) to submit proposals to the Commission. Further, Article 24 TFEU confers:

- a right to petition the European Parliament;
- a right to apply to the Ombudsman;
- a right to write to an EU institution in any EU language and to receive an answer in the same language.

These rights can be exercised only if the citizen is aware of them. This means having arrangements for the dissemination and obtaining of information and it raises the concept of 'transparency'. To that end, citizens are granted certain rights. Thus Article 11(1) TEU provides that there must be an opportunity to citizens and representative associations to know and publicly exchange views on all areas of Union action. Article 11(2) says there is to be open, transparent and regular dialogue with representative associations and civil society. Article 11(3) authorizes one million citizens of different member states to invite the Commission, acting within its powers, to submit a proposal for a legal act.

Between the EU and Its Member States and the Rest of the World

The relationship between the EU and its member states and the rest of the world is set out in Article 21 TEU and subsequent articles. For example, Article 21(1) says:

> The Union's action on the international scene shall be guided by the principles which have inspired its own creation, development and enlargement, and which it seeks to advance in the wider world: democracy, the rule of law, the universality and indivisibility of human rights and fundamental freedoms, respect for human dignity, the principles of equality and solidarity, and respect for the principles of the United Nations Charter and international law.

That Article was introduced by the Lisbon Treaty. Another relationship lies in trade and the EU Common Commercial Policy. Thus, Art 206 (TFEU) says:

> By establishing a customs union … the Union shall contribute, in the common interest, to the harmonious development of world trade, the progressive abolition

> of restrictions on international trade and on foreign investment, and the lowering of customs and other barriers.

We have here a complex set of arrangements of infinite detail and constant flux. It is not possible here to do more than make a brief mention that they form part of the picture of relationships and invite study through accessing the EU portal: http://europa.eu.

Between the EU Institutions and Their Staff

The sixth and last relationship identified here is of a different order. It is internal to the institutions and concerns the role of the institutions as employer. The institutions need high-quality staff in order to function. Traditionally they recruited their personnel through written competitions organized by the European Personnel Selection office (EPSO) (http://europa.eu/epso). The institutions are given power to employ staff by the TFEU Treaty, for example, Article 336 TFEU says:

> The European Parliament and the Council shall, acting by means of regulations in accordance with the ordinary legislative procedure and after consulting the other institutions concerned, lay down the Staff Regulations of Officials of the European Union and the Conditions of Employment of other servants of the Union.

The Staff Regulations lay down the detailed provisions governing the conditions of employment (grades, salaries, promotion, pensions, conditions of service) (http://eur-lex.europa.eu/LexUriserv/LexUriserv.do?uri=CONSLEG:1962R0031:20080501:EN:PDF). In so doing they define the relationship between the institution as employer and its staff. The Staff Regulations contain a balance between the requirements of the institution and the needs of the staff to be able to work quietly and efficiently and with a degree of protection. The Staff Regulations are an important text in a context of multiculturalism and multilingualism as they strive for equality of treatment for all. Among other things they provide for a Staff Committee comprising members elected by staff to provide a voice for matters affecting the personnel. Internal institutional balance is aimed at as regards administrative matters and issues such as promotions through a system of joint committees with equal numbers of members appointed by the administration (i.e. management) and the Staff Committee representing the staff. The Staff Committee, as a body created by a legal instrument, is governed by the Staff Regulations, and EU law, as regards its functions. On the other hand, the staff has freedom to join trade unions and these have a role in defending staff interests, assisting individuals encountering problems and, on a more general level, participating in negotiations in respect of conditions of employment and changes to the Staff Regulations. If one considers that the vast majority of EU officials have moved from another member state and so are generally in a weaker position on the job market, the existence of the unions also helps to preserve the overall balance and ensure the avoidance of serious problems at an early stage. Their principle activity is discussion and negotiation, both of which are staple ingredients in the EU method. Along with the Staff Committee and information provided by the administration, they play a role in informing staff about their rights and obligations, as well as assisting individuals in difficulty.

The EU Policy of Providing Information

The EU is conscious of the need to provide information and makes a great deal of it available, not only to persons involved in its processes, but also to the media and the general public. Thus, there is publication of all EU legislative acts in 23 languages in the Official Journal of the European Union in both paper and electronic form (http://publications.europa.eu/eur_lex/index_en.htm). Anyone can obtain information on virtually everything relating to the EU by visiting the Europa website (http://europa.eu). In addition anyone can visit the institutions to look at the physical premises. Every year in May there is an open day on a Saturday in Brussels for visitors to come in person to the EU institutions there. Throughout the year the institutions receive visitor groups from all parts of the world. Each institution has an information service dedicated to producing information materials and a web search soon reveals the large amount of information available, produced not just by the institutions but also by universities and other groups; for example, the European Information Network or the ETUI EU Information Service (http://www.europe.org.uk/info). Lastly, the EU institutions regularly grant access to people asking to see copies of internal documents, and Regulation (EC) No 1049/2001 of the European Parliament and of the Council of 30 May 2001 regarding public access to European Parliament, Council and Commission documents (OJ L 145, 31 May 2001, p. 43) provides in Article 17(1) for each institution to report annually on the number of cases in which the institution has refused to grant access to documents.

Conclusion

When one considers issues of power, transparency and control within the context of the European Union and its organization, as evidenced by the treaties establishing it, it becomes apparent how these themes lie at the heart of the way in which the EU has been structured. They provide evidence of modern methods using tools of language and law, as well as economic and political theory. Yet, on a broader scale, these themes require a context, or framework, in which to enter into their dynamics. That context comes into being through the creation of relationships between participants, in what can be considered a 'game' that takes place between participants or 'players'. The dynamics of each game depends on the number of participants and on the rules which are laid down for the conduct of the game: that is the function of law and legal texts. The actual dynamics and day to day activities take place within that context and vary and fluctuate according to the events which happen as part of life (see, for example, *European Voice* newspaper: http://www.europeanvoice.com/).

In the European Union, member states share their state power with institutions they have created together. These assist the member states to exercise control over activities they cannot control alone. In order for the arrangements to function there needs to be information about the activities. That is necessary so people know their rights and obligations and in order to ensure there is democratic control through the parliaments who represent the populations. The EU is very complex and involves an intricate structure of arrangements. These revolve around issues of sharing of power, sharing of control and sharing of information. In a system founded on the Rule of Law it is important to maintain a high level of consent to be bound. The EU in its latest stage of development, as evidenced by its legislative texts, is striving to continue in its 50 year footsteps.

References

Berry, E. and Hargreaves, S. 2007. *European Union Law*. Oxford: Oxford University Press.

Blockmans, W. 1997. *A History of Power in Europe*. Antwerp: Fonds Mercator Paribas.

Commission Directorate-General for Translation. [Online]. Available at: http://ec.europa.eu/dgs/translation/index_en.htm [accessed: 20 February 2011].

Davies, N. 1996. *Europe: A History*. Oxford: Oxford University Press.

European Voice. [Online]. Available at: http://www.europeanvoice.com/ [accessed: 20 February 2011].

Gallas, T. 1999. 'Coredazione e traduzione giuridica nella legislazione multilingue, in particolare quella comunitaria'. 43 Quaderni di Libri e riviste d'Italia, la Traduzione, Saggi e documenti (IV), 135-147.

German Constitutional Court and Lisbon Treaty Ratification. 2009. [Online, 2 July]. Available at: http://eulaw.typepad.com/eulawblog/2009/07/german-constitutional-court-and-lisbon-treaty-ratification.html [accessed: 17 June 2010].

http://curia.europa.eu [accessed: 20 February 2011].

http://definitions.uslegal.com [accessed: 20 February 2011].

http://eur-lex.europa.eu/en/index.htm [accessed: 20 February 2011].

http://eur-lex.europa.eu/LexUriServ/LexUriServ.do?uri=CONSLEG:1962R0031:20080501:EN:PDF [accessed: 17 June 2010].

http://europa.eu [accessed: 20 February 2010].

http://law.suite101.com/article.cfm/what_was_van_gend_en_loos_about [accessed: 17 June 2010].

http://news.bbc.co.uk/2/hi/europe/4592243.stm [accessed: 10 August 2011].
http://publications.europa.eu/eur_lex/index_en.htm [accessed: 17 June 2010].
http://www.coe.int [accessed: 17 June 2010].
http://www.europe.org.uk/info [accessed: 17 June 2010].
http://www.unizar.es/euroconstitucion/Treaties/Treaty_Const.htm [accessed: 17 June 2010].
http://www.un.org [accessed: 17 June 2010].
http://www.whats-your-sign.com [accessed: 20 February 2011].
Official Journal of the European Communities L 145, 31 May 2001, p. 43.
Official Journal of the European Union L 236 of 23 September 2003.
Official Journal of the European Union C 310 of 16 December 2004.
Official Journal of the European Union L 157 of 21 June 2005.
Official Journal of the European Union C 306 of 17 December 2007; rectification in Official Journal C 81 of 29 March 2010.
Official Journal of the European Union C 115, 9 May 2008.
Official Journal of the European Union C 83, 30 March 2010.
Official Journal of the European Union C 84, 30 March 2010.
Poels, J. 2003. *Illustrated Guide to Flags*, 47. London: Salamander.
Richardson, J. 2006. *European Union: Power and Policy-making*. Abingdon: Routledge.
Robertson, C.D. 2009. 'Multilingual Law: What Is It? How Is It Made? How Is It Used and Applied? (with reference to EU practice)'. *Curriculum, Multilingualism and the Law*. Zagreb: Globus, 373-395.
Robertson, C.D. 2010. 'EU Law and Semiotics'. *International Journal for the Semiotics of Law*, 23, 145-164.
Van Gend en Loos v. Nederlandse Administratie der Belastingen [1963] ECR 1.

Chapter 8
Toward an Objective Means of Measuring Governmental Legitimacy

M. Douglass Bellis

Statement of the Problem

Individual freedom seems to conflict with the requirements of governmentally imposed order. Outright prohibitions, regulations, taxes and procedural impediments seem to expand to fill whatever space government is allowed to occupy and hamper the individual in the quest for self-expression and happiness. Perhaps Rousseau was not greatly exaggerating when he said 'l'homme est né libre et partout il est dans les fers' (1762/1993: livre 1, chapitre 1).

But few prefer anarchy. A government, by providing a common means to resolve disputes between individuals and among groups within a society, increases personal security on average for its population, even if some injustice remains unremedied (Hobbes 2000: Chapter XIII and Confucius 2008).[1]

Yet government can create injustice as well as fail to remedy it. The same powers that can be used to correct an injustice can also be used to oppress. Government power can be hijacked by elite groups or individuals who turn the apparent rule of law into a cover for pillage or to satisfy their private grudges in unfair ways.

How can we resolve this theoretical and practical conflict between the need for an ordered and predictable authority and the fundamental rights we all possess by virtue of our humanity? How do we draw correct boundaries in a particular society between the rights of individuals and the power of the state?

Where the Answer Should Lie

The answer, if there is one, must lie in the moral philosophy by which we determine the legitimacy of government in general.

1 Hobbes was perhaps the first in the Western tradition to make this point explicitly, in the Leviathan, and ties it to our natural equality. From our natural equality it follows none has any inherent authority over anyone else. Each must protect himself from wrongs committed by others. Because of this, if no authority is established, society is reduced to a war of all against all. But this idea is also implicit in Confucius in the Analects, for whom social order and harmony are the basis of society (Lunyu 2.4).

Such questions of moral philosophy are often dismissed out of hand in modern times as insolvable.[2] In other cases, the questions are begged by resort to a conventional but subjective consensus (at least in 'Western' democracies) that the legitimacy of government is based on how 'nicely' it behaves. Does it torture or kill its people? Does it provide a non-corrupt system to solve their individual disputes with each other and the government itself? Does it accord them most of the items on a conventional list of rights and privileges that nice governments afford their peoples? Does it allow them, however indirectly, to express their opinions on how the government is doing, and in some manner allow those opinions to result in a change of government personnel when the opinions are sufficiently negative?

To most Western observers, these measures are pretty good indications of a government's legitimacy. However, no explanation is offered for why such things should be fundamental.[3] Consequently, a great departure, if temporary, or a long-term departure, if minor, is often tolerated as being consistent with overall legitimacy. And why not, since the consensus is a fuzzy one based on subjective results rather than some clear theory of human society and the place of government within it?

This means, however, that the determination of which departures are beyond the pale is left in obscurity, or to a similar subjective consensus (if one can be found) of like-thinking Western or Westernized observers. It is not surprising that other observers, perhaps Chinese ones for example, might argue that this basis for government legitimacy rests on the unexamined provincial views of an unrepresentative subset of the human population, and, ultimately, on the peculiarities and perhaps shortcomings of that subset's arbitrary cultural norms and unproven assumptions.

Original Theoretical Self-assurance of European Political Theory

But vagueness and uncertain premises for fundamental political theory were not always in the past characteristic of 'Western', by which we mainly mean European, thought. In fact, political theory in the West seemed in rather rude good health during the eras starting with the Renaissance and continuing through the Age of Reason. During those eras, characterized by the advancement of reason in the investigation of nature and the modernization of the Western European understanding of the Christian religion, writers such as Locke (1980), Pufendorf (1927) and Montesquieu (1950)

2 Perhaps this is in part because there are so many cultures in the world, now all aware of each other. Social anthropology has led some to conclude that all moral values are relative to the society in which they develop and can only with great difficulty be judged in terms of another society or universally.

3 Perhaps because of the general belief in moral relativism, it seems to many individuals unnecessary to examine the foundations of one's moral values. They are simply a given and may be arbitrary. But then on what basis, other perhaps than superior force, can we demand others share them?

presented confident assertions that government must be founded on the consent of the governed and that divisions of powers within government made government more accountable to its real masters, the people, and helped minimize unjust or ineffective government, and so increased human happiness. These assertions in turn were premised on the natural social equality of humans and their transcendent worth as individuals, and the binding legal nature of fundamental governmental norms arising from these premises. From this, there emerged both a consensus in favour of human freedom and some theoretical measures for the success of a given government structure in protecting that freedom. This consensus, while developed in the context of a somewhat diverse European culture, purported not to be limited to that culture, but of universal import and founded upon nature itself. Those functional measures of governmental legitimacy that were derived from this theoretical base still seem to be reflected in the modern Western consensus on what constitutes governmental legitimacy, though the theoretical base itself is not.

This earlier philosophical theoretical basis was not morally neutral or based on a simple if unexplained preference for an ill-defined 'nice' behaviour. It seems ultimately to have reflected a belief that increasing the control of humans over the planet (and perhaps ultimately over themselves) was a morally desirable outcome. Today either or both of those outcomes are often deemed either undesirable or false.[4]

While the original theoretical basis did not rest primarily on a theological base, it was often influenced by parallel contemporary developments in religious thought, as shown in Locke's *Second Treatise* and Pufendorf's *De Officio Hominis et Civis* (1927). Most of those theological issues do not appear to have as great an intellectual salience today as they once did.

Yet we have mostly retained the conclusions of this original philosophical theoretical basis for determining the extent to which government is legitimate, while we have dropped their intellectual and quasi-religious moral underpinnings. In doing so, we seem to have lost any theoretical basis for an objective and more exact measure for governments' legitimacy. This makes cross-cultural discussions of such legitimacy difficult. Without some sort of agreed upon ideas as to what human society and government are for, and how they may be legitimately instituted, all conclusions about their legitimacy take on a fundamentally subjective cast.

Nineteenth and Twentieth Century Collapse of 'Western' Political Thought

But perhaps there were good intellectual and historical reasons for at least a part of this loss of the theoretical underpinnings of Western political thought, reasons that have to do with both the intellectual and the historical developments that arose,

4 Global warming, mass extinctions, and other environmental catastrophes are tied to humanity's increasing mastery over the planet through science. Humanity is the first species that has clear power, through nuclear weapons, literally to destroy the planet. Nor is it readily apparent that greater knowledge has led to greater self control.

at least in part, from the very philosophical assumptions on which the consensus was based. Without examining and understanding those assumptions, we cannot separate what is valuable in these philosophical conclusions from what was incidental error arising from the limited context in which they were first formed. We therefore seem unable to capture a solid ground in our own times on which to stand a consensus we may feel intuitively is correct in its application.

Over time, philosophical ideas become oversimplified parodies of themselves and are reduced to clichéd slogans. They are misapplied to the point that the misapplications become mistaken for the idea itself, and the idea becomes discredited by the contradiction between its supposed applications and the promise it seemed to hold in theory. So perhaps it should not surprise us that even very sound ideas weather badly over time.

Further, in the case of this particular set of ideas about how to establish the legitimacy of government, the assumption that reason, applied to the demonstrated truths of nature, would both reinforce the moral teachings of religion and clarify human problems in such a manner that self-evident solutions would emerge for them, eventually came to be questioned.[5] We at first thought our scientific learning was an exact representation of nature, but it turns out to be, as best as we can tell, simply a probabilistic approximation of it (Goldstein 2005).[6] The impeccable logic of our reason, if applied to uncertain premises, yields less than certain results.[7]

That uncertainty might undermine both the moral and theoretical validity of our conclusions in the social sphere even more than it has in the physical sciences, especially if we somehow conclude that other means could lead us to more sturdy ones. As most people feel emotions more intensely in connection with political questions than they do in connection with scientifi c investigations, emotional reactions based on the received values of a cultural group or on a religious belief are more likely to govern our evaluation of political matters, and feel intuitively right to us. The attractions of emotion as a substitute for reason are, to a person seeking certainty, therefore very great. Certainty is appealing in political matters because those matters require immediate action in circumstances where full information is difficult or impossible to obtain and time for reflection is scarce. It is a natural

5 Perhaps that may be due to the uneven distribution of that greater knowledge, but even in individual cases, we probably all can think of someone who is very intelligent, learned and capable, who nonetheless uses those powers to aggrandize themselves and harm others.

6 Einstein in the early twentieth century destroyed our belief in the Euclidean simplicities we had previously assumed were time and space. Heisenberg, Bohr and others later through the uncertainty principle and quantum mechanics call into doubt even our theoretical possibility of observing and describing nature completely and exactly. One can see why such applications of reasoning might at some point shake one's confidence in reasoning itself.

7 Indeed, the impeccability of reason itself has come under question since Gödel in the 1930s showed that mathematics, which many thought the purest form of reason, requires unproved premises in order to exist, and so does not rest on provable foundations.

human impulse to grasp for any base for certainty in those circumstances. Our instincts and unexamined beliefs can give us such a base.

A similar transformation of expectations has occurred with regard to religion intellectually, though it must be noted that various forms of religion can provide just the sort of emotional base that in some cases has come to be a substitute for reason. While the new or revived learning that appeared during the European Renaissance and Reformation periods at first may have fortified and purified religious convictions in those who had that learning, it came to be seen over the centuries since then as questioning those convictions in an ever more fundamental fashion (Descartes 2000; Hume 2009; Hume 1993).[8] A strict Cartesian epistemology leaves little room for any religion, much less a revealed one.

This transformation has resulted in some cases in what some might see as an enlightened tolerance of the varieties of religious experience as all tending, in lesser or greater degrees, to reflect a more transcendental spirituality imbedded in humans and perhaps corresponding to some fundamental reality (Wright 2009).

In other cases the transformation has resulted in a firm conviction that there is no transcendental spiritual being at all (Dawkins 2006), and consequently no basis in one for political theory. If there is any basis for political theory, it must be a fundamentally material and physical one, winnowed by natural selection rather than purposeful cause, and presumably providing no particularly privileged place to the human species over others.

But these are more recent developments of a trend that had its beginnings in the late eighteenth century. In the earlier forms of these developments, the greatest good for the greatest number, however subjectively defined, gained appeal as a basis for political philosophy, as this approach assumes a moral end for society without attempting to find that end in religious or other teleological imperatives. The nineteenth-century Utilitarians reflected this development (Fuller et al. 2010; Mill 1874, 1999),[9] during a period in which the scientific method began very generally to replace theological givens as the foundation of knowledge.[10]

---

8 Rene Descartes, with a severe epistemological reductionism, laid the groundwork for this development in his *Discours de la Methode*. Hume, starting with somewhat similar epistemological premises, further discredited the claims of the then widely followed versions of Christianity.

9 Jeremy Bentham and John Stuart Mill dispensed with arguments based ultimately on religious assumptions, but still retained the notion of human worth, assuming that what made people happy was the proper measure of what was good in government. Since not all could always be happy, the greatest happiness for the greatest number amounted to the greatest good for the greatest number and so in theory could be calculated without reference to specific value structures. But it was hard to see how, if the greater number were happiest when the lesser number were their slaves, this pragmatic approach could ultimately give us a measure of governmental legitimacy, unless we are willing to argue that slavery is in some cases good.

10 While throughout the seventeenth and eighteenth centuries scientific method commanded the intellectual heights for the learned, the average person probably was little

Later, when even the ability of that method to describe nature exactly came into question, the subjective premises of a utilitarian approach had perhaps an even greater attraction, even if they could be based on nothing more than subjective, perhaps even selfish, emotion (James 1999; Dewey 2007).[11]

In still other cases, the intellectual tension between science on the one hand and religion and other theories of reality on the other, resulted in cognitive dissonance for those brought up not to question the received religious tradition of their group, but taught by science to question everything else. The psychological effects of such a dissonance can perhaps lead to a dangerous combination of a hardened fanaticism and a sophisticated practical capability to manipulate the fruits of technology in the service of intolerance.

In many traditional societies, and perhaps particularly those in which the new or revived learning we have been discussing was not among their formative cultural underpinnings, religious tradition remains a central bond of the individual to broader aspects of that individual's ethnic and individual identity. At first, learning about modern science and its practical applications may seem unrelated to the religious tradition of an individual coming from such a society. However, the premises of scientific learning potentially present an alternative explanation of the world and people's place in it, just as they historically did for the West as a whole. The same psychological pressures result and these have consequences for political and social theory.

In addition, even where education in science is relatively rare, increasingly easy transportation and communication brought about by technological change (whether that change was created through outside investment or at the behest of modernizers within a society) puts in place opportunities to see other ways of life that implicitly question some aspects of traditional society, including any religious views. So even where the 'Western' or European consensus may not be explicitly held to be true, the traditional society's assumptions, whatever they are, may fall into question. Or, to the extent there is a reaffirmation of local religious norms as part of a rejection of foreign cultural elements, there develops a kind of uneasy acculturation between elements of a 'modern' worldview and the traditional one.

If there is to be a common theoretical ground for the adoption of the modern Western consensus as to what constitutes legitimacy for government actions, it will not be found in the religious beliefs of Europeans as they were at the time of the original formation of that consensus. Worthy as those beliefs may in fact be, they no longer seem viable even to most Europeans. The course of intellectual

---

aware of what it was and little concerned about its applications. By the mid-nineteenth century, the popular understanding of the uses of the scientific method was quite general, though a full acceptance of it remained, and perhaps still remains, only among the learned.

11 At least in the American context, it is interesting that Pragmatism as a philosophical movement (William James and John Dewey) occurs just as relativity first appeared on the scene. Perhaps this can be seen as a further generalization of trends first evident in Utilitarianism.

history in Europe, and in the wider world as it became influenced by European culture, has seen a tension between the assumptions of intellectual debate and the role of religion in supplying fundamental principles. This tension contributes to the difficulty of maintaining the theoretical basis on which the Western consensus for judging governmental legitimacy is based. But it is the premise of this chapter that the non-religious aspects of the original theoretical basis can supply a needed objective standard for measuring governmental legitimacy.

This same ease of exposure to the outside world, which in modern times has caused cultural conflict and cognitive dissonance in the 'non-Western' world also caused questioning in Europe itself, beginning during the nineteenth century and still continuing, of some of the religious traditions that previously had been deeply entrenched in European culture. As a result, the certainty of many of the premises on which Europe's liberal traditions were based was also damaged because Europeans became aware of other, seemingly successful, religious and philosophical world views. The influence of Asian religious thought, especially Hindu and Buddhist, on nineteenth-century German scholars (Dumoulin 1981) led to a broader acquaintance with, and respect for, that thought among educated people wherever the 'Western' academic tradition penetrated.

Besides the broader intellectual crisis in the West as to the theoretical validity of reason as an intellectual tool and religion as the basis of morals, the chequered history of the expansion of rational and experimental approach to human affairs, both in Europe and elsewhere as its intellectual force expanded since the Renaissance and Reformation periods, has also served to undermine the philosophical premises of what we have been calling in this chapter the consensus. In the seventeenth and eighteenth centuries, the intellectual triumph of Whig and other liberal thought among the elites of Europe, and its contradiction with the human inequality then clearly visible in European society, produced at least a temporary collapse of the old order, in which that same elite had dominated political theory and political practice. Far from resulting in the general emancipation of Europe, the revolutionary ferment led to bloody chaos, then dictatorship, then almost universal war. This in turn led to a restoration of what we might call illiberal political theory and practice.[12] It constituted, in Europe, a long-lasting rejection, even among revolutionaries, of the prior liberal views and practice. Such views and practices were considered naïve at best, at worst as cynical tools to confuse or enslave the masses. Much of the rest of the world had never had such views to begin with, so even as the intellectual influence of Europe expanded in the nineteenth century, the earlier premises of political philosophy became lost in the dustbin of history.

In that century, new ideologies arose in Europe, sometimes egalitarian in principle, but mostly romantic and either anarchic or tyrannical in practice.[13] In the twentieth century, these ideologies would harden into totalitarian despotisms

12 Historically this was manifested in the Congress of Vienna and the Holy Alliance, both occurring after the defeat of Napoleon.

13 Anarchism and Communism, in a number of their forms, were among these.

that led the continent, and ultimately the world, into world wars and strife-filled division.[14] A good part of the world's population sank into a government-enforced enslavement that (for many) ended mostly because of its own internal contradictions. All of these belief systems of the nineteenth and twentieth centuries seemed to agree that earlier liberal thought, while perhaps sentimentally appealing, could hardly have application in the real world of famine and strife.

The reorganization of the nations of Western Europe after the Second World War led to the adoption in them of many of the forms of liberal government that had arisen out of the earlier European philosophical consensus, and to a reassertion of the values of that consensus. This was in part in reaction to the horrific results of fascist and Nazi political thought and practice, but was also influenced by the role of the United States in Western European reconstruction after the war. It did not necessarily amount to an adoption of the original enlightenment premises, but only of the 'modern' consensus as to how government behaviour should be measured. This may explain in part why the consensus in modern times is strongly affirmed but seemingly lacks a theoretical foundation. European scholarship had moved on from the foundation but perhaps European society shuddered at the horrors in its recent past and eagerly accepted values which unequivocally condemned those horrors.

An Isolated Remnant of Earlier Political Thought

Why was the influence of the United States in the reconstruction of Europe after the Second World War in the direction of a reassertion of political principles long since rejected by European thinkers as naïve or intellectually untenable?

Perhaps oddly, one part of the world on the periphery of European society in the last half of eighteenth century self-consciously formed its governmental institutions on the claimed basis of the very same 'Whig' or 'liberal' philosophy that began to be discredited very soon after the coalescing of those institutions. But so geographically isolated was the United States in those times from the mainsprings of European thought and experience that ideas discredited in the old world held on in the new. Further, the experience of the new world was more consistent with the idea of the primacy of the individual over the collective. Largely composed of transients from many differing cultures, European, African and Asian, each American community was a shifting combination of persons who might choose to change their location on short notice for any of a variety of reasons, and often did so in the early days of the United States down through at least the nineteenth century. To such people it was self-evident that individual choice preceded governmental authority.

14 One hardly wishes to linger over the sad history of twentieth-century Europe, with its Nazi, fascist and communist dictatorships and the wars and atrocities they brought.

In most cases, whatever the relevant group of neighbours decided among themselves was the only effective government they had during these earlier times. Attempts by more formal and distant powers to impose an external will were frustrated both by the logistical difficulties of doing so and the firm resistance of the people they sought to control. Government was seen in the colonies, and then the dubiously United States they formed, as simply a convenience for the governed to combine for common needs to whatever extent and in whatever manner they saw fit. The small size of the population and often its interdependence put natural limits on the claims of the commonality on the individual, who in any case could and did leave a community judged too oppressive.

But this was not anarchy. In each community, however defined, the collective ultimately imposed its values through the formal and informal tyranny of the majority, as de Tocqueville (2001: Chapter 15) explained. The population at large embraced the enforcement of the rules because they considered the rules to emanate from themselves. Actual government force seldom provided that enforcement, though vigilantism sometimes did.

The American Exception to the March of Theory

What did the American take on Pufendorf (1927) and Locke (1980), one that persisted for more than a century after it was largely rejected in Europe, look like?

In some ways, it was not so different from the modern 'consensus' in its operative forms. But its premises were much clearer. Many of them continue to be widely accepted at all levels in the American population even today, which sometimes makes for surprising turns in American debates over political issues.

That these premises held on is somewhat surprising, given that most of the current population of the United States is either itself immigrant, or relatively recently descended from immigrants, from countries which, for the most part, do not share those premises. But as we shall see shortly, it is natural for an immigrant to think of government in these terms.

The first and most important of these assumptions is that human individuals have rights that are not defined by the society in which they happen to reside, but precede it and are superior in obligation on the society to any additional rights conferred, or in some cases duties imposed, by the society itself. Only by their consent to membership in that society do they accept its rules in return for its protection, and then only to the extent those rules remain consistent with the prior fundamental rights.

This consent may be granted by forming a new society, something that now rarely happens but was once common in the American experience from the Mayflower Compact onward. Or people can consent to a government by immigrating to an existing society they find more conducive to the preservations of their freedoms. For most people that is perhaps little more than saying that the society entered is the one most conducive to allowing them to live the sort of life they aspire to live. Virtually the entire present population of the United States is either itself immigrant, or relatively recently descended from someone who entered its society either as an immigrant or at its fairly recent formation as a polity. This experience, then, of choosing the government under which one lives, contributes to the persistent salience (mentioned above) of the idea of consent as the basis for government.

The typical decision to immigrate to the United States is today more often based on material goals, but from time to time even now, and much more frequently in the past, the basis also included non-material motives as well, such as a desire to practice a religion or for artistic freedom. To the extent it arose from religious motivation, this history is perhaps a factor in the continuing broadly religious character of the American people as compared to people in some other parts of the world.

But the most common form of consent is the consent granted by continuing to live in the society into which you were born. Among the general population in America only a few decades ago, political dissent from the currently popular views was commonly greeted with a 'If you don't like it here, move to Russia [or whatever country was thought to mirror the philosophy of the dissident].' It might also be expressed as 'Go back where you came from.' This latter was based on the implicit assumption that every person here had an ancestral homeland to which they might return. That is an indication of how deeply a part of the American *volksgeist* this presumption remains. In other parts of the world where the forms of government have been influenced by American practice, the values that come from basing government on consent have gained great sway, but the premise on which they are based remains somewhat cloudy. Even within the United States, the concept of government by consent of the governed may receive more lip service than understanding. Making a more explicit use of this ultimate measure, rather than measuring by the existence of any given formal institutions, would result in a more objective, and perhaps in an easier to measure, index of governmental legitimacy.

How Consent Works in Practice

The inherent rights that precede society include the 'natural' right to do whatever an individual may wish so long as it does not impinge on the similar rights of others.[15] This can lead to many difficult cases of apparent and sometimes even real conflict. Needing a mechanism to resolve such conflicts is indeed a strong inducement to creating a government. During the period before government is established over a given territory, or when all government fails within it, there is no common judge and enforcement mechanism, that is, no government, each individual must interpret their own rights for themselves, with the likelihood of disputes being

15 This is the 'natural freedom' to which Hobbes, Pufendorf, Locke and others refer.

resolved by force.[16] This creates a powerful inducement to consenting to some form of government, perhaps even an imperfect one. Having a chance to have your dispute resolved by an impartial judge and then enforced by the collective force of the community generally is better than having to rely exclusively on your own strength and cunning. The greater predictability of such a society is conducive to the creation of wealth as well, if for no other reason than the greater clarity of the rules that apply within it and the procedures for obtaining redress when those rules are broken. This in part arises from the fact that there must generally be a wide general knowledge of what the rules of a society are among its members before we can rationally say those members have consented to them.

But there is a poorly machined gear in this theory of legitimate government. Given the real-world choices one has, and the inconvenience of changing one's country, one may consent at least provisionally to a defective government that is sometimes unjust. But this also can explain how governments can be partially legitimate, and provide a means of testing relative as well as 'absolute' legitimacy.

Here we have the key to a relatively objective measure of governmental legitimacy that resolves down to one idea: legitimacy resides in the consent of the governed to the *form of*, if not all the outcomes provided by, the government. Further, if the individual does not actively participate in the formation of society or did not change residence in order to be a part of a polity, the fact the individual stays resident implies an initial, conditional consent. (A corollary is that there must also be an effective right to emigrate from the territory controlled by the government.) If consent criterion is met by the objective facts on the ground, then the government must be considered fundamentally legitimate, at least as to those citizens so consenting. However the consent must be at a reasonably high level throughout society before the society overall can be said to be one to which its members consent.

This requirement of consent is not a formalistic legalism, so that a consent given at a point in time is then indefeasible. It also follows that a government can be legitimate as to some of its citizens and illegitimate as to others.

Legitimacy is neither proven nor disproven by any particular rules or procedures a government may adopt, so long as consent is real, and the fundamental human rights of its citizens, or some class of them, are not knowingly violated. So having jury trials may or may not be fundamental. It may be that the people of a given society overall may even choose legitimately to forgo certain rights that some individuals among them would otherwise consider important. Either maintaining or forgoing any one right does not in itself raise questions of the society's legitimacy, as long as the general consent of its members to the overall structure and results of government is in effect and no one's fundamental human right is violated. The current 'Western' consensus about how a legitimate government should look, to

16 We find this situation has arisen in recent times in various 'failed states', such as Somalia.

the extent it is not grounded on this principle, may be idiosyncratic to the cultural norms of the countries that consensus has grown up in.

Once you have the fundamental condition of legitimacy, consent, the government will have great flexibility in recognizing or rejecting some rights and duties or even whole areas of governmental activity, such as those relating to natural resources and the economy, as conducive to the reasons the society was formed. An individual cannot be deemed to give up, by entering society, certain of that individual's 'fundamental' freedoms, though perhaps that individual can forfeit even those by their wilful misconduct in violation of the norms they have legitimately agreed to follow by entering or remaining in a given society.

How Human Rights Fit into Legitimacy

What these fundamental freedoms are is perhaps not so hard to deduce in the light of the two main conditions of governmental legitimacy. Among them are the rights needed to continue to be making an informed judgment and giving informed and effective consent to continued membership in the society. Freedom of expression and association is surely fundamental, in the sense it is required for making informed judgments about, and maintaining informed consent to, the workings of the established government. Freedom to participate in political life is a part of this, though the forms political life may take will vary from society to society. As we have already observed, freedom of travel is also necessary, not only as a part of the free flow of ideas, but in order to effectuate the right of emigration.

There is another, related, class of fundamental rights: those rights, the furtherance of which the society must be presumed to have been formed to achieve. An individual cannot be thought to consent to be a slave. Once made a slave, that individual is at permanent war with any master and with the society that enforces the condition of slavery. Slavery is not simply to be found in the formal master and slave relationship, but can be seen in many situations in which an individual does not have an individual first right to the fruits of that individual's own labour. An individual may in some manner consent to part with a portion of them in order to obtain the benefits of the society that creates the conditions in which they are produced. Likewise an individual may, through some promise or fault, and after due process, be judged to owe them to another.

But an individual who conceives her fundamental rights violated and does not seek to emigrate when having the practical option of doing so acts at her own peril in fighting a war with a society that seeks to enslave that individual or otherwise violate that individual's fundamental rights. And in general societies hold the upper hand in such wars! Worse, unless her appraisal of her rights is objectively valid by reference to fundamental principles, her war is simple rebellion, and a violation of her fundamental agreement with society. We should not lightly take up arms against even an oppressive society, much less one that is doubtfully so.

In this context, it is interesting to think about the place of nonviolent resistance. Since it is non-violent, it is not war against society, even if it is wrongheaded or unjustified. Even if you are unpersuaded it is a fundamental human right, surely it is a useful tool for raising questions about fundamental human rights. No wise government will try to suppress it, even though such a government may in non-violent ways enforce equal laws that non-violent resisters may break.

So while some would say that fundamental human rights ultimately rest on religious beliefs, and some would have recourse to documents like the 1948 Universal Declaration of Human Rights, we can perhaps construct a surer theoretical framework by recourse to the ancient doctrine of consent, even if it is dressed in some new clothes and stands without some of its earlier religious or rationalist underpinnings.

Perhaps the only relatively objective argument for human rights and their relationship to government power we can find is built on the fundamental premise of the consent and equality of the governed.

How Can the Premise of Consent Be Tested?

The premise that government's legitimacy rests on consent, if accepted, does not relieve us from obtaining accurate information about a given government and the mores of its society, not to mention the objective state of its population's satisfaction with it, in order to determine its relative legitimacy. That process is difficult and subject to error. But given enough reliable facts, we should in principle be able to evaluate a society and its government pretty effectively, regardless of the cultural setting in which it arises. We should also be able to determine which violations of human rights render it partially or wholly illegitimate, and gauge appropriately our possible sanctions, if we consider it appropriate to intervene through whatever legal means may be available. While in most cases, the failure of a government to maintain the consent of those it governs is mainly a matter for it and them to determine, in extreme cases our common humanity, or the threats posed to others by a failed state, may justify our intervention. Our own convenience, economic interests or political preferences, however, never create such a justification.

Some Caveats and an Appeal to Utility

Of course, the premise that the consent of the governed is the base of government legitimacy might itself be open to question. So far we have offered it primarily as a hypothesis, which seems to fit the known facts well. Without a common religious faith affirming it, or scientific proof of the sort natural science perhaps cannot be expected to provide, there is still a possibility it is simply not valid. Even so, the theory may be a useful tool for discussion.

Perhaps human individuals do not have intrinsic worth and the commonality's convenience may at its will trump the individual's necessity. I think such a view is morally wrong. Others may not. But I believe most people's conscience, whatever may be their cultural roots, pushes against this view. In retrospect every tyranny comes to be abhorred, no matter how credible its original claims may have seemed about being instituted for the good of the many. In any case, people who come from differing religions, and some who have no religion at all, can affirm that the consent of the governed is the only basis for legitimate government. But ultimately, we need not decide whether our own personal cultural traditions or religious convictions include such values in order to use this sort of analysis.

We do so because of its practical utility, and the potentially objective tool it provides us for discussion with each other. As a practical guide it does not so much depend on any single cultural tradition, but has some plausible roots in many, and perhaps in all. So measuring consent seems like a good place to start, particularly because so many answers to questions about governmental, otherwise perplexing, can be deduced from it for any given society and a given set of facts about its culture and people.

For those who cannot agree that consent of the governed is the basis for government's legitimacy, then the issue is joined and we must await the judgment of experience in seeing how the theory operates in practice as a guide for us. But it is interesting that each society, imperfect as it may be in recognizing human economic and personal freedom, seems to progress materially in rough alignment with the extent of that recognition relative to its own past. Even where rough approximations such as free elections and lack of corruption in government replace the rule of consent, over all there seems to be a rough correlation (Barro 1996). Again, practical considerations seem to encourage us to use this approach.

In accepting the standard of consent, we can also admit we do not have an entirely value-free means of measuring government legitimacy. We do, however, have a much more objective way of measuring that legitimacy if we accept the fundamental premise that individuals define the powers of government, not government the rights of individuals.

The Implications of the Premise that Individuals Define the Powers of Government

A result of accepting this premise is that we can explain some of the apparent flexibility we see in practice as regards to deciding if a government is overall, or in some particular, acting in a legitimate manner, without losing a single standard for what is 'legitimate'.

With regard to individual disputes, the just punishment of most crimes and the fair enforcement of most contracts are surely preferable to a situation in which most crimes go unpunished and most contracts are effectively unenforceable. We most likely would find that a government that mostly provides justice in fact has the consent of a strong majority of its citizens as to the manner in which it governs. Even those few disappointed by injustice might reasonably consent to the form of governing and to some possibility that it will not in each case work properly, given human fallibility, so long as the flaw is not so grave that those few could not be said to have consented to a grossly unjust (as to them) system. So it may not matter in a society that a few crimes go unpunished or sometimes someone is unfairly punished for a crime that person did not commit if most people feel, correctly, that the criminal justice system is fundamentally fair.

If a means for bettering the criminal justice system is found, though, even a government that provides a fairly high degree of justice in its proceedings might be called into question, especially when there is a widespread public perception of persistent and fixable unfairness. In other cases, even a single instance of injustice, perhaps in taking a life as a punishment for a crime of which the executed individual is innocent, calls consent into question, not just the consent of the wrongly executed but that of the other citizens in whose name the execution occurs.

A society where consent exists at one point for the imposition of the death penalty may later lose that consent, and some of its legitimacy as more people become aware of the capability of the criminal justice system to bring about an unjust conviction of the innocent, and consequently the imposition of that penalty on innocent persons. This is true even where at first the legitimacy of that society was entirely secure. Even at first, though, at least to the individual who is the victim of such an injustice, the argument that the individual can ever consent to it seems unpersuasive. To that extent the government must be illegitimate. But a government can be illegitimate in part without completely losing its rightful authority overall.

This technique of starting with consent allows us to measure, perhaps even quantify, legitimacy, to the extent we can get valid data. Basing our measure of legitimacy on consent probably means that any given society only has a relative legitimacy, not an absolute one. But it is one that can be compared with the same country over time or with other countries without resort to unidentified criteria or arbitrary criteria incapable of abstract justification. It is interesting that the governments we are most likely to suspect of being illegitimate are often the same ones that prevent the effective gathering of polling information. Perhaps this is in some sense an admission of illegitimacy?

Of course, it is unlikely that any numerous or heterogeneous society has ever had the informed consent of each and every one of its members. Nor is that necessary for the theory to work. It is not surprising that society, like biological organisms might evolve over time toward something less likely to create dissention and unstable government, and that such an evolution would be correlated to greater and greater degrees of popular consent. If we are correct in saying that the importance of the consent of the governed is in fact founded in nature, as we may suspect, then any situation that leads to widespread social discontent but does not allow for peaceful change is unhealthy for the social organism. Perhaps it is not too much to say that such a situation is 'unnatural'. This is more a warning than a value judgment, though there are those who would feel it is both. A society not based on consent might be less likely to survive in competition with others more fully implementing the rule of consent. (Or perhaps those individuals in the society with less implementation of consent will be less likely to prosper and so want to change their society to one with a greater implementation of consent.) At any given time, the effective norm for successful societies might be different, but the competitive pressure probably is in the direction of greater and greater efficiency at obtaining greater and greater degrees of consent. It ought to be possible to measure this over time and so test the theory.

In some cases, as perhaps with the death penalty, what at first might have been an individual matter of justice may over time become a more general public and political dispute. It is the job of government to provide appropriate forums for resolving both such types of dispute.

For public and political disputes, as long as appropriate forums exist and are functioning efficiently, the government is probably legitimate overall, even though the resolution of any single dispute may be problematical. At any given time, various factions in a society, while basically agreeing on the form of government, may be strongly various as to what that government should in fact do without that situation in itself damaging the legitimacy of the government. If open debate is allowed, and the opportunity to resolve the debate, at least tentatively and from time to time, perhaps in elections or in the adoption of new laws, exists, the government structure overall is likely to have a high degree of consent, though the society it governs is not strongly agreed on a course of action.

Such a society may be stable and unified, though very contentious. Maintaining the consent of the governed over time, however, may require continuing progress toward resolving the contentions, if by no other means, then perhaps by trial and error!

A population that is hungry and impoverished, especially if those conditions arise from the failures of government, will not ultimately tolerate the continued existence of that government. Of course, popular perceptions of what constitutes an acceptable level of poverty may vary, so keeping its population in ignorance of the living standards of populations under other governments is a fundamental, if ultimately unattainable, imperative for an ineffective government. As a practical matter, such a government must become a tyranny, limiting the freedoms of travel and communication that would inform its population of the government's defects. To the extent it does so, such a government is acting outside the limits of legitimate government. We each can, I suspect, still think of examples of such governments in the world today, though perhaps their number is dwindling, as our Darwinian analysis might lead us to expect.

Once the population is fed, and the means of escaping poverty established (whether or not the poverty itself persists), a government has managed to meet the minimum requirements for legitimacy under the *salus populi* test. But by doing so it paradoxically raises the bar for itself. One area in which it does so is often in the need for greater transparency.

One Application of Rule of Consent: Conflicts Relating to Transparency

One area of government practice that many find central to determining its legitimacy is the degree of 'transparency' it allows surrounding its operations. How can we use the tool of consent theory to answer the question of how openly a government must disclose its decision-making process and the details of its operations to its people?

When government is based upon the consent of the governed, the apparent conflict between the rights of the governed and the powers and transparency of the government largely evaporates. Once again we can find, using the overall measure of consent, a great variety in the practices of states equally legitimate, because their respective peoples may validly consent to differing substantive and procedural rules.

Where trust in the mechanisms of government is great, as determined by the people in the context of their own society, less openness is still consistent with the consent of the governed. The constitutional convention that proposed the present constitution of the United States was conducted entirely in secret, but the public in each state by their votes approved the result, which seems to most observers to have been overall a legitimate establishment of a government by consent.

Another area where the people may well consent to differing degrees of openness in government is that of foreign policy and natural security issues. The public could reasonably decide that an open public debate might actually be harmful to national security.

But all decisions about transparency, like others, are subject to the consent rule. The people must give their informed consent before it is ever appropriate to hide from them any part of the public business. The requirement for informed consent means that the people must have continuing access to sufficient government information to determine whether they may in fact trust the government without greater transparency. How can that consent be considered informed if the government itself through secrecy in its operations, keeps the people unaware of what the true issues are and how the government chooses to approach them?

While in theory a government may have consent without having any ongoing public forum in which public issues are routinely debated, it seems unlikely many such exist.[17] Without open public debate, which among other things is a powerful education for the people, private debate cannot flourish in a modern largely

---

17 Perhaps ancient Sparta? But one expects that much more informal debate went on there than is found in historical records available to us at this remove. Then, too, given the limited numbers of people involved, private debate may have sufficed. As to the Helots, of course, Sparta could not have been said to be legitimate in any case.

populated country. Without private debate, consent is as likely to be lost through ignorance and misunderstanding as through government wrongdoing. Neither the government nor the governed are advantaged by such a result.

The people of each society may choose the level of transparency that works best for it, and yet still have enough information to judge whether or not to change that level. The ultimate decision, whether informed or not, must be in the hands of the people, though, in order to satisfy the rule of consent. A wise government will not lightly deny them any information that might be relevant to obtaining and maintaining that consent.

Conclusion

While some degree of open and free elected government seems required to obtain the consent of the governed, it is that consent, and not any specific forms of obtaining it, which ultimately determines the degree to which we can say the government is legitimate. No tyranny can long hide its illegitimacy behind a consent that was obtained through fraud or was based on premises no longer existing.

We should not be fearful to use the measure of consent, which is culturally neutral in substance (even if the forms through which effective consent may be given may be specific to each culture). Whether we base our decision to use this means of measuring government on our own religious or other cultural beliefs, or simply on its ability to predict in a consistent manner the legitimacy of governments and government behaviour we have a standard that we can rely on with relative certainty, if only we can find out the required facts.

As countries with legitimate governments are both more likely to prosper over time and to be more stable partners on the world stage, we take into account questions of legitimacy when dealing with them. It seems immoral not to do so, but even if morality is set aside, it seems unwise. In any event, the many cultures of the world, as they become more economically and often socially interrelated, even integrated, need a common idiom through which to discuss their differences and come to a mutual respect based on a shared principle.

This has been an effort to provide the basis for one.

References

Barro, R.J. 1996. 'Democracy and Growth'. *Journal of Economic Growth*, 1, 1-27.
Confucius. 2008. *The Analects*. Oxford: Oxford University Press.
Dawkins, R. 2006. *The God Delusion*. New York: Houghton Mifflin.
Descartes, R. 2000. *Discours de la Méthode*. Paris: Garnier Flammarion.
Dewey, J. 2007. *Democracy and Education*. Fairford: The Echo Library.

Dumoulin, H. 1981. 'Buddhism and 19th Century German Philosophy'. *Journal of the History of Ideas*, 42(3), 457-470.

Fuller, C., J.E. Crimmins and Philip Schofield. 2010. *Church-of-Englandism and Its Catechism Examined: The Collected Works of Jeremy Bentham*. Oxford: Oxford University Press.

Goldstein, R. 2005. *Incompleteness: The Proof and Paradox of Kurt Gödel*. New York: W.W. Norton.

Hobbes, T. 2000. *Leviathan*. Paris: Gallimard.

Hume, D. 1993. *An Enquiry concerning Human Understanding*. Indianapolis, IN: Hackett.

Hume, D. 2009. *Dialogue and Natural History of Religion*. New York: Oxford University Press.

James, W. 1999. *The Principles of Psychology*. Bristol: Thoemmes Press.

Locke, J. 1980. *Second Treatise on Civil Government*. Indianapolis, IN: Hackett.

Mill, J.S. 1874. *A System of Logic*. New York: Harper & Brothers.

Mill, J.S. 1999. *On Liberty*. Peterborough, ON: Broadview Press.

Montesquieu, V. 1950. *De l'Esprit des Loix*. Paris: Les Belles Lettres.

Pufendorf, S. von. 1927. *De officio hominis et civis juxta legem naturalem libri duo*. New York: Oxford University Press.

Rousseau, J.J. 1993. *Le contrat social ou principes du droit politique*. Paris: Editions Flammarion.

Tocqueville, A. de. 2001. *Democracy in America*. New York: Signet Classics.

Wright, R. 2009. *The Evolution of God*. New York: Little Brown and Co.

PART II
Visualizing and Contextualizing Transparency, Power and Control

Chapter 9

Battle of the Sexters: Teens Celling Sex in a World Wide Web of Conflicting Laws, Values and Social Norms

Michelle L. Wirth

Introduction

It is not clear why George was determined to pursue the case against the girls. In the end, some people insinuated he was blinded by the same photographs that he knew lured human vermin to children. Maybe it was chivalry that compelled George to try to save the girls from themselves. The problem was, George didn't know he was vulnerable, and there was no one there to save George.

George Skumanick grew up in Wyoming County, Pennsylvania, the grandson of immigrant coal miners and the son of a mechanic and a short order cook. He graduated from Tunkhannock Area High School in 1979, went on to college and returned home after he earned his law degree in 1986. Three years later he was appointed to replace the District Attorney (DA) of Wyoming County by Brendan Vanston, who resigned as DA to become a judge in the Court of Common Pleas in the same county.

In most states in the US, a DA is elected by residents of the county to prosecute people on behalf of the state. A DA proves his or her mettle by being 'tough on crime', prosecuting people for criminal conduct where there is probable cause that they might have broken the law. Although a DA has 'prosecutorial discretion', generally speaking the more convictions a DA wins, the better the DA is considered to be at doing the job. The DA and voters share an unspoken assumption that they and their loved ones are not the criminals.

A DA's power to determine whether to charge a person with a crime and prosecute a case 'gives them more control over the fate of those accused of a crime than a judge or jury' (Culp 2009). In theory, voting on whether to remove a DA by electing someone else is the citizen's opportunity to hold the DA accountable. In practice, however, citizens rarely get this opportunity because in 85 per cent of elections the incumbent runs unopposed. When voters have a choice between two or more candidates, they often do not have access to comprehensive quantitative information on which to base their choice, and in contested elections incumbent DAs still win re-election 69 per cent of the time. Overall, 95 per cent of DAs win re-election (figures drawn from Culp 2009). It turns out that 'media coverage of prosecutorial scandals is one of the few factors that significantly reduces a prosecutor's chances of reelection' (Bibas 2009: 986).

Mr Skumanick avoided the election hurdle when the outgoing incumbent appointed him to fill the position. In November 1989, the residents of Wyoming County elected incumbent DA Skumanick and thus retained him as the chief law enforcement officer of their county. DA Skumanick avoided being the subject of public scandal and media scrutiny for two decades as he prosecuted over 10,000 criminal cases in a hometown so small it shared a judge with a neighbouring county (Rudolf and Baker 2009). By the time he got the fateful call from the school officials at the Tunkhannock Area High School, DA Skumanick's career encompassed five elected terms and his sixth potential term was on the horizon.

DA Skumanick's campaign materials created the impression of an attorney who built a career by following the letter of the law to protect the vulnerable. He was a founding board member of the Children's Advocacy Center of Northeastern Pennsylvania and served on the Child Abuse Coalition and Juvenile Prosecutors Network of the Pennsylvania District Attorney's Association. He taught courses in criminal procedure, and on laws pertaining to cyber crime and sexual exploitation cases. He also presented educational programmes to students and conducted in-service trainings to teachers[1] so it was not unusual for the police to call him when school officials found nude and semi-nude photos of local girls on the cell phones of schoolboys. When he answered that call, this hometown DA had no cause to imagine that his work would be critiqued with the nationally published news headline, 'How Not to Prosecute a Sexting Case' (Bazelon 2010).

This case was catapulted from its small town origins to national headlines based on the strength of the conflict between past and prevailing interpretations of what constitutes child pornography, and ideas of who is a child pornographer and who is a victim. This chapter reviews the case and introduces a method of semiotic analysis that can be used to tease out key terms, their meanings and the influences that give the terms their meanings, to guide the construction of compelling frameworks and persuasive arguments.

How Not to Prosecute a Sexting Case

In October 2008, teachers at Tunkhannock Junior and Senior High schools confiscated cell phones from students who violated the school district's policy, which prohibited use of cell phones in the school. They searched five cell phones and found 100 images of nude or semi-nude students. Teachers called the police, who contacted DA Skumanick for advice on how to proceed. These authorities were concerned that students were unknowingly exposing themselves to the

1 *Miller et al. v. Skumanick* (2009) Temporary Restraining Order Hearing, 2009. [Online: American Civil Liberties Union of Pennsylvania]. Available at: http://www.aclupa.org/downloads/TranscriptTROhearing.PDF [accessed 25 June 2010].

risks inherent to 'sexting', the production and electronic distribution of sexually suggestive photographs and cell-phone text messages. In response, DA Skumanick and other law enforcement officers held an assembly at each of the schools to warn students of the danger. Officials sent letters warning parents and informing them that incidents of sexting had been confirmed at the schools.

The DA's office sent letters by certified mail to the parents of the kids on whose cell phones the photographs were found, and to the parents of the girls whose images were found on the cell phones. The letter informed parents that their child had 'been involved in dissemination of child pornography', and that there would be a meeting 'with all identified juveniles'[2] held at the Wyoming County Court House.

Members of 17 families attended the meeting held at the same courthouse in which DA Skumanick had prosecuted over 10,000 criminal cases. After he spoke about the dangers of sexting, DA Skumanick suggested that parents compel their children to accept a plea bargain in which they would go on probation and take a course of classes, reiterated that children who did not successfully complete the course would face felony criminal charges, and offered to clear the charges for any child who successfully completed the course and probation.[3]

A man stood up, the father of a girl threatened with felony charges as a result of appearing in a photograph in which she was pictured wearing a bikini. He asked how his daughter could be prosecuted for this; he didn't see anything wrong with the photograph. DA Skumanick answered, 'It was provocative.' The father asked, 'who [is] deciding what is provocative?'[4] One parent claimed that DA Skumanick replied, 'I could charge everyone here with felonies, we are doing the right thing and offering this class, and that's the law, and if you don't like it, too bad.'[5]

DA Skumanick informed the crowd that juvenile offenders do not get a jury trial in juvenile court.[6] He gave parents two weeks to let him know whether they would agree to the terms of probation.[7] Most of the parents took the probation offer. The parents of Marissa Miller, Grace Kelly and a girl given the pseudonym 'Nancy Doe', however, chose 'to bring the community's attention to bear upon their trials'[8] by suing the DA in federal court.

---

2 *Miller et al. v. Skumanick* (2009) Temporary Restraining Order Hearing, 2009, 13.

3 *Miller et al. v. Skumanick* (2009) Temporary Restraining Order Hearing, 2009, 22-23.

4 *Miller et al. v. Skumanick* (2009) Temporary Restraining Order Hearing, 2009, 23.

5 *Miller et al. v. Skumanick* (2009) Temporary Restraining Order Hearing, 2009, 24.

6 *Miller et al. v. Skumanick* (2009) Temporary Restraining Order Hearing, 2009, 29.

7 *Miller et al. v. Skumanick* (2009) Temporary Restraining Order Hearing, 2009, 24.

8 *McKeiver v. Pennsylvania*, 403 US 528 (1971) 553-556.

Caught between Being a Girl, and a Hard Place

Marissa Miller was 12 years old when she had a summer slumber party in her hot attic bedroom.[9] She and her friend Grace Kelly were in their white bras, one of them holding a telephone, the other making a 'peace' sign, when a friend used a digital camera to snap a photo of the girls from the waist up.[10] When Mrs Miller saw the photo, she told the girls they were 'goofballs'. She suspects that the friend who took the photo might have posted it on MySpace or Facebook, from which it was downloaded and eventually distributed to a classmate's cell phone. The Millers can't be sure – the photograph was taken three years before the threat of charges, and Marissa never possessed the image.

Nancy Doe appears to have stepped out of the shower just before she wrapped a white towel around her body, below her breasts,[11] and took a self-portrait.[12] She said she did not intend for the photograph to end up on the cell phone on which it was found more than one year later.[13]

DA Skumanick considered the girls to be accomplices in the production of child pornography.[14] He had no evidence that the girls distributed the photographs.[15] He intended to prosecute the girls if they did not take the plea deal.[16]

DA Skumanick found himself facing the girls in court at an emergency hearing. In March 2009 the American Civil Liberties Union (ACLU), on behalf of the girls and their parents, filed a motion with the United States District Court in which it requested that the Court issue a Temporary Restraining Order[17] [TRO]. They filed the motion pursuant to federal statute 42 U.S.C. §1983, Civil Action for Deprivation of Rights. The court had jurisdiction over the matter through federal statute 28 U.S.C. §1331, Federal Question.

With this change in jurisdiction, the girls changed their legal standing from being potential defendants in a juvenile court case within a state appellate system, to being plaintiffs in a civil case in federal court with a shorter appellate path to the US Supreme Court. The ACLU's successful motion also made DA Skumanick

9 *Miller et al. v. Skumanick* (2009) Temporary Restraining Order Hearing, 2009, 18-19.

10 *Miller et al. v. Skumanick* (2009) Memorandum, 2009, 6. [Online: American Civil Liberties Union of Pennsylvania]. Available at: http://www.aclupa.org/downloads/MillerTROorder33009.pdf [accessed 25 June 2010].

11 *Miller et al. v. Skumanick* (2009) Memorandum, 2009, 7.

12 *Miller et al. v. Skumanick* (2009) Temporary Restraining Order Hearing, 2009, 38.

13 *Miller et al. v. Skumanick* (2009) Temporary Restraining Order Hearing, 2009, 48.

14 *Miller et al. v. Skumanick* (2009) Memorandum, 2009, 8.

15 *Miller et al. v. Skumanick* (2009) Temporary Restraining Order Hearing, 2009, 66.

16 *Miller et al. v. Skumanick* (2009) Temporary Restraining Order Hearing, 2009, 44.

17 *Miller et al. v. Skumanick* (2009) Temporary Restraining Order Hearing, 2009, 56.

a defendant in federal court. As a prosecutor, he was not used to being in this position.[18]

The District Court issued the TRO under circumstances that had the order serve as a preliminary injunction and allowed DA Skumanick to seek an Interlocutory Appeal from the Third Judicial Circuit Court (Circuit Court).[19] If the Circuit Court affirmed the preliminary injunction, then the DA would be enjoined from filing charges against the girls and their parents unless he established probable cause, at which point he could move to have the court vacate the injunction.[20] If the Circuit Court did not affirm the preliminary injunction, then the DA could press charges against the girls, who would have an adjudication hearing in front of Judge Vanston in the Court of Common Pleas,[21] where they might be adjudicated delinquent.

There are no sentencing guidelines in juvenile court in Pennsylvania.[22] The adjudication 'delinquent' is a designation made in lieu of a criminal conviction. A juvenile court disposition, the parallel to a criminal court sentence, could include confinement in an out-of-home placement such as a juvenile correctional facility, 'disqualification from military service, "Megan's Law" sex offender registration, and enhanced sentencing for adult crimes' (Cleland 2010: 61). The disposition can be for up to four years initially, although the court can retain jurisdiction over a child until she or he becomes 21 years of age (Pennsylvania District Attorneys Association 2010). The sex offender registration requirements 'can extend well into adulthood' (Bowker and Sullivan 2010).

If the girls chose instead to take the juvenile court equivalent of a plea offer – called an 'informal adjustment' – they could be on probation for six to nine months, during which time they could be subjected to random drug testing.[23] They would also be required to complete an educational course, held for two hours per week for five weeks. The course curriculum would cover 'what it means to be a girl in today's society',[24] including issues such as 'sexual violence and harassment and its implications for the victim and the community', 'gender identity and specifically

18 *Miller et al. v. Skumanick* (2009) Temporary Restraining Order Hearing, 2009, 10-11.

19 *Miller et al. v. Skumanick* (2009) Appellant Brief, U.S. Court of Appeals Third Circuit, 1. [Online: American Civil Liberties Union of Pennsylvania]. Available at: http://www.aclupa.org/downloads/AppellantBrief.pdf [accessed 25 June 2010].

20 *Miller v. Mitchell*, 598 F.3d 139, 145 (2010) 154.

21 *Miller et al. v. Skumanick* (2009) Temporary Restraining Order Hearing, 2009, 52, 53.

22 *Miller et al. v. Skumanick* (2009) Temporary Restraining Order Hearing, 2009, 59; *see also Miller et al. v. Skumanick* (2009) Verified Complaint, 7-8. [Online: American Civil Liberties Union of Pennsylvania]. Available at: http://www.aclupa.org/downloads/MillerComplaintfinal.pdf [accessed 25 June 2010].

23 *Miller et al. v. Skumanick* (2009) Temporary Restraining Order Hearing, 2009, 10.

24 *Miller et al. v. Skumanick* (2009) Temporary Restraining Order Hearing, 2009, 27.

the conflicting messages society and the media send young women' and 'how advertisers "use" women to sell products'.[25]

Marissa Miller believed she did not do anything wrong, and she did not want to be charged with a felony. Mr Miller was concerned about having to fight criminal charges, and believed that taking the plea deal was the safest bet.[26] Mrs Miller objected to the requirement that the girls write an essay regarding what they did, why it was 'morally wrong'[27] and 'how it affected the victim in the case'.[28] As Mrs Miller saw it, her daughter was the victim. She asked, 'Who is to say what it is to be a girl in today's society?'

Necessity is the Mother of (Re)Interpretation: A Case for Semiotic Legal Analysis

Court documents for this case provide an intimate view of the conundrum that has stymied parents, law-enforcement officials and courts across the nation. The documents, which include appellate briefs and a hearing transcript, are public records and have been published and made available for free on the Internet by organizations such as the ACLU.[29] These documents reflect a conversation amongst the judge, the attorneys, the girls and their parents. Theirs is part of a larger conversation in law, in media, and in adult and adolescent social circles, about what it means to be a child, a child pornographer, a perpetrator or a victim.

As the US Supreme Court explained in 1803, 'Those who apply the rule to particular cases must, of necessity, expound and interpret that rule. If two laws conflict with each other, the Courts must decide on the operation of each.'[30] What is a court to do when a law appears to conflict with itself? How can a court, or an attorney, proceed when the facts of the case appear to conflict with prevailing interpretations of the rule?

An advocate can frame an issue in a way that is conducive to a jury or judicial tribunal seeing that an idea that was once out of step with its time is now an idea whose time has come. As Robertson Davies noted, 'The eye sees only what the mind is prepared to comprehend' (Davies 1951: 154). Research suggests that people do not see facts simply because they exist; they see facts when the facts fit a

25 *Miller et al. v. Skumanick* (2009) Reply Brief, 2009, 5-6. [Online: American Civil Liberties Union of Pennsylvania]. Available at: http://www.aclupa.org/downloads/Skumanickreply.pdf [accessed 25 June 2010].

26 *Miller et al. v. Skumanick* (2009) Temporary Restraining Order Hearing, 2009, 21.

27 *Miller v. Mitchell*, 150.

28 *Miller et al. v. Skumanick* (2009) Temporary Restraining Order Hearing, 2009, 27.

29 *Miller et al. v. Skumanick*. [Online: American Civil Liberties Union of Pennsylvania]. Available at: http://www.aclupa.org/legal/legaldocket/milleretalvskumanick [accessed 25 June 2010].

30 *Marbury v. Madison*, 5 U.S. (1 Cranch) 137 (1803) 177.

frame of reference that the interpreter – be it a judge, jury, viewer or reader – finds credible. Thus, a viewer is likely to disregard facts that do not fit with the viewer's frame of reference, or world-view (Bostrom 2005: 1-2).

This prompts the question, 'who is doing the seeing?' Whose thinking counts, and what are the key factors? Dr Mary Frances Berry said:

> [E]veryone has stories, including lawyers, judges, and jurors. Stories provide a frame of reference that determines what each of us believes is true about the law. They also shape law and how it is enforced. ... Whose story counts in legal decisions rests heavily on who controls political and economic power, in a process that is circular and progressive. The stories of the powerful are the only ones that count, and the counting further enhances the power of the tellers in the economic and political arena. ... The interaction between stories and the interpretation of legal rules is a process. We change the law not by focusing exclusively on formal legal rules but by changing the experiences, and eroding the myths and stereotypes, that underlie each person's stories. (Berry 1999: 4, 19)

A successful advocate first determines who is in power, and who or what has the ability to influence people in power. Successful advocates then create a framework that allows influential people to hear the issue in a way that fits their existing worldview, acknowledges their values, and guides them to see and interpret facts in a way that recommends an outcome favourable to the advocate's aims.

How does an advocate determine the key factors and the defining frameworks? J.M. Balkin suggests:

> Legal semiotics will allow us to clarify hidden tensions in the law and assist us in the continuing refinement of our moral and legal intuitions. ... The discovery of moral tensions within the law – justifications which point in opposite directions in different areas of the law – suggests that we should rethink our policy choices in those different areas, or that we must redescribe them under an alternative or more general theory in which they can be understood as consistent. (Balkin 1991: 7)

Semiotic legal analysis, the practice of identifying both the key terms that highlight the points of contention and the various frameworks that shift their meanings, is a starting point to influence those interpretations.

As times and perceptions change, an idea that was once ahead of its time may be an idea whose time has come. Even an issue that has been ruled upon and soundly decided can yet be the object of an argument with merit. When the US Supreme Court issued a ruling in the case of *Lawrence v. Texas*,[31] it overturned the

---

31 *Lawrence v. Texas*, 539 U.S. 558 (2003).

precedent it set just 17 years earlier in *Bowers v. Hardwick*.[32] The Court referred to the 'emerging awareness' and 'emerging recognition' of the nature of the issue underlying both cases, as reflected in more recent law, traditions and scholarship. The Court went on to say:

> The foundations of Bowers have sustained serious erosion from our recent decisions in Casey and Romer. When our precedent has been thus weakened, criticism from other sources is of greater significance. In the United States criticism of Bowers has been substantial and continuing, disapproving of its reasoning in all respects, not just as to its historical assumptions. ... To the extent Bowers relied on values we share with a wider civilization, it should be noted that the reasoning and holding in Bowers have been rejected elsewhere. ...[33]

The US Supreme Court has adopted new meanings in areas where the circuit courts had unanimously adopted a different meaning. Where circuit courts are split on an issue, there is also an opening to advocate for an emerging meaning (DuBois and Sweitzer 2010: 3). Where the circuit courts are not split on an issue, a dissenting opinion may yet provide the roadmap to a future winning argument. Even dicta regarding a matter on which the court did not rule may highlight frameworks to illuminate and deconstruct when presenting the matter in a future case.

A Method of Legal Semiotic Analysis

A legal semiotic analysis can be guided by several questions:

- What arguments or interpretations are asserted?
- What key factors – such as identities, roles or definitions – are implicit or explicit in those assertions?
- What are the prevailing and emerging meanings of those factors?
- What are the frameworks – the perspectives or world-views – that give the terms their prevailing and emerging, or contested, meanings?
- What changes (e.g. in technology and in power) have occurred since the time the law first came into effect, or significantly was reinterpreted, that may account for the present legal challenge?

To construct a compelling proposal, advocates can consider:

- Which framework is most consistent with the intentions of the legislature at the time the law was written; with the prevailing judicial standards; and with public sentiment?

---

32 *Bowers v. Hardwick*, 478 U.S. 186 (1986).

33 *Lawrence v. Texas*, 576-577.

- Are there assumptions underlying the key factors or frameworks that are at odds with one another in the current fact pattern, or with what was widely believed to be true at the time the law was written or most recently interpreted?
- If so, within what framework, or from what perspective, are those aspects not in conflict?
- If the conflict cannot be reconciled, which value should prevail, for what reason, and to what intended consequence?

An advocate who has answered these questions will be equipped to identify, or create, a framework in which the key facts favour the advocated outcome. An advocate can use the framework when crafting legal arguments, proposing legislation, and framing issues in the media. Below, the questions above are applied to the sexting case at hand to reveal the frameworks that compete when an old law is applied under new circumstances.

The Status of This Case

The Circuit Court did not issue binding legal precedent on the issue of whether children can be prosecuted under the statute *Sexual Abuse of Children*, 18 Pa.C.S. § 6312 (hereafter referred to as 18 Pa.C.S. § 6312), for voluntarily appearing in pornographic self-portraits. The legal documents reflect a consensus, although not unanimous, that children cannot be prosecuted under the statute for producing pornographic self-portraits, for the same reasons (discussed below) that they cannot be prosecuted solely for agreeing to appear in child pornography despite an absence of coercion.[34] A review of these documents can yield insights that can inform the creation of constructive arguments regarding related matters.

The presence of an issue regarding the possible violation of First Amendment rights compelled the appellate court to 'conduct an independent examination of the factual record as a whole'.[35] When DA Skumanick appealed the lower court's issuance of the preliminary injunction, he filed an appellate brief in which he promised not to bring charges against Marissa Miller and Grace Kelly, and pursued issues relating to pressing charges against Nancy Doe and her mother, Jane Doe. The District Court pointedly did not issue a ruling regarding whether Nancy Doe's appearance in the photographs was a constitutionally protected activity.[36] In reviewing an appeal from a preliminary injunction the Circuit Court 'generally [does] not go into the merits any farther than is necessary to determine whether the moving party established a likelihood of success'.[37] Accordingly the Circuit Court, in the words of one newspaper columnist, 'decided not to decide'

34 See *Commonwealth v. Kitchen*, 814 A.2d 209 (Pa. Super. 2002).

35 *Miller v. Mitchell*, 598 F.3d 139, 145 (2010) (citation omitted).

36 *Miller v. Skumanick* (M.D.Pa. 2009). No. 3:09cv540. 30 March 2009, 23.

37 *Miller v. Mitchell*, 147.

whether the photos in the sexting case are constitutionally protected free speech (Gorenstein 2010).

Although neither party briefed the issue at hand before the Circuit Court,[38] the Court asked the parties to present a supplemental briefing regarding whether children can be prosecuted for charges stemming from appearing in child-pornography voluntarily, under 18 Pa.C.S. § 6312.[39] In its published opinion the Circuit Court commented on aspects of the arguments that attorneys made in the supplemental briefing and on related arguments the attorneys made in the prior TRO hearing.[40] The District Court also offered commentary, reflected in the transcript of the TRO hearing and in its published opinion, which offers insight into the potential that exists to present arguments with merit regarding this matter.

What Are the Arguments or Interpretations Asserted?

The ACLU argued that even if the photographs in question were deemed to be pornographic, by virtue of appearing in pornographic photographs the children are *per se* victims and as such are excluded by law from being prosecuted as producers or accomplices. The ACLU also argued, 'child pornography cannot occur in the absence of abuse of a real child in the making of the images'.[41]

DA Skumanick asserted that the plain language of 18 Pa.C.S. § 6312 does not distinguish between who took the picture and who appears in it, such that a child who takes a pornographic self-portrait can be prosecuted under the statute.[42]

What Key Factors – such as Identities, Roles, or Definitions – Are Implicit or Explicit in Those Assertions?

During the TRO hearing, the judge remarked, 'You know, it seems like the child here or the children seem to be the victim, the perpetrator and the accomplice. I mean, does that make any sense? How does that make sense?'[43] Thus the judge put a fine point on what media coverage consistently highlighted as a compelling incongruity and the crux of the problem facing courts, law enforcement officers, parents and children across the country.

Court documents reflect the variety of meanings and underlying assumptions that different parties in this legal action ascribed to the terms 'victim', 'perpetrator' and 'accomplice'. These meanings are applied explicitly and implicitly. The implicit meanings can be gleaned in the process of reconciling the incongruity

---

38 *Miller v. Mitchell*, 148.

39 *Miller v. Mitchell*, 148.

40 *Miller v. Mitchell*, 153.

41 *Miller et al. v. Skumanick* (2009) Appellees Brief, U.S. Court of Appeals Third Circuit, 32.

42 *Miller et al. v. Skumanick* (2009) Temporary Restraining Order Hearing, 2009, 64.

43 *Miller et al. v. Skumanick* (2009) Temporary Restraining Order Hearing, 2009, 62.

that exists for interpreters – be they judges, attorneys or parents – as they contrast the people upon whom the meanings have historically been applied and the circumstances to which they have been applied, to the people and circumstances to which they are being applied in the case at hand.

What Are the Prevailing and Emerging Meanings of Those Factors?

The prevailing meaning of the key terms 'victim', 'perpetrator' and 'accomplice' is reflected in Pennsylvania laws that consider children who appear in child pornography to be 'victims rather than perpetrators'.[44] Pennsylvania law considers a child's pornographic appearance in a photograph taken by another person, to constitute abuse.[45] The Pennsylvania statute regarding accomplice liability, *Crimes and Offenses; Liability for Conduct of Another* 18 Pa.C.S. § 306(f) (2008), states:

> Unless otherwise provided by this title or by the law defining the offense, a person is not an accomplice in an offense committed by another person if: (1) he is a victim of that offense; [or] (2) the offense is so defined that his conduct is inevitably incident to its commission.

The Anderson law dictionary defines 'inevitable' as 'that which cannot be foreseen or prevented, e.g., an accident'.

Pennsylvania common law deems that a child who appears in a pornographic image taken by another person is a 'victim', even if the child consents.[46] This interpretation of the statute was stated in the opinion of *Commonwealth v. Kitchen*, which the ACLU cited in their appellate brief.[47] In that case, the person who consented to be photographed when she was a child was, at the time the photographs were taken, old enough by law to consent to have sex with the man who took the photographs. She had consensual sex with him, lived with him, became pregnant by him, bore their child and raised the child with him.[48] The court pointed out that the pertinent state statute prohibits children from giving legally effective consent, and explained, '[O]ur legislature recognizes that the inexperience of youth prevent[s] intelligent judgment in matters of morality.'[49] The court stated, '[N]o one can legally take pornographic photographs of a child, regardless of whether the child consents.'[50] What set of values is honoured by referring to children as

44 *Miller et al. v. Skumanick* (2009) Appellees Brief, U.S. Court of Appeals Third Circuit, 13.

45 *Commonwealth v. Kitchen*, 814 A.2d 209, 213 (Pa. Super. 2002).

46 *Commonwealth v. Kitchen*, 213.

47 *Miller et al. v. Skumanick* (2009) Appellees Brief, U.S. Court of Appeals Third Circuit, 31.

48 See *Commonwealth v. Kitchen*, 212.

49 *Commonwealth v. Kitchen*, 213.

50 *Commonwealth v. Kitchen*, 213.

victims when they volunteer to appear in pornographic photographs, even self-portraits, but not when they volunteer to have sex, procreate or marry with adults?

Novel application of a definition is one hallmark of an emerging meaning. In this sexting case, DA Skumanick defined the girls as producers, or accomplices in the production of child pornography. The ACLU characterized this interpretation as 'well beyond the terms of the statute, or of any recorded application of it'.[51]

The ACLU argued that the children in the case at hand could not be prosecuted as accomplices because Pennsylvania law deems them to be victims in regard to the pornographic photographs in which they appear.[52] The ACLU simultaneously argued that prohibited 'child pornography cannot occur in the absence of abuse of a real child in the making of the images'.[53] Thus the ACLU juxtaposed the terms 'victim' and 'abuse'. The ACLU's reliance on *Ashcroft v. Free Speech Coalition* in support of the latter proposition is a novel application of the case.

In *Ashcroft* the US Supreme Court considered whether the federal statute 18 U.S.C. §2251, Child Pornography Prevention Act of 1996 (CPPA) violated the First Amendment right to freedom of speech. CPPA prohibited the creation, distribution or possession of 'sexually explicit images that appeared to depict minors but were produced without using any real children'.[54] The Court held the CPPA to be overbroad and unconstitutional;[55] in order to prosecute under federal law, the child pornography in question must have been produced using real children, not 'virtual' children. Pivotal to the court's ruling was the fact that no children were used to create the images in question; the court reasoned that the images were therefore created without the abuse of real children.

The facts of *Ashcroft* are distinct from *Miller*, but the case may still be instructive. *Ashcroft* did not raise the question of whether a child who takes a pornographic self-portrait has abused him- or her-self or committed a sexual offense, and the court did not comment on whether there are circumstances under which the use of a child to create child pornography would not constitute *per se* abuse. A dissenting opinion, however, contained an argument that could be used in future cases. Three of the seven Supreme Court justices dissented in part from the ruling above:

> The Court has long recognized that the Government has a compelling interest in protecting our Nation's children. This interest is promoted by efforts directed against sexual offenders and actual child pornography. These efforts, in turn, are

---

51 *Miller et al. v. Skumanick* (2009) Appellees Brief, U.S. Court of Appeals Third Circuit, 31.

52 *Miller et al. v. Skumanick* (2009) Appellees Brief, U.S. Court of Appeals Third Circuit, 32.

53 *Miller et al. v. Skumanick* (2009) Appellees Brief, U.S. Court of Appeals Third Circuit, 32.

54 *Ashcroft v. Free Speech Coalition*, 535 U.S. 234 (2002).

55 *Ashcroft v. Free Speech Coalition*, 258.

> supported by the CPPA's ban on virtual child pornography. Such images whet the appetites of child molesters[.][56]

Thus Justice Sandra Day O'Connor, Chief Justice William Rehnquist and Justice Antonin Scalia presented an argument in support of prohibiting child pornography that was made without intrinsically abusing children.[57]

The Juvenile Law Center (JLC), a non-profit organization located in Philadelphia, Pennsylvania, filed a brief as *amici curiae* in support of the ACLU's position. The JLC argued that in 'sexting', where children voluntarily take and distribute their own sexually explicit photographs, they are not 'exploited *victims*' as they are in 'conventional' child pornography.[58] They asserted, however, that a child who voluntarily takes and sends a 'sexting' photo of herself does become a 'victim of exploitation' if the photograph is then widely disseminated by other people.[59]

What Are the Frameworks – the Perspectives or World-views – that Give the Terms Their Prevailing and Emerging, or Contested, Meanings?

A common view reflected in the *amici* brief, media coverage and research articles is that the sexually suggestive photographs of teenagers that constitute 'sexting' are what happens when teenagers use cell phones as a vehicle for their 'expression of normal adolescent sexual exploration'.[60] During a televised interview that premiered on a major television network, broadcast journalist Julie Chen asked DA Skumanick if the *Miller* case wasn't just a case of 'kids being kids, not realizing they were committing a crime' (Chen 2009). Several newspaper accounts include quotes from adults to the effect that they would have done the same thing if the technology existed when they were young. What factors, if any, distinguish 'sexting' from 'child pornography' in popular culture and in the law?

The case of *New York v. Ferber*[61] was the first time that the US Supreme Court examined 'a statute directed at and limited to depictions of sexual activity involving children'.[62] The Court described the context in which federal and state prohibitions of child pornography were created:

> [C]hild pornography and child prostitution have become highly organized, multimillion dollar industries that operate on a nationwide scale. [Over 260]

---

56 *Ashcroft v. Free Speech Coalition*, 264.

57 *Ashcroft v. Free Speech Coalition*, 260.

58 Brief of Juvenile Law Center as Amici Curiae in Support of Appellees, *Miller et al. v. Skumanick* (2009), 16.

59 Brief of Juvenile Law Center as Amici Curiae in Support of Appellees, 16, n. 9.

60 Brief of Juvenile Law Center as Amici Curiae in Support of Appellees, 20.

61 *New York v. Ferber*, 458 U.S. 747 (1982).

62 *New York v. Ferber*, 753.

> magazines depict children, some as young as three to five years of age. … The activities featured range from lewd poses to … rape, incest and sado-masochism. In Los Angeles alone, police reported that 30,000 children have been sexually exploited (Citations omitted).[63]

The Court noted that states have a 'particular and more compelling interest in prosecuting those who promote the sexual exploitation of children'[64] and that accordingly, 20 states (including Pennsylvania) passed laws that 'prohibit the distribution of material depicting children engaged in sexual conduct without requiring that the material be legally obscene'.[65] Implicit was the belief that the people who exploited children to make child pornography were adults, or at least not the self-same children who appeared in the photographs. In the *Miller* case, DA Skumanick challenged this implicit assumption and asserted that the practice of sexting makes children vulnerable to sexual exploitation in many of the same ways as child pornography.

What Changes Have Occurred between the Time the Law First Came into Effect, or Significantly Was Reinterpreted, That May Account for the Present Legal Challenge?

The pivotal change that has occurred since the federal and state child pornography laws were passed is that many children now possess and regularly use camera cell phones, the internet, web-cameras and personal computers. These technologies were not accessible to the general public at the time the laws were passed in the 1970s and early 1980s. Cell phones are now so cheap that they are commonly given to children; in 2004, 18 per cent of American 12-year-olds surveyed owned a cell phone, and by 2009 that percentage increased to 59 per cent (Lenhart 2009: 2). As the National Crime Prevention Council put it, many teens now have lives on the internet. Other researchers note: 'Nearly 90% of youth aged 12 to 17 communicate via e-mail and 75% communicate via instant messaging, and nearly half (48%) report using these methods of communication every day' (Burgess-Proctor, Patchin and Hinduja 2009).

The second change is in new understandings in the field of neuroscience that are relevant to the issues at hand. Neuroscientists recognize that the physiology that has viewing pornographic images of children 'whet the appetite of child molesters'[66] is also at work in the brains of children. Due to mirror neurons, found in the pre-motor cortex, actions that children see and imagine may impact their brains almost as if they had taken the action. Neuroscientist V.S. Ramachandran explains:

63 *New York v. Ferber*, 781, n. 1.

64 *New York v. Ferber*, 761.

65 *New York v. Ferber*, 749.

66 *Ashcroft v. Free Speech Coalition*, 264.

> If I reach out and pull an object, [a] neuron will fire, commanding me to pull that object. These are called motor command neurons that have been known for a long time. [A] subset of these neurons, maybe about 20 percent of them, will also fire when [a viewer is] looking at somebody else performing the same action. So, here is a neuron that fires when I reach and grab something, but it also fires when I watch [someone else] reaching and grabbing something. And this is truly astonishing. Because it's as though this neuron is adopting the other person's point of view. It's almost as though it's performing a virtual reality simulation of the other person's action. (Ramachandran 2009)

A study of the effect of pornography on neuroanatomy demonstrated that 'looking at still pictures of naked people trigger[s] our mirror neurons into action, as the brain [pretends] that it [i]s actually having sex, and not just looking at smutty pictures' (Lehrer 2009, commenting on Ponseti et al. 2006).

The phenomenon of children exploring their sexuality by taking pornographic self-portraits and distributing them on the internet has a different impact on brain development than the comparatively private sexual explorations and expressions of children in the past. Norman Doidge, MD, states:

> The comparatively tame softcore pictures of yesteryear – women in various states of undress – now show up on mainstream media all day long, in the pornification of everything, including television, rock videos, soap operas, advertisements, and so on. … Softcore pornography's influence is now most profound because, now that it is no longer hidden, it influences young people with little sexual experience and especially plastic minds, in the process of forming their sexual tastes and desires. … Pornography, delivered by highspeed Internet connections, satisfies every one of the prerequisites for neuroplastic change. (Doidge 2007: 102-103)

Doidge defines 'neuroplasticity' as 'the idea that the brain can change its own structure and function through thought and activity' (Doidge 2007: xix). Children who view pornographic images of themselves or other children through 'sexting' or other means may, neurologically, have their brains and their expectations shaped by what they see. This may lend credence to the argument presented by justices in *Ashcroft*, that even child pornography made without intrinsically abusing children could be uniquely influential on and damaging to children.

Conclusion

The prohibition against children giving legally effective consent in posing for pornographic photographs was coupled with the assumption that a child who appeared in such a photograph was a victim of another person, ostensibly an adult. Access to technology has made it possible for children to create and distribute pornographic self-portraits, and some children are inclined to do so. In light of these developments it is necessary to reconsider the interpretation of the terms in, and the application of, legislation designed to protect children from sexual exploitation. The semiotic legal analysis presented in this chapter has identified a number of questions to consider, including: If a child initiates the creation and distribution of pornographic self-portraits, is the child a victim? If the child is a victim, of what or whom is the child a victim? Given that viewing child pornography is deemed to, in the words of the US Supreme Court, 'whet the appetites of child molesters',[67] what legal consequences if any should befall a child who distributes pornographic self-portraits? Are parents and legal guardians complicit if they provide their child with the technology used to create, distribute, save and view images of child pornography? If so, should parents be held liable?

Epilogue

In April 2009, it was reported that 54-year-old Georgia resident Steven Swanson, a businessman, husband and father of two, was slated to be extradited from Georgia to Tunkhannock, Pennsylvania for trial on five counts of criminal solicitation and corruption of minors (Koviack 2009). A parent who had received the letter that DA Skumanick sent to the parents of children in the school district decided to check her daughter's cell phone and found a photograph of her 14-year-old daughter, naked from the waist up.[68] An FBI investigation revealed that Swanson met the girl in a chat room on the internet, and from Georgia managed to coerce the girl into providing fully nude and sexually suggestive self-portraits. Swanson planned to travel to Pennsylvania to have sex with the girl for what would be her first sexual experience.

Meanwhile police in Pittsburgh, Pennsylvania investigated claims that a 16-year-old student downloaded over 50 images of child- and adult-pornography onto his cell phone and shared them at school (Monahan 2010). Police characterized the images as being 'deeply disturbing and very explicit' and said that some of them appeared to feature children as young as eight or nine years old. When asked why he did it, the boy replied, 'I have no idea.'

In November 2009, the citizens of Wyoming County, Pennsylvania voted DA Skumanick out of office (Wyoming County Press Examiner 2009).

In August 2010, Pennsylvania state representative Seth Grove proposed legislation to prohibit minors from sexting. The law would create penalties that range in severity 'from a summary offense much like a traffic ticket to felony charges' (Wilson 2010). Representative Grove framed the issue thus: 'The goal … is not to send children to juvenile jail for petty pranks but to create a law to protect them from themselves – and one another. We want to make sure these

67 *Ashcroft v. Free Speech Coalition*, 264.

68 *Miller et al. v. Skumanick* (2009) Reply Brief of Appellant, 10-11.

pictures don't victimize kids even more.' The Pennsylvania District Attorneys Association supports the legislation. Andy Hoover, legislative director for the ACLU of Pennsylvania, characterized the legislation as a 'law [that] would allow the government to overly intrude in children's lives'. He presented an alternative, though not mutually exclusive framework for the issue: 'Teaching kids about their sexuality is the job that belongs to parents and educators, not prosecutors.'

References

Balkin, J.M. 1991. 'The Promise of Legal Semiotics'. *University of Texas Law Review*, 69, 1831-1852.

Bazelon, E. 2010. 'How Not To Prosecute a Sexting Case'. *Slate*. [Online, 18 March]. Available at: http://www.slate.com/id/2248281/ [accessed 18 April 2010].

Berry, M.F. 1999. *The Pig Farmer's Daughter and other Tales of American Injustice: Episodes of Racism and Sexism in the Courts from 1865 to the Present*. New York: Knopf.

Bibas, S. 2009. 'Prosecutorial Regulation versus Prosecutorial Accountability'. *University of Pennsylvania Law Review*, 157(4), 959-1015.

Bostrom, M. 2005. *When Facts Don't Fit the Frame*. [Online: Frameworks Institute]. Available at: http://www.frameworksinstitute.org/assets/files/eZines/facts_don%27t_fit_the_frame.pdf [accessed 24 March 2010].

Bowker, A. and Sullivan, M. 2010. 'Sexting: Risky Actions and Overreactions'. *FBI Law Enforcement Bulletin*, 79(7), 27-31.

Burgess-Proctor, A., Patchin, J.W. and Hinduja, S. 2009. 'Cyberbullying and Online Harassment: Reconceptualizing the Victimization of Adolescent Girls', in *Female Victims of Crime: Reality Reconsidered*, edited by V. Garcia and J. Clifford. Upper Saddle River, NJ: Prentice Hall, 162-176.

Chen, J. 2009. *Teen Sues DA Over Sexting Case*. [Online: CBS News]. Available at: http://www.youtube.com/watch?v=Zhsl5j_BJk4 [accessed 30 June 2010].

Cleland, J.M. 2010. *Investigation of the Juvenile Justice Scandal in Luzerne County, Pennsylvania: Interbranch Commission on Juvenile Justice Final Report*. Philadelphia, PA: The Unified Judicial System of Pennsylvania.

Culp, C.V. 2009. 'Voters often Underinformed in DA Contests'. *Waco Tribune-Herald*. [Online, 14 December]. Available at: http://stage.www.wacotrib.com/news/Voters-often-underinformed-in-DA-contests.html [accessed 9 May 2010].

Davies, R. 1951. *Tempest-Tost*. Harmondsworth: Penguin.

Doidge, N. 2007. *The Brain That Changes Itself: Stories of Personal Triumph from the Frontiers of Brain Science*. New York: Penguin Books.

DuBois, A. and Sweitzer, B. 2010. *Anders Briefs and Related Issues on Appeal*. [Online]. Available at http://fd.org/pdf_lib/Anders_Briefs.pdf [accessed 28 November 2010].

Gorenstein, N. 2010. 'Court Averts Free-Speech Issue on "Sexting"'. *Philadelphia Inquirer*, 18 March, B1.

Koviack, D.C. 2009. 'Georgia Man To Be Extradited on Child Porn Charges'. *The Rocket-Courier*, 30 April.

Lehrer, Jonah. 2009. *Porn and Mirror Neurons*. [Online: The Frontal Cortex]. Available at: http://scienceblogs.com/cortex/2009/08/porn_and_mirror_neurons.php [accessed 15 December 2010].

Lenhart, A. 2009. *Teens and Sexting: How and Why Minor Teens Are Sending Sexually Suggestive Nude or Nearly Nude Images via Text Messaging*. Washington, DC: Pew Research Center.

Monahan, F.R. 2010. 'This just in: April 22-29'. *Pittsburgh City Paper*. [Online, 22 April]. Available at: http://www.pittsburghcitypaper.ws/gyrobase/Content?oid=oid%3A78230 [accessed 1 July 2010].

Pennsylvania District Attorneys Association. 2010. 'Press Release: Pennsylvania District Attorneys Respond to ACLU's Opposition to Commonsense Changes in "sexting" law', 4 February.

Ponseti, J., Bosinski, H.A., Wolff, S., Peller, M., Jansen, O., Mehdorn, H.M., Büchel, C. and Siebner H.R. 2006. 'A Functional Endophenotype for Sexual Orientation in Humans'. *NeuroImage*, 33(3), 825-833.

Ramachandran, V.S. 2009. *The Neurons That Shaped Civilization*. [Online: TED]. Available at http://www.ted.com/talks/vs_ramachandran_the_neurons_that_shaped_civilization.html [accessed 4 October 2010].

Rudolf, M.J. and Baker, R.L. 2009. 'Vanston, Skumanick Leaving after Two Decades'. *Wyoming County Press Examiner*. [Online, 30 December]. Available at: http://wcexaminer.com/?p=7421 [accessed 28 November 2010].

Wilson, T. 2010. Pa. Working to Outlaw Teen Sexting'. *Philadelphia Inquirer*. [Online, 2 August]. Available at: http://www.philly.com/philly/news/homepage/20100802_Pa__working_to_outlaw_teen__sexting_.html?viewAll=y [accessed 2 August 2010].

Wyoming County Press Examiner. 2009. *You Be the Judge*. [Online, 30 December]. Available at: http://wcexaminer.com/?p=7425 [accessed 1 July 2010].

Acknowledgements

Thank you to Professors Jan Broekman and Anne Wagner, who made this possible, and to Professors William Butler, Jay Mootz and William Pencak for their encouragement. Editor Christoph Hafner deftly identified for deletion all the parts that no one wants to read. I am indebted to Jennifer Bonacci, Thomas J. Cordaro, Lea Clark, R.T. Peck, Janet Syphan, Holly O. Vaughn and Eric Wirth for their assistance. Julie Mickens graciously bestowed the benefits of her keen eye and journalistic expertise. Above all, I am grateful to Madeleine Hershey for her love, insight, encouragement and generosity. Her astute reading and material contributions to drafts helped me bridge the gap. All errors are my own.

Chapter 10
Visualizing the Terrorist Risk in President Bush's War on Terror and Peter Jackson's *The Two Towers*

Anita Lam

Introduction

> I know. It's all wrong. By rights we shouldn't even be here. But we are. It's like in the great stories, Mr Frodo, the ones that really mattered. Full of darkness and danger they were. And sometimes you didn't want to know the end. Because how could the end be happy? How could the world go back to the way it was when so much bad had happened? (Jackson 2002)

> The last time I spoke here, I expressed the hope that life would return to normal. In some ways, it has. In others, it never will. Those of us who have lived through these challenging times have been changed by them. We've come to know truths that we will never question: evil is real, and it must be opposed. (Bush 2002a)

> … and night fell on a different world. (Bush 2001b)

As night fell on 11 September 2001, it was said to have fallen on a different world, one in which everything had changed irrevocably. Following this theme of irrevocable change, post-9/11 America was represented as a world apart from the nostalgically remembered pre-9/11 America – namely, as a world in which the experience of vulnerability, insecurity and suffering was brought unexpectedly home to a developed nation previously lulled by the promise of an ever-safer world. This experience was burned into the flood of images surrounding the media depictions of the events of 11 September 2001 and subsequent depictions of the al-Qaeda terrorists in grossly simplified enemy images (Beck 2002). Al-Qaeda terrorism became used as *the* case study to redefine terrorism as a risk beyond price (Ericson 2007), which fed into a reconceptualization of the political significance of imagining the future in the United States (De Goede 2008). In post-9/11 America, risk has become an all-encompassing term through which the state imagines and acts as if it knows the future and can do something about it, even though this future is thought to contain ungovernable and statistically unpredictable catastrophes (Ericson 2007). To avoid another terrorist attack caused by the state's 'failure of the imagination' (National Commission on Terrorist Attacks upon the United States 2004), the American state needs to engage its catastrophic imagination[1] (Clarke 2006), by imagining the worst possible interpretation of future events.

In this chapter I explore the semiotics of a particular formulation of the catastrophic imagination, by asking the following question: what visual and discursive signs are deployed immediately after the events of 11 September 2001 in order to help the American mass audience imagine the terrorist risk, thus enabling certain kinds of state action? In answering this question, I investigate a particular moment of synergy between political culture and popular culture, in which the catastrophic risk of al-Qaeda terrorism became culturally resonant due to the intertextual relations between former President George W. Bush's official political narrative of the War on Terror and Peter Jackson's film adaptation of J.R.R. Tolkien's *The Lord of the Rings: The Two Towers* (2002). It will be argued that the paratext formed by the film's marketing campaign was implicitly shaped by the moral-political rhetoric used in President George W. Bush's public speeches about the War on Terror. Because this marketing paratext frames a particular reading of the filmic narrative, *The Two Towers* will be analysed as a conscious piece of fiction that reproduces, in cinematic terms, the risky type associated with the al-Qaeda terrorist. Because President Bush's speeches also informed anti-terrorist policies, this chapter will end with an analysis of the film's visualization of the Eye of Sauron, which parallels the US Department of Defense's visualization of its counter-terrorist surveillance programme, the Total Information Awareness (TIA) programme. The military programme invoked the spectre of a global surveillance state in its attempt to make all terrorist threats transparent to a sovereign state power that could then presumably control and govern such threats.

Risk and the Catastrophic Imagination

With the rise of risk management in the 1990s, the concept of risk has become pervasive in political discourse, organizational communications and everyday practices. The basic idea underlying the concept is simple. Risk refers to threats or dangers attributed to persons, technologies or nature. This threat is articulated as a probability about whether it will manifest as adverse consequences for a specified party or not. It is important to note that designating something as a risk or someone as risky can have legal implications. Because risk is a multidimensional concept, legal implications can vary depending on the manifestation of risk. The authority

1 Similarly, Richard Grusin (2004) uses the term premediation to refer to the particularly post-9/11 and American practice of imagining or mapping out as many possible futures as can be plausibly imagined. This practice of imagining the future has been tied to techniques of risk management (De Goede 2008), particularly in the management of terrorist risks.

with power and control over a particular risk varies with the manifestation of that risk.

According to John Adams (2003), risk can have three distinct manifestations. First, risk can be directly perceptible. For example, the al-Qaeda terrorist risk could be directly observed by the American public through repeated news footage of the hijacked planes crashing into the Twin Towers. It can be argued that, as a result of its widespread perceptibility, this was the precise moment at which the al-Qaeda terrorist risk became real for most of the American public. Law tends to be the authoritative means through which directly perceptible risks can be controlled, but as such, is only a reactive response to such risks. Secondly, risks can also be perceived through science, a perspective not privy to laypersons but instead managed by professional experts. The TIA programme, run by the US military and its attendant professionals (discussed later in this chapter), can be considered an institutional attempt to manage the future risks associated with terrorists, such as al-Qaeda, through quantified probabilities of future terrorist attacks. Lastly, the third category of risk – virtual risk – is one in which the veneer of sufficient knowledge is stripped away since it comes about in the context of uncertain scientific knowledge. Virtual risks may or may not be real, but they have real consequences if a sufficient number of people believe them to be true. Specifically, the virtual nature of the terrorist risk involves the anticipation of intentional catastrophe (Ericson 2006, 2007), and it is this anticipation of collective threat that underlines exhortations to engage the catastrophic imagination as a proactive means for prevention.

While Geoffrey Skoll (2007) argues that the state shapes the meaning of and public discourses on terrorism through the law, law seems to be most applicable to directly perceptible (past) acts of terrorism, rather than virtual (future-oriented) terrorist risks. Instead, it can be argued that law 'failed' to imagine the terrorist events until they had passed, not taking any lessons from various Hollywood disaster films that had rehearsed the coming catastrophe.[2] What is particularly noteworthy about the post-9/11 American cultural landscape is the dominance of the catastrophic imagination, which is now used as a security technique to visualize virtual, catastrophic risks (e.g. terrorism). Because cultural work is not only performed by security experts and policymakers but also by the entertainment

2 This general argument notes how similar the events of 9/11 are to the events imaged in fictional Hollywood disaster movies. For example, Baudrillard (2001) claims that these Hollywood films have fostered a particularly American hyperreality that has influenced images and ideas of global terrorism. Similar arguments have been made by Masco (2008), Petersen (2005) and Žižek (2002). Methodologically, this general argument tends to trace representations of large-scale catastrophe to pre-9/11 Hollywood films, suggesting that it was not a 'failure of imagination' *per se* that doomed America. Instead, 'failure' lay in the shortcomings of a particular imagination that dismissed certain eerily prescient pop cultural representations (e.g. Tom Clancy's novel *Executive Orders*, and Edward Zwick's film *The Siege*) as merely 'entertainment' (Salter 2008).

industries, the catastrophic imagination is not an area monopolized by law alone. Instead, it builds on the language of risk and risk management (Salter 2008), and is at least partially formulated and informed by Hollywood representations of catastrophe. As Joseph Masco (Masco 2008) writes that popular Hollywood nuclear films of the 1980s and 1990s informed contemporary American security culture, by building the nation through the image of itself in ruins, it is important to note that films offer a means of representing the ultimately unrepresentable (e.g. large-scale catastrophe). As such, they are also a premier means for making visible the invisible al-Qaeda terrorist (Watts 2006), especially since this 'new' terrorist threat is characterized by the sleeper cell scenario (Ericson 2007). For example, Der Derian (2005: 30) describes how shortly after 9/11, the Californian Institute for Creative Technologies gathered Hollywood screenwriters and directors to 'create possible terrorist scenarios that could be played out in their Marina del Ray virtual reality facilities'. In short, the filmic images of terrorist and the aftermath of terrorist attacks stood in for the inevitable failure of the imagination to conceive of the end of a society or a nation (Masco 2008).

As context (here understood as a combination of culture and history) gave meaning to the terrorist event (Skoll 2007), it also gave meaning to the catastrophic imagination. That is, the cultural context expands and contracts the imagination, which serves as a reservoir for virtual 'worst case' scenarios (Clarke 2006). Given the cultural contingency of the catastrophic imagination, the scope and content of the imagination varies in different times and places, particularly under different pop cultural and sociopolitical contexts. In the context of post-9/11 America, Peter Jackson's filmic adaptation of *The Two Towers* cinematically translates the virtual terrorist risk into a directly perceptible risk on the big screen for a mass audience, and as such offers an observable manifestation of how this risk was imagined in dramatic and catastrophic terms. And it is to this culturally resonant representation of the terrorist risk in *The Two Towers* that I will now turn.

Peter Jackson's *The Two Towers*: Interpretation and Paratext

Peter Jackson's film adaptation of *The Two Towers*, the second instalment in *The Lord of the Rings* trilogy, opened in theatres in North America on 18 December 2002. While the film garnered both enormous box office success[3] (indeed, it still is one of the highest grossing films of all time) and almost-across-the-board critical success (as measured by positive film reviews) at the time of its release, its reception in 2010 can be considered a little less enthusiastic. Nearly a decade after the theatrical release of *The Two Towers* and the events of 9/11, critical re-evaluation of the film in 'end of the decade best of' lists of films made between

3 Of the $900 million dollars that the film has grossed in worldwide ticket sales, one-third of this amount was accounted for by domestic ticket sales (e.g. U.S. and Canada) according to Box Office Mojo (www.boxofficemojo.com).

2000 and 2009 suggests that *The Lord of the Rings* trilogy rarely made the cut. While Jackson's trilogy seemed like the dominant movie-going experience in the first half of the millennial decade, the world has since changed:

> Maybe the immense hype surrounding the trilogy's release and all the attendant marketing burned itself out … Maybe the context in which the films were launched – the early Bush era, just after 9/11, when the 'War on Terror' hadn't yet become a dreary mixture of Orwellian gag-line and grinding reality – is now so deep in the cultural past that the movies have lost the invisible penumbra of meaning that seemed so strong at the time. (O'Hehir 2010)

I want to take seriously the possibility that what made *The Two Towers*[4] so meaningful to a post-9/11 American audience, and subsequently what made the film so successful at that time but not as much now, was its cultural resonance with public discourse shortly after 11 September. In order to understand the cultural resonance of *The Two Towers* at this particular moment in time, I would like to consider understanding as interpretation within a temporal distance, taking some cues from Hans-Georg Gadamer. That is, my inquiry is an attempt to 'clarify the conditions in which understanding takes place' (Gadamer 1975: 263), where an examination of those conditions entails an examination of the pre-conceptions in the mind of the interpreter. This Gadamerian framework assumes that understanding is not simply a reproductive but productive process, and that it is produced by particular interpreters. The following analysis takes the film's American marketers as the interpreters of note: they produce a marketing paratext that frames a particular understanding of the film, which in turn reproduces the pre-conceptions of the official political narrative of the War on Terror. That is, the marketers' pre-conceptions are likely to have included the President's political speeches, which were floating around in the collective conscious of public culture during the film's marketing campaign.

Generally, a paratext is a secondary text that is used to position the primary text – here, the film – in ways that will influence its reception (Genette 1997). In film marketing, the paratext precedes the film's release and can serve to frame a reading of the film itself. In creating the film's paratext, marketers do not necessarily create national concepts and feelings so much as tap into what already exists. As a couple of clever marketers once said, 'To be successful today, you must touch base with reality. And the reality that counts is what's already in the prospect's mind' (Ries and Jack 1986: 5). The reality that counted most in the context leading up to this particular film's theatrical release was America's War on Terror. Moreover, it is plausible to conceive of the film's marketing as acknowledging this particular reality since the marketing division of New Line Cinema, the company responsible

4 *The Two Towers* is also an interesting case study because Peter Jackson filmed the entire *Lord of the Rings* trilogy between 1999 and 2000, such that principal photography occurred prior to 9/11. However, the films themselves were released into a post-9/11 context.

for distributing *The Two Towers*, is itself American.[5] From a temporal perspective in which cause precedes effect, President George W. Bush's speeches precede the film release of *The Two Towers*, which suggests that it is the American audience's reception and interpretation of the film that connects the two narratives. That is, *The Two Towers* is not a deliberate piece of fiction that attempts to portray the reality of terrorism *per se*, but it can be interpreted as such.[6]

Two elements of the film's paratext are especially significant: the film's title and its tagline. Although the film title, *The Two Towers*, refers to Tolkien's novel published in 1954, roughly five decades prior to the 9/11 attacks, it is noteworthy that this title actually hit cultural nerves in 2002 as some Americans interpreted it as a reference to the Twin Towers of the World Trade Center. Shortly prior to the film's official release, a petition had appeared online to rally support for 'renaming *The Two Towers* to something less offensive' (Klerck 2001). Addressed to Peter Jackson, the petition, garnering approximately 4,000 signatures, claimed that it was morally repugnant and unforgivable for a film title to reference the attacks on the World Trade Center in a post-9/11 world. Although Peter Jackson himself had at one point considered changing the film title in the aftermath of the terrorist attacks (Sherwin and Jack 2002), it is noteworthy that no change in title resulted despite the heightened cultural sensitivity that characterized the post-9/11 film-making environment, especially circa 2001 to 2002, in which cinematographic shots of the Twin Towers were digitally removed from the background shots of other major feature films (e.g. *Spider-Man* and *Collateral Damage*).

As the film's title potentially alluded to the Twin Towers, *The Two Towers*' tagline sold the film as 'an epic adventure of good and evil set in a time of uncertainty' (New Line Cinema 2002). As the middle segment of a film trilogy, in which the beginning had passed and the ending had yet to manifest, *The Two Towers* represented that 'time of uncertainty', and in doing so also reflected the uncertain limbo in which post-9/11 America found itself, a time at which the beginning of the War on Terror had been declared but the end of this war had yet to manifest. This experiential theme of uncertainty underlies both the notion of virtual risk (Adams 2003) and the terrorist risk in particular, especially if terrorism is understood to be the politics of uncertainty (De Goede 2008; Ericson 2007). If the paratext formed by the film's marketing campaign ensured that the film would resonate with its American audience, it can also be said to highlight the film's three particular intertextual references to the Bush administration's official political narrative regarding the War on Terror, hereafter referred to in shorthand as the Bush narrative.

---

5 While it is often noted that much of the production of *The Lord of the Rings* film trilogy made use of Australian and New Zealander talent, its primary marketing campaign was designed by an American company.

6 It has been noted that fictional entertainment programmes are able to more accurately portray the reality of terrorism than the news, especially in cases where there are state-imposed legal restrictions on interviewing terrorists (Schlesinger et al. 1983).

The Epic Adventure: Apocalypse and the Present

As stories that predict the end of the world, apocalyptic stories are prominently featured in contemporary American politics, risk discourse and speculative fiction, of which *The Two Towers* is an example. The impulse to 'save the world', explicitly found in speculative fiction and implicitly found in risk discourse, can only come from a Judeo-Christian and Western culture[7] that believes that the world can end, because it conceives of history – with its linearly constructed temporal categories of past, present and future – as a vector bound to 'time's arrow' (Delumeau 1999). From this premise of saving the world and thus saving the future, we need to note two things: what is entailed by the concepts of 'world' and the 'future'. In this instance of post-9/11 America, the 'world' is understood to mean treasured ways of being. The 11 September terrorist attacks were understood as attacks on 'our [American] way of life, our very freedom' (Bush 2001a). Similarly, in his attempt to persuade the otherwise peaceable Ents to war, Merry understands the War of the Ring to be necessary in preserving 'all that was once green and good in this world' (Jackson 2002). For Merry, a hobbit, 'all that is green and good' is symbolized by his home and his way of life in the (green) Shire.

In representing an implied future, it is noteworthy that both *The Two Towers* and the Bush administration begin their narratives *in medias res* (i.e. in the middle of the story) and in doing so, mark their narratives as epic in the format set down by the Ancient Greek Homeric poems. With this format of starting in the middle, the present is articulated and understood only in relation to a particular understanding of the past and an imagined future. *The Two Towers* articulates its present as a re-enactment of a past task (i.e. the destruction of the One True Ring and with it, the Dark Lord Sauron) that ought to be accomplished successfully if Middle-earth is to have a good future. Similarly, for America, their past has defined where they currently (and proactively) stand in relation to the terrorist threat: 'This nation [US], in world war and in Cold War, has never permitted the brutal and the lawless to set history's course' (Bush 2002b). As the 'brutal and lawless' terrorists are deemed 'heirs of all the murderous ideologies of the 20th century … [following] in the path of fascism, and Nazism' (Bush 2001b), the terrorist threat is represented as continuing the threat of previous enemies faced by the United States of America – namely, enemies that America has successfully defeated before. Moreover, it is America's present response to the terrorist threat that will rewrite its future, as 'our country will define our times, not be defined by them' (Bush 2001b).

---

7 Other cultural-religious systems (e.g. the religion of the Ancient Greeks, Hinduism and Buddhism) conceive of a cyclical course of affairs rather than a linear understanding of time as past, present and future.

Good versus Evil; Light versus Darkness

In considering the Bush narrative as one that is written through a series of political events of speech-giving, it should be noted that the development of such a political event depends on a dialectic interaction between its political imperative and its moral-aesthetic imperatives (Wagner-Pacifici 1986). In the case of the Bush administration's political handling of the War on Terror, the political imperative – a narrative about risk management decisions – interacts with an aesthetic-moral imperative derived from Apocalyptic Christianity. Like *The Two Towers*, the Bush narrative can also be read as a symbolic tale modelled on Armageddon, the final battle of good and evil foretold in the Book of Revelation.

As Tolkien, regularly described as a 'devout Christian' (Rearick 2004), built his possible world with reference to a Judeo-Christian moral framework, the world envisioned in the Bush narrative alludes to the same system of morality, largely because George W. Bush is a president known for carrying his Christian faith into his public service (Singer 2004). As a result, the Bush narrative understands good and evil in Christian terms, using the binary construction of good versus evil to cleave the world into two 'Fellowships'. As the Fellowship fighting for and on the side of 'Good', America and its civilized allies are opposed to 'an axis of evil' (i.e. Iraq, Iran and Korea) (Bush 2002a), which serves as a breeding ground for terrorists. In this conflict of good and evil, 'there is no neutral ground' (Bush 2001c): 'either you are with us [America], or you are with the terrorists [axis of evil]' (Bush 2001b). Cinematically reproducing this binary worldview, *The Two Towers* pits the Fellowship of the Ring against the dark forces of Sauron. Although there are many towers in *The Two Towers*, the film's title refers to the union of Barad-dûr and Orthanc. As the Dark Lord Sauron rules atop Barad-dûr and his second-in-command, the Dark Wizard Saruman rules from the tower of Orthanc, the union of these two particular towers constitutes an 'axis of evil' against which the Fellowship of the Ring battles. While the Fellowship of the Ring might be considered an instance of transnational cooperation (e.g. it unites the races of Hobbit, Man, Dwarf and Elf into a single alliance), it is primarily premised on the old Western Alliance between humans and elves (Jackson 2003). The term 'Western Alliance' has a particular resonance in the post-9/11 context, particularly in terms of how America has conceived of her allies such that 'civilized nations' are largely defined as being Western nations.

In politically designating terrorists as 'evil' enemies of the United States of America, President George W. Bush asserts that this evil has a face that can be seen (Bush 2001a). Because evil can be seen, it is not some intangible, subjective moral perspective, but something that is real (Bush 2002a). Following the argument that 'seeing is believing', evil becomes something beyond metaphysical speculation: evil becomes ultimately visual, visible and observable. The visual then is not only sovereign among the senses, but particularly implicated in the representational practices that make state sovereignty possible (Amoore 2007). If a state's security is dependent on its representational practices that can identify and delineate 'us' from 'them', then it requires a visuality that can classify and categorize people into images and imaginaries (Amoore 2007). Thus, the political narrative about the War on Terror maps the battle between good ('us') and evil ('them') with imagery, particularly the images of light versus darkness. In doing so, this choice of visually transparent[8] imagery coincides with representations of the forces of good versus evil in *The Two Towers*.

The moral and aesthetic imperatives of political narrative intertwine when the imagery of light and darkness are understood in a Judeo-Christian framework. When America is understood as a beacon of light that 'no one will keep … from shining' (Bush 2001a), and the terrorists are associated with areas of darkness (i.e. 'caves and other entrenched hiding places') (Bush 2001b), the battle of good and evil is essentially visualized as a battle of light against darkness. Within the Judeo-Christian moral landscape, the use of terms such as darkness comes from scriptural images, in which darkness characterizes an individual's alliance with evil.[9] In *The Two Towers*, the Uruk-hai, Orcs under the command of the Dark Wizard Saruman, are represented as monsters born from the mud of Isengard's cave-like underground. In contrast to the appearance of the White Wizard Gandalf – a wizard with brilliantly white hair, garbed in white robes, and armed with a white staff and a white steed (Shadowfax) – who heads the Caucasian-looking Fellowship of the Ring, these Orcs constitute a 'risky' type due to their semiotic connection with the dark and the dirty. In visually translating Tolkien's light and dark imagery to the silver screen, Peter Jackson has created a white-and-black colour coding of 'good' forces and 'evil' forces.[10] That is, the forces of evil visually appear dark: the ugly Orcs, foot-soldiers of the forces of darkness, have charred skin, bleed black blood, and can only labour and battle under the cover of darkness.[11] The dark and hideous appearance of the Orcs is an easy marker of their 'evil' status, harking back to the same types of 'observations'

8 Here, I am using 'transparent' as a synonym for 'easily seen through or detected' because of obvious visual manifestations. In doing so, I'm highlighting how 'transparency' has been linked to the visual through its association with photography. For example, the *Oxford English Dictionary* defines transparency as 'a picture, print, inscription, or device on some translucent substance, made visible by means of a light behind'.

9 Yet the imagery of light and darkness can also take on different meanings. For example, the light can also symbolize the pure and the clean, whereas the dark represents the impure and the dirty. From Mary Douglas' anthropological perspective (Douglas 1966), dirt is essentially disorder in the eyes of its beholder. If terrorism is understood to be intentional catastrophe, then it intends to disrupt the (Western) world as we know it. In disrupting the order of the world, in which liberty is coded as purity in the American language and context, terrorists can be symbolized by dirt and represented as pollutants (Hacking 2003).

10 As part of the film's marketing campaign, the New Line Cinema website for *The Lord of the Rings* actually separates the cultures of Middle-earth into belonging to either the Forces of light (here visibly white) or the Forces of darkness (www.lordoftherings.net/legend/cultures/).

11 According to the 'Orc Facts' provided by the official *Lord of the Rings* website, the cannibalistic Orcs weaken in sunlight, only enjoy the pain of others, and are visibly hideous (www.lordoftherings.net/legend/cultures/).

used by 19th century anthropology. Specifically, this early form of criminal anthropology assumed that monstrosity manifested on the body, and could then be read from the body (Cole 2001), which is not so very different from the Bush administration's claim that evil is similarly visible and identifiable. As charges of racism have been flung as a result of Jackson's particular use of colour-coding in his visual representation of the races of Middle-earth (Whitaker 2006), similar charges have been made with respect to the targeted treatment of Muslim, Middle-Eastern and South Asian men following the 9/11 attacks in the United States (Mathur 2006). While Tolkien alluded to literary-moral archetypes associated with light and darkness in *The Lord of the Rings*, the cinematic translation of these archetypes proves problematic in much the same way that visual translations of the Bush narrative can lead to state implementation of policies that include an element of racial profiling (e.g. surveillance of Muslim neighbourhoods and mosques, and the random questioning and detaining of Muslim men by the FBI) (Bonikowiki 2005).

In writing President Bush's 'axis of evil' speech, speechwriter David Frum suggests that 'in a country, where almost two-thirds of the population believes in the devil, Bush was identifying Osama bin Laden and his gang as literally satanic' (Singer 2004: 208). As President Bush is credited with spearheading the rise of the Christian Right in contemporary post-9/11 America, it should be noted that fundamentalist religiosity has been integral to the portrayal of 'evil' terrorists and to precautionary logic in American political culture (Dershowitz 2006; Ericson 2007). The precautionary logic is articulated by President George W. Bush in the following excerpted speech:

> Understanding the threats of our time, knowing the designs and deceptions of the Iraqi regime, we have every reason to assume the worst, and we have an urgent duty to prevent the worst from occurring … There is no easy or risk-free course of action. Some have argued we should wait – and that's an option. In my view, it's the riskiest of all options, because the longer we wait, the stronger and bolder Saddam Hussein will become. (Bush 2002b)

As the precautionary logic has legitimated pre-emptive strikes on the enemy, it has justified the American mission to discover and destroy Iraq's 'weapons of mass destruction' before these weapons can be used against the United States. Similarly, the Fellowship of the Ring's mission is essentially pre-emptive. The Fellowship is united in preventing the Dark Lord Sauron from rising and taking corporeal form. In destroying the One True Ring, the Fellowship is destroying Sauron's 'weapon of mass destruction' – that is, the ultimate source of his power – and with it, the possibility that Sauron can use the Ring to 'make the last war that will cover all the world in shadow' (Jackson 2002: Smeagol), even though this 'shadow' alludes to metaphorical darkness rather than the shadow of a 'mushroom cloud' feared by President Bush (Bush 2002b). In short, both narratives emphasize the necessity of carrying out pre-emptive missions in order to 'save the world', justifying their missions through precautionary logic and the ability to easily visualize the dark and evil enemy.

The All-Seeing Eye: Surveillance and the Total Information Awareness Programme

While the Bush narrative of the War on Terror closely follows the film's paratext of being an 'epic adventure of good and evil set in a time of uncertainty', the film additionally captures the technological dream of post-9/11 American surveillance schemes as one particular way to resolve that uncertainty. In short, *The Two Towers*' representation of the Eye of Sauron parallels the visualization of the Total Information Awareness (TIA) programme. Revealed to the world in 2002 – the same year that *The Two Towers* was released – the TIA project was an example of a counter-terrorism programme that served the Bush administration's goal of strengthening the nation's intelligence capabilities 'to know the plans of terrorists before they act, and [to] find them before they strike' (Bush 2001b). Originating from the US Department of Defense, it was a programme for researching, developing and integrating technologies to virtually aggregate data across different sources of surveillance, and to mine these data for the purpose of producing risk profiles on terrorists and terrorist groups, based on which proactive action could be taken (Whitaker 2006). As a central data mining system, the TIA project symbolized the totalizing potential of a global surveillance state (Whitaker 2006), putting it in line with how Jackson has portrayed the Eye of Sauron as representative of the panoptic gaze. Michel Foucault (Foucault 1977) describes the panoptic gaze as the ideal surveillance mechanism, by drawing out these implications from Jeremy Bentham's Panopticon, an architectural design for a model prison. In the Panopticon ('All-Seeing'), there is a peripheric ring in which the inmate is totally seen without ever seeing his or her gazers. In the tall, central tower at the centre of this peripheric ring, the prison guard sees all the inmates without ever being seen himself or herself. In constructing this panoptic surveillance apparatus – what Foucault has called a 'house of certainty' (Foucault 1977: 202) – it reasserts a measure of control through some degree of certainty, which has been described as sorely lacking in the case of terrorism, or the politics of uncertainty (Ericson 2007).

In examining the cinematic representation of the Eye of Sauron, it is remarkable how its visual components are also used in the logo of the TIA programme. Both highlight how surveillance is a panoptical formula of power through transparency (Cole 2001), where transparency is metaphorically related to representations of light. The striking similarities between the Eye of Sauron and the logo of the TIA programme, both of which image/imagine surveillance as an extension of the eye of the sovereign, include the following.

First, there is a depiction of the All-Seeing Eye, which morally alludes to the All-Seeing Eye of God (in some ways, the ultimate sovereign) as it sits atop an incredibly tall architectural structure. In *The Two Towers*, the (mostly) incorporeal

Sauron is represented by a large, fiery eye that is suspended between the (devilish) horns found at the top of the 5,000 feet-tall tower of Barad-dûr in Mordor (the Dark Land). The All-Seeing Eye is represented in its Americanized form in the TIA logo as an eye embedded at the apex of a pyramid and from which light radiates, which is a symbol that is also found on the back of the American dollar bill. From observing the logo, one could interpret the pyramid as being especially tall because it is represented as slightly larger than the image of the globe. Both Eyes capitalize on a top-down approach to surveillance, which reiterates the word's French etymology (*sur* + *veiller* = to watch from above).

Second, the All-Seeing Eye is scanning the world: in the TIA logo, the world is represented by a globe; whereas in *The Two Towers*, the Eye of Sauron scans the flat surface of Middle-earth. Third, the Eye scans the world with a beam of light. As the Eye of Sauron scans the Middle-earth with a red beam of light for the One True Ring, the TIA Eye scans the globe with a yellow beam of light, in which case the image of the light might include semiotic associations to moral goodness and purity. Fourth, while the Eye is theoretically All-Seeing, its gaze (as operationalized by the geographical location of its light scan) is restricted to 'dark' areas of the world. In *The Return of the King* (2003), the third instalment of the film trilogy, the Eye of Sauron has been envisioned as the 'lighthouse of Mordor'. That is, the Eye's roving gaze is only depicted as scanning the Dark Land of Mordor for the Ring. Similarly, the TIA Eye is shedding light on the 'dark' area of the world: rather than scanning Western countries (e.g. North America, Australia and Western Europe), it is scanning Africa, the Middle East and Asia, presumably geographical locations that have been associated with the 'axis of evil'. If recent military interventions in the Third World are seen as violent attempts to expand America's surveillance coverage into obscure threatening corners of the world, then the imagery of 'darkness' has an additional meaning. In contrast to the luminosity and transparence of the developed world, the darkness associated with the less developed world results from their being less plugged into sophisticated communications technologies and networks (Whitaker 2006).

While the One True Ring in *The Lord of the Rings* has often been interpreted as a metaphor for the corruption of absolute power, its particular visualization in *The Two Towers* suggests an additional meaning, one that is related to surveillance schemes such as the TIA programme. Functionally speaking, wearing the Ring does not necessarily accord its wearers power *per se*. Instead, the Ring's effect is to make the wearer invisible to the world, but hypervisible to the Eye of Sauron. In drawing the All-Seeing Eye's gaze and commanding its attention, the Ring functions as a tracking device for surveillance technologies. As a piece of jewellery connected to a surveillance apparatus, the Ring has real-world analogues. For example, individuals serving their sentences in the community have worn ankle bracelets for electronic monitoring purposes. In certain instances, these ankle bracelets have been hooked up to the all-seeing gaze of a global-positioning satellite system that determines where the individual is geographically located at any one moment in time. By putting its wearer under targeted surveillance, the One True Ring provides its sovereign controller (i.e. Sauron) with what Michel Foucault has called power-knowledge (Foucault 1980), so that power and knowledge are inextricably linked to disciplinary technologies, such as the panoptic gaze of surveillance. This interpretation is facilitated by reading the TIA programme's motto – '*Scientia est potentia*' ('knowledge *is* power': a statement that equates knowledge with power) – as neatly summing up the goal of surveillance technologies in post-9/11 America. That is, since the terrorist risk was conceived in America as resulting from an informational deficit (Ericson 2007), the solution was to ensure that the state never lacked such knowledge again, tying the power of the state to unprecedented powers of surveillance (here understood as *the* knowledge or intelligence-gathering strategy). As such, the power of surveillance under a sovereign ruler would make the world transparent in order to visibly find and identify terrorist risks, but the power-knowledge discovered through surveillance would not itself be transparent to those identified as such risks (Cole 2000).

Conclusion

President George W. Bush asserted that '[f]or America, 9/11 was more than tragedy – it changed the way [Americans] look at the world' (Bush 2006). One could interpret this statement as suggesting that Americans look at the world differently because they are more likely to look at it in dramatic terms,[12] relying increasingly on the catastrophic imagination. As the catastrophic imagination is embedded in parallel deployments in political culture and popular culture, this paper conceptualized a film's marketing paratext as the means through which popular culture could meet political culture in a particular cultural context.

If culture involves the stories that we tell ourselves about ourselves (Geertz 1973), the striking synchronicity between the stories told by the Bush administration and by Jackson's film adaptation implies that they can be read as representative of post-9/11 American culture. If *The Two Towers* belongs to the literary genre of speculative fiction, which is one means of making the familiar strange and the strange familiar, then the strange world of Middle-earth is also a familiar one because of its intertextual relations with the post-9/11 world envisioned in the Bush narrative. Both narratives impose a plot on a time characterized by uncertainty, where this plot is modelled on the symbolic battle between Good and Evil. Invoking the Judeo-Christian notion of Armageddon, both plots resonate because they include moral-aesthetic archetypes (e.g. Good versus Evil, Light versus Darkness, and the All-Seeing Eye) that interact with a particular political imperative. Given the rise of the concept of risk and risk management decision-making in the wake

12 The choice of calling the events of 9/11 'a tragedy' might also be construed as way to describe 9/11 as a tragic drama. For some philosophers (e.g. Aristotle), tragedy is the highest literary art form.

of 9/11, the Bush administration's political imperative has been formed out of precautionary logic and the catastrophic imagination – a political imperative that is also inherent in the Fellowship of the Ring's pre-emptive mission. Although it served the precautionary imperative, the Total Information Awareness programme was visually mirrored in Jackson's representation of Sauron, fashioning Uncle Sam into the Dark Lord. While civil libertarians might imagine themselves as a Fellowship that had successfully destroyed the possibility of the Dark Lord's totalizing reign, it should be noted that component parts of the TIA programme live on in other preemptively-oriented state initiatives (e.g. Lifelog). As risk profiles are increasingly used for post-9/11 policing and surveillance purposes, the 'risky' individual must bear the pain of being designated 'risky'. Similarly, the individual who possesses the One True Ring must bear the burden of such a possession, where the burden manifests as risk of being under surveillance (e.g. monitored by the Eye of Sauron) and/or potential death and torture. In the latter case, it should be noted that Gollum, a Ring-bearer in *The Lord of the Rings* trilogy, is tortured by Sauron's army for information, which makes a striking parallel to reports of the CIA's secret torture (or 'interrogation') of terrorist suspects for information (about alleged terrorist plots) in post-9/11 America (Grey 2006). Like the One True Ring, an idea that combines notions of knowledge, power and truth, risk is ultimately construed as a symbolic totem or device that might either save or destroy our world, either bringing us closer to the light of transparent revelation through surveillance schemes, or binding us to the darkness associated with the state's abuse of power and control.

References

Adams, J. 2003. 'Risk and Morality: Three Framing Devices', in *Risk and Morality*, edited by Richard V. Ericson and Aaron Doyle. Toronto: University of Toronto Press, 87-103.

Amoore, L. 2007. 'Vigilant Visualities: The Watchful Politics of the War on Terror'. *Security Dialogue*, 38, 215-232.

Baudrillard, J. 2001. 'Spirit of Terrorism', translated by Dr. Rachel Bloul. *The European Graduate School*. [Online]. Available at: http://www.egs.edu/faculty/baudrillard/baudrillard-the-spirit-of-terrorism.html [accessed 14 April 2007].

Beck, U. 2002. 'The Terrorist Threat: World Risk Society Revisited'. *Theory, Culture and Society*, 19, 39-55.

Bonikowski, B. 2005. 'Flying while Arab (Or Was It Muslim? Or Middle Eastern?): A Theoretical Analysis of Racial Profiling after September 11'. *The Discourse of Sociological Practice*, 7, 315-328.

Bush, George W. 2001a, 11 September 2001. 'Presidential Address to the Nation'. *CNN*. [Online]. Available at: http://archives.cnn.com/2001/US/09/11/bush.speech.text/ [accessed 18 March 2010].

Bush, George W. 2001b, 20 September 2001. 'Address to the Joint Session of Congress and the American People'. *CNN*. [Online]. Available at: http://archives.cnn.com/2001/US/09/20/gen.bush. transcript/ [accessed 18 March 2010].

Bush, George W. 2001c, 7 October 2001. 'Presidential Address to the Nation'. *CNN*. [Online]. Available at: http://archives.cnn.com/2001/US/10/07/ret.bush.transcript/ [accessed 18 March 2010].

Bush, George W. 2002a, 29 January 2002. 'State of the Union Address'. *CNN*. [Online]. Available at: http://archives.cnn.com/2002/ALLPOLITICS/01/29/bush.speech.txt/ [accessed 18 March 2010].

Bush, George W. 2002b, 7 October 2002. 'President Bush Outlines Iraqi Threat'. Cincinnati: Cincinnati Museum Center.

Bush, George W. 2006, 11 September 2006. 'Presidential Address to the Nation'. *About.com: US Politics*. [Online]. Available at: http://uspolitics.about.com/od/speeches/a/9_11_bush.htm [accessed 18 March 2010].

Clarke, L. 2006. *Worst Cases: Terror and Catastrophe in the Popular Imagination*. Chicago, IL: University of Chicago Press.

Cole, D. 2000-2001. 'Secrecy, Guilt by Association, and the Terrorist Profile'. *Journal of Law and Religion*, 15, 267-288.

Cole, S.A. 2001. *Suspect Identities: A History of Fingerprinting and Criminal Identification*. Cambridge, MA: Harvard University Press.

De Goede, M. 2008. 'Beyond Risk: Premediation and the Post-9/11 Security Imagination'. *Security Dialogue*, 39, 155-176.

Delumeau, J. 1999. 'Back to the Apocalypse', in *Conversations about the End of Time*, edited by Umberto Eco, Stephen Jay Gould, Jean-Claude Carrière and Jean Delumeau. London: Penguin Press, 45-94.

Der Derian, J. 2005. 'Imaging Terror: Logos, Pathos and Ethos'. *Third World Quarterly*, 26, 23-37.

Dershowitz, A.M. 2006. *Preemption: The Knife that Cuts Both Ways*. New York: W.W. Norton.

Douglas, M. 1966. *Purity and Danger: An Analysis of the Concepts of Pollution and Taboo*. New York: Routledge.

Ericson, R.V. 2006. 'Ten Uncertainties of Risk-management Approaches to Security'. *Canadian Journal of Criminology and Criminal Justice*, 48, 345-357.

Ericson, R.V. 2007. *Crime in an Insecure World*. Cambridge: Polity Press.

Foucault, M. 1977. *Discipline and Punish: The Birth of the Prison*. New York: Pantheon.

Foucault, M. 1980. *The History of Sexuality, Volume I: An Introduction*. New York: Vintage Books.

Gadamer, H. 1975. *Truth and Method*. London: Sheed and Ward.

Geertz, C. 1973. *The Interpretation of Culture*. New York: Basic Books.

Genette, G. 1997. *Paratexts: Thresholds of Interpretation*. New York: Cambridge University Press.

Grey, S. 2006. *Ghost Plane: The True Story of the CIA Torture Program*. New York: St. Martin's Press.

Grusin, R. 2004. 'Premediation'. *Criticism*, 46(1), 17-39.

Hacking, I. 2003. 'Risk and Dirt', in *Risk and Morality*, edited by Richard V. Ericson and Aaron Doyle. Toronto: University of Toronto Press, 22-47.

Jackson, P. 2002. *The Lord of the Rings: The Two Towers*. New York: MMII New Line Productions.

Jackson, P. 2003. 'From Book to Script: Finding the Script'. *The Lord of the Rings: The Two Towers – Special Extended DVD Edition*. New York: MMII New Line Productions.

Klerck, K. 2001. 'Rename "The Two Towers" to Something Less Offensive Petition'. *Petition Online*. [Online]. Available at: http://web.archive.org/web/20021113001352/www.petitiononline.com/twotower/petition.html [accessed 18 March 2010].

Masco, J. 2008. '"Survival Is Your Business": Engineering Ruins and Affect in Nuclear America'. *Cultural Anthropology*, 23, 361-398.

Mathur, S. 2006. 'Surviving the Dragnet: "Special Interest" Detainees in the US after 9/11'. *Race and Class*, 47, 31-46.

National Commission on Terrorist Attacks upon the United States. 2004. *The 9/11 Commission Report: Final Report of the National Commission on Terrorist Attacks upon the United States*. New York: Norton.

New Line Cinema. 2002. *The Lord of the Rings: The Two Towers*. [Online]. Available at: http://www.lordoftherings.net/film/trilogy/thetwotowers.html [accessed 18 February 2006].

O'Hehir, A. 2010. '"Lord of the Rings": WTF Happened?' *Salon*. [Online]. Available at: http://www.salon.com/entertainment/movies/film_salon/2010/01/05/lotr_wtf/index.html [accessed 18 March 2010].

Petersen, P.S. 2005. '9/11 and the "Problem of Imagination": *Fight Club* and *Glamorama* as Terrorist Pretexts'. *Orbis Litterarum*, 60, 133-144.

Rearick, A. III. 2004. 'Why Is the Only Good Orc a Dead Orc? The Dark Face of Racism Examined in Tolkien's World'. *Modern Fiction Studies*, 50, 861-874.

Ries, A. and Jack, T. 1986. *Positioning: The Battle for Your Mind*, revised edition. New York: McGraw-Hill.

Salter, M.B. 2008. 'Risk and Imagination in the War on Terror', in *Risk and the War on Terror*, edited by Louise Amoore and Marieke de Goede. London: Routledge, 233-246.

Schlesinger, P., Murdock, G. and Philip, E. 1983. *Televising Terrorism: Political Violence in Popular Culture*. London: Comedia Publishing.

Sherwin, A. and Jack, M. 2002. 'Twin Tower Lobby Calls for Tolkien Title Change'. *The Times*, 12 December.

Singer, P. 2004. *The President of Good and Evil: The Ethics of George W. Bush*. New York: Dutton.

Skoll, G.R. 2007. 'Meanings of Terrorism'. *International Journal for the Semiotics of Law*, 20, 107-127.

Wagner-Pacifici, R.E. 1986. *The Moro Morality Play: Terrorism as Social Drama*. Chicago, IL: University of Chicago Press.
Watts, O. 2006. 'The Image and the Terrorist'. *Law Text Culture*, 10, 221-238.
Whitaker, R. 2006. 'A Faustian Bargain? America and the Dream of Total Information Awareness', in *The New Politics of Surveillance and Visibility*, edited by Kevin D. Haggerty and Richard V. Ericson. Toronto: University of Toronto Press, 141-170.
Žižek, S. 2002. *Welcome to the Desert of the Real*. London: Verso.

Chapter 11
Hearing and Belonging: On Sounds, Faiths and Laws

Massimo Leone[1]

Introduction: Sounds and Minorities

One of the most frustrating experiences a scholar can go through in Italy is trying to read a book while travelling by train. Upon entering a coach, the scholar will immediately find herself surrounded by passengers who relentlessly yell into their mobiles. The experience is particularly excruciating if the scholar understands Italian. After a few minutes, she will realize that no matter how acute her concentration power is, mental images evoked by the book will get contaminated by fragments of meaning from other people's lives: business information, intimate details, soccer opinions and endless small talk (Leone 2006).

Irritated by the impossibility of reading on Italian trains, for years I have been quarrelling with other passengers, spent a fortune in high-quality earplugs, and envied Swiss colleagues and their perfectly silent coaches. Then, all of a sudden, I had an illumination: I tried to see myself, or rather, I tried to hear myself from the point of view of the other passengers. I realized that while their loudly talking into their mobiles was an annoyance to me and to my desire to read, my longing for silence was an annoyance to them and their perpetual chitchatting. I realized that we were both in competition for the same scarce resource: the air in the coach meant as a potential channel of communication (Jakobson 1976; Jakobson and Waugh 1979).

On the one hand, I wished to keep this channel empty in order to use my book in a way that German philosopher Peter Sloterdijk effectively analysed in the first volume of his trilogy *Sphären*: as an instrument that enables the reader to create a protective sphere around her personal identity (Sloterdijk 1998). On the other hand, my fellow passengers wished to use the same channel in order to break the isolation of their personal identity through connecting it with the other pole of a conversation. One might argue that, at a different level, we were both seeking to achieve the same result: avoiding the feeling of solitude, which is often

1 This chapter was written also with the support of an Endeavour Research Award by the Australian Government. I thank Rick Mohr for inviting me to present a first version of this paper at the seminar of the Legal Intersections Research Centre at the University of Wollongong, Australia.

a remainder of death, by either silent immersion into a book or noisy involvement in a phone conversation.

However, the metaphysics of book reading and mobile small talk is not at stake here. What matters is that I realized that at least in present-day Italian trains, I am a minority. The way in which I would like to manage the sound space of Italian trains is not in the mainstream. Furthermore, I realized that like most minorities not only am I treated as a nuisance by other passengers but I am also insufficiently protected by the state. In other countries, Switzerland for instance, passengers can choose to travel in silent, mobile-free coaches. I often amuse Swiss colleagues by saying that this is the main reason for their academic superiority.

But why do silent coaches not exist in Italy? Probably, because the lobby of book readers is not strong enough to politically and economically justify their creation. However, this is not the point of the present paper. After all I could just purchase a mobile phone and participate in the national sport of loud phone conversation. I could join the majority. The point is that the entire public space and to a certain extent also considerable portions of the private space are exactly like an Italian train coach.

Given the physics of the production of sounds and the physiology of their perception, when sound space is used as a communication channel, it turns into a limited resource. By sound space here I mean a space in which sounds can be produced, perceived and potentially correlated with meaning. As I often tell my students in Italy, if you talk while I teach, you are stealing my channel. In this as in other examples, the limitedness of sound space is evident above all when its potential as a channel is privatized. My contract with the University of Torino implicitly says that during a certain number of hours per year the sound space of a certain classroom is mine and I have the exclusive right to use it as a communication channel.

However, owning a certain amount of sound space means that I can use this space to produce the sounds that I wish, but not that these sounds might be of whatever nature. From the legal point of view, one of the most interesting characteristics of the production of sounds is that they propagate through space. Therefore, owning a certain amount of sound space entails not only that I can use it to produce the sounds that I wish, but also that they must not propagate beyond the limits of this space. For instance, if I use a microphone when I teach, and my voice is so loud that it propagates into the classroom next to mine – as is often the case with the thin walls of Italian universities – I will steal the sound space, and therefore, the channel of my colleagues.

Technology for controlling the way in which sounds propagate through space is still primitive. Hence, sound spaces are usually conceived of as delimited by thresholds more than by frontiers. For instance, we would be quite annoyed if the neighbour's drill pierced the wall and intruded into our apartment, since we know that current drilling technology allows the driller to respect the frontier between the neighbour's space and ours. On the contrary, we accept that a certain amount of sounds produced in the neighbour's sound space penetrates into ours.[2]

Tolerance to the permeability of private sound spaces is, of course, not only a matter of technology, but also a matter of culture: the thresholds of sound spaces in Naples are more porous, I guess, than those in Sydney. One of the main reasons for legal controversies about private sound spaces in multicultural cities stems from the fact that neighbours with different socio-cultural backgrounds sometimes conceive of the thresholds of their sound spaces in different ways. This is an issue not only for private citizens, but also for those who elaborate legal prescriptions about sounds in multicultural societies.

Nevertheless, even with the biases of their socio-cultural backgrounds, citizens are usually quite aware that private sound spaces are a limited resource, that people compete for using them as communication channels, and that property of a sound space entails the right to produce sounds within the thresholds of such space. On the contrary, what citizens usually ignore is that the public sound space too is the object of constant competition among different agencies. The sounds of the public space in which we usually live are often so familiar to us that we tend to 'naturalize' them. In contemporary cities, for instance, we frequently perceive sounds of traffic, sounds of construction works, sounds of commercial advertising, etc. as if they were the sound of the wind, the sounds of birds, the sound of the rain.

The Semio-geography of Soundscapes

One of the purposes of a semio-geography of public soundscapes is to de-naturalize them by pinpointing the way in which they have been brought about through competition among specific social agencies. By 'soundscape' here I mean the series of sounds that usually characterize a certain sound space (Schafer 1994; Bull and Back 2005; Mikola 2007; Cossali and Brighenti 2008). By 'semio-geography' I refer to a contamination between semiotics and geography. The term 'semio-geography' is modelled after that of 'psycho-geography', first defined by Guy Debord as the study of the precise laws and specific effects of the geographical environment, consciously organized or not, on the emotions and behaviour of individuals (Debord 1955; Stein 1987; Stein and Niederland 1989; Coverley 2006; Self 2007). Similarly, semio-geography could be defined as the study of the way in which the environment is transformed into a fabric of signification patterns (Leone 2010a).

Some of the patterns that characterize the soundscapes of many contemporary cities are produced by religious agencies. This is particularly clear in certain urban environments. For instance, as a first year student at the University of Siena, in Italy,

2 The different reactions stem also from the different materialities of the intruding objects, and therefore, from the different expectations about their permanence in the alien space.

I realized too late that the tiny studio I had rented in the beautiful medieval town was adjacent to the bell-tower of a convent, and that the bell rang every morning at 6 a.m. to summon the local nuns for the office of Prime. My accomplishments as a young student owe a lot to my religious neighbours. Similarly, one of my most vivid memories of Marrakech is the sound of multiple *adhans*, the Islamic calls to prayer, reverberating through the medina at dawn.

However, contemporary urban soundscapes do not include only religious sounds like the ring of Christian bells or the voice of Islamic muezzins. In several Italian cities, for instance, some churches, including the one in front of my current house in Torin the habit of to keeping their doors wide open during the Mass, in order to eliminate or at least nuance the threshold between the religious inside of the temple and the lay outside of the city. Some parish priests even place loudspeakers in the churchyard in order to broadcast the sounds of the Mass in the street.

The injection of religious sounds in the public sound space of contemporary cities is problematic from both the political and the legal point of view, especially as regards the present-day multicultural and multi-religious societies. On the one hand, the political and the legal discourse must strike an equilibrium between those who, with more or less enthusiasm, welcome the presence of religious sounds in the public sound space and those who, on the contrary, object to it. On the other hand, the same political and legal discourse must also strike an equilibrium among different religious agencies competing for the production of sounds in the public sound space.

No genius is required to realize that the need for these two equilibria, the one between believers and non-believers and the one among believers, concerns not only sounds but every manifestation of religion in the public sphere (Leone 2010b). However, focusing on sounds, as well as on the other sensuous manifestations of religions in present-day multicultural and multi-religious cities, is necessary mostly in order to avoid a fallacy that studies on multiculturalism have frequently incurred: if we want to understand the way in which individuals and groups shape their existence in multicultural environments we must not consider them as disembodied agents, but as sensuous agents, as agents who exist in the environment by producing and receiving images, sounds, smells, tastes and contacts (Leone 2010c).

This is particularly urgent as far as the religious dimension of the social existence of individuals and groups is concerned: by disembodying religious agents, scholars do not adopt a neutral point of view, but rather project on their methodology the predominant religious sensibility of the 'Western' world, a disincarnated sensibility that ultimately stems from the Christian, and especially from the Protestant, conception of the religious body (Keane 2003).

The trend of sensuous scholarship has been already developed in human geography, for instance, by Paul Rodaway's book on *Sensuous Geographies* (1994), in anthropology, for instance by Paul Stoller's book on *Sensuous Scholarship* (1997), and partially also in multicultural studies, for instance, by research on everyday and sensuous multiculturalism carried out by Amanda Wise and other scholars predominantly in Australia and Canada (Wise, forthcoming). Nevertheless, to my knowledge, few researchers have thus far investigated the intersection between legal studies and sensuous scholarship.

'Western' Soundscapes and Nationalist Fantasies

I first became aware of the need to explore such intersection as I was analysing, thanks to a fellowship of the Australian government, legal controversies about the establishment of new places of worship in contemporary Australia (Leone 2009a). The main purpose of my research was to use the documents of these controversies, as well as the media coverage that they often generated, in order to understand how contemporary Australians react to the idea that their public environment might be modified by religious agencies, as well as in order to understand how these reactions interact with the Australian political and legal systems.

I was not surprised when I found out that reactions were particularly negative against religious minorities, and mostly against Islamic communities. Especially after 9/11, plans by Islamic groups to establish new places of worship in predominantly non-Islamic countries have been generally met with hostility (Humphrey 1989; Shadid and Koningsveld 1996; Isin and Siemiatycki 1999; Dunn 2001; Siemiatycki and Isin 2002; Allievi 2009). In my country, for instance, such plans have been often received with aggressiveness (Leone 2009b). I have exposed the main results of this investigation in other contexts and I will not reproduce them here (Leone 2009a).

However, I would like to point out that a particular aspect of these results *was* surprising to me. In Australia as well as in other countries, non-Islamic citizens have been objecting to the establishment of new Islamic places of worship by using more or less always the same arguments. As if all these objectors around the 'Western' world had contracted the same lawyers. One of these arguments turns around sounds. In transcripts of legal controversies in this domain, someone routinely complains that the planned new mosque might inject unwanted sounds in the public sound space, or even in the private sound spaces adjacent to that of the intended new place of worship.[3]

Islamic sounds are not objected to qua generic sounds, in terms of decibels characterizing their sound pressure level.[4] From this point of view, indeed, many other sounds in the public space of contemporary cities feature a higher level of sound pressure than Islamic sounds do, but are not as frequently objected to. A soccer stadium, for instance, probably produces louder sounds in the surrounding public environment than a mosque does. However, the establishment of new soccer

3 For instance in QPEC 068.

4 The local pressure deviation from the ambient (average, or equilibrium) pressure caused by a sound wave.

stadiums does not attract the same level of public hostility that the establishment of new mosques does. Nor are Islamic sounds objected to qua specifically religious sounds, qua manifestation of the religious dimension in the lay public space. From this point of view, indeed, many other religious sounds in the public space of contemporary cities are as loud as the Islamic ones. Citizens who object to the sounds that a new mosque might produce, do not object, for instance, to the equally loud sounds that Christian churches already produce in the same public environment.

On the contrary, Islamic sounds are objected to neither qua sounds nor qua religious sounds, but qua Islamic sounds. The same adjective recurs over and over again in complaints about the establishment of new Islamic places of worship both in Australia and in other 'Western' countries: *uncharacteristic*. Non-Islamic citizens in Australia as well as in other 'Western' countries claim that new Islamic places of worship should not be established in their neighbourhood because they are likely to produce uncharacteristic sounds, sounds that would spoil the character of the local soundscape.

I have already pointed out on other occasions that this argument concerns not only sounds, but the entire aesthetics of religious places of worship planned by Islamic minorities (Leone 2009a). In many legal controversies, for instance, non-Islamic Australian citizens claim that new Islamic places of worship might spoil the architectural, sometimes even the rural or semi-rural character, of their neighbourhood. I have also pointed out that these arguments should not be simply dismissed as racism coated in acceptable legal terms, but as manifestations of those nationalistic fantasies that Ghassan Hage has so effectively analysed in his books (Hage 1998). I will not repeat my considerations on this point.

On the contrary, I would like to emphasize that the intersection between sensuous scholarship and legal studies is fundamental from another point of view: it is only by studying the way in which the political and legal discourse of contemporary multicultural and multi-religious societies allows individuals and groups to modify the sensuous fabric of the public environment according to their cultural and religious sensibilities that we shall be able to grasp that which I would like to call the phenomenology of belonging in multicultural societies (Leone 2010c).

Toward a Phenomenology of Belonging

'Belonging' is a frontier-concept in the field of present-day multicultural studies on cities and religion. Although the idea of 'belonging' has been considered as central since the early development of city studies – for instance in *Human Communities* by Robert E. Park (1952) and in the other ground-breaking contributions of the Chicago 'urban ethnographers', both social researchers and policy makers currently believe that the concepts of 'sense of belonging' and 'feeling of belonging' urgently require further investigation.

Especially in societies with a long tradition in research on multicultural cities, such as Australia and Canada, it is increasingly found that the conceptual framework of 'cultural integration', predominant thus far in social research and policy making about social cohesion and harmony, is largely unsatisfactory in dealing with the challenges of the so-called super-diverse cities (Vertovec 2007). In order to bring about social cohesion and harmony, many social scientists and policy makers now contend that it is not sufficient that new citizens, for instance migrants, integrate their identities with the socio-cultural fabric previously created by the identities of old citizens. In the conceptual framework of 'cultural belonging', it is believed that social cohesion and harmony come about, on the contrary, when both old and new citizens feel that their identities are equally fundamental in shaping the socio-cultural fabric of the city in which they live. When they feel that they all belong to the city, and that the city belongs to them all.

Whereas in cultural integration, social cohesion and harmony are conceived as a situation in which no citizen feels *out of place*, and in which no citizen believes that her identity is incompatible with the pre-existent socio-cultural fabric of the city, in cultural belonging, social cohesion and harmony are conceived as a situation in which every citizen feels *in place*, and believes that her identity is not only compatible, but also consubstantial with the socio-cultural fabric of the city (Kobayashi and Peake 2000).

It is in this conceptual framework of belonging that several contemporary social scientists and policy-makers have started to reconsider the cultural dynamics of social harmony and disharmony in present-day multicultural cities. What does it mean when one feels that she belongs to the city, and what does it mean when one feels that the city belongs to her? What urban dynamics create and increase this sense and feeling of belonging, and what dynamics, on the contrary, decrease and destroy it? In what situations, and through what socio-cultural practices are new citizens, for instance, migrants, able to develop a sense/feeling of belonging toward the city in which they live, and in what situations, on the contrary, are they unable to do so? What is the relation between the way in which new citizens seek to develop a sense/feeling of belonging to the city, and the way in which old citizens try to maintain such sense/feeling?

When are these processes in competition (for instance, when the newer citizens secure opportunities to 'shape the city' in order to feel that they belong to it, the older citizens feel that they 'do not belong to it any more', because they are losing, or they believe they are losing, such power)? When are they, on the contrary, compatible? How do multicultural cities encourage or discourage senses/feelings of multiple belonging, and how does this affect the relation between old and new citizens, and between citizens with a feeling of single belonging and citizens with a feeling of multiple belongings?

Most important of all, how does the social articulation of this sense/feeling of belonging influence the participation of citizens in the creation of the economic, social and cultural fabric of the city? Do citizens who feel that they do not belong to the city act as merely passive citizens, whereas citizens who feel that they belong to it contribute actively to the social cohesion and harmony of the city? And what policies are the most suitable in order to bring about a 'common sense of belonging', and therefore a 'sense of common belonging' among all citizens?

In the last years, several social scientists have sought to answer these questions, for instance, by investigating the senses/feelings of multiple belonging in Hong Kong-born present-day Australian citizens (Mar 2004), or the way in which a common sense/feeling of belonging is currently developed in Australian multicultural suburbs (Wise 2005), or the role of senses/feelings of belonging in fuelling resilience in the poor neighbourhoods of present-day Los Angeles (Sánchez-Jankowski 2008), or the senses/feelings of belonging of families of Turkish origin in contemporary Germany (Bozkurt 2009), or by assessing anti-segregation housing policies in European cities (Bolt 2009; Van Kempen and Bolt 2009), or contestations that ensue from conflictive senses/feelings of belonging (Hage 2002; Ross 2009; Noble 2009), or by questioning the senses/feelings of belonging of new citizens of Chinese descent in the USA (Toyota 2010), but also by emphasizing the social tensions brought about by exclusive claims of belonging in the form of ideologies of autochthony (Gerschiere 2009).

It is my contention that developing the intersection between legal studies and a sensuous semio-geography is fundamental in order to analyse the phenomenology of belonging in present-day multicultural and multi-religious cities. The extent to which individuals and groups in a multicultural city feel that they belong to it and that, *vice versa*, the city belongs to them, also depends on the extent to which they are able to inject images, sounds, smells, tastes and contacts in the sensuous fabric of the public environment. In contemporary studies on Aboriginal soundscapes, I have come across a word that describes this process of creation of a feeling of belonging perfectly: 'interanimation'. Bradley and Mackinlay define it as follows:

> Through the sentience of their bodies, the Yanyuwa experience the different textures, scents, sounds of these places, and by utilizing their own in-depth knowledge of these phenomenal attributes are able to discern the place of places they are moving through. Thus this emplacement within the Yanyuwa world is not one of people creating places from a formless matrix or 'landscape', but instead describes a relationship where people and places exist as interrelated and co-dependent phenomena. Basso calls this 'interanimation': a process by which people animate places through their experience, emotions and knowledge. (Bradley and Mackinlay 2007: 79)

A multiculturalism where individuals and groups are allowed to express their cultural sensibility only in private or in specific cultural precincts, whereas they must refrain from any 'interanimation' of the public environment, seems to me a hypocritical multiculturalism, in which a majority keeps the cultural monopoly of the public space while revelling in an abstract rhetoric of cultural diversity.

The situation of Islamic minorities in many predominantly non-Islamic 'Western' countries is, from this point of view, paradigmatic. On the one hand, most non-Islamic opinion-leaders in these countries affirm that Islamic citizens are as entitled to express the religious dimension of their social identity as much as atheist, agnostic or Christian citizens do. On the other hand, though, most attempts at modifying the public environment according to an Islamic aesthetics are met with hostility and sometimes even with violent aggressiveness. As I have pointed out elsewhere, this is not a new phenomenon in history. For centuries, Jewish communities in Italy and elsewhere have been tolerated only on the condition that their impact on the public environment should be minimal (Leone 2010d: 254-268). Analogously, Islamic communities in present-day predominantly non-Islamic cities are tolerated but only on the condition that they are practically invisible or, as I will indicate in the last part of this chapter, inaudible.

Making Muslim Sound Space

Several studies have demonstrated that there is not such a thing as a single 'Islamic aesthetics' (Grabar 1983), and that Islamic individuals and groups in different historical periods and socio-cultural contexts show different ways of 'making Muslim space', to quote an excellent collection of essays on this topic (Metcalf 1996). Therefore, speaking of 'Islamic aesthetics', 'Islamic architecture' or 'Islamic sounds' is as meaningful as speaking of 'Christian aesthetics', 'Christian architecture' or 'Christian sounds'.

However, most scholars recognize that one of the most common limitations Islamic communities suffer in predominantly non-Islamic 'Western' countries concerns the impossibility to modify the public sound space. As Barbara Daly Metcalf puts it in presenting the collection of essays mentioned above:

> A particular absence in a largely non-Muslim environment is the lack of Islamic sounds, the sound of the *azan* (call to prayer) and the sound of the Qur'anic recitation, the latter especially marked in the nights of Ramadam. … (Metcalf 1996)[5]

Islamic citizens in predominantly non-Islamic cities often seek to reproduce some features of the public Islamic soundscape in their private sound space. As Barbara Daly Metcalf indicates:

> Catalogues from Islamic shops and newspaper advertisements aimed at Muslims are full of such items to create the sounds of an Islamic space. An electronic 'Azan Clock', for example, its digital display set in a replica of a domed mosque, can be set for the five daily prayers. Qur'anic tapes, produced in different styles and in different selections are widely available and certainly portable: as a poster

5 Quotations from Metcalf (1996) are from the electronic version without page numbers.

> at the Islamic Society of North America urged: 'Use Driving Time to Listen to Holy Qur'an'. (Metcalf 1996)

Michel de Certeau's theories on the 'invention of everyday life' would be suitable to analyse the quotidian strategies through which cultural and religious minorities around the world seek to overcome the limits on the manifestation of their social identity imposed on them by majorities (Certeau 1980). However, one might argue that these strategies are nothing but palliatives, confirming to those who carry them on that they do not belong to the place in which they live, and that the place in which they live does not belong to them.

Limitations to the way in which Islamic European citizens can modify the public soundscapes of the cities in which they live are particularly evident, as Stefano Allievi, one of the most prominent sociologists of contemporary Islam, indicated in a recent survey on 'Conflicts over mosques in Europe' (Allievi 2009: 48-49). Among the European countries whose Islamic population has considerably grown in recent years, mainly as a consequence of migration, only the Netherlands has officially recognized the *adhan* by voting a law in 1987 that granted to the Islamic call to prayer the same status of the Christian bells. Significantly, the only vote against this law came from three small Calvinist parties. However, there are no national prescriptions either on the number of times the *adhan* can be performed or on its volume. These matters are regulated by local authorities, usually in a restrictive way: in Amsterdam, for instance, the *adhan* can be performed only on Friday (Groenendijk et al. 1999).

In United Kingdom the *adhan* is often prohibited, and is allowed only in neighbourhoods with a strong presence of Islamic citizens. However, also in these cases non-Islamic citizens frequently complain about the audibility of the Islamic call for prayer. The mosque of East London, for instance, has been allowed to perform the *adhan* twice a day only thanks to the support of the local Anglican church (Eade 1996).

In Germany, several official documents declare that Christian bells and the Islamic *adhan* are both manifestations of the right of religious freedom and, within reasonable limits, deserve the same constitutional protection by the state, as it has been recommended in 1997 by both the *Bunderausländerbeauftragte*, the Federal Office for Foreigners, and the *Deutscher Städte und Gemeindebund*, the German Federation of Cities and Municipalities. However, these documents are usually interpreted in a way that grants constitutional protection to the *adhan*, but not to the loudspeakers that broadcast the *adhan*. Furthermore, the performing of the *adhan* is often received with hostility by non-Islamic citizens. For instance, in 1997-1998 some exponents of the evangelical churches of Duisburg started to diffuse a misinterpretation of the text of the *adhan*, claiming that it was a call against Christianity (Goldberg 2002; SpulerStegemann 2002; BeinhauerKöhler and Leggewie 2009).

In most European countries, including Belgium, France and Italy, where consistent Islamic minorities are present, Islamic representatives usually censor themselves and do not even dare asking permission for the performance of the *adhan*, knowing that such requests would attract the hostility of the non-Islamic majority and eventually worsen the conditions of life of Islamic individuals and groups.

In Norway mosques are allowed to broadcast the *adhan* once a week, on Friday, and with a sound pressure limit of 60 decibels (Larsson 2009), which is the average sound pressure of conversation at the distance of 1 metre.

In general, the *adhan* is performed in mosques and Islamic centres in Europe on special occasions and usually considered as an exceptional feature of the public sound space.

The only region of Europe where the *adhan* is performed on a regular basis is Bosnia-Herzegovina, which is also the only European state with an Islamic majority (Aksamija 2008).

In Australia, as well as in other predominantly non-Islamic 'Western' countries, almost all legal controversies concerning the establishment of new mosques involve complaints about the construction of minarets, the towers usually adjacent to a mosque, from the top of which the *adhan* is performed (Allievi 2009: 45-47; Haenni and Lathion 2009).

Minarets are not objected to exclusively qua potential sources of production and diffusion of Islamic sounds in the public space. Minarets are objected to also when Islamic communities wish to build them as purely decorative elements, without requesting the permission to use them in order to broadcast the *adhan*. Indeed, non-Islamic citizens in predominantly non-Islamic 'Western' countries often consider minarets, consciously or unconsciously, as a clearly visible architectural sign of the growing control that Islamic minorities might exert on the public space.

However, minarets are also related to that which contemporary musicologists define as 'soundmarks', that is, soundscape landmarks (Schafer 1994: 10; Lee 1999). For instance, Christian bell-towers, whose anthropological relevance has been effectively analysed by Italian ethnologist Ernesto de Martino (2002), are so central in the phenomenology of the public space not only because they are visible from everywhere, but also because sounds diffused from their top are potentially audible everywhere.

The idea that soon the minarets of European mosques might be used to broadcast *adhans* competing with secular or Christian sounds over the soundscapes of present-day European cities is currently received with hostility, at times even with aggressiveness, by many present-day non-Islamic European individuals and groups. Limitations are imposed on the construction of minarets everywhere in Europe, often with the clear intent to make them look shorter, and therefore, less symbolically present in the urban landscape than Christian campaniles or secular buildings (Allievi 2009: 45-47; Haenni and Lathion 2009).

Conclusions

On 29 November 2009, 57 per cent of the Swiss electors approved a constitutional amendment banning the construction of new minarets in the country, with retroactive effect on four existing Swiss minarets. This referendum and its results have been interpreted in different, sometimes opposite ways. My personal opinion is that it represents an alarming sign of both a social and a political phenomenon. At the social level, it indicates that the societies of many present-day European countries are increasingly prone to nationalistic fantasies according to which the control that cultural and religious minorities might exert on the public space must be minimized at all cost. Certain cultural and religious minorities, such as Islamic or Gypsy individuals and groups in Europe, are recurrently victims of such fantasies, for reasons which are too complicated to be analysed here.

At the political level, the Swiss referendum shows that such nationalistic fantasies, as well as politicians and other opinion-leaders who hijack them in order to increase their personal power, feed each other in a vicious circle whose worrying result is the growing incapacity of European democracies to protect the fundamental rights of their minorities.

As globalization and its migration flows increase the presence of cultural and religious minorities in 'Western' societies, intellectual, political, legal and educational efforts should be made to contrast the entrepreneurs of xenophobia and make sure that all individuals and groups, independently from their cultural and religious background, have equal access to the possibility of shaping the public space, including the public space of sounds, without having to betray their personal and social identity. Since the public space is a limited resource, negotiations and compromises will be needed.[6] However, it is evident that such negotiations and such compromises shall have to be different from what they are now, and bring about a fairer balance between the symbolical and material needs of majorities and minorities.[7]

Perhaps in the future, non-Islamic citizens in Western countries will not pay attention to *adhans* more than they do to Christian bells or traffic sounds. Perhaps in the future, Islamic sounds will perfectly belong to the soundscapes of 'Western'

6 The present chapter focused on 'Western' urban religious soundscapes, but it is evident that such negotiation efforts are needed in predominantly Islamic countries too, where some individuals and groups also wish to modify urban religious soundscapes in order to make them more plural and suitable for the rhythms of contemporary urban life: as an instance, consider the inversion of loudspeakers in Singapore's mosques (toward the mosque rather than toward the city) (Lee 1999) or the recent attempts to synchronize and standardize *adhans* in Egypt.

7 On the social tensions triggered by a plural urban religious soundscape when it does not correspond to a suitable equilibrium among different socio-cultural agencies, cfr Ivo Andrić's splendid description of Sarajevo's conflictive religious soundscape (Andrić 1946: 33).

cities. Perhaps in the future, this article will make no sense. I definitely hope so, but I cannot foresee if and when this future will take place. Of one thing, however, I am certain: Italian train coaches will never be silent.

References

Aksamija, A. 2008. '(Re)constructing History: PostSocialist Mosque Architecture in Bosnia and Herzegovina', in *Divided God and Intercultural Dialog*, edited by Zigmanov Tomislav (Ljubljana: Dijaški dom Ivana Cankarja (DIC) and KUD Pozitiv). [Online: Divided God]. Available at: www.pozitiv.si/dividedgod/ [accessed 14 February 2011].

Allievi, S. 2009. *Conflicts over Mosques in Europe: Policy Issues and Trends*. London: Alliance Publishing Trust.

Andrić, I. 1946. 'Lettera del 1920', Italian trans. in Nicole Janigro. *Dizionario di un paese che scompare. Narrativa della ex-Jugoslavia*. Rome: manifestolibri.

BeinhauerKöhler, B. and Leggewie, C. 2009. *Moscheen in Deutschland: Religiöse Heimat und gesellschaftliche Herausforderung*. Munich: Beck Verlag.

Bolt, G. 2009. 'Combating Residential Segration of Ethnic Minorities in European Cities'. *Housing and the Built Environment*, 24, 397-405.

Bozkurt, E. 2009. *Conceptualising 'Home': The Question of Belonging among Turkish Families in Germany*. Frankfurt and New York: Campus Verlag.

Bradley, J. and Mackinlay, E. 2007. 'Singing the Land, Singing the Family: Song, Place and Spirituality amongst the Yanyuwa', in *The Soundscapes of Australia: Music, Place and Spirituality*, edited by Fiona Richards. Aldershot: Ashgate.

Bull, M. and Back, L. 2005. *The Auditory Culture Reader*. Oxford and New York: Berg.

Certeau, M. de. 1980. *L'Invention du quotidian: Arts de faire, 1*. Paris: Gallimard.

Cossali, M. and Brighenti, A.M. 2008. *Soundscapes*. Monographic issues of *Squaderno*. 10 December 2008.

Coverley, M. 2006. *Psychogeography*. London: Pocket Essentials.

Debord, G. 1955. 'Introduction à une critique de la géographie urbaine'. *Les Lèvres nues*, 6, 11-15.

De Martino, E. 2002. *La fine del mondo*. Turin: Einaudi.

Dunn, K.M. 2001. 'Representations of Islam in the Politics of Mosque Development in Sydney'. *Tijdschrift voor Economische en Sociale Geografie*, 92(3), 291-308.

Eade, J. 1996. 'Nationalism, Community and the Islamization of Space in London', in *Making Muslim Space in North America and Europe*, edited by Barbara Daly Metcalf. Los Angeles and Berkeley, CA: University of California Press.

Gerschiere, P. 2009. *The Perils of Belonging: Autochthony, Citizenship, and Exclusion in Africa and in Europe*. Chicago, IL: University of Chicago Press.

Goldberg, A. 2002. 'Islam in Germany', in *Islam, Europe's Second Religion: The New Social, Cultural and Political Landscape*, edited by Shireen T. Hunter. Westport, CT: Praeger.

Grabar, O. 1983. 'Symbols and Signs in Islamic Architecture', in *Architecture and Community: Building in the Islamic World Today: The Aga Khan Awards for Architecture*, edited by Renata Holod and Darl Rastorfer. Millerton, NY: Aperture.

Groenendijk, K., Meyer, A., Penninx, R. and Rath, J. 1999. 'The Politics of Recognizing Religious Diversity in Europe: Social Reactions to the Institutionalization of Islam in the Netherlands, Belgium and Great Britain'. *Journal of Social Sciences*, 35(1), 53-68.

Haenni, P. and Lathion, S. 2009. *Les Minarets de la discorde:* Éclairage *sur un débat suisse et européen*. Golion: Infolio.

Hage, G. 1998. *White Nation: Fantasies of White Supremacy in a Multicultural Society*. Annandale, NSW: Pluto Press.

Hage, G. 2002. *Arab-Australians Toda: Citizenship and Belonging*. Carlton South, Vic.: Melbourne University Press.

Humphrey, M.T. 1989. 'Islam: A Test for Multiculturalism in Australia'. *Asian Migrant*, 2(2), 48-56.

Isin, E.F. and Siemiatycki, M. 1999. 'Fate and Faith: Claiming Urban Citizenship in Immigrant Toronto', *Working Papers of the Joint Centre of Excellence for Research on Immigration and Settlement – Toronto*, 8.

Jakobson, R. 1976. *Six leçons sur le son et le sens*, preface by Claude Lévi-Strauss. Paris: Éditions de Minuit.

Jakobson, R. and Waugh, L. 1979. *The Sound Shape of Language*. Bloomington, IN: Indiana University Press.

Keane, W. 2003. 'Semiotics and the Social Analysis of Material Things'. *Language and Communication*, 23, 409-425.

Kobayashi, A. and Peake, L. 2000. 'Racism Out of Place: Thoughts on Whitenessnd an Antiracist Geography in the New Millennium'. *Annals of the Association of American Geographers*, 90(2), 392-403.

Larsson, G. 2009. *Islam in the Nordic and Baltic Countries*. New York and London: Routledge.

Lee, T.S. 1999. 'Technology and the Production of Islamic Space: The Call to Prayer in Singapore'. *Ethnomusicology*, 43(1), 86-100.

Leone, M. 2006. 'All'inferno: I nuovi barbari, futuri borghesi'. *Golem l'indispensabile*, April. [Online] Available at: www.golemindispensabile.it [accessed 25 April 2011].

Leone, M. 2009a. 'Architectures of Transcendence: A Trans-Cultural Analysis of Legal Processes for the Construction, Modification, and Restoration of Places of Worship', in *Trans(l)egalité*, proceedings of the Conference of the Law and Literature Association of Australia, Griffith University in Brisbane, 2-5 December 2009, CD-Rom.

Leone, M. 2009b. 'Sustainable Religions in Contemporary Cities: A Semiotic Approach'. *International Journal of Environmental, Cultural, Economic, and Social Sustainability*, 5(3), 47-59.

Leone, M. 2010a. 'Legal Controversies about the Establishment of New Places of Worship in Multicultural Cities: A Semiogeographic Analysis', in *Prospects of Legal Semiotics*, edited by Anne Wagner and Jan Brockman. Berlin and New York: Springer.

Leone, M. 2010b. 'The Reasonable Audience of Religious Hatred: The Semiotic Ideology of Anti-Vilification Laws in Australia', in *Law and Religion in Public Life: The Contemporary Debate*, edited by Nadir Hosen and Richard Mohr. Oxford and New York: Routledge.

Leone, M. 2010c. 'On My Accent: Signs of Belonging in Multicultural Societies', in *Analysis of Cultures, Cultures of Analysis: Analisi delle culture, culture dell'analisi*, edited by M. Leone, numero monografico di *Lexia*, 5-6.

Leone, M. 2010d. *Saints and Signs: A Semiotic Reading of Conversion in Early Modern Catholicism*. Berlin and New York: Walter de Gruyter.

Mar, P. 2004. 'Ambivalent Loyalties: Tales of Trans/National Belonging', in *Proceedings of the 2nd Annual Conference of the Centre for Research on Social Inclusion*, edited by Michael Fine, Nicholas Smith and Amanda Wise, Macquarie University, 27-28 September 2004. Sydney: Centre for Research on Social Inclusion at Macquarie University.

Metcalf, B.D. 1996. *Making Muslim Space in North America and Europe*. Los Angeles and Berkeley, CA: University of California Press.

Mikola, M. 2007. 'Hearing Diversity: Representations and Sonic Landscapes of the Culturally Heterogeneous City', in *Everyday Multiculturalism Conference Proceedings*, edited by Selvaraj Velayutham and Amanda Wise, Macquarie University 28-29 September 2006. Sydney: Centre for Research on Social Inclusion. [Online]. Available at www.crsi.mq.edu.au [accessed 25 April 2011].

Noble, G. 2009. *Lines in the Sand: The Cronulla Riots, Multiculturalism, and National Belonging*. Sydney: Institute of Criminology Press.

Park, R.E. 1952. *Urban Communities: The City and Human Ecology*. Glencoe, IL: Free Press.

QPEC 068. 2004. *Kotku Education and Welfare Society Inc. v Brisbane City Council* (Planning and Environment Court of Queensland, 2004).

Richards, F. 2007. *The Soundscapes of Australia: Music, Place and Spirituality*. Aldershot: Ashgate.

Rodaway, P. 1994. *Sensuous Geographies: Body, Sense, and Place*. London and New York: Routledge.

Ross, M.H. 2009. *Culture and Belonging in Divided Societies: Contestation and Symbolic Landscapes*. Philadelphia, PA: University of Philadelphia Press.

Sánchez-Jankowski, M. 2008. *Cracks in the Pavement: Social Change and Resilience in Poor Neighborhoods*. Berkeley and Los Angeles, CA: University of California Press.

Schafer, R.M. 1994. *The Soundscape: Our Sonic Environment and the Tuning of the World*. Rochester, VT: Destiny Books.
Self, W. 2007. *Psychogeography*. London: Bloomsbury.
Shadid, W. and Koningsveld, S. van. 1996. *Muslims in the Margin: Political Responses to the Presence of Islam in Western Europe*. Kampen: Kok Pharos.
Siemiatycki, M. and Isin, E.F. 2002. 'Making Space for Mosques: Struggles for Urban Citizenship in Diasporic Toronto', in *Race, Space and the Law: Unmapping a White Settler Society*, edited by Sherene Razack. Ottawa: Between the Lines Press.
Sloterdijk, P. 1998. *1. Blasen*. Frankfurt am Mein: Suhrkamp.
SpulerStegemann, U. 2002. *Muslime in Deutschland: Nebeneinander oder Miteinander?*. Freiburg: Herder.
Stein, H.F. 1987. *Developmental Time, Cultural Space: Studies in Psychogeography*. Norman, OK: University of Oklahoma Press.
Stein, H.F. and Niederland, W.G. 1989. *Maps from the Mind: Readings in Psychogeography*. Norman, OK: University of Oklahoma Press.
Stoller, P. 1997. *Sensuous Scholarship*. Philadelphia, PA: University of Pennsylvania Press.
Toyota, T. 2010. *Envisioning America: New Chinese Americans and the Politics of Belonging*. Stanford, CA: Stanford University Press.
Van Kempen, R. and Bolt, G. 2009. 'Social Cohesion, Social Mix, and Urban Policies in the Netherlands'. *Housing and the Built Environment*, 24, 457-475.
Vertovec, S. 2007. 'Super-Diversity and Its Implications'. *Ethnic and Racial Studies*, 30(6), 1024-1054.
Wise, A. 2005. 'Hope and Belonging in a Multicultural Suburb'. *Journal of Intercultural Studies*, 26(1-2), 171-186.
Wise, A. Forthcoming. 'Sensuous Multiculturalism: Emotional Landscapes of Interethnic Living in Australian Suburbia'. *Journal of Ethnic and Migration Studies*. [Online]. Available at: www.crsi.mq.edu.au [accessed 14 February 2011].

Chapter 12
Terror *Australis*

Maria Giannacopoulos

In 2007 in a short essay contributed to a book titled *Law and Liberty in the War on Terror*, Phillip Ruddock, former Australian Minister for Immigration, quoted Sir John Latham, a former Commonwealth Attorney-General, who he says 'liked to quote Oliver Cromwell's statement on security matters that "being comes before well-being"' (quoted in Ruddock 2007: 3). In echoing the very essence of biopolitical governance he says 'the necessary premise of any constitutional order and system of government is that people are alive. Serious threats to national security must be addressed' (Ruddock 2007: 3). This quoting circle, which simulates a dialogue between white patriarchs who represent colonial militaristic and British ideas about law and governance, parallels the structure of Australian law and its self-serving internal dialogue that functions to produce it as a location free from violence in the name of security. Indeed, Ruddock reported that Australia's national security laws would not be 'overzealous' 'because our counter-terrorism laws have been modelled on the United Kingdom's long experience with dealing with terrorism in Northern Ireland' (Ruddock 2007: 7). Ruddock's reason for writing is to express that whilst not 'overzealous', the laws are necessary 'to protect against the global threat of terrorism' (Ruddock 2007: 3) which he says 'is one of the most serious threats we face' (Ruddock 2007: 3). Because the title of his essay, 'Law as Preventative Weapon against Terrorism' posits law as the means through which terror can be quashed, it functions to evacuate terror from the definition of white, Australian law. But Ruddock's use of language such as 'preventative weapon' betrays him since the idea of a weapon implies strength, force and power. The idea that the law can be a forceful weapon that eliminates terrorism from the national domain brings forth the seeming aporia that such law is implicated in war that is disguised in the language of civility. On 6 December 2005, in the context of the debate, or rather the former Howard government's attempt to stifle debate, in relation to the Anti-Terrorism Bill (No. 2) 2005, Senator Bob Brown expressed the impossible conditions faced by the Senate Committee in charge of debating the myriad of changes that within a matter of hours were to become law. He stated:

> We only need to reiterate what a farce this committee faces. We have 3.5 hours to debate not just extremely important amendments coming from the opposition and crossbenches but scores of amendments from the government itself, and they simply cannot be debated. So the Committee of the Whole is going to vote on amendments and, indeed, the legislation itself without having debated

> them. That is all the more poignant in view of the fact that we are talking about legislation which is to improve the security of this country and, according to the government, to balance the democratic values of this country with the right of people to have security … What we have here is the executive truncating the time for discussion in a way that is unprecedented in this parliament on a bill like this in the last 10 years. Moreover, the outcome of the debate is known before we get under way because every government member is going to support it and, what is more remarkable, the opposition is going to support it. The amendments will not get up. The final vote will be as the government has ordained it. That is the nature of the Senate in 2005.[1]

In this summation of Brown's protest of the proposed legislation, the key concerns of the current contribution are present. Brown in effect questions the meaning of democracy in the face of an increasingly securitized world but, importantly, because Brown's critique is located *before* the law, that is, in the period of the ostensible debate that is supposed to take place prior to the laws of a democratic nation being passed, his critique of the substantive law also makes visible the multiple forms of violence that *produce* the legislation enacted to control violence, that is, *terrorism* in the name of protection of the public. Bob Brown informed the Senate that the Greens would be moving an amendment to the Anti-Terrorism Bill (No. 2) 2005 to incorporate into its operations the International Covenant on Civil and Political Rights (ICCPR) as a way of ensuring that this be the 'measure by which courts might determine the fate of anybody brought forward for infringing this new security legislation'.[2] Brown highlights that Australia is a signatory to the Covenant, and that this legislation presents an opportunity to bring the international law document into the domestic law. However, the former Howard Government was insistent that that this was unnecessary since the legislation did not infringe on the international standards it had endorsed by signing the Covenant.[3] In this assertion the Howard government can be seen to be equating law with civil liberties even as it is the very means through which citizens are stripped of rights. Brown argues that just a few hours of debate around the question of how Australian democracy will be defended is farcical since this will erode civil liberties in the name of security. Brown warns:

> This legislation is a political document much more than a defence of Australians' security document. A very dangerous slide to McCarthyism is involved in this legislation being slammed and sledgehammered through the Senate today. We are in a new period of McCarthyism and we need to know that and understand it, and to worry that this time it will not be turned around.[4]

---

1 Hansard, Tuesday, 6 December 2005.
2 Senate Hansard, Tuesday, 6 December 2005.
3 Senate Hansard, Tuesday, 6 December 2005.
4 Senate Hansard, Tuesday, 6 December 2005.

Brown's warning whilst critical and urgent is problematic because it is informed by a confidence in the *proper* operations of the law. His position is that if the former Howard government incorporated the ICCPR into the legislation, then this would enable a just operation of the security legislation. Whilst it is tempting to agree with Brown's critique of the Howard regime, it is hard to ignore that this critique is underwritten by colonial and Anglocentric logic. I say this because his complaint pivots around the idea that the debate has been 'truncated' and 'guillotined' revealing an underlying assumption that if the proper procedure of the Senate discussion were followed then the law's operations would be less violent. I argue that Brown's is a colonial logic because it ignores the fact that proper rules and procedures can be followed, can be *lawful* but can still amount to racial violence for those against whom the law has always been used as a weapon. Brown's critique of the Howard government's outright contempt for the procedural aspects of law and parliamentary debate ignores the fact that even when law is deviated from, it is still law that is operating, which is to say, bypassing law is still within the realm of the *lawful*. Given that just four years prior to the moment from which Brown speaks, the executive 'truncated' debate and redefined the national boundaries of Australia to prevent the operations of human rights law in order to forbid asylum, the executive's power to deny law whilst being *lawful* cannot be properly seen as an aberration of law but rather as its logic and structure (see Giannacopoulos 2005). Senator Brown was not the only one who followed this logic which functions as law preserving violence since it effaces the violent constitution of law.

Labor Senator Ludwig also said that 'this is the most obscene thing' he has seen this government do.[5] For Ludwig 'obscene' is the practice of not upholding proper procedures for the passing of legislation, as opposed to the substantive changes that the legislation contains. He attempts to distinguish his party from the Greens by saying that:

> We do think, unlike the Greens, that you have to take the fight to the terrorists. You cannot take a backward step. You have to make sure that the people we entrust with our system to protect us and preserve our way of life have the necessary powers to ensure that they can root out these evildoers and put them behind bars and can prevent a terrorist attack so that we can have some measure of security and safety in Australia.[6]

Ludwig's position is critical towards the *procedural* actions of the Howard government, but the belief that law is a protective force of peace that can be used in the fight against violence that threatens it can be seen as the point of connection between these opposing political parties. The irony, that is perhaps lost on or is irrelevant to the Senators, is that the legislation that was passed in 2005 in relation

5 Senate Hansard, Tuesday, 6 December 2005.

6 Senate Hansard, Tuesday, 6 December 2005.

to terrorism was not so much law that protects the inside from the outside but rather re-marks the inside as a zone that can separate and distinguish those citizens who are 'protected' and those who are sacrificed in the name of that protection. These are legal processes that can now potentially do to citizens what has always been done to Indigenous peoples, aliens and refugees and that is to make them the basis upon which *security* is exacted. Greens Senator Kerry Nettle alerts the house to this when she says:

> … this legislation, for the very first time in Australia's criminal law, will allow people to be detained without trial or charge. We have already got that in immigration detention. People are locked up in immigration detention without being taken before a court, without being charged. In our immigration law, this government allows detention without trial and detention without charge.[7]

She then goes on to quote the President of the Law Council who is concerned that 'The control orders and preventative detention … allow Australians to be taken off the street and have their liberty curtailed for up to a year without charge. In other words, there is insufficient evidence to charge them and that makes a class of people unknown to the Australian law.'[8] Both of these critiques are necessary but not sufficient in addressing the full role that the law plays in such instances. Nettle rightly points out that the potential of such a law is to treat citizens the same way as refugees and as guilty before the fact of any crime. But does her critique suggest that prior to this piece of legislation the law already racially classified citizens? The framing of her critique which lays blame squarely on 'this government' functions to suggest that the issues with which she is dealing are the product of a particular government and not the effect of a particular system of law and governance. Her quoting of the President of the Law Council subtly indicates that a piece of legislation is *more* cause for alarm if it takes 'Australians' off the street as opposed to those seeking entry to the very category of Australian. The 'Australian' in the President of the Law Council's speech must be a white Australian, since Australian law is only innocent of the charges the President lays at the feet of this legislation if law is judged narrowly and on its own terms. By this I mean that if 'having their liberty curtailed' is understood more broadly as the series of practices that are the legal components of a colonial project of dispossession where the right to decide how the nation will be governed and who will be included at different historical junctures, then the statement declaring this an aberration of Australian law must be seen as Anglocentric in its operations of denying the racial and violent constitution of Australian law.

Senator Nettle goes on to say:

---

7 Senate Hansard, Tuesday, 6 December 2005.

8 Senate Hansard, Tuesday, 6 December 2005.

> This legislation for the very first time brings into Australian law concepts such as house arrest. Australians are not very familiar with the concept of house arrest … Members of the Burmese community who are now living in Australia came up and talked to me about this legislation because they understand well the impact of house arrest. This legislation allows for somebody – whomever it may be – to experience over 10 years of house arrest … That is what the military dictatorship in Burma has done to the leader of the democracy movement, whose party won the elections in 1990, and that is what this legislation gives the Australian government the power to do now or in the future.[9]

Despite living in Australia, the Burmese do not yet classify as Australian in Nettle's formulation. This is perhaps because they have not yet been granted citizenship by the state. At any rate her inclusion of this anecdote is to show, quite rightly, that the Australian government is behaving in ways that are analogous to a military dictatorship. But I take issue with this comparison for two reasons. The first is that there are many 'Australians' who have been granted citizenship by the Australian state but whose life experiences are drawn from other places in the world with their own unique political and social histories. Why doesn't Nettle consider that some Australians have non-Australian histories? Why does she homogenize all Australians as 'unfamiliar' with 'house arrest'? My contention is that she does this because who she is in fact speaking about when she says 'Australians' are in fact white Australians and by this conflation non-white Australians are positioned as 'ahistorical *tabula rasa* … devoid of prior histories of whiteness and racialised power' (Pugliese 2007). Further to this, Nettle, although a critic of the proposed legislation, reproduces ideas about law and democracy that give extremely narrow and legalistic meanings to terms like 'house arrest'. If one's home can become one's place of confinement where rights and liberties can be suspended by the authorities, then legal processes of colonialism which achieved Indigenous dispossession, can be seen to have brought about a state of 'house arrest' for entire peoples precisely by transforming, through the law, the home into prison. This is the foundation of Australian democracy. Nettle need not have looked as far as the Burmese example to find evidence for the suggestion that democracies can strip people to 'bare life' (Agamben 1998) as much as dictatorships can. But the colonial violence of the Australian state is what is continually effaced even by its so-called critics.

I have focused in some detail on the parliamentary debates around the Anti-Terrorism Bill because they assist in bringing to the fore another aspect of 'before' the law; the debate stage or the *democratic* process through which a Bill is transformed into an Act of law.[10] A critical reading of these debates reveals that even the critics of the process are instrumental in reproducing one of the primary

9 Senate Hansard, Tuesday, 6 December 2005.

10 For further discussion of the law in an Australian context, see Giannacopoulos (2007a).

myths of white law, that it is a location free from violence. Burke has argued in the context of security discourses and practices, that it is insufficient to question just the extremist enactments of security (Ruddock 2007: 3). It is imperative, he argues that 'mainstream critiques' (Ruddock 2007: 3) of security are also questioned because 'the surface appearance of lively (and often significant) debate masks a deeper agreement about major concepts, forms of political identity and the imperative to secure them' (Burke 2007: 3). The critics of the Anti-Terrorism legislation in 2005 can be seen to have been more interested in securing the proper procedures of law which in turn produce notions of law as democratic (as opposed to totalitarian) rather than in questioning the multiple forms of violence that this security legislation conceals and encodes. Andrea Smith's critical insight that when terror is made into a *crime* 'it actually serves to reproduce patriarchy and white supremacy by masking the sexism and racism of capitalism and the nation state' (Smith 2007: 47) is apt here. The politicians objecting to the Howard government's approach had no issue with the fact that the state could place terrorism *before* it, define it and in the process mask its own violent constitution. The legislation for and criminalization of terrorism is the means through which the state asserts its monopoly over violence.

The Anti-Terrorism Bill (No. 2) 2005 was also met with alarm by legal academic commentators who suggested that in pursuing its objectives the:

> preventative detention order regime breaches the human rights to be free from arbitrary detention and due process and cannot be said to be subject to an effective procedure of judicial review that provides adequate safeguards against violations of the human rights of the persons affected. (Byrnes et al. 2005)

Whilst these criticisms are incredibly important and draw attention to highly problematic aspects of the effects of the specific laws, they do not explicitly name the racial dimensions of this specific law as well as the way in which human rights concepts have been incorporated into the law as a means of denying them. This critique serves to position this particular legislation as 'bad' law since it is capable of breaching human rights protocols, leaving other laws and the violent nature of law itself un-interrogated. I suggest that these new laws warrant critical attention but this attention must also turn on what violence law is capable of, since violence is not external to law. To illustrate this point further I return to Philip Ruddock's defence of defence policy.

In a sentence that conjures Ruddock's period as Minister for Immigration, he states:

> Before turning to the specifics of Australia's response to terrorism, I would like to emphasise that preventative measures are not, as some critics have suggested, new to Australian law … the executive may take preventative steps with respect to asylum seekers, the mentally ill and people with infectious diseases … In the

> first and second world wars, regulations allowing internment of enemy aliens were upheld by the High Court as constitutionally valid. (Ruddock 2007: 3)

The government was trying to make this legislation appear *unexceptional* and in many ways it was. The executive 'may take preventative steps' because this discretionary power is enshrined in the Constitution, the document that founds the *independent* legal identity of the Australian state. Ruddock states, as a matter of legal fact, that racialized actions can be taken against refugees and aliens, without having to invoke the term 'race', because discrimination operates *as* law, as authorized by executive power. Ruddock addresses criticisms made of the Anti-Terrorism legislation by saying that 'it must be remembered that this is protective legislation … This approach is justified in light of the enormous threat which terrorism poses to our security' (Ruddock 2007: 4). He goes on to say that the rationale for preventative detention orders are the same as that of control orders, 'if there is credible evidence to satisfy a court that a person would be involved in a terrorist attack in the immediate future, the logical and responsible cause of action is to seek to contain and isolate that person to prevent an attack' (Ruddock 2007: 4). In order to silence his critics he uses the justification that needs no justification: protection. Even though the exact point of contention is the expansive reach of the Anti-Terrorism legislation that functions to produce the nation in a highly controlled and racialized manner, he suggests that the role of the legislation is to 'protect' which implies a sense of innocence for this process of effaced violence.

To the criticisms of the legal academics who say that there is not 'an effective procedure of judicial review' to protect the human rights of those affected by the Anti-Terrorism laws, he says with legal certainty and as proof of *lawful* practice that 'a recent constitutional challenge as to the validity of the parts of the legislation was unsuccessful' (Ruddock 2007: 3). Ruddock aligns himself with the Chief Justice in *Thomas v Mowbray*[11] to assert that the involvement of the courts amounts to the 'protection of human rights and not an abrogation from them' (Ruddock 2007: 6). I will return to this case shortly but I want to underscore here the way in which in this rhetorical move, human rights is equated with the operations of law which functions to suggest that Anti-Terrorism legislation *is* human rights legislation. Because the laws are designed to 'secure' and 'protect' the population from terroristic violence, the legislation is *protecting* the human right of the population to be secure. Burke's conceptualization of state power is apt here, both because he has identified the rationale used by the white sovereign state as well as the inadequacy of critiques of such action that are caught up in idealistic notions of the rule of law:

> sovereign states have long held and exercised such powers under the name of national security; as a normal sovereign prerogative available to executive government in the sphere of defence and foreign policy. Such powers are,

11 *Thomas v Mowbray* [2007] HCA 33.

> in short, not exceptional or 'outside' the law, but are all too often consistent with constitutional legal structures and grants of executive power. What this means is that a normative recourse to constitutionalism or the rule of law to counter such an apparent legal exceptionalism may be of limited value if the overarching ontology of security within which the rule of law takes shape is also not transformed. (Ruddock 2007: 10-11)

Here Ruddock was explaining the Constitution as the guarantor of liberty, but his lesson in the separation of powers reveals the way in which international events come to be present in the realm of domestic law:

> The ultimate safeguard of liberty in Australia is the Constitution along with the popular participation found in it … we are subject to the system of representative and responsible government, and separated powers, for which the Constitution provides. All action, whether it be legislative, executive or even judicial, is done under the Constitution in Australia. The response to terrorism is no different. (Ruddock 2007: 6)

Without yet mentioning it, Ruddock is engaging in a contest between opposing political systems. The system of which he is a representative is democratic, by virtue of a constitution that separates the three critical power concentrations: the legislature, the executive and the judicial. This didactic moment in Ruddock's text reveals the need to declare that this separation is a fact of democracy, even when the actions of the Howard government continually undermined this division of powers. I do not mean to suggest that they *improperly* used a *proper* system, if anything my argument is that the governmental actions were *proper* insofar as the constitution authorizes them, but it is this self generated logic, based on the *myth* of a separation of powers, that legitimizes and effaces an *improper*, violent and colonial system of governance. This violence is further effaced when Ruddock can, as a leader of a virtuous liberal democracy, go on to say that 'The Australian system of government is a strong one. Dicey thought that all federations were weak, and militant Islamists say the same thing about Western democracies' (Ruddock 2007: 7). From here it is impossible to know what the 'militant Islamists' say about Western democracies but it is possible to ascertain what Western democracies, as represented by Ruddock, say about 'militant Islamists'. This generic and homogenized category of 'militant Islamists' does not function as a real and identifiable group, but as an Orientalist (see Said 1995) construction generated by Ruddock, who here can be seen quite clearly to be saying that 'militant Islamists' are synonymous with terrorists, thereby revealing the racialized dimensions of the Anti-Terrorism legislation. The legislation is thus revealed to be racially supremacist but also legally and politically supremacist. By placing violence and terror outside of itself as something it judges and condemns the white state cleanses itself of colonial violence. The case of *Thomas v Mowbray* exposes the mythical claim of the separation of powers and Agamben's theory of the camp and of the state of exception is useful, but not without its limitations, in exposing the violence of the Western democratic Australian state. I will first discuss the racialized dimensions of the legislation whereby international events, that is, the global war on terror, get enacted in the Australian context and become encoded within Australian law. Unlike the domestic law's claim that Australian law is superior to international law and cannot be held captive to it, here the domestic law can be seen to embrace international developments, since the embracing of a war that announces Western democratic law to be antithetical to violence is consistent with the Australian state's colonial objectives and practices.

At the same time that these laws were being enacted, the *proof* that was needed to justify their importance in the national space came in the form of the Cronulla race riots where the 'militant Islamists' were understood as dangerous precisely because they were already within the national domain in the guise of 'Middle Eastern youth' threatening the white democratic order represented ably by young white men. Perera (2006: 41) has argued that 'Reimagined as "the homeland" in the context of the war on terror the already racially contested white site of the Australian beach produces compounding effects of exclusionary violence and xenophobia'.[12] The Sydney Morning Herald reported the battle for Cronulla beach as being between the 'mobs of youths chanting racist slogans and carrying Australian flags' who attacked the 'youths of Middle Eastern appearance' (SMH 2005a). Further reporting informed that 'a group later made its way back to Cronulla for a retaliatory strike, where men of Middle Eastern appearance are reported to have bashed a local man unconscious' (SMH 2005a). This particular representation does not burden white youths with *ethnic* descriptors. In sharp and deliberate opposition 'Middle Eastern' is properly capitalized as it is deployed to *give ethnicity* to the non-belonging youths. This framing of the battle for Cronulla beach continues the work of disavowing the connection between whiteness and violence even as the local youths are reported as being violent. The opposition set up in the reporting between the 'men of Middle Eastern appearance' who bashed the 'local man unconscious' repeats the familiar yet unspoken: the impossibility for youths *with ethnicity* to be local. This in turn creates the so-called locals as the un-raced, rightful owners of Cronulla beach. The beach is represented as being their possession to fight for. After all, if they chant racist slogans whilst carrying the Australian flag their violence comes to signify as something other than criminal *ethnic* violence. White violence at Cronulla beach is subtly sanctioned by creating a discursive distinction between legitimate violence and *ethnic* criminal violence. This legitimization of violence can be identified in the words of the former Prime Minister John Howard who said 'it's important that we do not rush to judgement about these events. I do not accept there is underlying racism in this country. I have always taken a more optimistic view of the character of the Australian people' (The Age 2005). Who are the 'Australian' people that Howard is optimistic about? Why should this event be shielded from immediate judgement? Who is it that can

12 For a further discussion of Cronulla, see Perera (2007) and Mitropoulos (2006).

occupy the position of *not* accepting that there is underlying racism in Australia? The white youths, although violent and racist, are cleansed in their violence by the carrying of Australian flags. The white youths, although violent in their actions are rendered innocent because their violence does not have a federal aspect.

The Anti-Terrorism Act (No. 2) 2005 Schedule 5 defines a 'serious terrorism offence' as amongst other things 'an offence against a law of a state' that has 'a federal aspect'. There is an aporia here, since all offences are deemed as such because they offend the laws of a state. So what is an offence with a federal aspect? Is it a crime against federation or a crime against the separation of powers? Is it a crime against the constitutional order or a crime against the democratic rule of law itself? Ruddock, as though imagining my line of questioning, said: 'If Australia did not have such preparatory offences and a terrorist act were to occur, the best we could expect from our criminal justice system would be convictions for murder' (Ruddock 2007: 5). Why wouldn't a conviction for murder be sufficient? The perpetrator would be deprived of their liberty and this could occur for the duration of their life. What harsher penalty could there be? But the point in a sense is not punishment which is what ordinarily takes place after a crime has been proven to have been committed. The point here is to circumvent established principles of law, *via law*, to bring punishment forward so that punishment precedes the crime as a way of preventing it. This process of criminalization which exceeds established principles of criminal law is the lawful way that legal and political dissent can be criminalized through the processes of law. The 'federal aspect', which is the qualification that enables this shift from established principles of criminal law, is thus revealed to be protecting not the population from violence by external terrorists, but functioning to protect the system of 'federalism' and its monopoly on violence through the terrorism that is encoded within Australian law. This point is made even clearer in Schedule 7 of the Act which defines 'seditious intention' as 'an intention to use force or violence to effect any of the following purposes':

> (a) To bring the Sovereign into hatred or contempt;
> (b) To urge disaffection against the following:
> (i) the constitution
> (ii) the government of the Commonwealth
> (iii) either house of Parliament
> (c) To urge another person to attempt to procure a change, otherwise than by lawful means, to any matter established by a law of the Commonwealth;
> (d) To promote feelings of ill-will or hostility between different groups so as to threaten the peace, order and good government of the Commonwealth.[13]

According to these legislative stipulations, it is impossible for the white youths to be considered terrorists, since terrorism is made synonymous with sedition and the

13 Anti Terrorism Act 2005.

white youths, like the laws themselves, are fighting to uphold the values of white law and democracy as represented by the Australian flag. In sharp distinction to this Pugliese (2006: 20) has observed that 'as underscored by the Cronulla race riots, subjects "of Middle Eastern appearance" are already within the current politically charged climate, figures who are tropically off the map: interlopers within the civic spaces of the nation'.

In Brighton-le-Sands where Bay Street was closed off and secured in what was a preview of the power of the Minister under 3UG of the Anti-Terrorism Act to declare a place be 'a prescribed security zone if he or she considers that a declaration would assist … In preventing a terrorist act occurring'[14] 'riot police were also called … to control groups of brawling youths who had reportedly thrown projectiles at police' (SMH 2005a). In Brighton-le-Sands the Australian flag had been burnt (SMH 2005b) making those who committed this action not only seditious but *internal* terrorists whose existence is antithetical to the liberal democracy in which they exist. Rockdale City Council, the council in which Brighton-le-Sands is situated, describes itself in official signs around the area as being situated on 'historic' Botany Bay. The violence done in the name of invasion and of empire is transformed and made static through the word 'historic'. And yet it was colonial images of violence supported by the flag of empire that came to mind as I watched the reporting of flag burning at Brighton-le-Sands. It was the British flag that Cook had forced into the earth upon invasion and it was in such manoeuvres that white sovereignty began to be violently asserted. As Schlunke (2002: 12) puts it: 'in 1770 James Cook arrived on the shores of Australia … The single ship was followed by a fleet and soon a flood. A systematic dispersal of Aboriginal people occurred which used massacre, reservations, diseases and "removal" of children amongst other techniques.' When framed in this way, the location of Botany Bay that appeared to be under threat by *ethnic* violence can be seen as having been constituted by a form of white sovereign violence which continues to be retrospectively legalized. The law relies on forms of visible disorder like the 'brawling youths' who need to be controlled by 'riot police' to continue to naturalize the law's function as restoring order and not as being implicated in the ongoing project of white sovereignty which requires all locations to be treated unproblematically as legitimately white possessions. Representations of *ethnic, terrorist* violence function to keep the concept of 'terrorism' glued to its 'eurocentric range of signification' (Pugliese 2006: 28). Pugliese (2006: 28) argues that terrorism 'must be wrenched' from its eurocentric meanings and 'understood in terms of that which is unfolding in the context of the coalition's war in Iraq. The magnitude of the terror unleashed by the "axis of the willing's" war in Iraq largely fails to register in the west.' In fact Australian law, at every one of its purportedly separate levels continually produces legal *truths* that justify the killing of civilians overseas in the name of domestic security.

---

14 Anti-Terrorism Act 2005.

In *Thomas v Mowbray* the High Court of Australia had to decide whether an order made by the Court under the Criminal Code, as amended through the Anti-Terrorism Act 2005 was invalid for the reason that the Act conferred upon the Court non-judicial power. It was alleged by the plaintiffs that there was no authority for such an order to be made because it was made via a breach of the separation of powers doctrine as enshrined in the Constitution. The interim control order had been made against Thomas who according to the judgement admitted that he had trained with al-Qaeda, a listed terrorist organization under section 4A of the Criminal Code. It was said that such training had 'provided Mr Thomas with the capability to execute or assist with the execution directly or indirectly of any terrorist acts'.[15] The majority of the High Court held that the powers conferred on the Court, authorizing the making of the control order *were* valid otherwise it would have been 'inappropriate to answer'.[16] This suggests that the Court *had* to find that the exercise of legislative power granting the Court (itself) power to work in unison with the will of the legislature was valid, given that they say that anything else would be 'inappropriate'. What then, resides in this category of the 'inappropriate'? This question is not addressed directly in the judgement of Chief Justice Gleeson because it comes too close, I argue, to exposing the *fiction* of the separation of powers. The Court in effect made a judgement about its own exercise of power and found that this was exercised validly, thereby the Court literally ruled in favour of itself. Whereas in the *Mabo (No. 2)* judgement the Court read its power *narrowly* (even if the effect was expansive and colonially violent) by saying that it could not inquire into the question of sovereignty as this would 'fracture the skeleton of principle', here the Court also upheld the 'skeleton of principle' of the Australian nation but this time by reading their powers as *extensive*, by finding that their own powers were valid.[17] Whilst the Court in *Mabo (No. 2)* ruled that the question of sovereignty was non-justiciable, here the High Court held, in effect, that the system by which this sovereignty is held is highly justiciable, especially since 'the controls set out in this interim control order statement will protect the public and substantially assist in preventing a terrorist act. Without these controls, Mr Thomas's knowledge and skills could provide a potential resource for the planning or preparation of a terrorist act.'[18]

To trace the aporetic logic of this judgement I hypothesize: what would have been the result if the Court had found that the power to make the order, as set out in the Anti-Terrorism legislation and the Criminal Code, was *invalid*? The Court's own response that such an answer would be 'inappropriate' suggests that the logic of the separation of powers, in this instance, functions to render *impossible* any other legal decision whilst also exposing the idea of a *separation* of powers as a

15 *Thomas v Mowbray* [2007] HCA 33.

16 *Thomas v Mowbray* [2007] HCA 33.

17 For further discussion of Mabo and non-justiciability of sovereignty, see Giannacopoulos (2007b).

18 *Thomas v Mowbray* [2007] HCA 33.

fiction. Would this outcome have been *inappropriate* because it departed from the will of the executive? Chief Justice Gleeson justifies the appropriateness of the uniformity between the Parliament and the judiciary by saying 'If, as in the present case, Parliament decides to confer a power on the judicial branch of government, this reflects a parliamentary intention that the power should be exercised judicially, and with the independence and impartiality which should characterise the judicial branch of government.'[19]

The Chief Justice defends the legislation by drawing upon democratic discourse, to suggest that the validity of the Court order is ensured because it manifests a 'parliamentary intention'. But as I attempted to show in the introductory part of this chapter, the 'parliamentary intention' was in fact the will of the executive. Although the Court was compelled to act in the interests of the executive, I do not want to fall into the reasoning that the Court was *coerced* by the executive as this would remove from view the way in which these seeming *coincidences* produce the myth of the separation of powers, even if in effect there is no separation. However, the Court is cunning in the way that it judges itself because if judged by the standards the Court *says* it is ruled and rules by, 'independence' and 'impartiality', then the decision that they did make, that the control order was valid, is actually quite inappropriate, since they judge in favour of themselves. Dyzenhaus and Thwaites would account for this by saying that the judiciary, like the legislature and the executive, demonstrate 'the compulsion of legality: the compulsion to justify all acts of state as having a legal warrant – the authority of law' (2007: 10). The use of the word 'compulsion' as the condition that brings about 'legality' confirms my analysis regarding the *lack* of separation of powers in two ways. Firstly, the term implies a form of behaviour that is irresistible and unavoidable. Secondly, 'compulsion', being the relative of *compulsory*, invokes the violent force of law. This is because there appears to be no choice available to those upholding white sovereignty as to whether the law will be brought to bear on a situation in a way that works to legitimate power. The judiciary's 'compulsion to legality' can be seen as the compulsion to preserve, as legitimate, the system of white sovereignty. This involves actions that ensure self-preservation for the judges but their actions amount to more than this since the judges are compelled to maintain the legitimacy of a violent colonial state. That their actions function as a compulsion, means that there is very little space remaining for critical inquiry about such actions. The *other* decision would have been *impossible* in the sense that it would fracture the 'skeleton of principle' that keeps their position guarded from critique and challenge. The *inappropriate* decision is one that decentres the white judiciary as having the right to decide what is legally possible. Even if judged as inappropriate, the decision of the High Court functions in line with the self generated logic that it is 'independent' and 'impartial' as though these concepts are universally good and not the categories through which white colonial law asserts itself and its legitimacy.

19 *Thomas v Mowbray* [2007] HCA 33.

Chief Justice Gleeson asserts:

> The power to make laws with respect to the naval and military defence of the Commonwealth and of the several States, and the control of the forces to execute and maintain the laws of the Commonwealth, is not limited to defence against aggression from a foreign nation; it is not limited to external threats; it is not confined to waging war in a conventional sense of combat between forces of nation; and it is not limited to protection of bodies politic as distinct from the public, or sections of the public.[20]

Here he is expanding the definition of 'defence' insofar as it can be legislated for with reference to the Constitution, with a specific emphasis on the way in which the sovereign nation can defend itself *as* a sovereign nation, in relation to its own population. The population within the white sovereign state can, or rather sections of it can, according to Gleeson's ruling, be treated as another state threatening the sovereignty of the nation would be treated. The *inside* of the nation can be seen as rezoned in terms of its *people* or *human* citizens and its *alien* citizens, thus animating Agamben's claim that 'where there is a People, there will be bare life' (Agamben 1998: 179). Whilst Agamben's theorizations of state power dovetail at many points with the central arguments in this chapter, I also want to raise some questions about Agamben's thesis on the camp as the 'materialisation of the state of exception' (Agamben 1998: 174). I want to preface these questions by acknowledging that Agamben's work in this regard is complex, compelling and important across numerous disciplinary locations. I argue that Agamben's theorization of state power is not limited because of its sustained focus on law as Burke (2007: 10) suggests, but rather because his analysis of law does not sufficiently complicate the relationship between colonial power and law. The questions I raise also stem from Agamben's conclusion in *State of Exception* about law's ability to be 'revived' and redeemed (Burke 2007: 11) if it can also be severed from violence (Agamben 2005: 88).

Agamben (1998: 166) raises the issue of the colony when he discusses the debates between historians about when the first camps appeared. Were the Spanish the first in Cuba, or the English in their imprisonment of the Boer population? From this, Agamben (1998: 166-167) concluded that what was of importance was that 'a state of emergency linked to a colonial war is extended to an entire civil population. The camps are thus born not out of ordinary law … but out of a state of exception and martial law.' My question here relates to the Australian colonial context and what would be defined and by whom as *ordinary* law under these circumstances? If the law is a key component of the normalization of a colonial order by the imposition of what is then thought of as *ordinary* law then what is the value of *ordinary* law as distinct from a 'state of exception'?

20 *Thomas v Mowbray* [2007] HCA 33.

The Anti-Terrorism Act is not a camp in the way that Agamben describes. His emphasis is on the way in which the 'camp consists in the materialization of the state of exception and in the subsequent creation of a space in which bare life and the juridical rule enter into a threshold of indistinction' (Agamben 1998: 174). Although the camp comes in many different configurations, the camp according to Agamben has a physical form. Importantly the form that the camp takes does not have to be in any way exceptional. In fact as Agamben argues, an 'apparently innocuous space' such as a hotel, or a sports stadium can, through the suspension of the 'normal order' (Agamben 1998: 174) turn a civil space into a space where atrocities are permitted. Joseph Pugliese extends Agamben's notion by arguing that 'Civil penality articulates the colonising of civic sites and civil practices by the state; it names the transmutation of hotel rooms and demountables into extensions of Australia's punitive and violent carceral apparatus' (Pugliese 2009: 155). Pugliese further argues that, 'The resignification of a hotel room in terms of a prison cell serves to violate the lexicon of the Australian vernacular; indeed, this linguistic turn instantiates what can only be called *vernacular violence*: this is a violence that is masked by its very ordinariness' (Pugliese 2009: 153). This argument is compelling and far reaching in its significance. Because Pugliese situates violence within the practices of everyday life, in the ordinary locations where life mundanely unfolds, he challenges our definitions of violence and therefore our ability to identify and assess our own complicity in the violence that unfolds everywhere around us.

Although a piece of law, specifically the Anti-Terrorism Act, cannot be understood strictly as a camp, it can certainly be understood as a location of effaced violence; effaced precisely because of its *ordinariness*. Under section 3UK of the Act, the state of legislated exception is defined as a ten-year period, that being the sunset clause of the legislation.[21] As such, the *ordinary* legislation passed in 2005, *ordinary* because its passing did not require the suspension of the *normal* order or of the Constitution but was an effect of procedures set out in that founding colonial document, gives the legislature, executive and judiciary the *lawful* option for ten years to suspend *normal* law by activating this legislation. In making this argument I want to underscore that this legislation, the way it is enacted and selectively deployed is only possible since the very ground upon which this takes place has been turned, through colonization, into the place of *ordinary* law and therefore of *ordinary* violence. The violent potential of the Anti-Terrorism Act is premised on the practices of Indigenous dispossession that have cleared the land of Indigenous laws so that *ordinary*, *singular*, white law can reign.

The Anti-Terrorism Act is unexceptional in the sense that it continues the work of colonization. The operations of *ordinary* law are always violent in the colonial context and not only when the Constitution is suspended. The Constitution, despite Ruddock's claim that Australian people voted for it (Ruddock 2007: 6), is the effect of Indigenous peoples being made bare life, so that the Australian nation

21 Anti-Terrorism Act (No.2) 2005.

might be founded and, in the context of this chapter, so that it may be further secured, whilst the Australian *people* are *protected.* In the context of an ongoing colonial project, violence and law cannot be prized apart as Agamben (2005: 88) suggests they can, because in the Australian context the law must ensure, through its legally violent processes, that white law remains the strongest form of violence in order to continue to secure the nation as a white possession. It is not up to those who have ruled and continue to rule the land with colonial violence to sit in judgement about violence and yet this is what colonial power allows them to do. National security and the legislation generated in its name, seek in the final analysis to secure the right of white colonial sovereigns to exercise violence over stolen lands. Moreton-Robinson has put it this way:

> As a regime of power, patriarchal white sovereignty operates ideologically, materially and discursively to reproduce and maintain its investment in the nation as a white possession. One of the ways in which the possessive investment manifests itself is through a discourse of security, which supports the existence, protection and maintenance of patriarchal white sovereignty. (Moreton-Robinson 2007: 88)

References

Agamben, G. 1998. *Homo Sacer: Sovereign Power and Bare Life*, translated by D. Heller Roazen. Stanford, CA: Stanford University Press.

Agamben, G. 2005. *State of Exception*, translated by K. Attell. Chicago, IL: University of Chicago Press.

The Age. 2005. 'Fresh Violence Rocks Sydney'. *The Age*, 13 December 2005.

Burke, A. 2007. *Beyond Security, Ethics and Violence: War against the Other*. London and New York: Routledge.

Byrnes, A., Charlesworth, H. and McKinnon, G. 2005. 'Human Rights Implications of the *Anti-Terrorism Bill* 2005'. [Online]. Available at: http://www.chiefminister.act.gov.au/docs/Stanhope_advice_20051018.pdf [accessed 25 April 2011].

Dyzenhaus, D. and Thwaites, R. 2007. 'Legality and Emergency: The Judiciary in a Time of Terror', in *Law and Liberty in the War on Terror*, edited by A. Lynch, E. MacDonald and G. Williams. Sydney: The Federation Press.

Giannacopoulos, M. 2005. 'Tampa: Violence at the Border'. *Social Semiotics*, Special Issue: *Charged Crossings: Cultural Studies of Law*, 15(1) (April).

Giannacopoulos, M. 2007a. '*Nomos Basileus*: The Reign of Law in a World of Violence'. *Australian Critical Race and Whiteness Studies Association (ACRAWSA) E-journal*, Special Issue: *The Borderpolitics of Whiteness*, 3(1). [Online]. Available at: http://acrawsa.org.au/files/ejournalfiles/67MariaGiannacopoulos.pdf [accessed 15 August 2009].

Giannacopoulos, M. 2007b. '*Mabo*, *Tampa* and the Non-Justiciability of Sovereignty', in *Our Patch: Enacting Australian Sovereignty Post 2001*, edited by Suvendrini Perera. Perth: API Network.

Mitropoulos, A. 2006. 'Under the Beach, the Barbed Wire'. [Online]. Available at: http://www.metamute.org/Under-the-Beach-the-Barbed-Wire [accessed 25 April 2011].

Moreton-Robinson, A. 2007. 'Writing off Indigenous Sovereignty: The Discourse of Security and Patriarchal White Sovereignty', in *Sovereign Subjects: Indigenous Sovereignty Matters*, edited by Aileen Moreton-Robinson. Sydney: Allen and Unwin.

Perera, S. 2006. 'Race, Terror, Sydney, December 2005'. *borderlands ejournal*, 5(1). [Online]. Available at: http://www.borderlands.net.au/vol5no1_2006/perera_raceterror.htm [accessed 25 April 2011].

Perera, S. 2007. '"Aussie Luck": The Border Politics of Citizenship Post Cronulla Beach'. *ACRAWSA e-journal*, 3(1). [Online]. Available at: http://www.acrawsa.org.au/ [accessed 25 April 2011].

Pugliese, J. 2006. 'Asymmetries of Terror: Visual Regimes of Racial Profiling and the Shooting of Jean Charles de Menezes in the Context of the War in Iraq'. *borderlands ejournal*, 5(1). [Online]. Available at: http://www.borderlands.net.au/vol5no1_2006/pugliese.htm [accessed 25 April 2011].

Pugliese, J. 2007. 'White Historicide and the Returns of the Souths of the South'. *Australian Humanities Review*, Special Issue: *Approaching Whiteness*, 42 (August-September).

Pugliese, J. 2009. 'Civil Modalities of Refugee Trauma, Death and Necrological Transport'. *Social Identities*, 15(1) (January).

Ruddock, P. 2007. 'Law as a Preventative Weapon Against Terrorism', in *Law and Liberty in the War on Terror*, edited by A. Lynch, E. MacDonald and G. Williams. Sydney: The Federation Press.

Said, E.W. 1995. *Orientalism: Western Conceptions of the Orient*. Harmondsworth: Penguin Books.

Schlunke, Katrina. 2002. 'Sovereign Hospitalities?' *borderlands ejournal*, 1(2). [Online]. Available at: http://www.borderlands.net.au/vol1no2_2002/schlunke_hospitalities.html [accessed 10 July 2009].

SMH. 2005a. 'Sydney's Racist Mob Violence Spreads'. *Sydney Morning Herald*, 11 December 2005.

SMH. 2005b. 'Two Refused Bail over Flag Burning'. *Sydney Morning Herald*. [Online, 23 December 2005]. Available at: http://www.smh.com.au/news/national/riot-fallout-flag-burning-charges-laid/2005/12/23/1135032159706.html [accessed 25 April 2011].

Smith, A. 2007. 'Unmasking the State: Racial/Gender Terror and Hate Crimes'. *The Australian Feminist Law Journal*, 26.

Chapter 13

'The Unbearable Whiteness of Beckham': Semiotics and Political Recoding of the Contemporary Celebrity

David Tan[1]

If the celebrity semiotic sign is recognized to represent the values of a majoritarian public, then the debate and opposition to these encoded ideals may be expressed by using the same signs in a 'recoded' manner, and such counterpublic uses can therefore be categorized as 'political speech'. Through an analysis of right of publicity claims, the author suggests that in order for political speech to be given adequate breathing space, it would be beneficial to understand how semiotic and cultural studies writings can contribute to the articulation of a robust First Amendment defence that adequately protects countercultural representations.

Introduction

Who is David Beckham? Or *what* is David Beckham? Physically he is a 34-year-old Anglo-Saxon male. Culturally, he is the White Knight. Gay Icon. Sex Symbol. Sporting Hero. David Beckham is the quintessential contemporary celebrity who is well-known to millions of people all around the world, from North America to Asia, from Europe to Africa.

According to Richard Dyer and many other cultural studies scholars, the celebrity is a sign that embodies particular meanings for the majoritarian public. Richard Dyer's extensive work on the movie star has been consistently hailed as being highly influential in the contemporary study of the meaning of celebrities in society. Celebrities can 'represent typical ways of behaving, feeling and thinking in contemporary society, ways that have been socially, culturally, historically constructed' (see Dyer 2004: 15-16).[2] In building on Dyer's arguments in examining the celebrity as a form of cultural power and its significance in identity formation,

---

1 PhD (Melbourne), LLM (Harvard), LLB B Com (Melbourne). I would like to express my appreciation to Professors Andrew Christie and Andrew Kenyon, Melbourne Law School, for their insightful comments on earlier drafts.

2 See also Dyer (1979: 3) (discussing how Hollywood, through its representation of movie stars, can reproduce the 'dominant ideology of Western society').

David Marshall observes that celebrities function as stable configurations of collective identity formations and act as 'icons of democracy and democratic will' (see Marshall 1997: 246). The courts have also noted that celebrities have become 'common points of reference for millions of individuals who may never interact with one another, but who share, by virtue of their participation in a mediated culture [as the audience], a common experience and a collective memory' (see Thompson 1990: 163).[3]

As illustrated in Roland Barthes' work, *Mythologies* (Barthes 1972: 110-111) a particular well-known individual, like David Beckham (the signifier), may be viewed as a sign that denotes 'celebrity' (the signified). The widespread media narratives and other forms of commercial and non-commercial circulation of the celebrity sign also result in a particular celebrity sign garnering certain connotations which make it distinctive *vis-à-vis* other signs.[4] Thus a celebrity sign like David Beckham is able to differentiate itself from other celebrity signs with an ascribed set of connotations; for example, the Beckham sign can connote attributes of sexual desirability and over time, the Beckham sign 'develops into a *metalanguage* and becomes a significant resource for cultural expression and critique' (Bosland 2005: 107).

Referring to Barthes' seminal work (Barthes 1972) as well as to Antonio Gramsci (e.g. Gramsci (1971) and Claude Lévi-Strauss (e.g. Lévi-Strauss 1967) Stuart Hall discusses the politics of signification (see Hall 1982: 70-74) and how ideological discourses of a particular society are classified and framed through semiotic signs within a 'pragmatic circle of knowledge' (Turner 2004: 103). In Barthesian terms, the celebrity image is seen to be a 'cultural narrative' or signifier that is synonymous with the dominant culture (Fuery and Fuery 2003: 93, 101). Due to the meticulously constructed public personae of many celebrities – particularly movie stars and sport icons – the semiotic signs of these well-known individuals are usually 'decoded' by the audience to represent a defined cluster of meanings. As a result of its publicly identifiable encodings, the celebrity semiotic sign also presents rich opportunities for alternative codings to challenge these 'typical ways of behaving, feeling and thinking in contemporary society' (Dyer 2004: 15-16) representative of majoritarian ideals.

According to Dyer's pioneering analyses, celebrities can have an ideological function of not only reiterating dominant values, but also concealing prevalent contradictions or social problems. More generally, cultural scholars have argued that 'identities can function as point of identification and attachment only *because* of their capacity to exclude, to leave out, to render "outside" abjected' (Hall 1996: 5).[5] This theme of popular subcultural resistance permeates the bulk

3 See also citations of Thompson in *ETW Corp v Jireh Publishing Inc*, 332 F 3d 915, 933 (6th Cir, 2003) ('*ETW Corp*'); *Cardtoons LC v Major League Baseball Players Association*, 95 F 3d 959, 972 (10th Cir, 1996) ('*Cardtoons*').

4 For a similar argument in relation to trademark, see Beebe (2004).

5 Emphasis in original. See also Hall (1997b).

of contemporary cultural studies (Marshall 1997: 46; Hall 1981: 239). What significance do all these observations have for the right of publicity and the First Amendment?

The right of publicity, broadly defined as the 'inherent right of every human being to control the commercial use of his or her identity' (McCarthy 2000: 3:1),[6] has been well-established in the United States for over 50 years.[7] It protects the burgeoning 'associative value' that well-known individuals bring to products and services (see Halpern 1995: 856, 859-860). The relevance of cultural studies here to right of publicity doctrine is the observation that different groups in society can use particular celebrity images in a variety of ways to represent their cultural identities and convey their political ideologies.[8] Hence the structural domination of a white Anglo-Saxon heterosexual male social identity – like the David Beckham sign – that occupies a privileged public identity suggests that other identities organized around being non-white, homosexual or female will have socially subordinate positions. The whiteness of the David Beckham sign is perhaps most starkly captured in the advertisement for Walt Disney theme parks where Beckham was portrayed as the gallant Prince Philip from the fairytale *Sleeping Beauty* astride a white stallion battling a dragon (Faber 2007; Walt Disney Company 2009). Other exemplars based on different combinations of race, class, gender, athleticism and sexual desirability also create multiple privileged social identities each valuing a particular ideological position over another. Thus a particular celebrity – like Beckham – who is symbolic of a privileged public identity can be seen to represent a majoritarian ideological position – a form of 'frozen speech' (see Barthes 1972: 112) – and is therefore open to a recoding challenge by minority groups to represent their cultural identities and convey their political ideologies.

This chapter argues that certain uses of the celebrity sign may be 'political speech' protected by the First Amendment, depending on content, form and context. It adopts the premise that the underlying rationale of the First Amendment is the advancement of a democracy where the public can freely participate in deliberating issues important to decision-making in a democracy. This is a plausible and well-supported view of the First Amendment. It further contends that the augmentation of this participatory theory of the First Amendment with cultural studies insights is likely to lead to better outcomes in cases because more speech of 'greater' constitutional value is protected – i.e. speech that contributes to

6 The right of publicity is articulated in the *Restatement (Third) of Unfair Competition* as follows: '[o]ne who appropriates the commercial value of a person's identity by using without consent the person's name, likeness, or other indicia of identity for purposes of trade is subject to liability'. *Restatement (Third) of Unfair Competition* § 46 (1995).

7 It was first recognized by the Second Circuit in 1953 that baseball players had a 'right of publicity' in their images. *Haelan Laboratories Inc v Topps Chewing Gum Inc*, 202 F 2d 866, 868 (2nd Cir, 1953).

8 I have explored this theme in an earlier work. See Tan (2008).

an increased awareness and debate of public issues – while speech of 'lesser' value need not be accorded the same level of protection.

The following section will show that First Amendment jurisprudence, especially Supreme Court decisions, supports an overarching approach to the First Amendment in terms of a participatory theory that places the highest constitutional value on political speech.

The section following that argues that the various tests formulated to give effect to First Amendment goals in right of publicity claims do not accord sufficient protection to political speech because they do not adequately address how uses of the celebrity identity may contribute to the advancement of democratic deliberation and debate. This is demonstrated through an analysis of the three main judicial tests presently used to articulate a First Amendment defence in publicity claims.

The next section contends that cultural studies writings on the political significance of the celebrity semiotic sign can assist the development of First Amendment jurisprudence and judicial tests in this area. It advances the analysis by recommending ways in which the three tests may incorporate relevant insights on the recoding potential of the celebrity sign especially as used by subaltern groups or counterpublics as an integral part of political and social identity formation.

The final section concludes that this use of cultural studies allows current First Amendment jurisprudence to be refined to protect political speech in a manner that more effectively negotiates the competing right of the celebrity individual to exploit the commercial value of his or her identity and the right of the public to use the celebrity sign as an expressive communicative resource in a participatory democracy.

Overview of the First Amendment

It has been noted by free speech scholar Rodney Smolla that '[c]ontemporary free speech doctrines are extraordinarily detailed and often confusing' and that '[m]odern First Amendment law abounds in three-part and four-part tests of various kinds' (Smolla and Nimmer 2008: 2:13; see also Post 2000: 2355) While it is not the purpose of this chapter to propose a systematic reconciliation or reconstruction of the contentious doctrines and rules of the First Amendment, this section argues that participatory understandings of democracy can provide a strong foundation for articulating an appropriate standard of protection for political speech under right of publicity laws.

Courts generally are concerned that the enforcement of publicity rights does not have a 'chilling effect'[9] on free speech. There are various theories of the First Amendment but this chapter adopts a participatory theory of democracy involving deliberation and debate for two key reasons. First, in addition to the centrality of

9 *Dombrowski v Pfister*, 380 US 479, 487 (Brennan J) (1965). See also Barendt (2005: 38), Schauer (1982: 80-85).

such an understanding in justifying free speech in any representative democracy, it is also an integral feature of many other prominent theories (Fallon 1999: 577-578). Second, US case law has consistently demonstrated the 'preferred position' of political speech at the apex of a speech hierarchy, and this in turn indicates the preeminence of participatory understandings of democracy (Barendt 2005: 20-21).[10] However, it should be noted that courts may also consider other justifications that cover non-political expressions as there is no single overarching theory that can account for the protection given to different types of speech.

Mutually supportive theories for the First Amendment have been said to rest on the tripartite goals of the Framers of the US Constitution that comprise sponsoring enlightenment or the discovery of truth, self-fulfilment and citizen participation in a deliberative democracy.[11] In its earlier conceptions, the First Amendment goal of enlightenment or the discovery of truth is represented most prominently by Oliver Wendell Holmes' theory of a 'marketplace of ideas' in which 'the ultimate good desired is ... reached by free trade in ideas',[12] and that 'the best test of truth is the power of the thought to get itself accepted in the competition of the market.'[13] The marketplace theory is perhaps 'the most famous and rhetorically resonant of all free speech theories' (Smolla and Nimmer 2008: 2:4) but it also exhibits a strong underlying democratic theory, evident in the oft-quoted phrase from *New York Times v Sullivan* that there is a 'profound national commitment' to the principle that 'debate on public issues should be uninhibited, robust, and wide-open'.[14]

However, the Supreme Court has more recently embraced a 'participatory theory of democracy' (e.g. Post 2000: 2371)[15] that is concerned with the enlightenment of public decision-making in a democracy through enabling public access to information and promoting public discourse.[16] Often known as the

10 It has also been called the 'most important theoretical approach to freedom of speech in the twentieth century' (Balkin 2004: 28).

11 Rodney Smolla argues that all three theories should be understood 'not as *mutually exclusive* defences of freedom of speech, but rather as *mutually supportive* rationales' (Smolla and Nimmer 2008: § 2:7). See also McCarthy (2000: 8:2-8:8); Smolla (1992: 14-17); Barendt (2005: 7-21).

12 *Abrams v United States*, 250 US 616, 630 (1919) ('*Abrams*'). See also *Whitney v California*, 274 US 357, 375 (1927).

13 *Abrams*, 250 US 616, 630 (1919).

14 *New York Times Co v Sullivan*, 376 US 254, 270 (1964) ('*NYT*') as quoted in *NAACP v Claiborne Hardware Co*, 458 US 886, 913 (1982) ('*NAACP*'); *Boos v Barry*, 485 US 312, 318 (1988) ('*Boos*'). The democratic variant of the marketplace of ideas theory was first discussed in *Thornhill v Alabama*, 310 US 88, 96, 101-102 (1940).

15 See also Barendt (2005: 18-21). Smolla refers to this as the 'democratic self-governance' rationale (Smolla and Nimmer 2008: 2:28).

16 E.g. *Virginia v Black*, 538 US 343, 365 (2003) ('*Black*'); *Reno v American Civil Liberties Union*, 521 US 844, 885 (1997) ('*Reno*'); *Hustler Magazine Inc v Falwell*, 485 US 46, 53 (1988) ('*Falwell*'); *Virginia State Board of Pharmacy v Virginia Citizens Consumer Council*, 425 US 748, 765 (1976) ('*Virginia Pharmacy*').

Madisonian ideal of deliberative democracy, different but related versions of this theory have been prominently championed by constitutional scholars like Robert Post (e.g. Post 1990, 1993, 2000), Cass Sunstein (Sunstein 1993: 17-23, 241-252; 2001: 6-9, 96-101, 239-243) and Jack Balkin.[17] Although the Supreme Court has never ruled that to qualify for the highest levels of constitutional protection speech must relate to self-government (Garry 2007: 519; Smolla and Nimmer 2008: 2:46) Justice Stephen Breyer, speaking in an extra-judicial capacity, has advocated an approach to constitutional adjudication centred on 'active liberty' similar to Post's participatory theory (Breyer 2002: 246). An acceptance of the participatory theory has important implications for the continuing development of judicial approaches in resolving the tension between free speech values and property rights in a right of publicity claim as it focuses not on an abstract notion of the quest for truth but on how the nature and content of communication can 'ensure that the individual can effectively participate in and contribute to our republican system of self-government'[18] where 'national identity [is understood] to be endlessly controversial' (Post 2000: 2369; Barendt 2005: 48-49).

This chapter concurs with the observation that 'where the doctrinal implications of different prominent theories ... collide, courts will tend to give priority to the participatory theory of democracy' (Post 2000: 2371).[19] The participatory theory clearly elevates political discourse to a special status at the top of the speech hierarchy and this is reinforced by Supreme Court decisions that consistently accord to political speech the highest constitutional value in the system of American democracy.[20] It seems that the Supreme Court has implicitly accepted the participatory theory with frequent pronouncements such as the First Amendment 'was fashioned to assure unfettered interchange of ideas for the bringing about of political and social changes desired by the people'[21] and 'the practice of persons sharing common views banding together to achieve a common end is deeply embedded in the American political process.'[22] Generally, political speech covers all discussion on public issues, especially if intended by

17 Balkin argues that the purpose of free speech is to promote a 'democratic culture' that is even broader than deliberation about public issues such that each individual has 'a fair chance to participate in the production of culture, and in the development of the ideas and meanings that constitute them and the communities and subcommunities to which they belong' (Balkin 2004: 4).

18 *Globe Newspaper Co v Superior Court*, 457 US 596, 604 (1982).

19 According to Schauer, the 'narrowness of the argument from democracy is also its greatest strength ... it does furnish several strong reasons for giving special attention and protection to political speech' (Schauer 1982: 44).

20 *Dun & Bradstreet*, 472 US 749, 759 (1985). See also *Morse v Frederick*, 551 US 393, 403 (2007); *Black*, 538 US 343, 365 (2003); *NAACP*, 458 US 886, 913 (1982); Smolla and Nimmer (2008: 16:1-16:2).

21 *Connick v Myers*, 461 US 138, 145 (1983); *NYT*, 376 US 254, 269 (1964); *Roth v United States*, 354 US 476, 484 (1957).

22 *NAACP*, 458 US 886, 906 (1982).

the speaker to influence governmental action.[23] Political speech has been defined by commentators as speech that has 'a reasoned, cognitive connection to some identifiable political issue that has the potential of entering the legislative arena' (Garry 2007: 516) or 'when it is both intended and received as a contribution to public deliberation about some issue' (Sunstein 1993: 130).

The First Amendment Defence in a Right of Publicity Claim

As Part II has shown, a preponderance of Supreme Court decisions and scholarly writings support the view that the central goal of the First Amendment is to advance democratic deliberation. Therefore, it follows that the defendant's use of the celebrity identity may be classified as political speech with the highest constitutional value if it contributes to democratic processes, and such uses should be accorded a greater value than artistic speech or entertainment. However, political speech does not occupy a paramount position in the current judicial tests which have been formulated to resolve the conflict between the plaintiff's proprietary right in identity and the First Amendment.

Limited Guidance from the US Supreme Court

The Supreme Court, in its only decision to have ever considered a clash between the right of publicity and the First Amendment, eschewed the heightened scrutiny doctrine used in the governmental regulation of speech cases.[24] *Zacchini v Scripps-Howard Broadcasting Co* was unusual on its facts because what was appropriated was the plaintiff's entire 15-second human cannonball act. Indeed the *Zacchini* decision may be distinguished from most right of publicity claims which involve an unauthorized use of name, likeness or other evocative aspects of identity rather than the performance value of identity (McCarthy 1995: 133; Ausness 1982: 989-990). Thus many commentators and courts have construed *Zacchini* to be of limited precedential value, relevant only to the rare situation where the plaintiff's 'entire act' has been appropriated (McCarthy 2000: 8:27; Jones 2006: 946).[25] As a result, as the following sub-section will show, lower courts have independently formulated their own tests to resolve the property-speech conflict. However, this chapter argues that *Zacchini* is important here because of its direct balancing approach to resolving the conflict between the plaintiff's property right and the First Amendment.

Despite the frequent rejection of case-by-case balancing in First Amendment cases involving state action, the *Zacchini* majority recognized that the proprietary

23 *NAACP*, ibid. 913-914; *Garrison*, 379 US 64, 74-75 (1964); *NYT*, 376 US 254, 270 (1964).

24 *Zacchini v Scripps-Howard Broadcasting Co*, 433 US 562 (1977) ('*Zacchini*').

25 *Comedy III*, 25 Cal 4th 387, 401 (2001).

right of publicity is not always trumped by free speech. The majority appeared to balance, on the one hand, the threat to the economic value of the plaintiff's performance and the impact of his ability to earn a living,[26] and the social purposes of preventing 'unjust enrichment' and providing 'an economic incentive ... to make the investment to produce a performance of interest to the public',[27] and on the other hand, the benefit of news and entertainment to the public.[28] However, without elaboration, the majority held that the plaintiff was entitled to compensation as the media was not always immunized by the First Amendment in right of publicity claims, a conclusion that was criticized by the dissent for its perfunctory brevity.[29]

In contrast to the majority opinion which focused on the economic value of the plaintiff's act and whether this value was taken by the defendant, the dissent looked to the intent of the media defendant as a starting point in their analysis. Nevertheless, both the majority and the dissent 'recognized that any formula to be used when deciding the First Amendment issue should be based on a consideration of the public's benefits and losses resulting in the absence of the privilege' (Wanat 2003: 255). This aspect of *Zacchini* is often ignored by judges and commentators who champion a particular test. For present purposes, it is notable that the *Zacchini* balancing approach can accommodate a participatory theory of democracy, where greater protection may be given to uses of the celebrity identity that promote attention to public issues and engender public debate.[30]

Judicial Approaches

Regardless of the judicial test ultimately used, the Circuit and state courts agree that if the defendant's use of the plaintiff's identity is categorized as protected 'core' speech – e.g. political speech, entertainment, art – then the defendant *may* be immune from liability; but if it is classified as commercial speech, the defendant will be liable for the commercial exploitation of the associative value of the plaintiff's identity. As this article is concerned with uses of celebrity identity in political speech, often by non-media speakers, three judicial tests most prominently used by non-media defendants to articulate a First Amendment defence will be examined – the direct balancing approach, the transformative elements test and the predominant purpose test.[31] At present, these approaches tend to ignore the

---

26 *Zacchini*, 433 US 562, 575-576 (1977). The plaintiff claimed that he suffered damage to the extent of US$25,000. Ibid. 575 (Fuery and Fuery 2003: 93, 101).

27 Ibid. 576-577.

28 Ibid. 578.

29 Ibid. 579 (Powell, Brennan and Marshall JJ).

30 See Part 4 below for a discussion of such uses as political speech by minority groups.

31 Other tests include the 'artistic relevance' test applicable to the title of artistic works and the 'relatedness' test proposed by the *Restatement (Third)*. E.g. *Rogers v*

political significance of the celebrity sign, and overwhelmingly focus on the *informational*, *artistic* and *entertainment* aspects of the defendant's use.

1. The direct balancing approach used by the Tenth Circuit in *Cardtoons LC v Major League Baseball Players Association* explicitly engages in the weighing of benefits and harms to determine if the public interest served by the First Amendment outweighs the public interest served by publicity rights.[32] Although it does not on its face accord special status to political speech, its open-ended nature potentially allows greater 'weight' to be given to political speech relative to art or entertainment that does not contribute anything of substantial value to democratic debate. However, its shortcomings lie in its potential for abstract application, as illustrated by the courts balancing what they perceive to be the public interests that the parties' rights represent rather than the direct benefits and harms to each party. Some courts in California[33] and the Eighth Circuit[34] have applied the direct balancing approach, but it is unclear if other courts are likely to follow suit.
2. The 'transformative elements' test, also known as the 'transformative use' test, was initiated by the California Supreme Court in *Comedy III*.[35] It draws from the first factor of the fair use doctrine in copyright law:[36] an unauthorized use of celebrity identity would be permitted if it was 'transformative'. However, its lack of clear guidelines can encourage judges to be art critics or to base decisions on external factors like the fame of the artist (Levine 2004: 216-219; Volokh

---

Grimaldi, 875 F 2d 994, 997 (2nd Cir, 1989); *Restatement (Third) of Unfair Competition* § 47 cmt c (1995).

32 95 F 3d 959, 972 (10th Cir, 1996) ('*Cardtoons*'). Legal commentator McCarthy has also endorsed this approach. (McCarthy 2000: 8:39).

33 *Gionfriddo v Major League Baseball*, 94 Cal App 4th 400, 409-410 (2001) ('*Gionfriddo*'); *Perfect 10 Inc v Cybernet Ventures Inc*, 213 F Supp 2d 1146, 1182-1183 (CD Cal, 2002).

34 *CBC Distribution & Marketing Inc v Major League Baseball Advanced Media LP*, 505 F 3d 818, 823 (8th Cir, 2007) ('CBC').

35 25 Cal 4th 387 (2001).

36 *Copyright Act 1976*, 17 USC § 107(1). See also *Campbell v Acuff-Rose Music Inc*, 510 US 569, 579-585 (1994) ('*Campbell*'); *Blanch v Koons*, 467 F 3d 244, 251-256 (2nd Cir, 2006); *Suntrust Bank v Houghton Mifflin Co*, 268 F 3d 1257, 1268-1269 (11th Cir, 2001); *Castle Rock Entertainment Inc v Carol Publishing Group Inc*, 150 F 3d 132, 142-143 (2nd Cir, 1998).

2003: 914-925).[37] As shown by recent California decisions,[38] the test is focused on visual transformation which can be overprotective of art and entertainment that contribute little to the discussion of public issues, but underprotective of political speech which may be contextually transformative (because of its recoding) though not visually transformative. The key question for courts adopting this test is 'whether the depiction or imitation of the celebrity is the very sum and substance of the work in question' (in which case the defendant is liable for commercial appropriation of identity) or 'whether a product containing a celebrity's likeness is so transformed that it has become primarily the defendant's own expression rather than the celebrity's likeness' (in which case the First Amendment trumps the plaintiff's claim).[39] The *Comedy III* court has also looked to determine whether the marketability and economic value of the challenged work derives primarily from the fame of the celebrity depicted.[40] It appears that a transformative use of identity may be determined by reference to the content, form and context of the expression. This suggests that contextual transformations – like the recoded use of a celebrity identity to challenge the majoritarian values that the celebrity sign represents – may merit First Amendment protection. But the court seems to contradict itself when it later emphasizes the primacy of visual transformation: that the inquiry is 'in a sense more *quantitative* than qualitative, asking whether the literal and imitative or the creative elements predominate in the work.'[41]

3. The usefulness of this test appears confined to visual depictions of the plaintiff, and the extent to which the defendant's use has departed from a realistic rendition of the plaintiff's likeness.[42] The judicial application of the test in *Winter*, *Kirby* and *ETW Corp* suggest that these rules do not necessarily entail greater awareness and discussion of public issues. On the other hand, political speech comprising literal depictions of celebrities that are recoded by counterpublics to express a particular viewpoint

37 See also *Cardtoons LC v Major League Baseball Players Association*, 868 F Supp 1266, 1272 (ND Okla, 1994) (the analysis loses integrity when only one of the fair use factors is considered).

38 E.g. *Kirby v Sega of America*, 144 Cal App 4th 47 (2006); *Winter v DC Comics*, 30 Cal 4th 881 (2003).

39 *Comedy III*, 25 Cal 4th 387, 406 (2001).

40 *Comedy III*, 25 Cal 4th 387, 407 (2001).

41 Ibid. 407 (emphasis added).

42 McCarthy is especially critical of the transformative elements test (McCarthy 2000: 8:72).

may not be sufficiently transformative under the present judicial approach. Hence the current test tends to overprotect artistic speech[43] but underprotect political speech despite the latter's greater constitutional value.

4. The predominant purpose test was employed by the Missouri Supreme Court in *Doe v TCI Cablevision*,[44] protecting an unauthorized use of identity if it was 'predominantly expressive' but finding an infringement of the right of publicity if it was 'predominantly commercial'. Although this test can offer significant protection to uses that convey predominantly expressive political speech, it currently makes no distinction between the constitutional values of political speech and apolitical art/entertainment, and does not provide clear criteria to resolve hybrid uses (e.g. where there is a mix of political speech and commercial speech – like selling of celebrity-related merchandise in connection with a political rally). The predominant purpose test is purportedly designed to address works that are both expressive and commercial (Levine 2004: 220) and may be stated thus:

> If a product is being sold that predominantly exploits the commercial value of an individual's identity, that product should ... not be protected by the First Amendment, even if there is some 'expressive' content in it that might qualify as 'speech' in other circumstances. If, on the other hand, the predominant purpose of the product is to make an expressive comment on or about a celebrity, the expressive values could be given greater weight.[45]

Unlike the transformative elements test, the mere presence of any visually expressive elements will not bar a right of publicity claim; for the defendant to escape liability, the use of the celebrity's identity must rise above bare transformation to significant expressive commentary.

While the predominant purpose test does not explicitly rely on a particular theory of the First Amendment, its focus on protecting expressive comment is compatible with a participatory understanding of democracy. It appears that the defendant's unauthorized use of a celebrity's identity will most likely be deemed 'predominantly expressive' if it contributed to debate on public issues or drew attention to the subordinate position of minority groups and, at the same time,

43 It is worth noting the Sixth Circuit's critical observation that: 'crying "artist" does not confer *carte blanche* authority to appropriate a celebrity's name' and 'crying "symbol" does not change that proposition and confer authority to use a celebrity's name when none, in fact, may exist.' *Parks v LaFace Records*, 329 F 3d 437, 454 (6th Cir, 2003) ('*Parks*').

44 *Doe*, 110 SW 3d 363, 373 (Mo banc, 2003).

45 *Doe*, 110 SW 3d 363, 374 (Mo banc, 2003) (citing Lee 2003: 500).

the celebrity's fan base has not been specifically targeted as potential customers of the defendant's product. In practice, the court's multi-factor analysis to determine whether expressive or commercial components predominate resembles the direct balancing approach. The judicial evaluation of the different factors in *Doe* may well have been performed under the rubric of 'direct balancing' where the constitutional value of the defendant's comic book, in terms of its critical commentary and contribution to debate about public issues, is taken into account, and policy considerations more openly discussed.

Identity Politics and the Celebrity: A Cultural Studies Perspective

If the celebrity semiotic sign is recognized to represent the values/ideals of a majoritarian public, then the debate and opposition to these 'encoded' values/ideals may be expressed by using the same signs in a 'recoded' manner, and such counterpublic uses can therefore be categorized as 'political speech'. In order for political speech to be given adequate breathing space, it would be beneficial to understand the free speech issues in publicity claims within the context of a First Amendment theory that 'preserves the independence of public discourse so that a democratic will within a culturally heterogeneous state can emerge under conditions of neutrality, and so that individuals can use the medium of public discourse to persuade others to experiment in new forms of community life' (Post 1990: 684).

The Celebrity Personality as a Political Site of Interpretive Practice and Contested Meanings

This section demonstrates that cultural studies perspectives can complement and augment a participatory theory of the First Amendment because uses of the celebrity identity by those who are 'subordinated' to communicate their disagreement with majoritarian values/ideals and to draw wider public attention to their social positions can be viewed as political speech. This contention was mooted three decades ago in Richard Dyer's star studies regarding the gay community's use of the Judy Garland star sign; and other scholars today can be seen to draw on the classic idea of the political significance of star signs, with the support of the general writings of Roland Barthes and Stuart Hall about recoding of semiotic signs. First mentioned in *Stars*, and later more thoroughly explored in *Heavenly Bodies*, Dyer's analysis of the use of the Judy Garland semiotic sign by the gay community provided a valuable foundation for subsequent studies on the use of celebrity personalities by subcultural groups in their identity formation (Rojek

2001: 70).[46] Described as a 'foundational observation' in the study of the cultural function of celebrities (Turner 2004: 103), Dyer claims that '[s]tars articulate what it is to be a human being in contemporary society' (Dyer 2004: 7). Most celebrities may be seen 'as representing dominant values in society, by affirming what those values are in the "hero" types (including those values which are relatively appropriate to men and women)' or as alternative or subversive types 'that express discontent with or rejection of dominant values' (Dyer 1979: 52).[47] His work on the politics and cultural dominance of whiteness (Dyer 1979) also exposes an Anglo-Saxon hegemony said to be characteristic of American society.

Dyer's *Stars* (1979) which laid the groundwork for the celebrity studies of Marshall (1997) and Turner (2004), appears to have influenced the thinking of legal commentators like Rosemary Coombe (1991, 1998) and Michael Madow (1993). In the later *Heavenly Bodies*, Dyer contends:

> Stars are also embodiments of the social categories in which people are placed and through which they have to make sense of their lives … categories of class, gender, ethnicity, religion, sexual orientation, and so on. (Dyer 2004: 18)

In highlighting the 'radical potential of the stars', Dyer further observes that there is a political dimension to the use of stars for repressed groups like 'the working class, women, blacks, gays – who have been excluded from the culture's system of representations in all but marginal and demeaning forms' (Dyer 1979: 183-184); the subordinated social groups are using these star signs which are associated with the dominant ideology to appropriate power for themselves in a democracy.

In the US, the 'structural barriers or limits of class [that] would obstruct [the] process of cultural absorption' have not assisted the 'democratic enfranchisement of all citizens within political society' (Hall 1982: 60). Reading culture politically can reveal how celebrity signs can 'reproduce the existing social struggles in their images, spectacle, and narrative' (Kellner 1995: 56). Indeed there is a significant emphasis in contemporary cultural studies on the notion of audience participation – be it their complicity or resistance – in the hegemony of cultural texts propagated by the media and other producers (Fiske 1996; Morley 1980; Ang 1991). It is in these studies of semiotic disruptions that one may find the relevant tools for establishing a conceptual framework within First Amendment doctrine that addresses the political agenda of the active audience. Individuals outside the majoritarian value-system often have an 'alternative foci of integration' and are thus defined as 'sub-cultural' or 'subaltern' or 'counterpublics' (Warner 2002:

---

46 'Judy Garland's iconic status in gay culture partly derived from her ability to cope with disapproval, rejection and marginalization' (see also Madow 1993: 194; Coombe 1991: 1876-1877).

47 See also Dyer (2004: 12) ('the star phenomenon reproduces the overriding ideology of the person in contemporary society').

119); and there is an increasing judicial recognition of these groups asserting their alternative views in the political sphere.[48]

Building on Jürgen Habermas's work on the public sphere (Habermas 1989; Calhoun 1992) Michael Warner's analysis of the struggles that bring individuals together as a public postulates that 'subaltern counterpublics' usually articulate alternative power relations with the dominant public defined by race, gender, sexual orientation and other subordinated status (Warner 2002: 44-63, 117-120). Counterpublics are 'counter' to the extent that they try to supply different ways of imagining participation within a political or social hierarchy by which its members' identities are formed and transformed (Warner 2002: 121-122). According to Warner, a counterpublic maintains 'an awareness of its subordinate status … [with respect] not just to ideas or policy questions but to the speech genres and mode of address that constitute the public' (Warner 2002: 119).

Each celebrity persona can be a powerful signifier that is synonymous with the dominant culture. Thus a counterpublic use of a particular celebrity persona can acquire a political dimension, and may be seen as a 'discursive space … for contesting and engendering the American character' (Sunder 1996: 164-165). Hall has also defined the taking of an existing meaning and reappropriating it for new meanings as 'trans-coding' (Hall 1997a: 270) and explained that repressed groups may use trans-coding strategies to reverse stereotypes, substitute 'negative' portrayals with 'positive' ones or contest subordinate representations from within (Hall 1997a: 270-275). For example, with reference to David Beckham, the dominant coding for the Beckham sign may be construed to represent not just sexual desirability, but also reinforcing the hegemony of *white heterosexual* desirability (thus excluding the representation of the *non-white non-heterosexual*). Viewed in this manner, those opposing this majoritarian signification may want to recode the Beckham sign to highlight their subordinate or hidden status in society, and to increase the visibility of their political participation through the use of the celebrity symbol. In the words of Garry Whannel, known for his writings on the signification of sporting celebrities, the image of Beckham that departs 'from the dominant masculinised codes of footballer style' may also represent 'a challenge to the heterosexual conformity of sport's modes of male self-presentation' (Whannel 2002: 202).

Thus, if one accepts that ideological challenges may be effected through certain recoded uses of the celebrity sign,[49] then one could use a celebrity sign

48 E.g. *Hurley*, 515 US 557 (1995) (where the defendants professed to express its members' pride as openly gay, lesbian and bisexual individuals and support their march in the New York St Patrick's Day parade); *Raymen v United Senior Association Inc*, 409 F Supp 2d 15 (DDC, 2006) ('*Raymen*') (where the defendants were protected by the First Amendment in the use of the plaintiff's images in an advertising campaign which challenged various public policy positions taken by the American Association of Retired Persons).

49 Arguments have been made regarding the use of trademarks and copyrighted works in a similar fashion. E.g. Coombe (1998).

like Beckham to interrogate the categories of whiteness, men, ruling class, heterosexuality and other dominant powers and forms that ideology legitimates, showing the social constructedness and arbitrariness of all social categories and the binary system of ideology (Kellner 1995: 61).

In summary, from a cultural studies perspective, the political agenda of counterpublics or subaltern groups may be best communicated to mainstream society through the use of widely recognized celebrity signs to which the public have ascribed particular representative values or characteristics. For example, with respect to gay and lesbian communities, legal commentator Madhavi Sunder explains:

> Central to this project is a cultural play with signs and symbols aimed, first, at illustrating that gays, lesbians, and bisexuals always have been and always will be part of the 'normal' operations of society and, second, challenging the normality of such operations by exposing the hidden homosexual. (Sunder 1996: 167)

Thus the celebrity signs that are constitutive of cultural heritage – like 'Judy Garland', 'Marilyn Monroe', 'Tiger Woods' and 'David Beckham' – each transcend the human individuals who bear these names, and are symbolic of the ideological hegemonies of social identities in contemporary society. Their recoding by counterpublics may be viewed as '[p]ractices of articulating social difference [that] are central to democratic politics' (Coombe 1998: 295; Warner 2002: 210). The next section will investigate when such practices ought to be categorized as political speech that merits the highest level of First Amendment protection.

Using Celebrity Signs within First Amendment Doctrine

Rethinking the use of the celebrity sign as political speech The recoding practices of subaltern groups may 'seem distant, if not utterly divorced from the legal regime of personality rights' (Coombe 1992: 386) and 'are neither readily appreciated using current juridical concepts nor easily encompassed by the liberal premises that ground our legal categories' (Coombe 1998: 6). But closer inspection reveals that through different modes of expressing the celebrity personality – like adulation, parody, satire and burlesque – subaltern groups are able to advance their political ideologies and assert alternative identities that 'affirm both community solidarity and the legitimacy of their social difference by empowering themselves with cultural resources that the law deems the properties of others' (Coombe 1992: 366). The participatory theory of the First Amendment supports the protection of the making of 'representations about self, identity, community, solidarity, and difference' or the articulation of political and social aspirations using the celebrity sign within a 'dialogic democracy' (Coombe 1998: 248-249) as political speech.

In First Amendment doctrine, such recoded circulations can be viewed as a form of political activism akin to Raymen v United Senior Association Inc,[50] characterized by their ability to 'reverse perceptions of social devaluation or stigma, articulate alternative narratives of national understanding, and challenge exclusionary imaginaries of citizenship.'[51]

In this light, the recoding of celebrity signs by gay and lesbian counterpublic groups may be conceived as political speech expressing an opposition to 'heteronormativity'[52] that embodies 'a constellation of practices that everywhere disperses heterosexual privilege as a ... central organizing index of social membership' (Warner 2002: 195). Similar arguments may be made for other subaltern categories of race, gender or class. For example, the celebrity signs of Tiger Woods or Jacqueline Onassis, as articulated through widely distributed photographic and televisual images, especially in advertising, embody certain values/ideals for the majoritarian public.[53] Therefore, their recoding, like an ironic use of the Tiger Woods' image by National Association for the Advancement of Colored People (NAACP)[54] to highlight the discrimination of coloured people or on T-shirts 'as an extensive ... message of social advocacy' to express their pride in being associated with a successful African-Asian American icon in a festival or parade,[55] can be categorized as political speech because of their pertinent viewpoints that significantly contribute to democratic participation and debate.[56]

However, conferring on such uses the status of political speech does not guarantee immunity from liability for every subaltern group or individual speaker who tacks on a political message to unauthorized uses of the celebrity sign. As McCarthy cautioned:

> [I]f all it took for a defendant to wrap itself in the First Amendment was to add an appropriate 'Express Your Support for ______' slogan on all celebrity merchandise, then the right of publicity to control the commercial property value in his or her identity would be destroyed. (McCarthy 2000: 7:22)

50 409 F Supp 2d 15 (DDC, 2006).

51 409 F Supp 2d 15, 32 (DDC, 2006). See also McLeod's explanation of how communities may use celebrity signs – like John Wayne – that represent a certain ideal in mainstream society as a 'resistive reading' (McLeod 2006: 658).

52 Heteronormativity has been defined as 'the institutions, structures of understanding, and practical orientations that make heterosexuality seem ... privileged' (Warner 2002: 188).

53 E.g. *ETW Corp*, 332 F 3d 915 (6th Cir, 2003); *Onassis*, 472 NYS 2d 254 (1984).

54 The mission of the NAACP is to ensure the political, educational, social and economic equality of rights of all persons and to eliminate racial hatred and racial discrimination. See NAACP (2010).

55 E.g. *Ayres*, 125 F 3d 1010, 1014 (7th Cir, 1997); *Heffron v International Society for Krishna Consciousness Inc*, 452 US 640, 647 (1981).

56 NAACP also seeks, *inter alia*, to 'remove all barriers of racial discrimination through democratic processes' (see NAACP 2010).

In assessing a publicity claim, especially in the context of advertising, courts should distinguish whether the recoding of the celebrity sign is 'genuinely a political statement' or an attempt to '*appropriate* "difference" ... in order to sell a product' (Hall 1997a: 273).[57] Accordingly, if one views the First Amendment as informed by a pragmatic cultural studies approach, regardless of whatever formulation the court adopts, one should consider: (i) the *content* of the expressive elements of the use of the celebrity personality (e.g. whether it was to advance a political cause or affirm the political identity of a particular social group); (ii) the *form* of expression (e.g. whether the use was commercial in the form of advertising, character merchandising or product sale, or non-commercial, or a hybrid); and (iii) the *context* of the use (e.g. whether it was to express a particular viewpoint at a parade, rally or some other public forum).[58]

Revisiting the current judicial approaches This section will focus on examining how the three main judicial tests can accommodate the classification of recoded uses of the celebrity identity as political speech within their analyses.

> **Direct balancing approach** Presently, the balancing test tends to be applied at an abstract level and does not clearly balance the benefit to the defendant speaker against the harm to the celebrity plaintiff, including the plaintiff's own First Amendment rights, if the right of publicity was not enforced. Of the three tests examined, its open-ended nature best allows courts to consider the content, form and context of the use of the celebrity identity and to explicitly evaluate the relative harms and benefits to the parties involved.[59] In recognizing the recoding possibilities of the celebrity identity for political speech, the factors that a court may consider include: (i) the primary motivation of the defendant speaker in using the celebrity plaintiff's identity; (ii) the nature of the defendant's commercial enterprise; (iii) the content of the defendant's expressive speech; (iv) the medium of the defendant's expression; (v) the occasion and location of the defendant's use; (vi) the presence of alternative avenues of communication; and (vii) the intended audience of the defendant's communication.

---

57 Emphasis in original.

58 The location of the speech is important. In *Ayres*, the selling of expressive T-shirts by the Marijuana Political Action Committee to be worn at City-sponsored festivals in Grant Park was held to be political speech. *Ayres*, 125 F 3d 1010, 1013-1014 (7th Cir, 1997).

59 After a lengthy review of various approaches to incorporate First Amendment considerations into right of publicity doctrine, McCarthy, citing the *Cardtoons* direct balancing approach with approval, has also concluded that one needs to 'meet the conflict head on' and '[t]he balance must be laboriously hacked out case by case' (McCarthy 2000: 8:39).

In evaluating the harm to the plaintiff, the court may consider: (i) the nature and extent of damage to the plaintiff's ability to exploit the associative value of his or her identity;[60] and (ii) whether the defendant's products were a substitute for products offered by the plaintiff or the plaintiff's authorized licensees.[61] This approach can better provide adequate breathing space to the freedoms protected by the First Amendment[62] and is compatible with the Supreme Court's current analysis involving speech on private property that requires balancing of the competing interests of the property owner and of the public with respect to the particular property to determine 'expressive access'.[63] For example, the majority's 'single-sentence attempt at balancing' in *ETW Corp v Jireh Publishing* was criticized by the dissent as falling 'woefully short of any meaningful consideration of the matter'.[64] As indicated above, a better approach to balancing is to consider the direct harms and benefits to the parties involved.[65] Rick Rush's depiction of Tiger Woods arguably constitutes the type of conventional depiction of the celebrity likeness in traditional merchandising that appeals to fans. Clearly the content of the defendant's expression may not be classified as political speech for African-American or Asian-American counterpublic groups; the sale of the prints was not in the context of expressing a particular viewpoint about social or political identity. When one weighs the relatively low constitutional value of the defendant's artwork against the interference with the proprietary publicity right of Woods, it appears that Jireh Publishing may not avail itself of the protection of the First Amendment.

Transformative elements test Under its present formulation as applied in *Winter* and *Kirby*, the transformative elements test may restrict subaltern groups from appropriating celebrity signs for the construction of their social identities in everyday activities unless the celebrity's likeness has been *visually* transformed. For example, the groups may be prohibited from using a literal depiction (e.g. a photograph) of a particular celebrity on silkscreened T-shirts or other merchandise bearing the celebrity's image

60 E.g. *Doe*, 110 SW 3d 363, 367 (Mo banc, 2003) (where the plaintiff introduced evidence that the defendant's use 'resulted in a diminution in the commercial value of his name as an endorser of products' and has in fact lost endorsement opportunities).

61 E.g. *Comedy III*, 25 Cal 4th 387, 405 (2001); *Cardtoons*, 95 F 3d 959, 97 (10th Cir, 1996); *Winter*, 30 Cal 4th 881, 890 (2003); Harder and Self (2005: 575-576).

62 E.g. *Boos*, 485 US 312, 322 (1988); *Falwell*, 485 US 46, 56 (1988).

63 E.g. *PruneYard*, 447 US 74, 82-88 (1980); *Hudgens*, 424 US 507, 518-521 (1976); *Lloyd Corp*, 407 US 551, 563 (1972). See also *Albertson's*, 107 Cal App 4th 106, 113-114, 123 (2003).

64 *ETW Corp*, 332 F 3d 915, 949 (Clay J) (6th Cir, 2003).

65 E.g. *Cardtoons*, 95 F 3d 959, 971-976 (10th Cir, 1996).

for sale to group members to highlight a public issue like the subordinated social position of the homosexual community.

However, depending on the identity of the speaker and the context of the unauthorized use, certain expressive uses of merchandise may qualify as political speech. For example, the sale of T-shirts by counterpublic groups like Lambda Legal[66] bearing the images of actors like Heath Ledger, Jake Gyllenhaal and Tom Hanks – who have been honoured at the Academy Awards for playing gay characters in critically acclaimed movies – to be worn at a Gay Pride Parade should be viewed as 'transformative' because the recoded meaning of the celebrity signs now carries significant political content. Moreover, in *Comedy III*, where the transformative elements test was first articulated, the court had emphasized that 'the transformative elements or creative contributions that require First Amendment protection ... can take many forms ... from heavy-handed lampooning to subtle social criticism'.[67] Thus, by examining the content, form and context of the impugned use, the transformative elements test may be adapted to protect non-visually transformative uses of the celebrity identity.

In a tenuous application of the test in *ETW Corp*, the majority concluded that the artwork was transformative because the work conveyed a message 'that Woods himself will someday join that revered group'[68] and it 'communicates and celebrates the value our culture attaches to such events'.[69] By attempting to analyse the constitutional *value* of the defendant's use, the Sixth Circuit appears to have refined the transformative elements test in a manner that contrasts sharply with the refusal of the California courts to do so. But Rush's painting of Woods conveys no discernible political expression that contributes to democratic deliberation, it does nothing to challenge the majoritarian ideals embodied in the Woods sign, and the Sixth Circuit should have found a right of publicity infringement.[70]

Predominant purpose test Under the predominant purpose test, non-governmental organizations and civic groups, like NAACP and Legal Lambda that highlight the subordinated position of minorities in American society and lobby the government for policy changes, are more likely

66 Lambda Legal is a national organization in the US committed to achieving full recognition of the civil rights of lesbians, gay men, bisexuals, transgender people and those with HIV through impact litigation, education and public policy work. See Lambda Legal (2010).

67 *Comedy III*, 25 Cal 4th 387, 406 (2001) (citing Andy Warhol's literal silkscreened celebrity portraits as a First Amendment-protected critique of the celebrity phenomenon).

68 *Comedy III*, 25 Cal 4th 387, 936 (2001).

69 Ibid.

70 See also criticisms of the application of the transformative elements test by the *ETW Corp* majority in Franke (2006: 970-974) and Sloan (2005: 918-920).

to benefit from the protection of the First Amendment than commercial enterprises. But to protect all speech that is 'predominantly expressive' does not make a distinction between speech that arguably has a higher constitutional value (because it contributes to public debate about political issues) and speech that has a comparatively lower value (because it merely entertains or is simply aesthetic). Again, in *ETW Corp*, *The Masters of Augusta* appears to be a commemorative work produced for sale to the public and does not contain 'expressions of value, opinion, or endorsement'[71] of significant democratic value. The work does not critically comment on a specific attribute of Tiger Woods – like his ethnic heritage or the values he embodies – or draw attention to political or social issues facing subaltern groups. Neither Rush nor Jireh Publishing had recoded the Woods sign, and the literal rendition simply reproduces the dominant preferred reading of the Woods celebrity sign as a national hero consistent with his *commercial* positioning. Consequently, the Sixth Circuit should have decided that the freedom of speech would not have been impermissibly abridged by the prohibition of the sale of the prints.

In contrast, if the NAACP or other subaltern groups had produced literal depictions of Woods for sale to support their advocacy efforts, such uses arguably may be construed as politically expressive. In these circumstances, the commercial nature of the sale of prints and any other products bearing Woods' likeness can be said to be incidental to the predominant purpose of constructing particular social identities for minority groups by these non-profit counterpublics which will in turn empower their political participation. But this does not mean that counterpublics have *carte blanche* to appropriate the identities of celebrities under the banner of political speech. Each case has to be evaluated based on the content, form and context of the use, and one needs to be on the lookout for defendants who tack on a political message to products that exploit the associative value of identity in the hope of securing First Amendment protection.

Summary and Conclusions

A participatory theory in which the First Amendment is seen to be advancing public decision-making in a democracy suggests that expressive uses of the celebrity identity, particularly by subaltern groups, that contribute to democratic processes have a higher constitutional value than either artistic speech or entertainment. This observation is reinforced by the Supreme Court's consistent positioning of political speech at the apex of the speech hierarchy. The semiotic analysis of politically expressive uses of the celebrity identity also augments the participatory argument

71 *Hurley*, 515 US 557, 573 (1995); *McIntyre v Ohio Elections Commission*, 514 US 334, 341-342 (1995).

that political speech ought to be given greater weight in the First Amendment defence as articulated in right of publicity claims.

The broad definition of political speech in First Amendment jurisprudence would easily encompass the recoding of celebrity signs by counterpublics that enables 'the practice of persons sharing common views banding together to achieve a common end [which] is deeply embedded in the American political process'.[72] As such, cultural studies can inform the revision of existing judicial tests to better take into account the content, form and context of politically expressive uses of the celebrity identity when engaging in an evaluation of the conflict between property and speech rights.

However, a cautionary note is warranted about the judicial use of semiotics and cultural studies. In reaching its decision in *ETW Corp*, the Sixth Circuit majority departed from the traditional examination of the clash between publicity and First Amendment rights, and attempted – in a most unsatisfactory and inadequate manner – to import cultural studies into its judicial reasoning. The court dedicated just three paragraphs to a cursory mention of the symbolic value of the celebrity sign and the associative value of Woods' identity,[73] without any discussion of the uses of the celebrity sign by audiences in their interpretive practices. If the court were to consider the political significance of recoded celebrity signs and the consequent constitutional value of the defendant's speech that incorporated Woods' identity, the outcome in *ETW Corp* might have been different. Unfortunately, the court devoted much of its analysis to the rationales for recognizing a right of publicity[74] instead of how social groups use the celebrity personality as a communicative resource in a manner that deserves First Amendment protection.[75] This type of brief reference to cultural studies as *ex-post facto* rationalization is not a desirable practice (Jones 2006: 957).[76] But, as this chapter has shown, judicial reference to cultural studies could be much more productive.

In conclusion, this chapter has demonstrated that cultural writings on the *political* value of the celebrity sign, its meaning and potential uses by counterpublics or subaltern groups, can add to the richness of First Amendment jurisprudence. It adds to the legal scholarship through its examination of the potential importance of the celebrity sign in political advocacy efforts and its illustration of how these

---

72 *NAACP*, 458 US 886, 906 (1982).

73 *ETW Corp*, 332 F 3d 915, 938 (6th Cir, 2003).

74 *ETW Corp*, 332 F 3d 915, 931-938 (6th Cir, 2003). Contra ibid. 955 (Clay J dissenting) ('Despite various commentary and scholarship … the fact remains that the right of publicity is an accepted right').

75 Passing comments were made with regard to the use of the celebrity personality as an important expressive and communicative resource to 'symbolize individual aspirations, group identities and cultural values', but no further analysis was undertaken of *what* particular uses merit First Amendment protection (ibid. 935).

76 '… in many instances the courts' reasoning is result oriented, with the court creating a test that validates the result it wants to reach in the given case'.

insights may be incorporated into the judicial tests. Courts like the Sixth Circuit can benefit from a structured analysis of how cultural studies may be meaningfully integrated into the First Amendment defence. Regardless of the confusing morass that may surround the application of First Amendment considerations to a right of publicity claim, recognizing the potential of the celebrity sign to function as a political site of contestations offers valuable assistance to the refinement of the current tests.

References

Ang, I. 1991. *Desperately Seeking the Audience*. New York: Routledge.

Ausness, R.C. 1982. 'The Right of Publicity: A "Haystack in a Hurricane"'. *Temple Law Quarterly*, 55, 977-1055.

Balkin, J.M. 2004. 'Digital Speech and Democratic Culture: A Theory of Freedom of Expression for the Information Society'. *New York University Law Review*, 79, 1-58.

Barendt, E. 2005. *Freedom of Speech*, 2nd edition. Oxford: Oxford University Press.

Barthes, R. 1972. *Mythologies*, translated by Annette Lavers. New York: Hill & Wang.

Beebe, B. 2004. 'The Semiotic Analysis of Trademark Law'. *UCLA Law Review*, 51, 621-704.

Breyer, S. 2002. 'Lecture: Our Democratic Constitution'. *New York University Law Review*, 77, 245-271.

Bosland, J. 2005. 'The Culture of Trade Marks: An Alternative Cultural Theory Perspective'. *Media and Arts Law Review*, 10, 99-116.

Calhoun, C. 1992. *Habermas and the Public Sphere*. Cambridge, MA: MIT Press.

Coombe, R.J. 1991. 'Objects of Property and Subjects of Politics: Intellectual Property Laws and Democratic Dialogue'. *Texas Law Review*, 69, 1853-1880.

Coombe, R.J. 1992. 'Author/izing the Celebrity: Publicity Rights, Postmodern Politics, and Unauthorized Genders'. *Cardozo Arts and Entertainment Law Journal*, 10, 365-395.

Coombe, R.J. 1998. *The Cultural Life of Intellectual Properties: Authorship, Appropriation, and the Law*. Durham, NC: Duke University Press.

Dyer, R. 1979. *Stars*. London: British Film Institute.

Dyer, R. 2004. *Heavenly Bodies: Film Stars and Society*, 2nd edition. London: Routledge.

Faber, J. 2007. 'David Beckham Endorsing Disney'. *CBS News Entertainment*. [Online]. Available at: http://www.cbsnews.com/stories/2007/01/26/entertainment/main2402436.shtml [accessed 5 November 2009].

Fallon, R.H. Jr. 1999. 'How to Choose a Constitutional Theory'. *California Law Review*, 87, 535-579.

Fiske, J. 1996. *Media Matters: Everyday Culture and Political Change*. Minneapolis, MN: University of Minnesota Press.

Franke, G. 2006. 'The Right of Publicity vs the First Amendment: Will One Test Ever Capture the Starring Role?' *Southern California Law Review*, 79, 945-991.

Fuery, P. and Fuery, K. 2003. *Visual Cultures and Critical Theory*. New York: Bloomsbury.

Garry, P.M. 2007. 'The First Amendment and Non-Political Speech: Exploring a Constitutional Model that Focuses on the Existence of Alternative Channels of Communication'. *Missouri Law Review*, 72, 477-524.

Gramsci, A. 1971. *Selections from the Prison Notebooks*, translated by Quintin Hoare and Geoffrey Nowell Smith. New York: International Publishers.

Habermas, J. 1989. *The Structural Transformation of the Public Sphere: An Inquiry into a Category of Bourgeois Society*, translated by Thomas Burger. Cambridge, MA: MIT Press.

Hall, S. 1981. 'Notes on Deconstructing the "Popular"', in *People's History and Socialist Theory*, edited by Raphael Samuel. London: Routledge, 227-239.

Hall, S. 1982. 'The Rediscovery of "Ideology": Return of the Repressed in Media Studies', in *Culture, Society and the Media*, edited by Michael Gurevitch, Tony Bennett, James Curran and Janet Woollacott. London: Methuen, 52-82.

Hall, S. 1996. 'Introduction: Who Needs "Identity"?', in *Questions of Cultural Identity*, edited by Stuart Hall and Paul Du Gay. London: Sage, 1-17.

Hall, S. 1997a. 'The Spectacle of the "Other"', in *Representation: Cultural Representations and Signifying Practices*, edited by Stuart Hall. London: Sage, 223-290.

Hall, S. 1997b. 'The Local and the Global: Globalization and Ethnicity', in *Culture, Globalization and the World System: Contemporary Conditions for the Representation of Identity*, edited by Anthony D King. Minneapolis, MN: University of Minnesota Press, 19-40.

Halpern, S.W. 1995. 'The Right of Publicity: Maturation of an Independent Right Protecting the Associative Value of Personality'. *Hastings Law Journal*, 46, 853-873.

Harder, C.J. and Self, H.L. III. 2005. 'Schwarzenegger vs. Bobbleheads: The Case for Schwarzenegger'. *Santa Clara Law Review*, 45, 557-580.

Jones, R.S. Jr. 2006. 'The Flip Side of Privacy: The Right of Publicity, The First Amendment, and Constitutional Line Drawing – A Presumptive Approach'. *Creighton Law Review*, 39, 939-960.

Kellner, D. 1995. *Media Culture: Cultural Studies, Identity and Politics Between the Modern and the Postmodern*. London: Routledge.

Lambda Legal. 2010. [Online]. Available at: http://www.lambdalegal.org/about-us/ [accessed 1 June 2010].

Lee, M.S. 2003. 'Agents of Chaos: Judicial Confusion in Defining the Right of Publicity-Free Speech Interface'. *Loyola LA Entertainment Law Review*, 23, 471-501.

Levine, J.K. 2004. 'Can the Right of Publicity Afford Free Speech? A New Right of Publicity Test for First Amendment Cases'. *Hastings Communications and Entertainment Law Journal*, 27, 171-232.

Lévi-Strauss, C. 1967. *The Scope of Anthropology*, translated by Sherry Ortner Paul and Robert A. Paul. London: Jonathan Cape.

Madow, M. 1993. 'Private Ownership of Public Image: Popular Culture and Publicity Rights'. *California Law Review*, 81, 127-240.

Marshall, P.D. 1997. *Celebrity and Power: Fame in Contemporary Culture*. Minneapolis, MN: University of Minnesota Press.

McCarthy, J.T. 1995. 'The Human Persona as Commercial Property: The Right of Publicity'. *Columbia-VLA Journal of Law and Arts*, 19, 129-148.

McCarthy, J.T. 2000. *The Rights of Publicity and Privacy*. Minneapolis, MN: Thomson/West.

McLeod, K. 2006. 'The Private Ownership of People', in *The Celebrity Culture Reader*, edited by P. David Marshall. New York: Routledge, 649-665.

Morley, D. 1980. *The Nationwide Audience*. London: British Film Institute.

NAACP. 2010. [Online]. Available at: http://www.naacp.org/about/mission/index.htm [accessed 1 June 2010].

Post, R.C. 1990. 'The Constitutional Concept of Public Discourse: Outrageous Opinion, Democratic Deliberation, and *Hustler Magazine v Falwell*'. *Harvard Law Review*, 103, 601-686.

Post, R.C. 1993. 'Meiklejohn's Mistake: Individual Autonomy and the Reform of Public Discourse'. *University of Colorado Law Review*, 64, 1109-1137.

Post, R.C. 2000. 'Reconciling Theory and Doctrine in First Amendment Jurisprudence'. *California Law Review*, 88, 2353-2374.

Rojek, C. 2001. *Celebrity*. London: Reaktion.

Schauer, F. 1982. *Free Speech: A Philosophical Enquiry*. Cambridge: Cambridge University Press.

Sloan, M. 2005. 'Too Famous for the Right of Publicity: *ETW Corp.* and the Trend Towards Diminished Protection for Top Celebrities'. *Cardozo Arts and Entertainment Law Journal*, 22, 903-932.

Smolla, R.A. 1992. *Free Speech in an Open Society*. New York: Alfred A Knopf.

Smolla, R.A. and Nimmer, M.B. 2008. *Smolla and Nimmer on Freedom of Speech: A Treatise on the First Amendment*. Minneapolis, MN: Thomson/West.

Sunder, M. 1996. 'Authorship and Autonomy as Rites of Exclusion: The Intellectual Propertization of Free Speech in *Hurley v Irish-American Gay, Lesbian and Bisexual Group of Boston*'. *Stanford Law Review*, 49, 143-172.

Sunstein, C.R. 1993. *Democracy and the Problem of Free Speech*. New York: The Free Press.

Sunstein, C.R. 2001. *Designing Democracy: What Constitutions Do*. New York: Oxford University Press.

Tan, D. 2008. 'Beyond Trademark Law: What the Right of Publicity Can Learn from Cultural Studies'. *Cardozo Arts and Entertainment Law Journal*, 25, 913-994.

Thompson, J.B. 1990. *Ideology and Modern Culture: Critical Social Theory in the Era of Mass Communication*. Stanford, CA: Stanford University Press.

Turner, G. 2004. *Understanding Celebrity*. London: Sage.

Volokh, E. 2003. 'Freedom of Speech and the Right of Publicity'. *Houston Law Review*, 40, 903-930.

The Walt Disney Company. 2009. 'Stars Play Out Disney Park Fantasies in New Images Unveiled by Annie Leibovitz: Photography Featuring Scarlett Johansson, Beyoncé and David Beckham Kicks Off Disney's "Year of a Million Dreams"'. [Online]. Available at: http://corporate.disney.go.com/corporate/moreinfo/beckham_parks012607.html [accessed 1 July 2010].

Wanat, D.E. 2003. 'Entertainment Law: An Analysis of Judicial Decision-making in Cases Where a Celebrity's Publicity Right is in Conflict with a User's First Amendment Right'. *Albany Law Review*, 67, 251-277.

Warner, M. 2002. *Publics and Counterpublics*. New York: Zone.

Whannel, G. 2002. *Media Sports Stars: Masculinities and Moralities*. London: Routledge.

Chapter 14
Warhol: Images of Infamy and Underpinning Power

Oliver Watts

> The shots of leading figures in economic life and other prominent people in straw hats and padded suits can only be distinguished from gangsters by the fact that they take their hats off when they enter the room while they exploit the robust speech of the gangster for sake of popularity. (Adorno 1991: 91)

> Andy's very royal. It was like Louis XIV getting up in the morning. The big question was whom would Andy notice. (Stein and Plimpton 1982: 201)

Introduction: Trauma, Pop and Ideology

It may seem blasphemous to see an ideological, political subject in Warhol's work. The traditional reading of Warhol is cool detachment. In Warhol though detachment *describes* the ideology of the hidden master signifier; his art of simulacrum highlights what underpins meaning. In merely repeating the Campbell's soup cans and other commodity products a complete levelling occurred between art and popular culture. The strength of Warhol's work in this vein was described by, among others, Thierry de Duve as an illumination that art, in the period of late capital, can offer no critique. Art becomes another commodity fetish, the connoisseur becomes the shopper, and art is exposed as a pure expression of 'exchange value', which Warhol directs the viewer to accept (de Duve 1989). The Warhol *Brillo Box* (1964) has become the quintessential exemplar of this comment on art and late capital (Danto 1997).[1] In contrast, the *Death and Disaster* series, of which the Jackie works are considered a part, need to be carefully examined in regard to setting Warhol in post-ideological, late capital. The subject matter is so closely connected to the law and society on its limit, through riot and violence, through sovereigns and 'great' criminals, that as a series it is difficult to ignore their commentary on the power of these political and juridical acts and images. On the whole Warhol's work is about equivalence, the electric chair is on par with a flower from *Woman's*

---

1 Arthur Danto sees the *Brillo Box* as the end of art history. For Danto the *Brillo Box* in its almost exact replication of the real object becomes pure philosophy, which Hegel had already set as the goal of art, for art to become pure Spirit. Danto writes, 'What makes *Brillo Box* a work of art is that it incarnates, expresses, whatever idea it does express, hence is idea and mere thing at once, a box transfigured if only into the idea of a box' (2004, 178).

Figure 14.1 Andy Warhol, *Thirteen Most Wanted Men*, 1964

Source: © Andy Warhol/Corbis.

Day; however, in this series Warhol consciously focuses on images that point to a failure in the smooth running of capitalist, disciplinary society. As Jacques Derrida and Walter Benjamin, have noted, the state's monopoly on violence is a breach of the smooth running of neutral, well-ordered bureaucracy. Indeed when disciplinary society *shows* that it has this power, the disciplinary method of control has failed; compared to the capillary power of normalization, violence is the sledgehammer supplement. These images of state violence and control though offer a small gap in the edifice of bureaucratic control where we may see still working the mythical sovereign authority. For this reason Warhol's *Death and Disaster* series may be used to find the 'mystical authority' still working but hidden in the administered world. Warhol seems to actively engage with showing this 'official' line, and how it underpins the images of disciplinary control. One such foray went so far as to engender official censor for the misuse and (dangerous) appropriation of state imagery; this work was Warhol's mural, *Thirteen Most Wanted Men* (1964). Particularly as its reception was *not* in the art gallery but in the public space at the New York State Fair (Figure 14.1), it more easily allows for a reading of critical and active social engagement. With this controversial mural, and I suggest in part the *Death and Disaster* series, Warhol enters into a dialogue with the political and social import of images. Pop art itself, as a socially engaged art allows for Warhol as an engaged citizen. Pop, Conceptualism and Minimalism countered Formalism by showing that an autonomous 'art for art's sake' was dangerously disconnected from political realities.

Pop explicitly added social references to art and started to work with political movements at the time – such as the response to consumerism, civil rights and the Vietnam War.

A number of theorists have seen Warhol as socially engaged. Looking at Warhol as a response to political upheaval, Hal Foster famously coined the term 'traumatic realism' to describe the images of violence and mourning in the *Death and Disaster* series, in relation to Warhol's response to the hysterical state of trauma at this time. For Foster (1995),[2] Warhol represents as clearly as possible an art of the mass subject who is chronically disconnected from the trauma of death and social realities of the day, where media has created a nihilism of equivalence. Against Foster, this chapter sees instead, Warhol's 'machinic' distance and repetitions as providing a space for critique, through Deleuzian notions of *differance* and simulacrum. Warhol's process is like a contemporary version of the *flâneur*, viewing the scenes (here the mediated spectacle) without losing the position of the individual as a point of critique. Walter Benjamin cites Fournel who saw the difference between the strolling but critical *flâneur* and the *badaud*, or gaper. Fournel writes:

> The simple flâneur is always in full possession of his individuality, whereas the individuality of the badaud disappears. [The world] … intoxicates him to the point where he forgets himself. Under the influence of the spectacle which presents itself to him, the badaud becomes an impersonal creature; he is no longer a human being, he is part of the public, of the crowd. (Benjamin 2003: 41)

Foster's (1995) characterization of the mass subject has more to do with the *badaud* than the individual; under the title of 'mass witnessing' he describes the 'strange new mass subjectivity' (1995: 48). Within the essay an alternative formulation of

2 Hal Foster relates his ideas of how Warhol reads images to Michael Warner's notion of the 'mass subject'. In this reading there is a new public sphere held together by shared mass mediated images and texts. The old body politic is done away with (i.e. the effigy) and ideology and politics no longer hold sway over the 'citizen'. This chapter, follows others who believe that the body politic is still a useful construct for understanding contemporary politics, see particularly Neocleous (2003).

the public sphere is noted but not followed, namely a 'pathological public sphere'. Footnoting Žižek, Foster correctly assumes that this recent move in art history would have ongoing support, and this chapter engages with this pathological approach (1995: n36 48). As for Deleuze, the simulacrum is not fully equivalent but is made up of moments of idiosyncrasy in place and time. The individual in Warhol is clearly not totally subsumed under the mass of imagery, and Warhol is very clear that we do not have to be fully sucked in.

Warhol read through a Lacanian lens, as suggested paradoxically by Foster, offers an alternative to Foster's account; Warhol mines the mass-mediated imagery for its underlying ideology and refuses to be seduced by it into an unthinking 'mass subject'. In Foucault's reading of power/knowledge, the administration of control over information, science and education are ways of normalizing and regulating the individual. There are two major provisos to this theory that Warhol helps explicate. First, each subject is a point of oppression under society's gaze, but the subject is also part of the capillary that exercises that gaze. The subject therefore may be the point of liberation as well as oppression. Foucault himself in his later work suggested that through the 'care of the self' the subject could resist normalization. Judith Butler's 'paradox of subjection' highlights this point, insisting that the law cannot fully account for the individual (Butler 1997). Following Foucault, through Lacan, Freud and Althusser, she alerts us to the paradox of subjectivity as founded on a subjection to language, images and laws. Through his repetition of images of the law Warhol plays with legal power and the symbolic order and it is the serial repetition of Warhol's imagery that forms the focus of this chapter.

Furthermore, it is here that we can examine the means by which Warhol uncovers the ideology that hides behind knowledge. This is another Lacanian corrective to Foucault's knowledge/power. Knowledge is never neutral, which Foucault would agree with. However, Lacan highlights that beneath knowledge, in the disciplinary society of late capital, is the hidden figure of the master, or master signifier that underpins the discourse of knowledge. It is this aspect of the underpinning ideology in the mass media that Warhol uncovers by obviously shifting the underpinning ideology of the society to his own signature and brand: brand Warhol. We will look at various strategies of 'signing' or marking the image 'as a Warhol'. Although for the sake of Law and Literature we will focus on images that have traditionally been seen as 'ideological or repressive state apparatuses' the notion of the logo works across all imagery. The theoretical understanding of Warhol from Foucault to Deleuze is that the copying or seriality is important not to highlight equivalence but indeed difference. Warhol's method is a process that we can bring to the law. So in Warhol's oeuvre it is the *process* of pinning meaning, rather than an image or mark of authority that is important. This method of multiple interpellation in Warhol is an ongoing process of marking difference. I have called this a process of branding, marking with the logo, but it is the ability of anything, all knowledge to be marked that is important here.

University Discourse and Advertising Imagery

To understand the fantasy that underpins the disciplinary society it is worth looking in more detail at Lacan's *mathème* for the university discourse. In it S2 (neutral knowledge) as agent addresses the *petit a* ('bare life' or a child-like cipher) to create, in the place of the product, the barred subject, \$. The master signifier or power itself is hidden below the line in the position of truth in the *mathème* (see Boucher 2006). Žižek (2003) gives a good example of how this *mathème* functions in the disciplinary society:

> Perhaps the exemplary case of the Master's position which underlies the university discourse is the way in which medical discourse functions in our everyday lives: at the surface level, we are dealing with pure objective knowledge which desubjectivizes the subject-patient, reducing him to an object of research, of diagnosis and treatment; however, beneath it, one can easily discern a worried hystericized subject, obsessed with anxiety, addressing the doctor as his Master and asking for reassurance from him. At a more common level, suffice it to recall the market expert who advocates strong budgetary measures (cutting welfare expenses, etc.) as a necessity imposed by his neutral expertise devoid of any ideological biases: what he conceals is the series of power-relations (from the active role of state apparatuses to ideological beliefs) which sustain the 'neutral' functioning of the market mechanism. (Žižek 2003)

My reading explores Warhol's imagery for multiple 'ideologies' that alternatively organize the field of language and knowledge. 'Warhol the Advertising Illustrator' is the key to understanding how Warhol critiques ideology; the way advertising works is exemplary of the university discourse. Although camp, detached and cool, Warhol's hidden joke is that we both know what is *really* being said. My strategy is borrowed from Matthew Sharpe's (2006) reading of advertising since the 1960s as exemplary of the university discourse. In a nutshell, we do not buy toothpaste, as we did in the 1930s, because the doctor says (the master discourse). Instead, Sharpe observes, after the 'Revolution' in advertising, we buy a product because 'it is as if the advertiser had winked at us across a crowded room' (2006: 306). The joke, or hidden meaning behind an advertisement means that the product and the viewer are of a like mind and therefore suited to each other. It is not merely the superficial look of advertising and commodity fetishism that Warhol appropriates. What Warhol does is use the double (or multiple) interpellation of the advertising image to ideological ends. He undermines the authority of the master discourse by connecting with the viewer through jokes and hidden messages, as in advertising. It is at once a mode of critique but also of friendship and kinship. Matthew Sharpe (2006) follows Baudrillard in suggesting that advertising is 'a tremendous effort to materialise the superego' (2006: 307). Lacan highlights that the superego is not S1 or the master signifier, but actually close to S2 or knowledge, as a means of enjoyment (so in the place of the agent, S2/S1). The jocular, cynical flavour of

Warhol's work already directly copies the new turn in advertising at this time to transgress against the 'conforming' or mass subject in ads that were fun and less authoritative – a mode still common today. It is only beneath the line, behind the message that the master signifier is found, hidden and repressed, as the logo (the S1 beneath the S2 knowledge, S2/S1). As Sharpe (2006) concludes, '… this is because logos function as pure master signifiers (S1) within the advertisements. They are there merely to tie everything together, not to add anything new. To put it differently, they do not exist, they function' (2006: 312). This Lacanian methodology gives us another way to access the idea of 'double interpellation', or multiple interpellation; the master signifier that underpins the meaning of the image may guarantee meaning in different ways.

We can use one of Warhol's own examples to see how the 'joke' and the hidden 'logo' work to create a connection with the viewer. Warhol's cover of *Art Forum*, March 1985, had a number of Life Savers on the page with a caption, 'please do not lick this page'. The ad works like this: because you know that you cannot and should not lick the page, you share a joke with the hidden big Other. You trust the big Other because of this shared joke and may then buy the product, in this case Life Savers. In Warhol's reformulation the joke is brought into the art world, which becomes another level of big Other. We get the joke of the joke in an ad on the cover of *Art Forum*. As art readers we see that it recalls many tricks famous in art history that play with mimesis (recall the Greek fable of the contest between Zeuxis and Parrhasius as to who could trick the other with their verisimilitude), and we share *this* joke. It is a direct copy of an ad but it also references Duchamp's *Please Touch* (1947) and Magritte's *This Is Not a Pipe* (1928-1929). We share the joke then with another big Other, here *Art Forum* readers/editors are drawn to another hidden ideological quilting point, the signature of Warhol signifying *not* Warhol as such (as in Foucault's author function) but ART. Warhol's attitude may not be a machinic copying but an advertiser's double-speak; it is a double speak that Warhol would have been very aware of. The signature, the signature techniques of screen-printing, the brand recognition of the silver bob, the silver grounds, and the signature line (borrowed from Ben Shahn) all collate under one logo. This Warhol logo functions by teasing and enticing recognition from the viewer, drawing us all in as friends under the cover of a joke.

A number of writers have connected Warhol's work with advertising in a formal way. Indeed it is well known that his first 'paintings' were used in a window display. By the 1980s Warhol again returned to advertising (Warhol and Hackett 1989). Some look at the formal similarities between the two oeuvres of Warhol's work, eliding the difference between the two modes, as Warhol himself seemed to do (see Buchloh 2003). It is the shift from advertising to art brand that I think is crucial to considering Warhol's work as a methodology of advertising. His brand, like the advertising brand, becomes the new master signifier, shared by the viewer who gets the joke. It is the 'quilting function of the logo or brand signifier' where logos function as 'pure master signifiers' (Sharpe 2006: 310-312).

I note too that this notion of a doubling or multiplying through repetition has long been seen as part of Warhol's method. Foucault and Deleuze's readings of Warhol focus on repetition as a mode of resistance and ethical play. Unlike Baudrillard, Deleuze's simulacrum is not so nihilistic, and the difference between the iterations of text or image explicate the possibilities of the singular rather than the essential. This is not limited to the singularity of the Warhol brand but it would encompass it. Warhol, for Deleuze (1994), 'pushed the copy, copy of the copy etc., to the extreme point at which it reverses and becomes a simulacrum (such as Warhol's remarkable "serial" series, in which all repetitions of habit, memory and death are conjugated)' (1994: 293-294). For Deleuze and Foucault, Warhol is able, through repetition and *difference*, to engage critically with the simulations of mass media. Foucault writes:

> This is the greatness of Warhol with his canned foods, senseless accidents, and his series of advertising smiles: the oral and nutritional equivalence of those half-opened lips, teeth, tomato sauce, that hygiene based on detergents; the equivalence of death in the cavity of an eviscerated car, at the top of a telephone pole and at the end of a wire, and between the glistening, steel blue arms of the electric chair. 'It's the same either way,' stupidity says, while sinking into itself and infinitely extending its nature with the things it says of itself; 'Here or there, it's always the same thing; what difference if the colours vary, if they're darker or lighter. It's all so senseless – life, women, death! How ridiculous this stupidity!' But in concentrating on this boundless monotony, we find sudden illumination of multiplicity itself – with nothing at its centre, at its highest point and beyond it – a flickering of light that travels even faster than the eyes and successively lights up moving labels and the captive snapshots that refer to each other to eternity, without ever saying anything: suddenly, arising from the background of the old inertia of equivalences, the striped form of the event tears through the darkness, and the eternal phantasm informs that soup can, that singular and depthless face. (1977: 189)

So for Foucault (1983) Warhol's serial images represent 'similitude' and the 'infinite and reversible relation of the similar to the similar' (1983: 44). Warhol is a key figure in showing that similitude points to the 'possibility of change' which Foucault calls difference, and it is Warhol's seriality that proves difference can present itself as an ethics of singularity and the self. The Lacanian notion of multiple interpellations based on varying master signifiers is similar. The copies – the branding of the self – put pressure on the transcendental reading of aesthetics as aesthetics of beauty, or as an image of transcendental truth or justice.

Advertising and Images of Law and Violence

The methodology of iteration and double interpellation brings an ideological critique to Warhol's work, which for some theorists is unfounded. Briefly, it is important to place this reading in relation to the large body of work on Warhol. The approaches to Warhol are generally split between referential (subject matter) and simulacral (nihilistic, detached, camp cynicism) analysis. In a Lacanian reading of Warhol as brand the two options can be elided. What we are looking for is the hidden fantasy, and myth, that underpins the law, which Warhol's work especially encounters.

For a start we will focus on images of state violence and surveillance. Already the ideological implications of these images, as opposed to a cow in a field or a large dollar sign, are pointing in a certain direction. We focus on these images though for the sake of their jurisprudential interest but the methodology of the underpinning brand/S1 will work with any image. For those that have looked at the politics in Warhol's work there is a general distrust of the simulacral contentions that an atom bomb may be equivalent in meaning(lessness) to a daisy. Simon Watney's (1989) far-reaching essay asks for a broader visual studies approach to Warhol, where the 'Warhol Effect' is based on a Foucauldian genealogy of ethics. Similarly, Rex Butler (2007) has pushed for a reappraisal of Warhol's art, suggesting that far from being the cynical Warhol of the simulacrum, it is worth looking at the artist as earnestly religious. Such an approach positions Warhol as a believer. Butler broadens his argument, following Hubert Damisch, to suggest that Warhol is trying to bring back art to an art before art – injecting contemporary art with magic. This is a very useful direction, and this paper opens up a reading not of religious icons but of Warhol's icons of the law. Many authors have taken Warhol's religiosity and faith as icon maker seriously (see Dillenger 1998; Adams 2004). To avoid commonplaces and return to our question of juridical images, we must engage with images that respond to state power rather than religion. And yet, as we know through Kantorowicz et al., the history of the state and religion is connected.

The state does authorize the languages and images of the law but as a hidden, repressed force. It is this force that this chapter finds as a point of interest in many of Warhol's images. The violence of the law is a particular limit case for the disciplinary society and it appears, in the number of images of state violence, that Warhol became aware of violence as an Achilles' heel. By borrowing from the advertiser's lexicon Warhol highlights this process of quilting the 'violent force' of the laws founding and its 'mystical authority' in a number of images, particularly in the *Death and Disaster* series. Walter Benjamin (1996) suggests that state violence becomes obvious in two types: as founding violence and as the conserving, preserving violence of ongoing repression, such as seen in the police *force*. It is the state's monopoly over violence, that Derrida (1992) finds lurking in the transcendental, 'mystical' authority of the law upon which this force is based. For our purposes then, the use of this force, is the small exceptional moment, when the founding force of the law shows itself in the disciplinary society. To put that into Lacanian terms, the use of violence, in the electric chair and atom bomb for example, allows us to see the hidden but operative master or S1. In Warhol's work the hidden unrepresented sublime object is the quilting point or authority of the founding violence. Agamben (2005), borrowing from Derrida, has poetically defined this force of law as the 'force-of-law' (2005: 38-39). In this reading the 'force-of-law' is a thing that can be played with in a Kafkaesque manner, or in relation to political power, 'be claimed' by either the state or the revolutionary powers (which act as counter-sovereigns). Violent force in this way is always extra-legal, a limit to the civilized functioning of the law. It is this juridical understanding of the law and violence that I want to tease out for Warhol.

Warhol's *Death and Disaster* series is usually read, in traditional art historical terms, as a twentieth-century vanitas. The celebrity is warned that, *Et in Arcadia Ego*, or roughly translated, 'I (death) am even here in Hollywood'. But violence and the state are perhaps an under-theorized theme in relation to these works. It is well documented that an alternative title for the *Death and Disaster* series was going to be *Death in America*; the explicit mention of the American state would have highlighted his socio-political concerns. To begin simply, the subject matter of this series correlates directly to many of the examples offered by Benjamin (and Derrida) as instances of sovereignty and the 'monopoly' of violence. *The Atomic Bomb* (1965), is an incredible metaphor for state-founding military power. The great criminal is present in *Gangster Funeral* (1963) and *Thirteen Most Wanted Men* (1964). The many riots that Warhol shows are evidence of the legally sanctioned strike or protest, here most commonly civil rights protest and in these images the concomitant act of police repressive violence. Finally, and most famously connected to Warhol, is the connection between violence, the state and the death penalty shown in his many iconic images of the *Electric Chair* (1963-1981). Looking closely at the electric chair teases out some of our concerns in a preliminary way. There are actually two electric chairs. The first one re-images a photo done in 1954 of the electric chair in Sing Sing used for publicity purposes. The room is shown *in toto* with the 'Silence' sign visible on the right of the image. Who speaks thus? Is it an ironic silence, a spectral silence (for there is only the chair), or is it the imperative of the disciplinary society? The image was created while there was some discussion over whether or not the State of New York should persist with the death penalty. In the year Warhol produced his electric chair they legislated for the cessation of the practice, so perhaps the image is celebratory of a newly passed statute. In the second version, the photograph is the same but cropped to focus on the chair itself. The images that Warhol produces are not merely repeated photographic images. For one thing they are life size, or, in the case of Warhol's electric chair, about three-quarter scale, enough to imply the absent body. This is perhaps why on revision Warhol cropped the chair out of its room. The room was not replicated in a 2-metre painting but the chair could be; in the end the image of the chair turns the gallery into the execution chamber. The chair also looks like a throne from a biblical or courtly painting; face on to the viewer the chair implies the sitter looking towards the viewer threateningly.

So for work that is all about the *surface* the abject is still present here, or to put it in another way, the image is still able to pierce the viewer with a certain violence and horror. What underpins this violence, or, is it pure violence with no clear underpinning? Who authors the image?

Thirteen Most Wanted Men and the Ideology of the Mugshot

The complexity of Warhol's methodology of the brand, his direct confrontation with state violence and the importance of art as a point of critique are present in *Thirteen Most Wanted Men.* There is no doubt that in this work Warhol played with this joke of double meaning. Proposed, completed and hung for the New York State Pavilion at the World's Fair of 1964 in Flushing Meadows, it was based on a New York State pamphlet that 'advertised' or 'promulgated' the State's 13 most wanted criminals. Warhol's transposition was composed of panels each with the screen-printed image of the wanted criminal on a silver ground. It was placed on the façade of the pavilion. In an uncanny nod to a breach in the 'neutrality' and 'scientific nature' of the mug shot, four of the 13 appear in a more casual and informal manner, from a personal snapshot because there was no official photo on file. On the one hand the work can be seen as an extension of the celebrity portrait, suggesting a certain fame or infamy. It can be seen in relation to what Crone (1970) calls the 'documentary series'. Alternatively it could be an extension of the *Death and Disaster* series where the work is situated within the procession of suicides, deaths, gangster funerals and other nefarious newspaper stories. In *Thirteen Most Wanted Men* the violence of the image itself is directed towards the criminal; the mug shot is the forensic, surveillance image *par excellence*. Warhol confuses the state utility of the image in re-imaging the mug shot.[3] The requisitioned mug shot also questions the law's monopoly on this sort of (violent) imaging. A particular area of ideological monopoly is the imaging of state violence and law. Benjamin writes:

> To counter it one might perhaps consider the surprising possibility that the law's interest in a monopoly of violence vis-à-vis individuals is not explained by the intention of preserving legal ends but, rather, by that of preserving law itself; that violence when not in the hands of the law threatens it not by the ends that it may pursue but by mere existence outside the law. (1996: 239)

By branding these violent acts, Warhol questions the authority of this violence, showing the violence of his images to be *without* moral value, and extra legal;

3 The work has an art historical precedent. In 1923, Duchamp had made a 'Wanted: $2,000 Reward' poster of himself with two mug shots, casting himself as a criminal allegedly wanted for running an illegal gambling operation. Underneath were written many aliases including Rrose Sélavy.

for Benjamin (1996) police violence and police mug shots are not legal in so much as they occur when the law (empirically) no longer can 'guarantee' order 'through the legal system' (1996: 243). But as a perverse corollary, what basis does the law found its authority on, if Warhol can so easily co-opt its process? It is this groundlessness that haunts the law's application because its own founding violence is without a real authority only a mythic one; in Derrida's terms the law is haunted by this spectre. It is this non-ideological point, this extra-ideological violence that is the antagonism or 'Symbolic Real' that Warhol explores in his images of violence. He attacks the fantasies that conceal this gap, critiquing the state through appropriation and re-branding. He draws us into his game; we know that the new image has been utterly altered although it still 'looks' the same. In the case of the *Thirteen Most Wanted Men* the loosening of the great criminal from the control of the police opens up the possibility of the outlaw celebrity, fun and the threat of the failure of the state monopoly. In fact when the work was censored Warhol (1980) wrote, 'Now I wouldn't have to feel responsible if one of the criminals ever got turned in to the FBI because someone had recognized him from my pictures' (Warhol and Hackett 1980: 72). It was important to Warhol that his art would not be 'useful' or 'disciplinary'.

The mural was eventually painted over or 'whitewashed'. There are a number of suggestions why the work was received so poorly. Phillip Johnson explained that the work was unsuitable because the images of the wanted men were out of date and some of the 'criminals' had been exonerated; he recalls that he and the Fair were concerned that there was a threat of libel. Contemporary articles had contradictory reports from both Warhol and Johnson, who publicly fought over the work. It is reported that Robert Moses wanted the work taken down so as to not offend the Italian constituents of New York. Warhol has suggested Rockefeller himself asked for its removal as Governor of New York. Second, there was the aesthetic outcry. The Fair felt that what Warhol had proffered was not art; the threat that Pop posed was that the artist could *directly* quote from life. In this case the quotation was exacerbated by the fact that what was quoted was not a trademark or commodified object, nor a celebrity or a magazine photograph, but in a very rare move for Warhol, a quotation from a state-authored image.[4] Kristin Fedders (2005) also lays emphasis on the public nature of the work. What Fedders adds is the notion of public space (particularly the Pavilion) in connection to how Pop was received. While the approach is admirable in its attempt to broaden art history's scope and respond to the cultural and physical context and framing of the work, Fedders conclusions are too centred on modernist art history. She notes that, 'Although Pop art drew its imagery from popular culture, when reinserted into the popular context of the Fair it proved either unrecognisable or offensive to

4 Other examples of such quoting include the little known suite of lithographs dedicated to Kennedy, *The Flash Suite* (1968), where the President's seal is copied, as well the series of banknotes in *192 One Dollar Bills* (1962), and his appropriation of official portraits in *Reigning Queens* (1985).

many members of the public, suggesting how unfamiliar the mass audience was with Pop art in 1963' (Fedders 2005: 4). Indeed the response was terrible, with many editorials unhappy with the subject matter, which they saw as unpatriotic, irresponsible, neurotic, parodic, absurd, bizarre and unrepresentative (Block 1963). Although Fedders is correct to look at the parergon of the work she neglects to see that perhaps the work was not received as art at all.

It is clear that this chapter contends that the censorship occurred mainly because the author(ity) underpinning the image was not 'official' and challenged the states monopoly on punishment and violence. What is the shock of the work, and why did it create a scandal? Beside the personal motivations of key players a few general assumptions can be made. Perhaps the greatest threat was that Warhol took the brochure of the state literally, as Žižek suggests, 'to the letter of the law'. If the state's intention was to make images (to create icons) of the criminals that needed surveillance/imaging by the state (and its obliging public) then what could have been the problem with this repetition? Can it not still work to promulgate the information (S2)? As a brochure it had what Žižek calls a reflective logic of ideology, creating a fear or a sense of community action. One agrees or responds because others respond in the same way. The brochure or ideological instrument is not to be seen only as an Althusserian interpellating ideological state apparatus but a rallying cry. As Žižek discusses, regimes can only rally behind common threats, the Mafioso being a particularly good one in 1964. The work shifted the register only slightly but with an effect that was shocking. The work's power was based on Deleuze and Foucault's point that the simulacrum is an effect of difference itself, it need not be 'authentic' nor alternatively directly parodic or transgressive. It is worth teasing out a few different outcomes of this process of differencing.

The Desirable Criminal

The first obvious reading from a pun in the title itself is a movement from the neutrality of the mug shot to an embodiment of libidinal force. The 'double coded' nature of this work has been illuminated by Richard Meyer who saw it as denoting a homosexual longing, moving between 'official surveillance and illicit desire' (Meyer 1994, 2002). If we follow Susan Sontag's definition of camp as seeing something 'tender' in the everyday then this is a camp doubling; like a saint he has seen the beauty and humanity in a mug shot. Meyer sees the internal gazes and the position of each head's gaze to be important where the men are looking at each other longingly across the grid. The viewer too is implicated by what Meyer sees as a homosexual gaze. The criminality is seen as an extension of gay criminality, and contextualizes the scandal by recounting that Warhol was under surveillance from the FBI for his films at this time; particularly those with illegal homoerotic content. Connections between Warhol's work and gay themes have been broadly established (see Silver 1992; Doyle and Flatley 1996). In this case the punning title of *Most Wanted Men*, shows an interplay between this more personal interpellation of homosexual desire and the interpellation of the state towards the 'good citizen'. By referencing in its 'double code' both the private and the public individual, Warhol makes a wonderfully succinct statement on the political realities of homosexuality at this time. In an inverted way, if we see the author of the image as the state, the repressed homosexual desire of Warhol (in the image) towards *Thirteen Most Wanted Men* becomes a guilty secret. Locating this desire within a supposedly disciplinary/neutral image offers one answer to the anxiety leading to censorship and the disavowal that the mural encountered.

The confusion of the juridical and the desirous image is also effected by the subject matter. The gangster is akin to Warhol, in that he too questions the monopoly of the violence of the state; he kills, steals and lives with impunity. It is this outlaw, sovereign quality that makes the gangster such a seductive subject in popular culture, turning Ned Kelly into Heath Ledger. To return to Benjamin (1996) on the 'great' criminal: 'The same may be more drastically suggested if one reflects how often the figure of the 'great' criminal, however repellent his ends may have been, has aroused the secret admiration of the public. This cannot result from his deed, but only from the violence to which it bears witness' (1996: 239). Similarly for Derrida the 'great criminal', which the *Thirteen Most Wanted Men* definitely are, shows the law's founding violence as threat (1992: 40); it is what he calls a 'strategy of rupture'. What Derrida (1992: 40) sees in the criminal, the famous criminal, is the 'radical contestation of the given order of the law, of judicial authority …'. What connects the originary sovereignty of the artist, lawmaker and criminal is Derrida's final word (1992: 40): 'The people's shudder of admiration before the "great criminal" is addressed to the individual who takes upon himself, as in primitive times, the stigma of lawmaker or the prophet.' Regardless of approach, Warhol's subject matter references the law at its limit. It is Warhol's subjects, from the 'great' criminal, to riots, the electric chair (death penalty), presidents and sovereign power, that have an uncanny connection to the examples used by Derrida in 'Force of Law'. For Derrida (1992: 15) the possibility of justice is a 'self-authorisation of law as the possibility of the exercise of deconstruction'. In this way Warhol's bold appropriation of Repressive State Apparatus as embodied in the public pamphlet suggests the 'self-authorisation of law'. The neutral imagery of the university discourse is shown to have an ideological underpinning, a mythic, kingly point beyond the law, on which it is authorized.

Erasing the Brand

All of Warhol's repetitions reinforce the power of the advertising joke, the private joke between the viewer from the perspective of the shared brand experience. What makes *Thirteen Most Wanted Men* such a telling case is that in this instance the original authorial voice responded in disgust and created an adversarial showdown, whereas usually Warhol's simulacrum kept rolling on. The controversy

Figure 14.2 Andy Warhol, *Double Elvis*, 1964
Source: © Andy Warhol/Corbis.

Against all protestations the work was finally censored, before the Fair (1980) even opened. The artist himself called it a 'whitewash' (Warhol and Hackett 1980: 71). But in the end it was not exactly a white wash. First, Warhol was asked to censor his own work, setting up the perverse scenario that Warhol would be his own executioner. Warhol could not stifle a last 'scaffold speech', a performance against the state, in painting over *Thirteen Most Wanted Men* in his signature silver paint. This silvered painting has not been theorized and should be seen as a work in its own right.

Warhol, at first, cheekily had the idea to replace the image with images of the censor, Robert Moses, the director of the Fair.[5] Lancaster recalls (1989: 199) 'Andy Warhol had the images painted over, and then decided to replace the work with a massive multiple portrait of Robert Moses.' Moses himself would become the subject of prohibition and expulsion, and would take the place of the criminal in a serial portrait of infamy. This suggestion was not accepted officially. It appears, though, that, Warhol did not wait for final approval and finished the work

5 Is there a joke here about a Golden Calf and iconoclasm; (Robert) Moses as the icon(oclast)? This reading may not be so farfetched with Moses at the time seen as the driving force of modernism in New York City, a latter day Haussmann, who was destroying the tenements to make way for the new.

regardless; there are two pieces of photographic evidence of The Robert Moses portraits that were never released for public exhibition. Like a private joke (think of Goya's *Nude Maja*, 1800), the Factory could laugh at the folly of the censor. Although stymied in public, Warhol was still free in his studio. This is perhaps a weak transgression but it suggests an alternative reading of the censored work. Warhol had *Thirteen Most Wanted Men* painted over in silver to produce another work, quickly and decisively, which as Lancaster suggests (1989: 199), 'anger had provoked'. The act of painting over the work with silver therefore should not be read as a final capitulation but a new beginning; the silver-wash should be seen as the compromise work, which Warhol accepted in the public sphere in lieu of the Moses work.

The silver paint is not merely a white wash but a metallic, shiny, iconic colour. It erases but sanctifies the *Thirteen Most Wanted Men*, like the curtain of the Jewish Torah, an ark or cabinet. Most obviously it is the potential ground of another work; it is the beginning of the repeat, creating a palimpsest as seen in religious manuscripts. Or is it the 'silver screen', 20 feet by 20 feet, in cinematic proportions ready to accept another image of filmic glamour. Finally, Warhol often produced multiple panel works that *did* involve monochromatic sections, such as one whole panel of silver, that in relation to the screen printed figure referenced an ongoing process of seriality (see Figure 14.2). This reading is supported by reports at the time which reported the silver work as a compromise, one headline reading, 'So Nothing satisfies Warhol' (Kincade 1965). The positive nothing, an active erasure in silver paint becomes a Warholian gesture of creation and censorship. The silvering is a symbolic act of screening or veiling, and becomes a reaction to the normative screen of Lacan. Here it is a normative screen marked by Warhol's singularity where the 'silver screen' becomes an alternative potential symbolic order, literally another 'grounding' master signifier. The silver paint becomes a point where outlaw and sovereign meet and accounts for a strategy of the Warholian brand. The normal, normative screen, the covering as phallus, is censorship by *black* paint not silver. Warhol has given us an alternative universe of individual will much like the fantasy of the 'great' criminal himself. It is interesting that the work was censored again. Marc Siegel (2003) describes its revival for the Berlin Fair in 2002. The one image Siegel uses for a page reproduction is the image of the *Thirteen Most Wanted Men*. Siegel notes that for the Berlin retrospective the *Thirteen Most Wanted Men* were reunited on separate canvasses as well as being heavily advertised. Siegel sees as significant the effect of 9/11 on the decision of the director of Berlin, Heiner Bastion, not to put the mural together again and instead to present the works as separate panels in a line. The mug shot of the 'great criminal' in relation to New York still had great terrifying power that needed sublimating and controlling.

Conclusion: The Silver Nothing instead of the Effigy

The silver painting becomes a metaphor of beginnings and the founding force of the law. It highlights, in Derridean terms, an aporia of the decision that must always make the law anew and reset the ground. The cognitive doctrine or idea, or in the case of a Derridean reading, the mystical founding force, is turned into artistic and cultural artefacts and rituals. It is through dealing with these artefacts and rituals that we internalize and believe the doctrine. State apparatuses act on us, through ideology, and are part of the process of legitimizing the founding violence. Douzinas (2005) writes, 'Most legal systems are the outcome of force, the progeny of war, revolution, rebellion or occupation. This founding violence is either re-enacted in the great pageants that celebrate nation and state-building or forgotten in acts of enforcement of the new law and the interpretation of the new constitution.' In other words the chasm of violence that haunts the law is covered by fantasmic supports which can be celebratory or repressive. *Thirteen Most Wanted Men* conflates both modes in the same image. Benjamin describes the utopian act as a striving always to separate the violence of the founding act and justice as a transcendental potential. But this contingency in the symbolic can, *contra* Derrida, never be achieved, if one follows the argument of Lacan. As Žižek explains (1994: 27), 'Such a reading of spectrality as that which fills out the unrepresentable abyss of antagonism, of the non-symbolisable real, also enables us to assume a precise distance from Derrida, for whom spectrality, the apparition of the Other, provides the ultimate horizon of ethics.' For Derrida, the promise of messianic justice, yet-to-come, is the goal of critique. The problem with this stance for Lacan, and later theorists in this mode, is that as Žižek states the spectre already shows itself as a withdrawal from the horror of completeness, of complete freedom. Surely a blank silver painting is the image of this always potential becoming, never to be completed. Perhaps, as in this case, bearing the trace of the painting/law underneath, it pushes forward into a new space. As the viewer we accept Warhol's role as his own brand but it is tempered by the possibility of others too, it is not a special position but one of many. In *Thirteen Most Wanted Men* Warhol really marks this position as the creator and censor of the image. But he shows that this process is always in a state of flux. Underneath all knowledge and imagery in the disciplinary society is not neutrality but a position, the position of the hidden master. Even for a moment in *Thirteen Most Wanted Men*, through his mode of simulacrum, Warhol shows that the image is indeed pinned by a repressive state ideology that hides behind the neutrality of the image. But unlike the hysteric Warhol does not really call for the master to appear, although in a fit of anger he started painting Moses over and over; in the end Warhol shows that the image of the law is really the erased and hidden master, an invisible force.

References

Adams, Ruth. 2004. 'Idol Curiosity: Andy Warhol and the Art of Secular Iconography'. *Theology and Sexuality*, 10(2), 90-98.

Adorno, Theodor. 1991. 'The Schema of Mass Culture', in *The Culture Industry*. London: Routledge.

Agamben, Giorgio. 2005. *State of Exception*, translated by Kevin Attell. Chicago, IL: University of Chicago Press.

Benjamin, Walter. 1996. 'Critique of Violence', translated by Edmund Jephcott, in *Selected Writings: 1913-1926*, edited by Marcus Bullock and Michael Jennings. Cambridge, MA: Belknap Press.

Benjamin, Walter. 2003. 'The Paris of the Second Empire in Baudelaire', in *Walter Benjamin, 1938-1940*, edited by Marcus Bullock and Michael Jennings. Cambridge MA: Harvard University Press.

Block, Adolph. 1963. 'Bizarre "Art" at Fair'. *New York Times*, 18 October.

Boucher, Geoff. 2006. 'Bureaucratic Speech Acts and the University Discourse: Lacan's Theory of Modernity', in *Jacques Lacan and the Other Side of Psychoanalysis: Reflections on Seminar XVII*. Durham, NC: Duke University Press, 274-291.

Buchloh, Benjamin. 1989. 'The Andy Warhol Line', in *The Work of Andy Warhol*, edited by Gary Garrells. Seattle, WA: Bay Press.

Butler, Judith. 1997. *The Psychic Life of Power: Theories of Subjection*. Stanford, CA: Stanford University Press.

Butler, Rex. 2007. 'Two Warhols', *Andy Warhol*, exhibition catalogue. Brisbane: Queensland Gallery of Modern Art, 60-69.

Crone, Rainer. 1970. *Andy Warhol*. London: Thames and Hudson.

Danto, Arthur. 1997. *After the End of Art: Contemporary Art and the Pale of History*. Princeton, NJ: Princeton University Press.

Danto, Arthur. 2004. *Disenfranchisement of Art*. Columbia: Columbia University Press.

de Duve, Thierry. 1989. 'Andy Warhol or the Machine Perfected', translated by Rosalind Krauss. *October*, 48, 4-58.

Deleuze, Gilles. 1994. *Repetition and Difference*, translated by Paul Patton. New York: Columbia University Press.

Derrida, Jacques. 1992. 'Force of Law: The "Mystical Foundation of Authority"', in *Deconstruction and the Possibility of Justice*, edited by Drucilla Cornell, Michel Rosenfeld and David Gray Carlson. London and New York: Routledge.

Dillenger, Jane. 1998. *The Religious Art of Andy Warhol*. New York: Continuum.

Douzinas, Costas. 2005. 'Violence, Justice and Deconstruction'. *German Law Journal*, 6(1) (January). [Online]. Available at: www.germanlawjournal.com/article.php?id=546 [accessed 1 April 2011].

Doyle, Jennifer and Flatley, Jonathan (eds). 1996. *Pop Out: Queer Warhol*. Durham, NC: Duke University Press.

Fedders, Kristin. 2005. 'Pop Art at the 1964/65 New York World's Fair (Philip Johnson, Andy Warhol, Roy Lichtenstein, James Rosenquist, Robert Indiana)'. Unpublished Doctoral Thesis, University of Pennsylvania.

Foster, Hal. 1995. 'Death in America'. *October*, 75, 39-59.

Foucault, Michel. 1977. 'Theatrum Philosophicum', in *Language, Counter-Memory, Practice: Selected Essays and Interviews*, edited by Donald Bouchard. Ithaca, NY: Cornell University Press.

Foucault, Michel. 1983. *This is Not a Pipe*, translated by James Harkness. Berkley, CA: University of California Press.

Kincade, Kit. 1965. 'Silver Square "So Nothing" at Fair, It Satisfies Warhol'. *New York World Telegram*, 6 July.

Lancaster, Mark. 1989. 'Andy Warhol Remembered'. *The Burlington Magazine*, 131(1032), 198-202.

Meyer, Richard. 1994. 'Warhol's Clones'. *Yale Journal of Criticism*, 7(1) (Spring), 79-109.

Meyer, Richard. 2002. *Outlaw Representation: Censorship and Homosexuality in Twentieth-Century American Art*. New York: Oxford University Press.

Neocleous, Mark. 2003. *Imagining the State*. London: Open University Press.

Sharpe, Matthew. 2006. 'The "Revolution" in Advertising and University Discourse', in *Jacques Lacan and the Other Side of Psychoanalysis: Reflections on Seminar XVII*. Durham, NC: Duke University Press, 292-314.

Siegel, Marc. 2003. 'Doing It for Andy'. *Art Journal*, 62, 6-13.

Silver, Kenneth E. 1992. 'Modes of Disclosure: The Construction of Gay Identity and the Rise of Pop Art', in *Hand-Painted Pop: American Art in Transition, 1955-1962*, edited by Russell Ferguson. Los Angeles, CA: Museum of Contemporary Art, 179-203.

Stein, Jean and Plimpton, George. 1982. *Edie: American Girl*. New York: Knopf.

Warhol, Andy and Hackett, Pat. 1980. *Popism: The Warhol Sixties*. New York: Harcourt Brace Jovanovich.

Warhol, Andy and Hackett, Pat. 1989. *The Andy Warhol Diaries*. New York: Warner Books.

Watney, Simon. 1989. 'The Warhol Effect', in *The Work of Andy Warhol*, edited by Gary Garrels. Seattle, WA: Bay Press.

Žižek, Slavoj. 1994. 'The Spectre of Ideology', in *Mapping Ideology*. London: Verso.

Žižek, Slavoj. 2003. '*Homo Sacer* as the Object of the Discourse of the University'. *Lacan Ink*. [Online]. Available at: www.lacan.com/hsacer.htm [accessed 1 April 2011].

Index

accountability 14
advertising 185, 230, 232-233, 247-249, 255
ambiguity 15
American 130, 132-134, 30, 166-167, 169-171, 173-177, 179, 196, 221, 222, 229, 230, 232-235, 237, 240, 251, 260
Australia 13, 14, 22, 24, 25, 170, 183, 187, 188, 190, 198-200, 202-210, 212-215

Bosnia-Herzegovina 193
Burmese 203

Canada 143, 168, 187, 189
canon law 52
ceteris paribus 36
Chinese 13-22, 26, 27, 29, 30, 126, 190, 198
Code (Criminal) 15-21, 29, 52, 61, 65, 210
colloquial speech 55
communication process 51
conditional assumption 33
contextual interpretation 24
contract 31, 32, 34, 35, 85, 86, 88, 90-94, 96-104, 184
Council of Europe 115
Cuba 212
cultural studies 217, 219, 220, 228, 229, 231, 233, 237, 238

democratic 18, 60, 62, 63, 67, 70, 71, 74, 75, 83, 118, 122, 200, 203, 206-208, 211, 218, 220-223, 225, 228, 229, 231, 232, 235, 236
dialectic relationship 87
Dialogism 85, 87, 90, 95, 106
Direct Balancing Approach 233

English 14, 15, 22, 23, 26, 27, 29, 31-33, 38, 41, 47, 48, 53, 56, 61, 70, 100-103, 117, 173, 212
EU 63, 64, 110-122
Euphemisms 80
European 30, 51, 52, 57, 61-66, 84, 109-112, 114-123, 126, 129-132, 178, 190, 192-195

First Amendment 155, 158, 217, 219-237, 239-241
Freedom 72, 136, 238, 240, 241
French 58, 100, 176

genre 48, 51, 52, 55, 58, 59, 86, 88, 89, 91, 93, 95-97, 100, 177
German 52, 57, 117, 122, 131, 143, 183, 192, 259
government legitimacy 126, 137, 138

Hong Kong 50, 109, 190
house of certainty 175
human rights 72, 76, 79, 119, 135, 136, 137, 201, 204, 205

Ideology 197, 239, 241, 243, 252, 260
Indian 25
institutional power-holders 32
International Contracts 31
Internet 69, 152, 160, 161
interpret 13, 24, 26, 29, 72, 134, 176, 177
Italy 183, 184, 185, 191, 192

judicial independence 69
justice 13, 14, 26, 29, 55, 67, 69, 70, 71, 81, 118, 138-140, 179, 208, 249, 255, 258
justification 15, 57, 63, 64, 68, 78, 82, 137, 139, 205

legal acts 59, 60, 63
Legal Conditionals 4
legal discourse 34, 35, 38, 39, 41, 43, 47, 48, 52, 64, 186, 188
legal systems 13, 14, 19, 27, 73, 117, 187, 258
legal texts 13, 62, 64, 69, 109, 117, 122
legislation 14, 15, 22-25, 29, 51, 52, 61, 63, 64, 66, 71, 112, 114, 116, 117, 199-206, 210, 211, 213, 214
legislative text 23, 25, 51, 59, 114
linguistic
  convention 13-15, 18, 21, 22, 27-29, 86-88, 90, 91, 93-95, 99, 104, 111-113, 213
  rules 13, 15, 22, 27, 51, 52, 57, 28, 29, 64, 73-75, 78, 89, 97, 103, 109, 114, 133, 117, 122, 135, 141, 172, 201, 211, 220, 226
  uncertainty 14, 21
Lisbon Treaty 110, 117-119, 122

media 27, 69, 147, 148, 152, 155, 121, 165, 187, 218, 224, 229, 245, 246, 249
mediation 88, 93
metalanguage 218
metaphor 78-9 90, 176, 251, 258
metatextual 53, 55
motiva evitentur 52, 61, 62, 64
multilegal 32, 47
multilingual 32, 47, 112

negotiation 47, 48, 89, 109, 111, 112, 114, 121, 194
Netherlands 84, 192, 196, 198
non liquet 29
Northern Ireland 199
Norway 193

ortyl 52-54, 58

Poland 56-60, 65, 66
polemic 67, 68
Polish 51-61, 64
polyphony 86-99, 104
Predominant Purpose Test 235
prima facie 76
psycholinguistic 43
public interest 21, 225
purposive interpretation 25

rationalization 96
religion 14, 126, 128-131, 134, 138, 171, 179, 186, 188, 229, 250
Renaissance 126, 129, 131
rhetoric 52, 58, 68, 69, 77, 79, 84, 166, 190
rights 18, 23, 28, 41, 74, 80, 83, 100, 109, 113-115, 119, 121, 122, 125, 126, 133-136, 138, 141, 165, 194, 200, 203-205, 220, 222, 225, 231-233, 235, 237, 245, 251
Roman law 23, 52, 64
rules 13
Russia 67, 68, 70, 72-74, 77, 78, 81, 83, 134
Russian 67, 68, 69, 70, 71, 76, 77, 78, 83

semio-geography 185, 190
semiotic 51, 88, 94, 97, 109, 173, 176, 217, 218, 220, 228, 229, 236
semiotic code 51
Semiotic legal analysis 153
signs 90, 93, 94, 109-112, 114, 116, 166, 209, 217, 218, 228, 229, 231, 232, 234, 235, 237
social custom 57
sound spaces 184, 185, 187
Spanish 212
speech act 51-62, 64
statute 70, 21-24, 251
Supreme Court 17, 150, 152-154, 158, 159, 220-225, 227, 234, 236
Swiss 183, 184, 194

terrorism 165-167, 170, 173, 175, 178, 180, 199, 200, 202, 204-206, 208, 209
terrorist 165-168, 170, 171, 175, 177-181, 201, 205, 208-210
Total Information Awareness program 166
transformative 224-227, 234, 235
transformed social practice 97
traumatic realism 245
Turkish 190, 195

United Kingdom 192, 199
United Nations 14, 115, 119
United States 58, 65, 132-134, 141, 165, 171, 172, 174, 180, 219, 221, 222
United States of America 58, 65, 171, 172

vague 14-19, 21, 22, 26, 27, 82
values 26, 38, 52, 61, 64, 68, 69, 71, 72, 74-76, 83, 126, 128, 132-134, 138, 200, 209, 217, 218, 222, 226-228, 231, 232, 236, 237
verdict 17, 52
vernacular violence 213

Wales 22

For Product Safety Concerns and Information please contact our
EU representative GPSR@taylorandfrancis.com Taylor & Francis
Verlag GmbH, Kaufingerstraße 24, 80331 München, Germany